Ichiro, Satchel, and the Babe

THE JOHNS HOPKINS UNIVERSITY PRESS

Ichiro, Satchel, and the Babe

MIKE ATTIYEH

The Johns Hopkins University Press
BALTIMORE LONDON

The Johns Hopkins University Press
2715 North Charles Street
Baltimore, Maryland 21218-4363
www.press.jhu.edu

Library of Congress Cataloging-in-Publication Data

Attiyeh, Mike
Ichiro, Satchel, and the Babe : more baseball's fun facts and serious trivia /
Mike Attiyeh.
p. cm.
Includes bibliographical references.
ISBN 0-8018-7264-2 (pbk. : alk. paper)
1. Baseball—Miscellanea. I. Title.

GV873 .A86 2003
796.357'02—dc21   2002040580

A catalog record for this book is available from the British Library.

To my cousin Suzie,
a truly beautiful human being

Contents

Introduction   ix

Spring Training   xv

Opening Day   xvii

First Season   1

First Postseason   143
First World Series   148

Second Season   155

Second Postseason   318
Second World Series   323

Barnstorming Tour   331
Acknowledgments   333
Bibliography   335

Introduction

Ichiro Suzuki, Satchel Paige, and Babe Ruth are among the most recognizable names professional baseball has ever known. Like pop stars Elvis and Madonna, Ichiro, Satchel, and the Babe are known to baseball followers by their first names. Each has come to embody the league he dominated, and each remains enshrined in our minds as a baseball icon. Together, they symbolize the gradual unification of baseball worldwide.

Ichiro become the first Japanese position player to make it to the majors, where he virtually duplicated the gaudy numbers he had put up in the Far East. He was a superstar in Japan, and his star has shone even brighter since he took the major leagues by storm in 2001, sweeping the American League Rookie of the Year and MVP awards that year while playing for a record-setting Seattle Mariners squad whose success captured international interest. A right fielder with dazzling speed, a good arm, and superb batting skills, Ichiro is an international figure whose success has opened the doors to a new nation of major leaguers.

The crowd-pleasing Satchel was the top gate attraction of the negro leagues. He relied on a blazing fastball to mow down rows of hitters and brazen, unrivaled showmanship to entertain millions of fans throughout America. Blessed with a tireless arm, the lanky righthander often pitched without rest to help promote the league and then turned on his charm to tell a great story afterward. After a long, celebrated, and sometimes frustrating negro league career, the resilient Satchel finally got his chance to play in the major leagues, following Jackie Robinson. Although Satchel wasn't the player who broke the color barrier, it was his—and Josh Gibson's—success in exhibition games and barnstorming tours against major leaguers that gave credibility to the negro leagues and aroused the prerequisite curiosity.

The Babe passed away more than a half-century ago and hasn't swung a bat since 1935, yet his name remains the single most recognized in the annals of baseball. Ruth's story is rooted in baseball lore. He emerged from an unstable childhood to become the best performer in the major leagues. After Ruth became established as the best left-handed pitcher in the American League, his bat opened eyes and prompted a position change to the outfield. Playing every day for the New York Yankees, the Babe popularized the long ball and gave the home run a personality similar to his own—loud, grandiose, and theatrical. In addition to changing the dynamics of the game and rescuing the sport from an infamous scandal, the Babe dominated baseball like no one else has with a power game never seen before and not seen since.

All of a sudden, however, the Babe's place appears less secure than that of Ichiro and Satchel. Ichiro will always be known as a pioneer among Japanese position players, and Satchel is regarded as the best pitcher in negro league history and an important figure in the integration process. But the Babe's place is on shakier ground these days. The Babe's unofficial stranglehold on the title of the best player of all time has been questioned of late with the surge of today's best player, Barry Bonds. And Bonds is definitely the best player my 35-year-old eyes have ever seen. But as a historian of the game, I pay as much attention as possible to those who played before my time.

To compare players from different eras is a difficult task, but research, statistical interpretation, and an organized structure make it possible. Other than accounting for factors such as ballpark configuration and ball texture, the best method, I believe, is by comparing a player against his peers from the same era. Whatever advantages the player enjoyed, or disadvantages the player had to cope with, his peers were helped, or hurt, by them as well.

For example, modern hype says that Bonds over the last two years has enjoyed the most dominant two-year stretch ever for a slugger. But a comparative study such as I have suggested shows otherwise. In 1920 the Babe drilled 54 home runs in a league that included no other 20–home run hitter, and his total was greater than that of every other *team* in the American League. He followed that feat with 59 home runs the next year, in a circuit that featured a runner-up total of 24. In 2001 Bonds crushed 73 home runs but did so in a league that also included a 64-homer slugger, a 57-homer slugger, and a plethora of 40-plus-homer sluggers. In 2002 Bonds didn't win the home run title.

Slugging percentage, you ask? In 1920 Ruth slugged .847, well ahead of the runner-up figure of .632, and more than double the league average of .407. In 1921 Ruth slugged .846, well ahead of the runner-up figure of .606, and almost double the league average of .424. In 2001 Bonds slugged .863 and more than doubled the league average of .422, but his runner-up slugged .737. In 2002 Bonds slugged .799, while his runner-up slugged .622 and the league average was .410. The Babe out-slugged his league average by a combined 862 points in 1920–21, whereas Bonds out-slugged his league average by a combined 830 points in 2001–2002. Even ignoring factors such as smaller parks and more tightly wound balls that favor today's offensive players, the Babe's accomplishments add up to a mountain of seemingly unreachable standards.

Much was made of Bonds' 46 home runs and .370 batting average in 2002, and for good reason, as that dual feat demonstrates a tremendous ability to hit for power while boasting a high average. But the Babe topped those figures in the same season five times, and that excludes his 60-homer campaign in 1927 and his .393 campaign four years earlier. The Babe wasn't just a slugger; he was a great batsman, whose powerful yet beautiful swing netted a .342 career average, 47 points higher than Bonds'. The Babe's record .690 career slugging average is almost 100 points better than Bonds'. The Babe's record career 1.16 OPS (on-base plus slugging percentage) is comfortably ahead of Bonds' 1.02. His .474 career on-base percentage (second only to Ted Williams) is well ahead of Bonds' .428. Bonds, who enters the 2003 season with 101 fewer home runs than Ruth in only 64 fewer at-bats, has averaged a home run every 13.59 at-bats over his career. The Babe homered every 11.76 at-bats. As Curt Schilling of the Arizona Diamondbacks has argued, "Barry is a superstar in any era. But I don't know if he hits 70 riding trains [home runs] playing in those old, huge parks, with a ball that's twice as soft as the new balls, with the older, larger strike zone. And let's face it, 15 years ago, you could drop a hitter and never think twice about it. . . . The game is just so different today."

Some members of the media claim that Bonds is the most feared hitter ever. Although it's impossible to quantify fear, again, the evidence does not support the hype. Since intentional walks were not counted prior to 1954, the Babe and Bonds can't be compared in this specific category (and Bonds' record of 68 intentional walks is thereby only a 47-year mark). But as far as total walks are concerned, Ruth was walked 2,062 times, or once every 5.15 plate appearances. Bonds has been walked 1,922 times, or once every 5.42 plate appearances. Bonds' walks in the 2002 postseason drew plenty of attention. But please don't tell this historian that no one has ever been so carefully pitched to in the postseason. Bonds walked 27 times in 17 games (1.59 passes per game), batting in front of Benito Santiago. In the 1926 World Series, Ruth drew 11 walks in 7 games (1.57 passes per game), batting in front of Lou Gehrig. I'm sure you'll agree that being walked with Gehrig on deck is a lot more impressive than being walked with Santiago on deck.

Also, much was made of Bonds' prodigious home runs during the 2002 World Series, and of his overall performance in leading his team to within six outs of the title. Many said Bonds' 485-foot home run in Game Two of the series may have been the longest in fall classic history, but, according to home run historian Bill Jenkinson, Babe's shot at St. Louis' Sportsman's Park during Game Four of the 1926 World Series measured 510 feet. And although Bonds redeemed five previous postseason failures with a spectacular 2002 postseason that earned him his first NL pennant, let's not forget that the Babe was a masterful postseason performer from the start. The Babe helped or led his teams to seven world championships, three times as a pitcher for the Boston Red Sox. In 10 World Series, Ruth batted .326, reached base more than 46 percent of the time, boasted a hefty .744 slugging average, homered 15 times, and was 3-0 with a minuscule 0.87 ERA over 31 innings on the mound. As you can see, Ruth's ledger doesn't need the hype.

The historical oversight brought about by Bonds' recent performances is not, I feel, intended as disrespect to Babe Ruth. People generally want to say that they saw the best ever in action, because this would increase their own value as fans or scribes or storytellers. As a consequence, they tend to favor modern players. Television networks, looking to boost ratings, encourage such hype.

Of course, if Bonds keeps playing at this supreme level, I may have to revisit the comparison. But for now, the Babe remains atop my list of the greatest major leaguers of all time. That's the truth. I have found the truth can almost always be discovered, if the effort is put forth. Most people don't have the time or the resources. That's where I come in. Welcome to *Ichiro, Satchel, and the Babe.*

Spring Training

Which former major league player once saved Cal Ripken Jr.'s life? (Look for question number 2 to find the answer.) Who is the only player in history to hold the single-season club record in batting average for three different franchises? (Question number 90.) With a .300 batting average being the meter stick, who got the best of whom: eight-time batting champion Tony Gwynn or four-time Cy Young Award winner Greg Maddux? (Question number 164.) When Roberto Clemente died in a plane crash, who took over in right field? (Question number 256.) Which major league home run king set a national high school record by returning four kickoffs for touchdowns in one game? (Question number 265.)

If you know the answers to any of these questions, then congratulations! You've just been hired as the manager of a miserable, cellar-dwelling team. Your job is to reconstruct the team, and you have two full seasons to do it: your contract calls for a two-year plan for transforming this club into a serious contender.

How can you do it? By not only reading *Ichiro, Satchel, and the Babe* but by playing it as well. You don't have to take the job, of course: you can simply read *Ichiro, Satchel, and the Babe* and enjoy its question-and-answer format. But if you're up to this managerial challenge, this is how it works: Each chapter (season) includes 162 questions (games). In the First Season, you must answer 92 questions correctly (win 92 games) to qualify for the postseason, and in the Second Season you must answer 88 correctly. Every correct answer is a win, and every incorrect answer is a defeat. The answer must be complete (matching answers must also be complete) and correct to obtain the win.

Included in the question format are trivia questions, matching questions, fill-in-the-blanks, true or false, fill-in-the-lineup, multiple choice, and more. All the facts are updated through the 2002 Major

League Baseball regular season and postseason. To keep you on your toes, the questions are not classified by any category or particular design. And a good number of questions deal with many matters at once. (This is not your ordinary baseball book.) The "Did You Know?" facts interspersed throughout the book are merely for information and entertainment and do not factor in the scoring.

If you gain entry into the postseason, you must win (answer) four League Championship Series games (questions) to advance to the World Series. To become a world champion, you must again win a best-of-seven series by answering four more questions correctly.

Think you can you handle it? If so, good luck, skipper, and don't forget that you will be judged on your performance when it comes time to decide whether you'll be tendered another contract. So use a piece of paper to keep track of your results and compare them to the manager's requirement for rehiring (as decided by your general manager), located after the completion of Season Two's postseason. Without further ado, let's throw out the first pitch and play ball!

Opening Day

Major League Baseball has featured 127 opening days throughout its glorious history, each one unique, each one full of promise, and each one delivering a new chapter. Although the structure of the game has remained the same over the years, there have been many changes since the inaugural 1876 season, and opening day is our first glimpse of what will be new.

The history of Major League Baseball is full of such examples. Here are a few:

—After Ban Johnson declared that his American League would compete with the National League, Johnson's circuit debuted as a major league on April 24, 1901, in Chicago, where the hometown White Sox beat the Cleveland Indians by a score of 8-2.
—More than 74,000 watched as Babe Ruth christened beautiful Yankee Stadium on April 18, 1923, with a three-run homer in a 4-1 New York victory over the Boston Red Sox, his former team.
—New baseball communities were officially born when expansion teams played their first game on opening day in 1961, 1962, 1969, 1977, 1993, and 1998.
—After the American League introduced the designated hitter rule in December of 1972, many watched with curiosity as New York's Ron Blomberg and Boston's Orlando Cepeda filled that role in the first-ever DH game on opening day 1973.
—On March 29, 2000, Major League Baseball broke new ground by opening its season overseas in Tokyo, where the Cubs outdueled the Mets, 5-3.
—On opening day 2001, the MLB season opened in San Juan, Puerto Rico, where the host Blue Jays defeated the Rangers in a game that

also featured the first contest for Alex Rodriguez after his signing of a $252 million, free agent contract with Texas.

—In keeping with tradition, the 2003 National League schedule will feature an opener in Cincinnati, where the Reds will unveil their brand new Great American Ball Park on the riverfront.

As you can see, a lot has changed over those years, yet a lot has remained the same. Players still argue with umpires even though umpires hardly ever reverse their original decision, peanuts and beer are still very much a part of the game, players are still treated like kings off the field, owners still try to buy pennants, and fans still fight over foul.balls.

I have a feeling that the future holds even more changes in store, changes that may alter the face of the game but never the foundation. So, in the spirit of opening day, here's a preview of what to expect over the next 50 years: By the year 2053, the gender barrier will be broken, Major League Baseball will be renamed, and the restructured league will include teams all over the world, including Japan, Australia, West Canada, Hawaii, and even Cuba. Every stadium will be equipped with a dome or retractable roof, eliminating almost any chance of a rain delay. Advanced nutrition and supplements will allow strong-willed players to play well into their mid-fifties, and thus to break a score of legendary career records. The ball will be wound so tight and move so fast, pitchers will wear gear on the mound, and umpires will call games from a field box via advanced technology. Players will be drafted as early as the ninth grade and given signing bonuses greater than Barry Bonds' 2003 contract. A player who is yet unborn will break the bank, commanding a six-year, $3 billion contract. Franchise fees will exceed $4 billion, and baseball journalists will finally command decent money.

Here are some opening day "Did You Know?" tidbits to get you warmed up:

◆ Did you know the St. Louis Cardinals on April 18, 1950, hosted the first major league opening day game to be played at night, defeating the Pittsburgh Pirates? According to *Baseball Chronology,* righthander Gerry Staley threw a six-hitter for the 4-2 victory, and Stan Musial and Red Schoendienst homered.

◆ Did you know the Philadelphia Athletics' Herb Pennock came within an out of an opening day no-hitter on April 14, 1915? With two out in the ninth inning, the southpaw yielded a single to Boston outfielder Harry Hooper, whom he joined later in the season as a teammate on the Red Sox. Pennock won the game, 5-0.

◆ Did you know Walter Johnson threw a 15-inning shutout on opening day, 1926, blanking the Philadelphia Athletics and outdueling Eddie Rommel, 1-0, at the age of 38? The marathon six-hitter, which biographer Jack Kavanagh called "the greatest opening day game anyone ever pitched," marked Johnson's seventh and final opening day shutout. Johnson's first opening day shutout took place 16 years earlier (also against the Athletics), as a fluke double prevented the "Big Train" from becoming the first pitcher to throw an opening day no-hitter. Because of an over-capacity crowd that spilled onto the field, an area down the right-field line in foul territory was sectioned off by rope. Wouldn't you know that in the seventh inning, Frank "Home Run" Baker lofted a routine drive to that area, where right fielder Doc Gessler looked prepared to make the catch. Then, as Kavanagh writes, "some clod whose foot stuck out from under the rope . . . tripped the outfielder." That was the only hit Johnson allowed in outdueling fellow future Hall of Famer Eddie Plank, 3-0. (Johnson was 9-5 in his 14 opening day assignments.) The NL record of opening day shutouts is three, shared by Rip Sewell, Chris Short, and Rick Mahler.

◆ Did you know Don Drysdale is the only pitcher with two career opening day home runs? Drysdale's season-greeting home runs opened the schedules of the 1959 and 1965 Dodgers.

◆ Did you know Eddie Mathews and Barry Bonds are the only two players to homer twice in each of the first two games of a season? Mathews accomplished the feat in 1958 en route to a 31-homer season, and Bonds did it in 2002 en route to a 46-homer season.

Ichiro, Satchel, and the Babe

First Season

◆ Did you know lefthander Jimmy Key was 7-0 on opening day assignments, the standard for most wins without a loss in season openers? The active Greg Maddux is 6-0.

◆ Did you know Minnesota Twins outfielder Brant Alyea enjoyed an opening day record seven RBI to start the 1970 season? With the performance, which helped Twins righthander Jim Perry win the opener, the platoon outfielder was on his way to career-best totals of 16 home runs, 61 RBI, and a .291 batting average.

1. *This rookie southpaw struck out Babe Ruth 10 times in their first 13 confrontations in 1922 and held the Bambino to a .190 average during his brief career. Name the left-handed screwballer who used his specialty pitch to master the one and only Ruth.*

    ANSWER: Hub Pruett
    Pruett, perhaps the first left-handed screwballer, retired Ruth in each of their first 11 official matchups, a stretch that included 10 strikeouts, a groundout, and two walks. Overall in 1922, Pruett whiffed Ruth 13 times in 21 matchups. During his three years in the American League, from 1922 to 1924, Pruett held Ruth to four hits in 21 official at-bats, striking him out 15 times, issuing eight walks, and yielding two home runs and a sacrifice fly.
    Pruett, who was studying medicine, pitched in the majors for seven years to pay for his studies. He received his M.D. at St. Louis University. The St. Louis Browns screwballer, who also had an excellent curve, was overused during one stretch in 1922 and never recovered. He retired with a record of 29-48 with an ERA of 4.63. In 1922 Pruett was 7-7 with a 2.33 ERA. He was a physician for well over forty years.

2. *One day back in 1972, a 12-year-old Cal Ripken Jr. faced death but was saved by this heroic third baseman. A regular in the Double-A Asheville Orioles clubhouse (managed by his father, Cal Ripken Sr.), Ripken Jr. was playing catch with this third baseman at McCormick Field when a gun shot whizzed by their heads. Almost simultaneously, another shot landed just in front of Junior's feet. After getting over the shock of the third shot, this future All-Star picked up Junior and carried him into the dugout, saving his life. Can you name this hero?*

ANSWER: Doug DeCinces

DeCinces, who found himself in a Baltimore Orioles uniform for the first time the following season, was the savior, according to a 1992 article in *Baseball Weekly*. Authorities later arrested a juvenile delinquent for shooting at the players from the Blue Ridge mountains.

The right-handed-hitting DeCinces assumed the Orioles' third-base duties in 1976 and became the Angels' hot corner man from 1982 to 1987. DeCinces, who was part of three division championship teams and a pennant winner in 1979, concluded his 15-year career with a .259 average and 237 home runs. His best season came in 1982, when he led the Angels to within one game of the American League pennant and achieved career highs of 30 home runs, 97 RBI, a .301 average, 42 doubles, 94 runs scored, and a .548 slugging percentage. DeCinces also registered 399 assists that year, the seventh highest season total by a third baseman and the highest since 1974.

3. *Who was the only player to hit for the cycle as a pitcher?*

ANSWER: Jimmy Ryan

On July 28, 1888, for the Cubs, Jimmy Ryan became—and yet remains—the only player to hit for the cycle while pitching. Ryan singled in the first, doubled in the second, homered in the fourth, and tripled in the fifth. A unique player in that he threw left-handed, played outfield, shortstop, and filled in occasionally at second and third base, the 19th-century right-handed slugger toed the mound 24 times in his career, starting 5 games. He won six of his seven career decisions, but he made a much bigger impact with his bat. A .306 career hitter over an 18-year career spent mostly on Cap Anson's Cubs teams, Ryan finished in the top ten in batting three times and in the top ten in slugging six times. During the 1888 season he enjoyed his best campaign, as he led the National League in home runs, total bases, slugging, doubles, and hits. In 1896 Ryan became the first player ever to be officially issued an intentional walk. He retired in 1903 with 2,502 hits, 451 doubles, 157 triples, 418 stolen bases, and 1,642 runs. His total of 118 home runs was an impressive figure for that era. His strong left arm came in handy, as he accrued a still-standing National League career record of 356 outfield assists.

4. *While pitching the first major league shutout of his career in 1970, this powerful youngster threw a masterful one-hitter in which he set a club mark with 15 strikeouts. Who was this flame-thrower and renowned strikeout artist?*

ANSWER: Nolan Ryan

Nolan Ryan set the Mets franchise record for strikeouts on April 18, 1970, against the Philadelphia Phillies. His record, though, stood for only four days before teammate Tom Seaver made Ryan's achievement seem less impressive by striking out 19 to tie the major league record. Ryan would later tie Seaver and Steve Carlton's record of 19 strikeouts on August 12, 1974, for the California Angels, with whom he had made a fresh start en route to grand achievements.

Ryan struck out 493 batters as a Met, before recording 2,416 whiffs for the Angels, 1,866 for the Astros, and 939 with the Rangers.

♦ Did you know the newly franchised New York Mets of the early 1960s got the idea for their pinstriped orange and blue uniforms by borrowing the orange from the Giants, the blue from the Dodgers, and the pinstripes from the neighboring Yankees? Original members of the short-lived Continental League, the Mets were accepted by Major League Baseball to play in New York, filling the National League void left by the departing Dodgers and Giants. Rather than risk a competing league, especially one presided over by the incomparable Branch Rickey, Major League Baseball decided to expand. Owner Joan Payson was awarded the Mets franchise, to debut in 1962. After two years in the Polo Grounds, the Mets moved into Shea Stadium, named after New York attorney William Shea, who had announced the formation of the Continental League in July of 1959.

5. *Match these catchers with their feats:*

1	Smokey Burgess	A	led the league in putouts six times
2	Randy Hundley	B	caught Harvey Haddix's near-perfect game
3	Jack Clements	C	caught a record 160 games in a season
4	Ray Mueller	D	caught 1,073 games, a record for left-handed catchers
5	Roy Campanella	E	shares the major league record of 155 consecutive games caught

ANSWER: 1—B, 2—C, 3—D, 4—E, 5—A

Randy Hundley must have taught his son Todd very well. Todd caught 150 games for the Mets in 1996 to become the 18th catcher to don the "tools of ignorance," or catcher's gear, that often in a season. The active Hundley has a way to go to catch up with his father in this category. The elder Hundley caught 160 games in 1968, 152 in 1967, and 151 in 1969. . . . Clements, a 17-year catcher who retired following the 1900 season, batted .286 over a career that also featured five top-ten finishes in the home run department. Clements remains the only left-handed receiver to catch 300 games. . . . Frankie Hayes co-owns the record of 155 straight games behind the plate. . . . Campanella, perhaps even better defensively than he was with the bat, caught 100 or more games in each of his last nine seasons, also throwing out an all-time record 57.4 percent of all the baserunners who dared try to steal on him over his 10-year career. According to Dave Smith of *Retrosheet*, which has tracked "the 1958–2000 seasons plus Roy Campanella's career since [it] has play-by-play data for all of his games," Campy has the top three single-season performances. Campy gunned down a single-season record 68.1 percent (32 of 47) in 1951. *Retrosheet* lists Ned Yost as the worst ever at throwing out baserunners, as 87.9 percent of all base stealers were successful off him over his six-year career.

◆ Did you know Jerry Goff, Geno Petralli, and Harry Vickers share the dubious record (from 1900 on) of six passed balls in a single game? On May 12, 1996, Goff, playing his first game of the season, tied the mark while performing for the Houston Astros. Incredibly, Petralli of Texas had also tied the mark, set in 1902 by Vickers, in 1987.

◆ Did you know Gary Carter holds the mark for fewest passed balls in a season by a catcher who caught at least 150 games? According to *The Sporting News Complete Baseball Record Book,* Carter's one passed ball in 152 games caught in 1978 is the standard.

6. *Only three players in major league history have compiled 300 home runs, 300 stolen bases, and 2,000 hits. The first was Willie Mays. The last was Barry Bonds. The other is:*

A Joe Morgan
B Bobby Bonds
C Andre Dawson
D Mickey Mantle
E Don Baylor

ANSWER: C

Dawson retired at the end of the 1996 season with 2,774 hits, 438 home runs, and 314 stolen bases. Bonds reached the 2,000-hit mark in 1999, to join Dawson and his godfather Mays in this elite group. Mays, however, had 3,283 hits, making him the only member of the 300-homer, 300-steal, and 3,000-hit club. Bonds joined another exclusive club in 1998, becoming the first player in history to reach 400 home runs and 400 stolen bases; no active player is a threat to join him in that circle. (And Bonds is on the cusp of a new dual-threat mark, standing seven steals away from unveiling the stratospheric 500-500 club.) Rickey Henderson, who has 1,403 stolen bases and 3,040 hits, concluded the 2002 season with 295 home runs.

◆ Did you know Paul Molitor joined Ty Cobb and Honus Wagner as the only players in history to collect 3,000 hits, 600 doubles, and 500 stolen bases?

◆ Did you know George Brett and Dave Winfield joined Willie Mays and Hank Aaron as the only players versatile enough to amass 3,000 hits, 300 home runs, and 200 stolen bases? Brett retired with 3,154 hits, 317 home runs, and 201 stolen bases. Winfield had 3,110 hits, 465 home runs, and 223 stolen bases. Mays stole 338 bases, and Aaron stole 240.

◆ Did you know George Brett is the only player with more than 3,000 hits (3,154), 300 home runs (317), 600 doubles (665), 100 triples (137), and 200 stolen bases (201)?

7. *Match these prolific hitters with their feats:*

1	Hank Aaron	A	hit the most homers during the 1960s
2	Duke Snider	B	had the most homers and RBI in the 1950s
3	Willie Mays	C	is the only player to homer in the All-Star Game and World Series off the same pitcher in the same year
4	Harmon Killebrew	D	his six stolen bases is a career All-Star Game record
5	Frank Robinson	E	led the league in homers four times

ANSWER: 1—E, 2—B, 3—D, 4—A, 5—C

Aaron surprisingly won "only" four home run titles. His 44 roundtrippers led the National League in 1957, 1963, and 1966, and he led with 39 homers in 1967. . . . Snider's 326 home runs and 1,131 RBI led the majors during the 1950s (yes, that's more than Willie, Mickey, Ted, or Stan). . . . Killebrew's 349 home runs led the majors during the 1960s. The record for most homers in a decade, set by Babe Ruth in the 1920s, is 467. Jimmie Foxx hit 415 in the following decade, and Mark McGwire smashed 405 in the 1990s. . . . Robinson homered off Pittsburgh's Doc Ellis in the 1971 All-Star Game and in Game One of the 1971 World Series, making Ellis a loser in each game. However, Ellis' Pirates came back to win the 1971 fall classic over Robinson's Orioles.

◆ Did you know the Mel Ott Trophy is given each year to the National League's home run champion? Ott, with a distinctive leg kick, took advantage of the dimensions of his home park to hit 323 of his 511 career home runs at the Polo Grounds. Although prodigious from gap to gap, the Polo Grounds' measurements down the lines were an easily reachable 280 feet or less, depending on the year. Yet Ott's biggest home run was hit on the road, in Washington's Griffith Stadium to be specific, with two out in the 10th inning of Game Five of the 1933 World Series. His solo home run to center field off the Senators' Jack Russell gave the Giants a 4-3 victory in the clinching contest. Although the Polo Grounds added a few home runs to Ott's total, the park also took away plenty of singles, doubles, and triples. Ott was also blessed with good eyes, leading the National League in walks six times.

8. *The 2001 World Series between the Arizona Diamondbacks and New York Yankees marked only the second fall classic in which a team entered the ninth inning of Game Seven with a lead and lost. Name the only other World Series.*

ANSWER: The 1997 World Series

In Game Seven of the 1997 series, the Cleveland Indians led 2-1 as closer Jose Mesa took the mound in the bottom of the ninth inning against the Florida Marlins. But Moises Alou greeted Mesa with a single to left. With one out, Charles Johnson singled Alou to third, and Craig Counsell lifted a game-tying sacrifice fly to knot the game at 2-2.

In the 11th inning, against Charles Nagy, a starter who had been called in for relief with two out in the 10th, the Marlins mounted another rally. Florida's Bobby Bonilla, who had homered earlier, opened the inning with a single off Nagy and, with one out, advanced to third when Counsell's grounder went through the legs of second baseman Tony Fernandez, who was screened by a lumbering Bonilla. Then, Jim Eisenreich was walked intentionally to load the bases, before Devon White hit a grounder to Fernandez, who forced out Bonilla at the plate, moving Counsell to third with two out. With Edgar Renteria at the plate, Nagy got ahead (0-1) but grooved the second pitch, which Renteria lined to center field for the game-winner, plating Counsell and sending a full house of 67,204 into a state of pandemonium.

Marlins reliever Jay Powell got the win for a hitless top of the 11th. Fernandez, who drove in both Indian runs with a two-run single in the third, had to endure some comparisons to Bill Buckner. For Renteria (who had three hits in the game), the series-winning single was his sixth walk-off hit of the year. For the Marlins, the dramatic win marked their 28th victory in their final at-bat for the year, a figure that includes 3 other such triumphs in the postseason.

The dramatics of Game Seven redeemed the sloppy play and poor pitching that plagued the first six contests, which received record-low television ratings. Overall, a series record 76 walks were issued by mostly inexperienced pitchers, 13 errors were committed, 81 runs were scored, and miserable weather marred the three middle games at Cleveland. But in the end a victorious and well played thriller gave a young franchise the coveted spot on the top of the mountain.

9. *This strikeout artist totaled a record-tying 12 one-hitters, 15 seasons of at least 200 Ks, three straight 300-K campaigns, and 215 double-digit strikeout performances. He is:*

A Rob Feller
B Nolan Ryan
C Lefty Grove
D Walter Johnson
E Steve Carlton
F Bob Gibson

ANSWER: B

With 186, Randy Johnson is fast approaching Ryan's record of double-digit strikeout performances. Sandy Koufax's 98 such performances are the third most ever. In 2002 Johnson whiffed 334 batters to reach 300 strikeouts for a record fifth consecutive season. In that season the "Big Unit" also registered his sixth 300-K season overall, matching Ryan.

In 1998 Curt Schilling whiffed exactly 300 batters to become the sixth pitcher with consecutive 300-K campaigns. Amos Rusie was the first to do so in 1890–91, followed by Rube Waddell (1903–4), Koufax (1965–66), Ryan (1972–74 and 1976–77), and Richard (1978–79). Johnson was the seventh.

Ryan in 1973 struck out 10 or more batters 23 times, a mark tied by the "Big Unit" in 1999, 2000, and 2001.

By the way, Johnson and Schilling became the first teammates to each strike out 300 batters in 2002.

◆ Did you know Grover Alexander never pitched a no-hitter during his illustrious career, which included a single-season record four one-hitters in 1915?

◆ Did you know that, in the three years prior to his rookie campaign in 1968, Ryan, a six-foot-two Texan, struck out a mind-boggling 445 batters in only 291 innings of work in the Mets' farm system?

10. *Which of the following perfect games was the first game of a double-header:*

A Sandy Koufax's
B Jim Bunning's
C John Lee Richmond's
D Cy Young's

ANSWER: B

Bunning's gem, on Father's Day no less, was the opening game of a twinbill on June 21, 1964. Ernie Shore's performance on June 23, 1917, which is no longer counted as an official perfect game, was also the first game of a doubleheader.

◆ Did you know in catching Jim Bunning's Father's Day perfect game in 1964, Phillies catcher Gus Triandos became the first receiver to catch a no-hitter in both leagues? Triandos, a 13-year major league catcher with a .244 lifetime batting average, caught Hoyt Wilhelm's no-hitter with the Orioles in 1958.

◆ Did you know Mike Witt pitched his 1984 perfect game on the last day of the regular season, that September 30th? The California Angels' six-foot-seven righthander struck out 10 Texas Rangers.

11. *Can you name the keystone combination that each earned a Gold Glove during consecutive championship seasons?*

ANSWER: Dave Concepcion and Joe Morgan

Shortstop Dave Concepcion and Hall of Fame second baseman Joe Morgan each won consecutive Gold Gloves for the 1975 and 1976 world champion Cincinnati Reds. Morgan (who won five Gold Gloves, in 1973–77) and Concepcion (who earned his five Gold Gloves from 1974 to 1977 and in 1979) played a huge role in the Big Red Machine's success. The 1975 Reds led the league in defense (by far), runs, and stolen bases and posted the third best team ERA. Also led by Gold Glovers Johnny Bench (1968–77) and center fielder Cesar Geronimo (1974–77), the 1975 Reds established a then-record 15-game errorless streak with the help of, arguably, the best middle defense in baseball history. (The Reds' 15-game errorless streak was later surpassed by the 1991 Cardinals' streak of 16 games.)

The 1976 Reds also led the league in defense (matching the 102 errors and .984 percentage of the previous year), as well as in stolen bases and every major offensive category.

◆ Did you know the 1999 New York Mets set records by committing just 68 errors and compiling a .989 fielding percentage? The error mark was 13 fewer than the previous record low, set by the 1998 Baltimore Orioles. The previous record for fielding percentage was .986, set by the 1995 Cincinnati Reds. New York's infield committed just 33 errors, 12 fewer than the previous record, set by the 1964 Orioles. First baseman John Olerud and third baseman Robin Ventura each made nine errors, while the keystone combination of Rey Ordonez (four) and Edgardo Alfonzo (five) combined for nine. The 1988 Twins' mark of 84 errors lasted 10 years. In 2000 the Indians set AL records for fewest errors (72) and highest fielding percentage (.98813).

◆ Did you know the Cincinnati Reds made the fewest errors in a season a record 20 times in the 20th century?

◆ Did you know the 1965 Minnesota Twins are the only team in history to lead their league in errors and still reach the World Series? Minnesota that season committed 172 miscues but still won 102 games. The Twins lost the World Series in seven games to the Dodgers.

12. *This Yankee holds the record for the longest hitting streak in World Series history and is among the top 10 in six major offensive categories during fall classic play. This clutch player also scored the 1953 World Series–winning run. Who is he?*

ANSWER: Hank Bauer

Bauer began his 17-game World Series hitting streak during Game One of the 1956 World Series and continued the hot stretch with a hit in every series game through Game Three of the 1958 World Series.

Bauer's World Series success is a story of adversity overcome. The Yankee right fielder's offensive performance was abysmal in his first four World Series (1949–52), as he went 7-for-57 (.123) with one extra-base hit, two runs scored, and five RBI. In the 1953 fall classic, Bauer contributed with six hits (.261) and six runs, including the series-winning run on Billy Martin's walk-off single in the ninth inning of Game Six, a 4-3 victory that netted the Yankees their fifth straight world championship. Platooning, the right-handed hitter batted .429 in the 1955 World Series. The following October, Bauer got a hit in all seven games, hitting his first World Series home run among his nine safeties. In 1957 he again got a hit in all seven games, homering twice and driving in six runs. In the 1958 fall classic Bauer slugged .710 in the seven-game set, homering four times (tying the then-record) with eight RBI. Over his last five World Series, Bauer batted .298 (39-for-131) with seven homers, 19 RBI, and 19 runs scored, in stark contrast to his first four classics.

Marquis Grissom of the Cleveland Indians had his World Series hitting streak stopped at 15 in 1997, after hitting safely in all 12 World Series games for the Atlanta Braves in 1995 and 1996.

Derek Jeter hit safely in all 12 postseason games in 1999 (including all four games in the World Series) to tie Bauer for the longest postseason hitting streak at 17. Jeter's postseason hitting streak ended at 17 in 2000, and, in 2001, his World Series hitting streak ended at 14, three shy of Bauer's standard, one behind Grissom, and tied with Roberto Clemente.

◆ Did you know Tris Speaker remains the only player in history to put together three hitting streaks of at least 20 games in the same season? Speaker accomplished this feat in 1912, during which he hit safely in a career-best 30 and had two other streaks of 20, according to the Baseball Hall of Fame. Pete Rose enjoyed a record seven hitting streaks of at least 20 games in his career. Speaker, Cobb, Chuck Klein, and Heinie Manush each had five such streaks. Ty Cobb and George Sisler remain the only two players in history with a pair of 30-game hitting streaks.

13. *The 1936 Yankees are the only team in history to boast five players who accumulated 100-plus RBI. Fill any two of the three blanks.*

> Lou Gehrig (152)
> A _____ _____ (125)
> Tony Lazzeri (109)
> B _____ _____ (107)
> C _____ _____ (107)

ANSWER: A—Joe DiMaggio, B—Bill Dickey, C—George Selkirk

The Mariners in 1996 came very close to matching the 1936 Yankees. Ken Griffey Jr. had 140 RBI, Jay Buhner, 138, Alex Rodriguez, 123, and Edgar Martinez, 103. Paul Sorrento was 7 RBI shy of the century mark.

14. *Boston's Tom Gordon set a major league record by converting 54 consecutive save opportunities, including his last 43 of the 1998 season. Can you name one of the two relievers whose record of 41 straight saves Gordon broke?*

ANSWER: Trevor Hoffman and Rod Beck

Trevor Hoffman of the Padres and Rod Beck of the Giants shared the record of 41 straight saves. Hoffman converted his last 8 chances in 1997 and first 33 in 1998. After saving all of his 28 opportunities in 1994, Beck continued the streak (which had begun late in 1993) into 1995, reaching 41 consecutive save conversions in May. Gordon, who also set a record for consecutive saves over the course of one season with 43 in 1998, stretched his record streak to 54 by converting his first 11 opportunities in 1999. After blowing a save on April 14, 1998, Gordon didn't waste another chance until June 5, 1999. Before Gordon, the record for consecutive saves in one year belonged to Cleveland's Jose Mesa, who converted his first 38 save opportunities in 1995.

The man whose record Beck edged is Dennis Eckersley. Since blowing a save on September 11, 1991, Eckersley saved his last four chances of that season and his first 36 in 1992. Eckersley's 40 consecutive saves shattered Rob Dibble's streak of 26 over the 1990 and 1991 seasons for the Cincinnati Reds. Eckersley turned the baseball world's attention to relieving in 1992 by sweeping postseason honors. The accurate side-armer won the AL Cy Young Award and the AL MVP Award after winning seven of eight decisions and nailing 51 saves in 54 chances (an incredible percentage of 94.4 percent) over 69 games. In addition, "Eck" struck out 93 batters and walked only 11 (an unbelievable strikeout to walk ratio of 8.5 to 1) in 80 innings.

Simply put, anyone describing Eckersley would soon run out of superlatives. When asked to do so, third base teammate Carney Lansford said, "We don't play to win. We play to bring 'Eck' in the game." The last time Eckersley was relieved prior to the 1993 season was on May 25, 1991. In 1992 Eckersley was so dominant and efficient that he allowed only two inherited runners to score and was called for only 290 balls to the 309 batters he faced.

◆ Did you know Trevor Hoffman's .888 career save percentage is the best ever? Entering the 2003 season, Hoffman has 352 saves in 396 opportunities. Hoffman surpassed Tom Henke's .8698 mark as best among those with at least 150 saves.

15. *Name the Brewers pitcher and catcher off whom Rickey Henderson stole his record-breaking 119th base during the 1982 season?*

ANSWER: Doc Medich and Ted Simmons

Medich and Simmons on August 27 of that year formed the battery off which Henderson eclipsed Lou Brock's single-season record of 118 steals, en route to a modern standard of 130. In fact, Henderson swiped 3 more bases that game. Opponents, however, soon came to focus on stopping Henderson to such an extent that he was only able to steal 3 bags that September after pilfering 127 through August.

When Brock made history with his record-breaking 105th stolen base on September 10, 1974, he victimized Philadelphia's battery of Dick Ruthven and Bob Boone twice that evening. Then, negro league Hall of Famer James "Cool Papa" Bell awarded Brock second base in a special ceremony.

When Maury Wills broke Ty Cobb's record of 96 steals on September 23 of the 1962 season, the victimized Cardinals battery was Larry Jackson and Carl Sawatski. Wills also stole more than one base on his record-setting day.

Cobb's stolen base success rate was 71.6 percent, Henderson's was 75.6 percent, Brock's was 78.1 percent, and Wills' was a most impressive 88.8 percent. At the time he claimed the record, Brock was 35 years old. Henderson was a young pup at 24, Cobb was 28, and Wills turned 30 that October 2.

◆ Did you know that no team from 1950 to 1956 stole 100 bases—a statistic that makes Maury Wills' 104 stolen bases in 1962 seem even more remarkable? Wills was to the stolen base what Babe Ruth was to the home run in the late 1910s and early 1920s, bringing the art back to the forefront. For his efforts, Wills was awarded the NL MVP in 1962. He also scored 130 runs, collected 208 hits, and won the Gold Glove at short that season.

16. *Since the All-Star Game MVP was instituted in 1962, only once has there been a co-presentation of the award. It happened in:*

A 1962
B 1979
C 1981
D 1975

ANSWER: D

The Cubs' Bill Madlock and the Mets' Jon Matlack shared the honor in 1975. In 1962 there were two All-Star Games, hence two separate MVPs. From 1959 to 1961 there were also two, but the All-Star Game MVP award didn't debut until 1962.

◆ Did you know Bill Madlock became the first major league third baseman in history to win more than one batting title in 1976, winning his second straight for the Cubs? Madlock won four batting titles, the first of which came in 1975 for the Cubs, with the last two benefiting the Pirates organization, in 1981 and 1983. George Brett and Wade Boggs have since joined the club with three and six, respectively.

17. *Hall of Famers Paul and Lloyd Waner were the first set of brothers to finish their careers with a .300 average (with at least 10 years each). Can you choose the only other duo?*

A Ed Delahanty and Jim Delahanty
B Joe DiMaggio and Dom DiMaggio
C Bob Meusel and Irish Meusel
D Joe Sewell and Luke Sewell

ANSWER: C

Bob and Irish Meusel had remarkably similar careers. Bob batted .309 and gathered 1,693 hits over a career that spanned 11 years, the first 10 for the Yankees. He appeared in six World Series for the Yankees, winning three. Irish, whose birth name is Emil, batted .310 and collected 1,521 hits over a career that also spanned 11 years. Irish appeared in four straight World Series for the Giants, winning the first two. Each played left field, batted right-handed, and had a little pop in their bats. Each led the league in RBI once. Bob hit 156 homers to Irish's 106, although the latter's career coincided with the Dead Ball Era.

Interestingly, Bob's Yankees squared off in the fall classic against Irish's Giants in three straight years, from 1921 to 1923. The elder Irish came away victorious the first two times, with Bob helping the Yankees win the franchise's first world championship in 1923. Irish had seven RBI in the 1921 and 1922 World Series, and Bob had eight RBI in the 1923 Series. Perhaps not coincidentally, the series outcome mirrored which Meusel brother performed best.

"Big Poison" Paul Waner hit .333 over 20 seasons, and "Little Poison" Lloyd hit .316 over 18 seasons. Lloyd couldn't quite join Paul as a member of the 3,000-hit club, finishing with 2,459 hits.

18. *Known for his slugging, this Hall of Famer held the career record in home runs and triples when he retired from Major League Baseball in 1897. Who is he?*

ANSWER: Roger Connor

A 19th century stalwart, Connor is known more for his lifetime total of 138 home runs, a record which was surpassed by Babe Ruth in 1921, than he is for his career total of 233 triples. His triples mark was surpassed by Jake Beckley in 1905 and by just three others since: Honus Wagner, Ty Cobb, and current leader Sam Crawford. The strong, left-handed first baseman was a consistent performer, producing great career power numbers despite leading the National League in homers just once and triples twice, with 18 three-baggers in 1882 and 20 in 1886. He added 22 three-baggers in 1887 and a career-high 25 in 1894. In nine different seasons, he totaled 15 triples or more. Connor batted .317 over an 18-year career that also featured a .397 on-base percentage and a .486 slugging percentage.

Although Connor left the majors in 1897, he didn't stop playing. He purchased the Waterbury club of the Connecticut League and attracted fans by inserting himself. Besides being the owner, Connor worked as the field manager and the team's 41-year-old first baseman. He wasn't just taking up space, either, hitting .319 in 1898 and leading the circuit with a .392 mark the following year at the age of 42.

19. *Match these thieves with their corresponding feats or inabilities:*

1	Ty Cobb	A	never stole second, third, and home in the same game
2	Robby Thompson	B	stole 743 bases (home 17 times)
3	Rickey Henderson	C	stole 722 bases (home 27 times)
4	Honus Wagner	D	stole second, third, and home in a game a record six times
5	Eddie Collins	E	was caught stealing a record four times in a 12-inning game

ANSWER: 1—D, 2—E, 3—A, 4—C, 5—B

On July 12, 1911, Cobb drew a walk off Athletics southpaw Harry Krause and then, on consecutive pitches, stole second, third, and home. Cobb believed that the more daring he was on the basepaths, the more havoc he created for the opposing defense and, therefore, the more miscues he caused. No baserunner took as many chances on the basepaths as Cobb, and no baserunner (Jackie Robinson, Lou Brock, and Rickey Henderson included) created as much havoc for opponents as the "Georgia Peach." Cobb ran the bases much as he lived life—with reckless abandon. . . . Thompson was gunned down on four straight steal attempts by Phillies' catcher Bo Diaz on June 27, 1986.

◆ Did you know the Cubs' Frank Schulte was caught stealing 9 times in 11 World Series attempts? In addition to that dubious fall classic mark, Schulte was caught stealing a record five times by Philadelphia Athletic catchers Ira Thomas and Jack Lapp in the 1910 World Series. His only two successful steals came in the 1908 fall classic against notoriously bad Tigers receiver Boss Schmidt.

20. *Perhaps no two Hall of Famers are mistaken for one another more often than George Kelly and Joe Kelley. Listed are some accomplishments achieved by one of the pair. Correctly select to whom the feats or distinctions belong, by indicating "GK" for George Kelly or "JK" for Joe Kelley.*

A boasted a career .317 batting average and .402 on-base average
B batted .297 over a career that featured four World Series appearances
C had five straight 100-RBI seasons from 1894 to 1898

D twice led the league in RBI and once in home runs
E finished in the top ten in slugging seven times
F twice finished in the top six in the NL MVP voting
G had 194 triples and 443 stolen bases
H was a great fielding first baseman during his career, spent mostly with the Giants
I was a left fielder for the powerhouse Baltimore Orioles of the 1890s
J was nicknamed "High Pockets"

ANSWER: A—JK, B—GK, C—JK, D—GK, E—JK, F—GK, G—JK, H—GK, I—JK, J—GK

The right-handed Joe Kelley, who played from 1891 to 1908, batted .300 for 11 straight years, knocked in at least 91 runs for 7 straight years and "boasted a powerful arm, great speed, and tremendous spirit and magnetism," according to the Hall of Fame. In the twilight of his 17-year career Joe Kelley served as player-manager for the Reds (for three years) and the Braves (for one year). . . . The six-foot-four George Kelly, who played from 1915 to 1932, hit at least 17 homers five straight years. Hall of Fame Giants manager John McGraw said Kelly delivered "more important hits for me than any player I ever had."

21. *Match these players with the historical events they participated in:*

1 Nolan Ryan — A is the only player to have participated in two unassisted triple plays

2 Paul O'Neill — B stole a modern record of 13 bases as a pitcher over his career

3 Jim Cooney — C is the only player to have been in uniform for three nine-inning, 19-strikeout games

4 Davey Johnson — D was the only player to hit behind all-time home run leaders Hank Aaron and Japan's Sadaharu Oh

5 Bob Gibson — E is the only player to have played on the winning side of three perfect games

ANSWER: 1—C, 2—E, 3—A, 4—D, 5—B

O'Neill, a right fielder, was in the lineup when the Yankees' David Wells and David Cone threw their perfect games, in 1998 and

1999, respectively, and when the Reds' Tom Browning pitched his gem in 1988. Reggie Jackson was on the winning side in the Jim Hunter and Mike Witt gems. . . . Ryan was in uniform for his 19-strikeout game on August 12, 1974, for Tom Seaver's performance on April 22, 1970, as well as for Steve Carlton's against Ryan's Mets on September 15, 1969. In his 1974 performance, Ryan was a strike away from a record 20th K as he built a two-strike count to the last batter. But rookie Rick Burleson made contact with Ryan's last offering, lining right back to the mound, where Ryan made the catch for the win, settling instead for a record-tying 19. . . . Cooney was erased on the bases when his Cardinal teammate Jim Bottomley lined into an unassisted triple play to Pirate shortstop Glen Wright on May 7, 1925. Cooney got his revenge when he turned his unassisted gem for the Cubs on May 30, 1927, against Pittsburgh.

◆ Did you know Alfredo Griffin is the only other player besides Paul O'Neill to appear in the box scores for three perfect games, doing so as a member of the losing team all three times? He batted against Len Barker (in 1981) while with Toronto and against Tom Browning (1988) and Dennis Martinez (1991) as a Los Angeles Dodger.

22. *Choose this tough pitcher who struck out Mickey Mantle in 12 of their 16 official confrontations, limiting "The Mick" to but three hits:*

    A Early Wynn
    B Billy Pierce
    C Dick Radatz
    D Herb Score
    E Mike Garcia

ANSWER: C

The hard-throwing, right-handed Radatz had the advantage of pitching to a left-handed Mantle (a switch-hitter, who was naturally right-handed). Radatz, who never started a game, broke in with the Red Sox in 1962 and led the American League in appearances (62) and saves (24) to earn the Fireman of the Year Award as a rookie. He improved to 15-6 with 25 saves and a 1.97 ERA in 1963, and 16-9 with 29 saves and a 2.29 ERA in 1964, earning an All-Star selection each year. During that 1964 season, Radatz struck out 181 batters in 157 innings for a still-standing major league record by a reliever. (Rich Gossage holds the NL mark of 151 Ks in 133 innings for Pittsburgh in 1977.) This power reliever concluded his solid, seven-year career with 122 saves, a 52-43 record and more than a strikeout per inning.

◆ Did you know Dan Quisenberry won the Rolaids Relief Man Award a record five times? Rollie Fingers won it four times, as did Bruce Sutter. Rawly Eastwick (NL) and Bill Campbell (AL) were the winners in the year of the award's inception, 1976.

23. *Match these players with their distinctions:*

1	Dallas Green	A	is the only player to hit a home run in the first and last at-bat of his career
2	Jack Hamilton	B	homered in his first at-bat and tripled in his second season, his only home run and triple in a 21-year career
3	Hoyt Wilhelm	C	was the only pitcher to yield a grand slam to Pete Rose
4	John Miller	D	was the only pitcher to yield a home run to Tommie Aaron but not to Hank

ANSWER: 1—C, 2—D, 3—B, 4—A

Green posted a 20-22 career ledger over eight years before becoming a successful manager, guiding the Phillies to the 1980 world title. . . . Wilhelm retired with an .088 career batting average, getting 38 hits in 432 at-bats. His homer came off the Braves' Dick Hoover. . . . Amazingly, Miller's home runs in his first and last at-bats were his only career home runs. Miller made his debut for the Yankees in 1966 and, after not playing in 1967 and 1968, played for the Dodgers in 1969. Overall, Miller collected 10 hits in 61 at-bats. . . . Tommie Aaron, a first baseman and outfielder for the Braves, never batted above .250 and never hit more than eight homers in his seven major league seasons.

◆ Did you know Earl Averill and Hoyt Wilhelm are the only players among the elite group of 87 who homered in their first major league at-bat to later make the Hall of Fame? Of the 87, Gary Gaetti tops the list with 360 career home runs. Although accounts of how many players homered in their first major league at-bat vary, home run guru David Vincent of the Society for American Baseball Research (SABR) assures me it is 87.

24. *The Big Red Machine has to rank among the best teams of all time. The 1975 Reds went 108-54 and won a classic World Series against the Red Sox, and the 1976 Reds went 102-60, dominating the post-season as well. However, their lineup is well known and would not pose a challenge to you buffs. So you'll be asked about the 1939 Yankees, who defied all odds (after having won the world championship the previous three years) and knocked off every club gunning at them with an emphatic 106-45 mark, despite losing Lou Gehrig to Amyotrophic Lateral Sclerosis (ALS) and playing without an injured Joe DiMaggio for six weeks.*

What made the team so hard to beat was the organization's commitment to winning and the professional attitude toward a common goal each player inherited upon donning the pinstripes, along with the undeniable aura that accompanies them. It was from the same blueprint that the 1949–53 Yankees were created. The players were so unselfish and goal-oriented, even great teams in other sports, such as the NBA's Boston Celtics of the 1960s, are measured against them. Every player knew that the world championship was the goal, and every one thought of the team first and himself second. In the nostalgic documentary When It Was A Game *(produced by cable television's Home Box Office), narrator Peter Kessler related an anecdote in which Yankee manager Joe McCarthy was asked why he liked his second baseman Joe Gordon so much. "I'll show you why I like him," McCarthy responded before calling Gordon over. "What's your batting average?" McCarthy asked. "I don't know," replied Gordon. "What's your fielding average?" asked McCarthy. "I don't know," Gordon answered. McCarthy, then, told the interviewer, "That's why I like him. All he does is come to beat you. OK? Multiply that by nine; that's a tough outfit to beat." With hard-working General Manager Ed Barrow pulling the strings, the 1939 Yankees clubhouse was full of such professionals. The team scored 411 more runs (967-556) than it allowed—the greatest difference outside the 19th century. Below is the 1939 Yankees' defensive alignment. Fill in the blanks, and name the winningest pitcher on the 1939 squad:*

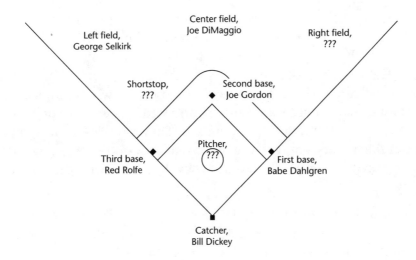

ANSWER: Shortstop, Frank Crosetti; Right field, Charlie Keller; Pitcher, Red Ruffing

Ruffing, who was 21-7, and six others reached double figures in wins in 1939. Righthander Atley Donald was the second leading winner for the Yankees, earning 13 victories among his 16 decisions. Lefty Gomez, Bump Hadley, and Monte Pearson each won 12, spot starter Steve Sundra won 11 of 12, and Oral Hildebrand was 10-4.

Keller and Selkirk flip-flopped in the corner outfield spots, and Tommy Henrich filled in at right field and center. But the rookie Keller received the most playing time in right, responding with a .334 batting average, a .447 on-base percentage, a .500 slugging mark, and 83 RBI in 111 games. The left-handed-swinging Keller continued his hot hitting by clubbing a rookie record three home runs in the subsequent World Series while slugging an outrageous 1.187 to help the Yankees sweep the Reds. Had the World Series MVP trophy existed back then, Keller would have easily won it. Henrich, who didn't play in the World Series due to injury, also proved valuable during the regular season, playing in 99 games and batting .277 with 57 RBI. Nicknamed "Old Reliable" for consistent play throughout his career, Henrich was also a solid defensive player, certainly more skilled with the glove than either Keller or Selkirk.

Crosetti, who played on eight world championship teams and

coached for nine others, was a part of a record 23 pennant winners, either as a player or coach. Crosetti played from 1932 to 1948 and began coaching in 1947, a post he held through 1968.

The 1998 Yankees were very similar to their predecessors in that no player cared who got the deciding hit or the win, as long as the team was victorious. Manager Joe Torre said, "There's no one name that comes to mind but the team itself. They have this inner conceit about them. They know they're good, but they don't really care about telling people how good they are. They don't care who gets the winning hit."

◆ Did you know the 1987 world champion Twins were actually outscored during the regular season, 806-786? The only other division or pennant champion (since 1876) to be outscored was the 1984 AL West champion Kansas City Royals club (686-673). Each of the seven teams in the AL West that year was outscored, a dubious distinction. The 1981 Royals team was also outscored, 405-397, for the season, but it was not outscored during its post-strike second-half title. The Royals did not win their division, anyway, losing to Oakland in the Division Series.

25. *Match these players with their unusual feats:*

1 Fred Odwell	A	is the only player to play in an All-Star Game and later umpire one
2 Ty Cobb	B	is the only player besides Rusty Staub to homer in his teens and his forties
3 Mickey Owen	C	is the only slugger never to homer again after winning a home run title
4 Lon Warneke	D	is the only player to homer in the All-Star Game but not during that regular season

ANSWER: 1—C, 2—B, 3—D, 4—A

Odwell, a left-handed slugger who played in the outfield for the Reds from 1904 to 1907, hit a league-best 9 homers in 1905 and retired with the lowest career home run total (10) for a home run champion. . . . Owen, who hit 14 career homers with a season-high of 4, failed to homer in 421 regular-season at-bats during the 1942 regular season. He contributed in other ways, though, finishing fourth in the National League MVP vote thanks to great defense behind the plate, unselfish play (18 sacrifice bunts), and surprising speed on the basepaths (a comfortable career high of 10 steals). . . . Warneke, a three-time 20-game winner who gained recognition by helping the Cubs into the 1932 and 1935 World Series, became an umpire after he returned from World War II. He retired with a 193-121 ledger.

◆ Did you know umpire George Moriarty, a former Detroit Tigers player as well as manager, was allowed to arbiter the 1935 World Series between the Tigers and Cubs? A below-average batter who possessed good speed and solid defensive skills at third base, Moriarty played for Detroit from 1909 to 1915. Following a 13-year major league career, Moriarty managed the Tigers in 1927 and 1928 before embarking on a 22-year career as an American League umpire. Realizing this, the Cubs players and coaches kept an eye on Moriarty and rode him every chance they got, reminding him to be honest throughout the six-game series, won by the Tigers. The Cubs rode Moriarty for good reason, as it turned out. In Hank Greenberg's autobiography, *Hank Greenberg,* the Hall of Fame first baseman (with Ira Berkow's help) wrote, "When [Moriarty] was umpiring third base . . . he coached me on how to take a lead so I could steal home."

26. *By now you know the Boston Red Sox were once called the "Pilgrims," and perhaps you know they were also called the "Americans," "Puritans," and "Plymouth Rocks," as well as the "Speed Boys," before they permanently chose their current name in 1907. Match these current franchises with their original team name.*

1	San Francisco Giants	A	Blues
2	Baltimore Orioles	B	Gothams
3	Philadelphia Phillies	C	Atlantics
4	Cleveland Indians	D	Brewers
5	Los Angeles Dodgers	E	Quakers

ANSWER: 1—B, 2—D, 3—E, 4—A, 5—C

The Giants, then in New York, were first called Gothams in 1883. . . . The current Orioles franchise began as the Milwaukee Brewers in 1901, moved to St. Louis and became the "Browns" in 1902, and then moved to Baltimore in 1954 as the Orioles. . . . The Phillies began as the Quakers in 1883, posting a horrible 17-81 ledger in their inaugural season. . . . The Indians were first called the Blues, not to be confused with the 1800s Cleveland Blues of the National League or other unrelated and defunct Blues franchises during the 19th century. . . . The Dodgers began as the "Atlantics" of the American Association in 1884. . . . The 1907 Red Sox went 59-90 despite the new name, finishing in seventh place. Hall of Fame third baseman Jimmy Collins was the team's leading hitter for average (.291), and Hall of Famer Cy Young won 21 games with a 1.99 ERA.

27. *Match these 19th-century stars with their career totals:*

1	Jack Beckley	A .308 batting average, 1,357 runs
2	Billy Hamilton	B .344 batting average, 915 stolen bases
3	Dan Brouthers	C 2,853 hits, 1,718 runs, .339 average
4	King Kelly	D .342 batting average, 106 homers, 205 triples, 1,523 runs
5	Jesse Burkett	E .308 batting average, 1,600 runs, 1,575 RBI

ANSWER: 1—E, 2—B, 3—D, 4—A, 5—C

All five are in the Hall of Fame. Beckley and Brouthers were first basemen, and Hamilton, Kelly, and Burkett were outfielders. . . . "Big" Dan Brouthers was perhaps the most intimidating player in the 19th century, leading the league in slugging seven times and in batting five times. Brouthers, who hit as many as 14 homers in a season (1884), is credited with hitting the longest home run in the 1800s, clobbering a pitch completely out of Capital Park. Despite hitting .344 in 1896, Brouthers quit the Philadelphia Phillies over a salary dispute. He returned eight years later for five at-bats with the New York Giants, his 11th team, at the age of 46. . . . Kelly was without a doubt the flashiest and most flamboyant offensive performer of the 19th century, exciting fans with a good bat and a hectic style of baserunning that confused opponents and prompted the famous chant, "Slide, Kelly, slide." An integral member of seven pennant-winning clubs, five on Cap Anson's Chicago clubs of the 1880s, and three second-place teams, Kelly won two batting titles, swiped 315 bases, and led the National League in runs three straight seasons, in doubles three times, and on-base percentage twice. Although a poor fielder, Kelly displayed a rare brand of versatility by splitting time between right field and catcher, and by playing every position on the field throughout a 16-year career that ended following the 1893 season.

◆ Did you know Hall of Fame second baseman Bid McPhee refused to wear a glove throughout his first 14 major league seasons? McPhee, recognized as the best second baseman of the 19th century, batted .272 over his 18-year career and consistently ranked atop the league in defensive categories.

Although gloves became generally used by 1886, his fifth season, McPhee refused to wear them for another decade, for reasons relating to machismo.

28. *This outfielder holds the major league record of 392 consecutive error-less games and 938 consecutive errorless chances. Is he Devon White, Ken Griffey Jr., or Darren Lewis?*

ANSWER: Darren Lewis

Lewis, a center fielder, made his debut on August 21, 1990, with the Oakland A's before being traded across the bay to the San Francisco Giants that December. He didn't commit his first error in the majors until June 30, 1994, against Montreal, nearly four years after his debut (he played in 25 games in 1990, 72 games in 1991, 100 games in 1992, 136 games in 1993, and 59 games in 1994 before his first miscue). The errorless span also covered a National League record 369 games and 905 chances since 1991.

To give that streak its proper due, consider that Johnny Damon holds the AL record with 592 consecutive errorless chances, from August 27, 2000, to August 31, 2002.

29. *Match these pioneering Hall of Famers with their heritage:*

1	Roberto Clemente	A	first Venezuelan inducted
2	Ferguson Jenkins	B	first Canadian inducted
3	Jackie Robinson	C	first Latin American inducted
4	Chief Bender	D	first Indian inducted
5	Luis Aparicio	E	first African American inducted, in 1962

ANSWER: 1—C, 2—B, 3—E, 4—D, 5—A

Jenkins won at least 20 games seven times, including each year from 1967 to 1972. In 1974 Jenkins won a career-high 25 games for the Texas Rangers in his first AL season. . . . Bender, one of the very best pitchers in the clutch, capped a great career by earning induction into the Hall of Fame in 1953, a year before he died. A clean-living man, Bender retired with a 210-127 ledger compiled over a 16-year career that featured six campaigns of at least 17 wins and a trio of seasons with the league's best winning percentage. Bender also won six World Series games. . . . Aparicio earned election almost exclusively by his brilliant defensive play at short. Displaying great range and a quick, smooth release, Aparicio led the American League in fielding eight times, tying him with Everett Scott and Lou Boudreau for the major league record. His 8,016 assists are the second highest by any player at any position (only Ozzie Smith has more). The eight-time All-Star is regarded as the best defensive shortstop pre-Ozzie.

◆ Did you know Ferguson Jenkins remains the last pitcher to win 20 games and drive in 20 runners in a season? In 1971 Jenkins won 24 games for the Cubs while also driving in 21 runs and slamming six homers.

◆ Did you know Larry Walker in 1997 became the first native Canadian to earn a league MVP honor, winning the NL award by a landslide. Walker also surpassed many of Jeff Heath's Canadian records, including most career home runs (Walker enters the 2003 season with 335), most career RBI (Walker enters the 2003 season with 1,133), most career hits (Walker enters the 2003 season with 1,863), most home runs in a season (49), most RBI in a season (130), and most stolen bases (33) in a season.

◆ Did you know Andres Galarraga became Venezuela's career home run leader and career RBI leader in 1997? Galarraga surpassed Tony Armas when he hit his 252nd homer on April 30, and surpassed Dave Concepcion when he drove in the 951st run of his career. In 1996 Galarraga also surpassed Armas' Venezuelan single-season mark of 43 homers by clubbing 47. In 1998 Sammy Sosa set new marks for a Latin American in most of the single-season power categories with a 66-homer, 158-RBI, and 416–total base campaign. Sosa would later set new marks with 160 RBI and 425 total bases.

30. *In his record-setting 2001 season, Barry Bonds belted 39 home runs by the All-Star break, more than anyone else in history through that point. When Mark McGwire in 1998 hit 37 by the break, whose record did he tie?*

    A Jimmie Foxx
    B Dave Kingman

C Reggie Jackson
D Roger Maris
E Babe Ruth

ANSWER: C

Jackson hit only 10 more home runs over the rest of the 1969 campaign and finished with 47, third in the American League. McGwire went on to hit 33 more en route to his 70. Bonds blasted 34 more for a staggering total of 73. According to Lyle Spatz of the Society for American Baseball Research, Hank Greenberg (1938) and Albert Belle (1995) shared the record for most home runs hit after the All-Star break (36) before McGwire drilled 37 in 1999. McGwire is the only player in history to hit 30 home runs before the All-Star break four times.

31. *Match these early stars with their career average and position:*

1	Hughie Jennings	A	career .292-hitting second baseman
2	Jack Glasscock	B	career .290-hitting shortstop
3	Deacon White	C	career .312-hitting shortstop
4	Fred Dunlap	D	career .273-hitting second baseman
5	Bobby Lowe	E	career .291-hitting left fielder
6	Sherry Magee	F	career .303-hitting third baseman/catcher

ANSWER: 1—C, 2—B, 3—F, 4—A, 5—D, 6—E

Jennings, who had five consecutive seasons of at least 125 runs scored and three consecutive 100-RBI seasons for the Baltimore Orioles during the 1890s, retired with a .390 on-base percentage and 359 stolen bases. The competitive Hall of Famer went on to a stellar managerial career, guiding the Tigers to three straight pennants, from 1907 to 1909 (in his first three years as manager, a feat yet to be duplicated), and the 1924 Giants into the World Series as well. . . . Glasscock enjoyed six .300 seasons, won the 1890 batting title, twice led the league in hits, and swiped 372 bases during a 17-year career spent mostly with the defunct Cleveland Blues and Indianapolis Hoosiers. Nicknamed "Pebbly Jack" for his habit of picking up pebbles, Glasscock solidly fielded his shortstop position, playing bare-handed. He also was among the first players to back up throws at second base, as well as to signal in advance who would cover on a play at second. . . .

White, who established himself as the best bare-handed catcher in the late 1870s and then as an excellent third baseman in the 1880s, led the National League in batting average, RBI, slugging, hits, and triples in 1877. A magnet for success, White helped Cap Anson win the inaugural 1876 NL pennant—after heavily contributing to Harry Wright's three straight National Association titles—and rejoined Wright the following year in the National League for a fifth straight pennant. The left-handed batter didn't slug much but played every position at one time or another and provided field leadership in abundance. White was clearly one of the era's top-echelon players. That's why it's difficult to understand the decision of the newly structured Veterans Committee, which in 2002 submitted a list of 200 players it will re-review for inclusion in the Hall of Fame, not to recommend White for the Hall. Their list includes some marginal All-Stars from the modern era yet omits unquestionable stars such as White, Glasscock, Dunlap, and Sherry Magee. . . . Dunlap, who played from 1880 to 1891, put together a trio of .300 campaigns but made a name for himself primarily with outstanding defensive play at second base. The smooth fielder comfortably bested the league average in range factor (chances per nine innings) and fielding percentage during each of his first nine years. In 1884 Dunlap enjoyed one of the best and most complete campaigns of the 19th century, playing for the St. Louis Maroons in the Union Association. "Sure Shot" led all second basemen in fielding percentage, range factor (6.41), double plays, assists, and putouts, and led the entire circuit in batting average (.412), slugging (.621), hits (185), home runs (13), runs (a whopping 160), total bases, and extra-base hits. . . . Lowe did a little bit of everything: he used his good range and sure hands to field well, swiped 302 bases, scored at least 100 runs three straight campaigns, and hit for occasional power from the lead-off position (à la Brady Anderson). A key member of the famous Boston Beaneaters of the 1890s, Lowe helped lead the Beaneaters to five pennants in the 1890s and teamed with first baseman Fred Tenney, shortstop Herman Long, and Hall of Fame third baseman Jimmy Collins to form arguably the best infield of the 1800s. . . . Magee, a well-rounded ball player who distinguished himself in the Dead Ball Era, led the National League in RBI four times, won the 1910 batting crown, and led the league in extra-base hits three times and slugging twice. A consistent performer,

Magee finished among the top 7 in homers seven times, in the top 10 in batting six times, in the top 10 in OPS (on-base plus slugging percentage) eight times, and the top 8 in extra-base hits 10 times. In 1919 the right-handed slugger ended a 16-year career that also featured 2,169 hits, 1,182 RBI, 425 doubles, 166 triples, 441 stolen bases, and 260 sacrifices. In the field, Magee completed the full package with great range, a sure glove, and an outstanding right arm. A Phillies left fielder from 1904 to 1914, Magee was traded to the Braves in 1915 at his own request before settling with the Reds in 1917, for whom he played in the victorious 1919 World Series. The only knock on Magee was his temper, which got the best of him on July 10, 1911, when he punched out umpire Bill Finneran and was suspended, originally for for the entire season, before his suspension was reduced and he was allowed back five weeks after the incident. In 1928 Magee came full circle, becoming an umpire. He tragically died the following March after contracting pneumonia.

◆ Did you know Hall of Famer and 19th-century star Cap Anson was loved and respected by so many that a total of $50,000 was raised by the fans and the Cubs as a gift following his retirement in 1897?

32. *This Hall of Fame second baseman played only 1 game at second during his first four years and only 26 games throughout his first five seasons. He is:*

A Joe Morgan
B Rogers Hornsby
C Nap Lajoie
D Eddie Collins
E Frankie Frisch

ANSWER: B

Hornsby was dealt by St. Louis to the New York Giants in 1926 for Frisch after the Cardinals refused to pay his enormous salary demand of $150,000 over three years. His ill remarks directed at management for scheduling an exhibition game during a heated pennant race also had something to do with the trade.

"Rajah" played mostly shortstop and third base during his first five seasons. For all his great feats, the volatile and irreverent Hornsby was traded two other times—and the trades didn't involve other Hall of Famers. In January of 1928, deemed too strict a disciplinarian as player-manager, he was traded to the Boston Braves for Shanty Hogan and Jimmy Welsh. Ten months later, Hornsby was dealt to the Chicago Cubs for Socks Seybold, Percy Jones, Lou Legett, Freddie Maguire, Bruce Cunningham, and $200,000.

In August of 1932, Hornsby was fired as player-manager of the Cubs 99 games into the season. Hornsby had apparently collected money from his players to bet on horses. When the players demanded their money back, Hornsby lost control of his club. The Cubs caught fire at the end of the season and won the NL pennant, later refusing to award Hornsby a World Series share.

◆ Did you know Rogers Hornsby was a minority owner of the St. Louis Cardinals when the organization traded him to the Giants in 1926? Being a club shareholder, Hornsby made the process very difficult for the Cardinals, whose troubles soon convinced Major League Baseball to deny active players any share in team ownership at all. Hall of Famers John McGraw, Frank Chance, and John Montgomery Ward, reportedly, were part-owners as players, although Ward's ownership was of his team in the Players League in 1890. David Stevens' fine book, *Baseball's Radical for All Seasons,* details Ward's career and part-ownership of the Brooklyn club, for which he also managed and started at shortstop, batting .337 with 134 runs scored, 189 hits and 63 stolen bases. Ward performed so well that the covering writers referred to the team as "Ward's Wonders."

33. *Which team owned the major league's best record when the 1994 season was abruptly halted by the strike?*

ANSWER: The Montreal Expos

The Montreal Expos owned an excellent 74-40 ledger and looked like a sure bet to earn their second postseason appearance when labor strife ended that season. The Expos were 3½ games better than the next best team in the majors (the Yankees), and 6 better than the next best team in the National League (the Braves). Due to financial instability, the Expos were later forced to part with much of the talent that gave them such a solid foundation, moving stars such as Pedro Martinez, Larry Walker, John Wetteland, Cliff Floyd, Moises Alou, Jeff

Shaw, Ken Hill, and Marquis Grissom. The Expos are now being out-drawn by some minor league teams amid suggestions of relocation.

The Expos went to the postseason for the first—and only—time in 1981, coming within one run of reaching the World Series, as they suffered a heart-breaking 2-1 defeat to the Los Angeles Dodgers in the decisive Game Five of the NL Championship Series. Montreal advanced to the NL Championship Series in that strike-shortened campaign by defeating Philadelphia three games to two in a specially created Eastern Division Series. Ace Steve Rogers outdueled the Phillies' Steve Carlton twice, beating "Lefty," 3-1, in the opener and hurling a six-hit shutout in the finale. Gary Carter homered twice and drove in six runs in that series, and closer Jeff Reardon saved the Expos' first two wins.

In the NL Championship Series, Rogers won his only start against the Dodgers, a seven-hitter in Game Three. The right-handed Rogers was so relied on by manager Jim Fanning (who had taken over with 27 games left in the second half of the season) that he was summoned in relief to start the top of the ninth inning of a tied Game Five. Meanwhile, reliable closer Jeff Reardon was fresh, healthy, and waiting in the bullpen. A tired Rogers then allowed a solo homer to Rick Monday in that ninth, bringing to an end the Expos' most successful season. Two decades later, the franchise was on the brink of extinction.

The issue of contraction came up as Commissioner Bud Selig tried without success to eliminate two teams—the Montreal Expos and Minnesota Twins—in the offseason after the 2001 campaign. Selig said that the elimination of two teams was necessary to stop industry losses, which he claimed added up to $232 million. *Forbes* magazine, though, reported that Major League Baseball earned $75 million in 2001 rather than losing $232 million as Selig had claimed, a drastic difference of more than $300 million. Selig, former owner of the Brewers, again faced accusations of a conflict of interest, since the Brewers could have benefited financially if the Twins were contracted. Selig still argues that the team is no longer in his name, but he did remain CEO of the Brewers during the six years he served as interim commissioner, then handed the team over to his daughter (Wendy Selig-Prieb, a non-investor), and may regain control of the Brewers once his term as commissioner is over. In my opinion, Milwaukee is much more deserving of contraction than Minnesota. Milwaukee has the smallest television market in the majors, smaller than that of eight minor league teams. Also, the Twins' television market is twice the size of the Brewers', as is Minnesota's metropolitan area.

◆ Did you know Major League Baseball has not contracted since 1899, when the Cleveland Spiders, Washington Senators, Louisville Colonels, and Baltimore Orioles were cut loose from the 12-team National League? The Spiders (a horrible .134 winning percentage), the Senators (49 games behind), and the Colonels (two games under .500) were struggling organizations and had losing records that year. The Orioles, however, had just posted their sixth straight winning record in 1899, 86-62. In fact, that Baltimore franchise had won three straight NL pennants from 1894 to 1896 and went 90-40 in 1897 and then 96-53 in 1898. But Baltimore's owners (manager Ned Hanlon was among them) moved many of their great players following the 1898 season over to a franchise they also owned in Brooklyn, named the Superbas, and transferred the rest of their desirable roster after the 1899 season. The 1900 National League included the Brooklyn Superbas, Pittsburgh Pirates, Philadelphia Phillies, Boston Beaneaters, Chicago Orphans, St. Louis Cardinals, Cincinnati Reds, and New York Giants.

34. *While playing for four different teams, this player has been a member of a division champion each year from 1991 on, with the exception of the strike-aborted 1994 season. Name him.*

ANSWER: David Justice

Justice started in right field for an Atlanta Braves franchise that won the NL West Division from 1991 to 1993 and then the NL East in 1995 and 1996. He then moved on to the Cleveland Indians, who won the AL Central from 1997 to 1999, with Justice splitting time between left field and designated hitter. In 2000 the New York Yankees pulled the trigger on a deal to acquire Justice from the Indians, and his potent left-handed bat and plate discipline helped them win the AL East in 2000 and 2001. Justice played the 2002 season for the AL West Division champion Oakland Athletics. He enters the 2003 season with career marks of 305 home runs, 1,017 RBI, a .378 on-base percentage, and a .500 slugging average.

Justice, who made his debut in 1989, won the NL Rookie of the

Year Award in 1990, hitting 28 homers with a .373 on-base percentage and a .535 slugging average. His 40 homers and career-high 120 RBI helped the Braves win 104 games in 1993, and his 33 homers, 101 RBI, and career-best .329 mark helped the Indians reach the World Series in 1997. In 2000 his two-team total amounted to 118 RBI and career highs of 41 home runs and 306 total bases. In the subsequent AL Championship Series, Justice earned series MVP honors with two homers, two doubles, eight RBI, and a .538 slugging average to help the Yankees defeat the Seattle Mariners in six games for the AL pennant. His 1995 Braves and 2000 Yankees teams won the World Series.

Tom Glavine and John Smoltz have also played on a division champion each year since 1991, not including the 1994 strike season, doing so for the Atlanta Braves.

35. *Vida Blue and Jim "Catfish" Hunter have allowed four career All-Star Game home runs. But _____ was tagged for a record three homers in a single All-Star Game. Name him.*

A Jim Palmer
B Lefty Gomez
C Atlee Hammaker
D Gaylord Perry

ANSWER: A

In the 1977 mid-summer classic at Yankee Stadium, Palmer was hammered by Joe Morgan, Greg Luzinski, and Steve Garvey during the National League's 7-5 victory. Palmer also holds the dubious career All-Star Game mark with seven walks issued. Incidentally, Morgan's home run led off the game, the fourth of five lead-off home runs in All-Star Game history. The four others to lead off a mid-summer classic with a homer are Frankie Frisch (1934), Lou Boudreau (1942), Willie Mays (1965), and Bo Jackson (1989).

◆ Did you know that Sammy Sosa has never homered in his 11 career All-Star at-bats, batting an atrocious .091? The 2000 Home Run Derby champion has also struck out four times in All-Star competition through 2002.

◆ Did you know Randy Johnson is one All-Star Game start away from tying the record for pitchers? Johnson, whose four starts leave him one shy of the record shared by Lefty Gomez, Robin Roberts, and Don Drysdale, has started twice for each league and has been selected nine times. Overall, he is 0-0 with a 0.82 ERA (11 innings, four hits, two walks, and 11 Ks) in seven All-Star appearances.

36. *Match these players with their distinctions:*

1	Ernie Lombardi	A	was the first player to reach the 100-RBI mark at the break
2	Hank Greenberg	B	held the major league record of 23 consecutive losses until Anthony Young shattered his mark
3	Don Buford	C	won a record 18 games by the All-Star break
4	Clifton Curtis	D	was the easiest player in history to double up
5	Wilbur Wood	E	was the hardest player in modern history to double up

ANSWER: 1—D, 2—A, 3—E, 4—B, 5—C

Lombardi was doubled up 261 times during his 5,260-at-bat career, or once every 20.1 at-bats. . . . On the other hand, Buford was only doubled up 33 times during his 4,553-at-bat career, or once every 138.0 at-bats. . . . Greenberg had an amazing 103 RBI by the 1937 All-Star break en route to 170 for the season. In 1998 Texas' Juan Gonzalez became the second player to top 100 RBI before the All-Star break, reaching 101 en route to 157. Greenberg's first half spanned only 76 games, whereas Gonzalez had played in 87. . . . Wood's total of 18 wins at the midway point of the 1972 season was the most since the inception of the All-Star break in 1933. . . . The Mets' Anthony Young snapped his 27-game losing streak on July 28, 1993, to improve his record to 1-13. Young had last won on April 19, 1992, a drought spanning 74 appearances.

37. *Match these sluggers with their power feats:*

1	Ralph Kiner	A	the first second baseman to have back-to-back 30-homer seasons
2	Frank Howard	B	one of only four players to hit a home run over Tiger Stadium's left-field roof

3	Jim Rice	C	the first player to homer six times over a three-game stretch and seven times over four straight games
4	Ryne Sandberg	D	the last American Leaguer to have amassed 400 total bases in a single season
5	Tony Lazzeri	E	hit a record eight home runs in four games

ANSWER: 1—E, 2—B, 3—D, 4—A, 5—C

During a scorching hot streak in 1936, Lazzeri homered once on May 21 (before an off-day), once in the first game of a doubleheader on May 23, twice in the second game that day, and three times on the 24th. Eight others have joined Lazzeri in homering at least six times over three consecutive games: Ralph Kiner (twice), Gus Zernial, Frank Thomas of the Mets, Lee May, Mike Schmidt, Manny Ramirez, Barry Bonds (twice), and Shawn Green (with a record seven from May 23 to 25, 2002). Kiner's two streaks (in 1947) were more impressive than Bonds' two streaks, since Kiner's were separate—almost a month apart—whereas Bonds' overlapped. Kiner was flat-out torrid during the last two months of the 1947 season. On August 16, he tied Lazzeri's then-record of seven homers over a four-game span. On September 12, he slugged his eighth homer over a four-game span, eclipsing the record he had shared for a month. Zernial, Howard, and Bonds have also homered seven times over four games, but no one has matched Kiner's eight. . . . Harmon Killebrew (1962), Cecil Fielder (1990), and Mark McGwire (1997) are the others to duplicate Howard's prodigious 1968 feat. The most famous home run to clear Tiger Stadium's right-field roof came off the bat of Reggie Jackson, whose light tower–destined moon shot in the 1971 All-Star Game off Doc Ellis helped give the American League its only victory between 1963 and 1982. . . . Rice had 406 total bases (25 doubles, 15 triples, and 46 home runs) in 1978. Todd Helton, who in 2000 became the 16th different player to reach the 400 total-base mark, was among four players to accomplish the feat in 2001. Sammy Sosa, Luis Gonzalez, and Barry Bonds were the others. Gonzalez and Bonds were newcomers to the 400-total-base club, bringing the membership to 18. Helton and Sosa are the latest additions to the exclusive membership of multiple 400 total-base seasons, a group that is headed by Lou Gehrig, who had five such seasons. Chuck Klein had three and Babe Ruth had two, as did Rogers Hornsby and Jimmie Foxx.

38. *Match these hurlers with their accomplishments:*

1	Tom Seaver	A	is the only pitcher with 3,000 strikeouts and fewer than 1,000 walks
2	Nolan Ryan	B	became only the second pitcher to win the Cy Young and Rookie of the Year Award
3	Fernando Valenzuela	C	became baseball's first player to be paid $1 million per year
4	Ferguson Jenkins	D	didn't strike out in eight career at-bats against Nolan Ryan

ANSWER: 1—B, 2—C, 3—D, 4—A

After the 1978 season, Rose tested the free-agent market and received a four-year deal worth $810,000 per year for the first million-dollar contract. A year later, Ryan received the first $1 million per year contract ($4.5 million over four years), a deal negotiated by agent Richard Moss—the same man who helped Fernando Valenzuela become the first player to earn a million-dollar deal via arbitration in 1983. . . . Valenzuela's feat of not striking out in eight at-bats versus Ryan is remarkable considering Ryan whiffed 1,174 different major leaguers, including 31 Hall of Famers. By comparison, Atlee Hammaker struck out 13 times against Ryan in 18 at-bats.

39. *In 1996 three clubs (the Baltimore Orioles, Seattle Mariners, and Oakland Athletics) surpassed the mark of 240 home runs set by the 1961 New York Yankees. In 1997 the Mariners set yet a new record with 264. Can you name one of the two teams that shared the record before the 1961 Yankees?*

ANSWER: The 1947 Giants and 1956 Reds

The 1947 Giants hit 221 homers, as did the 1956 Reds. Johnny Mize (51), Willard Marshall (36), Walker Cooper (35), and Bobby Thomson (29) were the biggest Giants contributors. The biggest Reds contributors were Frank Robinson (38), Wally Post (36), Ted Kluszewski (35), Gus Bell (29), and Ed Bailey (28).

In 1996 the Orioles shattered the record with 257. The Mariners clubbed 245 roundtrippers, and the Athletics added 243. In Seattle's record-breaking 1997 campaign, Ken Griffey Jr. belted 56 homers, Jay Buhner crushed 40, Paul Sorrento hit 31, Edgar Martinez, 28, Alex Rodriguez, 23, and Russ Davis, 20, to highlight a power lineup. The Mariners' record streak of four straight 200-homer seasons lasted from 1996 to 1999.

The Rockies tied the NL single-season home run mark in 1996 and surpassed it with an NL record 239 the very next year.

The 1996 teams took advantage of allegedly watered down pitching following developments such as expansion, smaller ballparks, smaller strike zones, and perhaps a "juiced" ball.

◆ Did you know the Oakland Athletics hit 14 grand slams in 2000, breaking the mark of 12 set by the 1997 Atlanta Braves and equaled by the 1999 Cleveland Indians. In 1996 the Seattle Mariners and Baltimore Orioles each hit 11, surpassing the previous mark of 10 set by the 1938 Tigers and equaled by the 1987 Yankees, the 1995 Mariners, and the 1995 Brewers.

40. *Match these pitchers with their distinctions:*

1	Whitey Ford	A	has the best winning percentage of any 300-game winner (.680)
2	Hoyt Wilhelm	B	the oldest to win 20 games, at 42
3	Satchel Paige	C	started the opening game of a World Series eight times
4	Lefty Grove	D	gave up Ted Williams' first hit
5	Warren Spahn	E	the only reliever to win the ERA crown
6	Red Ruffing	F	the Hall of Fame pitcher with the fewest major league strikeouts (290) among those inducted for their pitching

ANSWER: 1—C, 2—E, 3—F, 4—A, 5—B, 6—D

The knuckleballing Wilhelm won the first of two ERA titles in 1952, his rookie season with the New York Giants. He baffled batters with an ERA of 2.43 in 71 appearances spanning 159⅓ innings. That year, Wilhelm also won 15 of his 18 decisions (for a league-best .833 winning percentage) and saved 11 games. Interestingly, Wilhelm qualified for the ERA title just twice, winning each time. In the only year he spent predominantly as a starter (with 27 starts), Wilhelm fashioned a league-leading ERA of 2.19 and a ledger of 15-11 in 1959 for the Baltimore Orioles. He became the first pitcher to win an ERA title in both leagues. The year before, on September 20, 1958, he no-hit the Yankees. Of his 143 career wins, a record 124 came in relief. Wilhelm pitched till just before his 49th birthday. . . . Paige's major league strikeout totals are misleading, as he entered the majors late in his baseball career after giving his heart and soul—two decades' worth—to the Negro National and American Leagues. In fact, Paige is the negro leagues' career leader with 1,177 strikeouts. Paige made his NNL debut with the Pittsburgh Crawfords in 1931 and his major league debut 17 years later. . . . Grove, who also led the American League in winning percentage five times, won exactly 300 games against just 141 defeats. His 31-4 season in 1931 also gives him the best single-season winning percentage among 30-game winners.

◆ Did you know that Satchel Paige once walked the bases loaded on purpose to face his best friend Josh Gibson in the ninth? Paige proceeded to strike out the pernicious Gibson, with two men already out, for the victory. Paige didn't win all the battles between the two, though. According to William Brashler, author of *Josh Gibson,* the slugger claimed he could hit .400 against Paige and .700 "in the pinches." The book further reveals Josh once homered off Paige and then yelled to him, "If you could cook, I'd marry ya." Hilarious!

41. *Can you name the only brother tandem to hurl a combined shutout?*

ANSWER: Rick and Paul Reuschel

Brothers Rick and Paul Reuschel of the Chicago Cubs combined to shut out the Dodgers, 7-0, on August 21, 1975. Rick went the first 6⅓ innings, and Paul closed the door. Rick, the starter, went 11-17 that year. Paul, the reliever, finished the season with five saves and a 3.50 ERA in the first of his five years in the majors. Rick won 214 big-league games in a 19-year career, including 20 for the Cubs in 1977, 19 for the Giants in 1988, and 17 in the Giants' pennant-winning 1989 season. Paul won 16 games and saved 13 over five years for the Cubs and Indians. Each was right-handed.

In another brotherly note, almost a half-century earlier, on May 3, 1927, the Dodgers' Jesse Barnes and the Giants' Virgil Barnes engaged in the first pitching matchup of brothers in major league history, according to Baseball Library. The elder Jesse entered the game in relief and pitched seven strong innings to give Brooklyn a 7-6 triumph over New York. Virgil, who started the game for the Giants and allowed 12 hits, took the loss. Jesse Barnes, a two-time 20-game winner who led the National League with 25 victories in 1919 and was a key member of two New York Giants world championship clubs during the early 1920s, retired in 1927 with a 152-150 ledger. Virgil, younger by five years, pitched for nine seasons, mostly for the Giants, and compiled a 61-59 record with an ERA of 3.66. The brothers were teammates on the Giants from 1919 to 1923. If you're wondering about Stan and Harry Coveleski, they refused to pitch against each other.

◆ Did you know Greg and Mike Maddux became the first brothers in history to face each other, as rookie starting pitchers on September 29, 1986? The Cubs' Greg won, 8-3, over Mike and the Phillies.

42. *Of the 14 times a player has hit four home runs in a game, only one used an inside-the-park to aid his tremendous feat. Can you name the player?*

ANSWER: Ed Delahanty

In fact, two of Delahanty's four homers for the Philadelphia Phillies on July 13, 1896, were inside-the-park, according to home run researcher David Vincent. In that game Delahanty amassed a then-record 17 total bases, a mark since surpassed only by Joe Adcock and Shawn Green.

Delahanty is not among those who hit their four homers in consecutive at-bats within a single game, a feat accomplished only by Bobby Lowe, Lou Gehrig, Rocky Colavito, Mike Schmidt, and Mike Cameron.

Including at-bats over more than one game, 30 different players have homered in four straight at-bats a total of 32 times, most recently a quartet of players in 2002. Of those 30 players, one actually performed the feat over a four-game stretch sprinkled with four walks—Ted Williams, from September 17 to 22, 1957.

◆ Did you know Ed Delahanty is the only player to have a four-double game as well as a four-homer game? Delahanty's record-tying game of four doubles was on May 13, 1899, three years after his four-homer performance.

◆ Did you know Pat Seerey came the closest to a pair of four-homer performances? Three years before his four-homer game, Seerey homered three
times and blasted a triple to Yankee Stadium's "Death Valley" in left-center
for the Indians during a July 13, 1945, game. Three years and five days later,
Seerey, then an overweight White Sox outfielder, blasted four home runs, the
last in the 11th inning of a wild, 12-11 slugfest victory at Philadelphia. Chuck
Klein and Mike Schmidt also hit their fourth homer in extra innings.

43. *Can you name the only two players to hit four consecutive home runs
twice?*

ANSWER: Ralph Kiner and Mike Schmidt

Kiner's streak took place over two games each time. Kiner
homered in his last at-bat on August 15, 1947, and followed that up
by homering in his first three at-bats against the Cardinals the next
day. He repeated the feat two years later by homering in his last two
at-bats on September 11, 1949, and his first two at-bats on September
13 (after an off-day).

Schmidt hit four consecutive homers in Chicago on April 17,
1976. Then, on July 6, 1979, Schmidt hit one out in his last at-bat before homering in his first three plate appearances on July 7, against
the Giants in Veterans Stadium. Schmidt went on to homer in each
of his next two games. Talk about red hot.

44. *Can you name the only player to play on three 100-game losers in the
same season?*

ANSWER: Johnnie LeMaster

In 1985 LeMaster played on the 62-100 Giants, the 60-102 Indians, and, last but not least (no pun intended), the Pirates, who finished with a 57-104 ledger.

A Giant for his first 10 years, the shortstop had not been a member of a last-place team until 1984, his 10th season. LeMaster batted
.128 in a combined 94 at-bats for the three squads in 1985. The .222
career hitter homered just 22 times over a 12-year career that began
with a homer in his first major league at-bat in 1975. Defense was
LeMaster's stronger skill, although he didn't stand out in that department either.

45. *Which college did Jackie Robinson attend?*

A UCLA
B USC
C New York University
D Mississippi State University

ANSWER: A

In addition to baseball, Robinson excelled in track and field, football, and basketball at UCLA. Some even claimed that baseball was Robinson's worst sport. Robinson graduated from UCLA and went on to become a veteran of World War II. For his accomplishments, honor, courage, and role in history, Robinson earned many awards and honors, including Commissioner Peter Ueberroth's decision in 1987 to rename the Rookie of the Year Award in Jackie's name.

46. *Which team sported the only lineup comprised wholly of rookies?*

A 1977 Toronto Blue Jays
B 1962 New York Mets
C 1963 Houston Colt 45's
D 1977 Seattle Mariners

ANSWER: C

On September 27, 1963, the Colt 45's lineup featured nine rookies: Brock Davis (left fielder), Jim Wynn (center fielder), Aaron Pointer (right fielder), Rusty Staub (first baseman), Joe Morgan (second baseman), Sonny Jackson (shortstop), Ernie Fazio (third baseman), Jerry Grote (catcher), and pitcher Jay Dahl. Houston lost by a 10-3 score to the Mets in the Astrodome. As part of a late-season experiment, Houston manager Harry Craft played 15 rookies before sending in his first veteran (pinch-hitter Carl Warwick) in the eighth inning. The average age of his starting lineup was 19 years and four months. For Dahl, who was 17, the game marked his only major league appearance. Sadly, Dahl died in a car accident on June 20, 1965, in Salisbury, North Carolina, at the age of 19.

Of the bunch, Morgan, of course, earned entry into the Hall of Fame, and Staub, Wynn, and Grote became All-Stars. The left-handed-hitting Staub earned seven All-Star selections over a 23-year career that included stints with seven different teams and featured 2,716 hits, 499 doubles, 292 home runs, 1,466 RBI, and a .362 on-base percentage.

Wynn used every inch and ounce of his five-foot-nine, 165-pound frame to earn three All-Star invitations over a consistent and productive 15-year career. The diminutive Wynn, who was nicknamed "Toy Cannon" for his powerful swing and stellar throwing arm, hit 291 home runs despite playing most of his career in the spacious Astrodome, where he enjoyed seven of his eight 20-homer campaigns. A disciplined as well as powerful hitter, Wynn fatigued pitchers with six campaigns of at least 100 walks, twice leading the National League in that category. Wynn's cannon arm netted him 139 career outfield assists and 40 double plays from the outfield.

Grote was a solid defensive catcher who earned two All-Star invitations for the New York Mets. Mostly a singles hitter, Grote batted .282 in 1968, his first All-Star season, and .295 in 1975. However, it was behind the plate that Grote impressed, handling the Mets' plentiful pitching talent with aplomb throughout his 12-year tenure in New York.

◆ Did you know outfielder Harry Craft caught the last out in Johnny Vander Meer's second consecutive no-hitter? Craft also was responsible for the installation of the two-foot screens inside the "foul" poles, after he hit a disputed home run to left field at the Polo Grounds in 1939. Soon afterward, NL president Ford Frick made the screens mandatory in every NL park, and the American League later followed suit.

47. *In the famous poem "Casey at the Bat," the final score was:*

A 3-2
B 5-3
C 4-2
D 4-3
E 6-4

ANSWER: C

Written by Ernest Thayer, this poem first appeared in print on June 3, 1888, in the *San Francisco Examiner* and was made famous by William deWolf Hooper, a singer and monologist.

◆ Did you know Jack Norworth, who wrote the lyrics to "Take Me Out to the Ball Game" in 1908, didn't see his first ball game until 34 years afterward? Albert Von Tilzer wrote the music to the song.

48. *This manager holds the National League record for most World Series and All-Star Games won:*

A Tom Lasorda
B Walter Alston
C Sparky Anderson
D John McGraw

ANSWER: B

Alston won four fall classics and seven All-Star games in accruing a career ledger of 2,040-1,613, for a .558 winning percentage. Alston's 9 All-Star Games managed trail only Stengel's 10, and McCarthy's 7 are third. Incidentally, Joe Torre in 2001 became the first manager from either circuit to win his first four trips to the mid-summer classic.

◆ Did you know Bobby Cox's 30 victories in League Championship Series play (against 31 losses) are the most of any manager? In 1996 Cox surpassed Sparky Anderson's 18 wins in League Championship Series play (against 9 losses). Cox also holds the mark of 27 NL Championship Series victories. Joe Torre holds the mark for AL Championship Series victories (20), with a record overall LCS winning percentage of .741. Torre is 20-7 in AL Championship Series competition and 0-3 in NL Championship Series play. Tony LaRussa also has 20 LCS wins for the second best total, two more than Anderson. Tommy Lasorda and Whitey Herzog each have 16 wins in 30 League Championship Series games. Earl Weaver shared the mark for AL Championship Series victories (15) with LaRussa before Torre's dominant stretch.

49. *Most of the print and attention given to baseball's on-field happenings are about great accomplishments. Little notice is given to the underachievers' feats. Can you name the player with the lowest batting average over the course of a 300-at-bat (minimum) season?*

ANSWER: Bill Bergen

This dubious distinction belongs to Bill Bergen, a Brooklyn Dodger catcher who hit a record-low .139 during the 1909 season—

a measly 48 hits in 346 at-bats. The Society for American Baseball Research (SABR) found that Bergen, in that 1909 season, went 46 straight at-bats without a hit, a stretch believed to be the worst ever by a position player. Bergen also claims the lowest career batting average with a minimum of 2,500 at-bats. Over his 3,028 at-bats (from 1901 to 1911), the right-handed hitter eked out 516 hits for an anemic .170 lifetime batting average and a feeble .395 career OPS (on-base plus slugging percentage). Among those with at least 3,000 at-bats, only Duane Kuiper (with one) homered less often than Bergen (two).

Bergen remains widely recognized as the worst-hitting starter in history. In compensation, he was a solid defensive catcher; he called a good game, caught a pair of no-hitters, and once nailed seven would-be base stealers in a game. Bergen was so bad offensively, however, he was sometimes penciled in the ninth slot of the batting order—behind the pitcher!

Owners of the second through fifth worst career batting averages are: Billy Sullivan Sr. (.212), Dal Maxvill (.214), Bobby Wine (.215), and Dave Duncan (.217). Wine came to bat 3,172 official times, managing a mere 682 hits. Duncan was 617-for-2,885. Maxvill was 748-for-3,443, and Sullivan was 777-for-3,657. In 1970 Maxvill may have had the least productive offensive season ever, hitting .201 and slugging .223 while setting dubious major league records for fewest hits (80), doubles (5), and extra-base hits (7) among those who played at least 150 games.

As unproductive as these batters were, it was another player who came to symbolize poor hitting: Mario Mendoza. The career .215-hitting shortstop (over 1,337 at-bats, spanning nine seasons) was so inept with the bat he inspired the phrase "Mendoza line," representing a batting average below .200 or between .200 and .215, depending on your source. The phrase was born amidst a three-year drought for Mendoza, from 1975 to 1977, in which he featured batting averages of .180, .185, and .198. George Brett coined the phrase, as a way of describing "the point in the Sunday paper batting statistics where the batters' averages were below Mendoza's," according to Baseball Library. Various definitions have been adopted since.

◆ Did you know a shortstop named John Gochnaur may very well have been the worst player of all time? After an 11-at-bat first year with Brooklyn,

Gochnaur hit .185 with 48 errors in a full season (459 at-bats) with Cleveland in 1902. In 1903, Gochnaur hit .185 (in 438 at-bats) with an AL record 98 errors. On cue, 1903 was his last major league season. The following year he batted .161 in 285 at-bats and fielded poorly for San Francisco of the Pacific Coast League. Not much better were Ray Oyler, Frank Emmer, Bill Bergen, Jack Nabors, Aloysius Travers, Rich Morales, and Anthony Young.

◆ Did you know Rob Deer's .179 average in 1991 was the lowest in history among those with 400 at-bats, eclipsing Ed Brinkman's .185 in 1965?

◆ Did you know pitcher Bob Buhl went hitless in 70 at-bats in 1962? The right-handed Buhl batted .089 for a career that spanned 14 years.

50. *Match these World Series walk-off heroes with the pitchers who surrendered these series-ending hits or runs:*

1	Goose Goslin	A	scored on Johnny Miljus' wild pitch
2	Billy Martin	B	doubled off Pat Malone
3	Bing Miller	C	singled off Clem Labine
4	Earl Combs	D	singled off Larry French

ANSWER: 1—D, 2—C, 3—B, 4—A

Goslin's walk-off hit to right field drove in Mickey Cochrane with the winning run as the Tigers beat the Cubs 4-3 in the clinching Game Six of the 1935 World Series. Cochrane singled with one out in the ninth off French, Chicago's starter, before moving to second on Charlie Gehringer's groundout to first. . . . Martin's game-ending hit to center field drove in Hank Bauer with the winning score as the comeback-minded Yankees beat the Dodgers 4-3 in the clinching Game Six of the 1953 World Series. After the Dodgers had tied the game at 3-3 in the top half of the ninth on the strength of Carl Furillo's two-run homer, Bauer started the bottom half for the Yankees with a lead-off walk against the hard-throwing Labine. Yogi Berra followed by lining out to right before Mickey Mantle's infield hit advanced Bauer to second. Martin followed with his 12th hit of the series. . . . Miller's walk-off double drove in Al Simmons to cap a dramatic, three-run ninth and give the Athletics a 3-2 triumph in the clinching Game Five of the 1929 World Series. With one out in the bottom of the ninth, Philadelphia's Max Bishop singled off Malone,

Chicago's starter. Mule Haas followed with a two-run homer to right field, tying the game. Cochrane grounded out for the second out, but a tiring Malone then served one to Simmons, who doubled off the wall. After Jimmie Foxx walked intentionally, Miller followed with a long drive off the wall that pushed home Simmons to end the series. . . . Combs' run in the bottom of the ninth gave the Yankees a 4-3 victory, completing a four-game sweep in the 1927 World Series. Combs started the inning with a walk off Miljus, the Pirates reliever, then advanced to second on Mark Koenig's bunt single. Then, the first of two wild pitches Miljus would deliver moved Combs to third and Koenig to second. After walking Babe Ruth intentionally to load the bases, Miljus struck out Lou Gehrig and Bob Meusel. After getting ahead of Tony Lazzeri, Miljus looked in charge and capable of escaping his own jam. But his next pitch, on an 0-1 count to Lazzeri, was errant, allowing Combs to score with the winning run. The 1927 fall classic remains the only World Series to end on a wild pitch.

51. *Match these early greats with the colleges they came from:*

1	Lou Gehrig	A	Bucknell University
2	Harry Hooper	B	Columbia University
3	Christy Mathewson	C	Michigan
4	Joe Sewell	D	St. Mary's (in San Francisco)
5	George Sisler	E	Alabama

ANSWER: 1—B, 2—D, 3—A, 4—E, 5—C

Due in large part to his intelligence, background, and manner, Mathewson became America's first modern sports hero. The talented, handsome, religious, articulate, and clean-cut Mathewson dispelled the myth that Major League Baseball was for those who could not otherwise function in society. From an affluent family that put him through a private school and Bucknell University (where he was selected class president), the blond, blue-eyed all-American refused to pitch on Sundays because of his religious beliefs. All this and more is shown in Eddie Frierson's one-man play "Matty," in which Frierson plays Mathewson and many other characters, including the interesting John McGraw. If you haven't seen the play (directed by Kerrighan Mahan), you're missing a dear chapter in your baseball life. . . . Eddie

Collins, like Gehrig, graduated from Columbia University. . . . As a left-handed pitcher brimming with excellence, Sisler was an incredible 50-1 for Michigan. . . . Hooper's teammate (and outfield partner) Duffy Lewis also graduated from St. Mary's, and the other third of this outfield trio (one of the best and, probably, the smartest), Tris Speaker, attended a college near his home town in Texas before leaving without a degree. Even their manager Bill Carrigan received a diploma from Holy Cross. Some earlier stars graduated as well. Fred Tenney, a career .295 hitter over 17 years, was one of the first college graduates (1894 class at Brown University) to achieve baseball stardom. Swift center fielder Roy Thomas (1894 class at Penn) also helped work against the stereotype that stars on the field couldn't be stars in the classroom (and vice versa). After graduating, the Phillies' left-handed singles hitter began a 13-year career in 1899, leading the National League in walks seven times and on-base percentage twice while boasting five .300 campaigns, a quartet of 100-run seasons, and a bevy of defensive accomplishments. In the field, Thomas' tremendous range allowed him to lead the National League in putouts three times, and he twice led in total chances before retiring with the highest career fielding percentage among all outfielders. He also retired with a .413 on-base percentage and a then-outstanding .972 fielding percentage. . . . Other 19th-century stars, such as Jim O'Rourke (Yale, 1887), Monte Ward (Columbia, 1894) and John Lee Richmond (Brown, 1880; M.D. at NYU, 1883), also graduated from college and achieved success on the playing field.

♦ Did you know Cap Anson attended Notre Dame's prep program from 1866 to 1868 and Iowa's prep program from 1869 to 1870 but never graduated?

♦ Did you know that it was Harry Hooper who convinced manager Ed Barrow to play Babe Ruth in the outfield for the Red Sox in 1919? Hooper, Boston's team captain, confided this fact to interviewers for the book *The Glory of Their Times,* by Lawrence Ritter.

♦ Did you know Al Lopez is the oldest living Hall of Famer? The 1977 inductee celebrated his 94th birthday on August 20, 2002. Buck Leonard, Rick Ferrell, and Charlie Gehringer, the three previous, have died over the past nine years. Leonard died at the age of 90 in 1997, and Ferrell and Gehringer each passed away at the age of 89 in 1995 and 1993, respectively. Joe DiMaggio was the second oldest Hall of Famer when he passed away in March of 1999 at the age of 84.

◆ Did you know the last living major leaguer born in the 1800s, Chet Hoff, passed away on September 17, 1998, at the age of 107? Karl Swanson, who was born on December 17, 1900, took over as the oldest living major leaguer, but he passed away in the spring of 2002. Ralph Erickson celebrated his 100th birthday on June 25, 2002, before passing away two days later. Willis Hudlin (96) and Joe Cascarella (95) also died in 2002. Billy Werber (94) is now the oldest living player.

52. *Can you name the Yankees utility infielder whose harmonica playing caused manager Yogi Berra to erupt in anger on the team bus, turning the team's focus around en route to the 1964 AL pennant?*

ANSWER: Phil Linz

On August 20, Linz was playing the harmonica in the bus when Berra (angered at the Yankees' fourth straight loss to the White Sox) ordered Linz to stop playing "Mary Had a Little Lamb." Berra, who was maligned in the papers as "too soft" a manager, thought his team wasn't pulling its weight and was in no condition to be "partying," 4½ games back in third place. The incident seemed to spark the Yankees, who won 30 of 43, including 22 of their 28 games in September, to win the pennant by one game over the White Sox (98-64), with the Hank Bauer–managed Orioles (97-65) placing third. (It also didn't hurt that Mickey Mantle came back after his leg injury.) Linz's bat caught fire as well. The "punch and Judy" right-handed hitter who finished his career with a .235 average (11 career home runs in 1,372 at-bats, or 1 homer every 125 at-bats) exploded for two home runs, one double, four singles, and five runs scored in the Yankees' defeat at the hands of the Cardinals during the 1964 World Series.

Incidentally, legend has it that when Linz asked what Berra said, Mickey Mantle told him, "He said play it louder." After he did, Berra, thinking Linz ignored his request, confronted Linz. But Jim Bouton, in his insightful and revolutionary book *Ball Four*, refutes that part as made up.

53. *It's not difficult to remember the 1975 Reds' lineup. The Reds' anony-mous starting pitching, however, is another matter. Nary a pitcher from that staff won more than 15 games, as six hurlers started be-tween 19 and 32 contests. Can you name three of the six starters?*

ANSWER: Don Gullet, Gary Nolan, Jack Billingham, Fred Norman, Pat Darcy, and Clay Kirby

The left-handed Don Gullet started 22 games and was an in-spiring 15-4. Nolan (15-9 and 32 starts) and Billingham (15-10 and 32 starts) accounted for 211 and 208 innings, respectively, to lead the team. The southpaw Norman (12-4 and 26 starts) and righthanders Darcy (11-5 and 22 starts) and Kirby (10-6 and 19 starts) combined for a 4.50 ERA and a 1-2 record in only 14 innings pitched during postseason play.

◆ Did you know Gary Nolan's career fielding percentage of .989 trails only Don Mossi's .990 among pitchers?

54. *Mickey Mantle (536) and Eddie Murray (504) are the two greatest switch-hitting home run hitters of all time. Match these four switch-hitters with their home run totals:*

1	Chili Davis	A	314
2	Reggie Smith	B	287
3	Bobby Bonilla	C	350
4	Ruben Sierra	D	276

ANSWER: 1—C, 2—A, 3—B, 4—D

Chipper Jones has a great chance of climbing the ladder, enter-ing the 2003 season with 253 homers. Ted Simmons (248), Ken Sin-gleton (246), and Mickey Tettleton (245) are eighth, ninth, and tenth, respectively, through 2002. Also, Bernie Williams has 226.

Murray's total of 1,917 RBI is far ahead of Mantle's 1,509 for the all-time lead among switch-hitters. In fact, Murray's total is seventh on the all-time list, just 73 away from third-place Lou Gehrig and 380 behind all-time leader Hank Aaron. Murray fell just 83 RBI shy of joining Aaron and Babe Ruth as the only members of the 2,000-RBI club.

◆ Did you know Eddie Murray is the only man to reach the 500-homer plateau and never hit at least 40 homers in a season? Murray's career-best single-season figure was 33, accomplished for the 1983 world champion Orioles. Similarly, Stan Musial finished with 475 home runs despite never hitting 40 homers over the course of a season. He hit 39 in 1948.

55. *Match these pitching pairs with their distinctions:*

1 Oakland's Todd Van Poppel and Chicago's Wilson Alvarez	A the only pitchers to clinch a postseason berth with a no-hitter
2 Bobo Holloman and Joe Cowley	B the last complete game of their career was a no-hitter
3 Phil Niekro and Don Sutton	C their matchup marked the first in which each starting pitcher was born in the 1970s
4 Mike Scott and Allie Reynolds	D their matchup marked the first first encounter of 300-game winners

ANSWER: 1—C, 2—B, 3—D, 4—A

Cowley's no-hitter on September 19, 1986, for the White Sox was his last win, as he lost his last two decisions that year and all four with the Phillies in 1987. Holloman won two more games after his no-hitter in May 1953 but threw no more complete games. . . . Many remember Scott's no-hitter over the Giants (2-0) on September 25, 1986, to clinch the NL West, and no one who witnessed the 1951 pennant race can forget Reynolds' 8-0 no-hitter over the Red Sox to clinch the pennant on September 28, 1951.

◆ Did you know Wilson Alvarez of the White Sox threw a 7-0 no-hitter over the Orioles on August 11, 1991, in only his second major league game? In his first start, two years earlier with Texas, Alvarez couldn't retire a single batter. Alvarez faced five Toronto Blue Jays, allowing two home runs, another hit, and two walks.

56. *On August 25, 1922, the Chicago Cubs were 26-23 winners over the _____. The Cubs, in fact, led 25-6 in the fourth inning and barely held on to record the 27th out with the bases loaded. The 49 runs scored in this game still represents a single-game major league record.*

ANSWER: Philadelphia Phillies

The game included 51 hits, 23 walks, and 10 errors but lasted just three hours and one minute. Chicago's Cliff Heathcote reached base seven times, tying a modern NL record. Hack Miller, another Cubs outfielder, hit a pair of three-run homers. Leading 11-6 after three innings, the Cubs poured on the scoring with a 14-spot in the fourth inning, grabbing a 19-run bulge. Tony Kaufmann earned the win for the Cubs, who had nine players scoring at least twice. Jimmy Ring was the loser for the Phillies, who featured 13 players scoring at least one run.

57. *Match these unknown heroes with their heroics or feats:*

1	Johnny Kucks	A	had 144 RBI in 1950—one short of the rookie mark
2	Horace Clark	B	set a record for AL second basemen by leading the league in assists six straight years
3	Walt Dropo	C	won Game Seven of the 1956 World Series
4	Myril Hoag	D	tied a still-standing record with six singles in a nine-inning game

ANSWER: 1—C, 2—B, 3—A, 4—D

Kucks, a 23-year-old righthander, three-hit the Dodgers and, with the help of a grand slam by Bill Skowron, led the Yankees to a 9-0 victory for the 1956 world championship. A second-year hurler, Kucks went 18-9 during the regular season and had already pitched in relief in each of the first two games of the series. . . . Clark played all-out defense for the Yankees, pacing the junior circuit in assists each year from 1967 to 1972. Clark, who fielded an impressive .983 for his career at second base, never won a Gold Glove, as Bobby Knoop of the Angels and Davey Johnson of the Orioles combined to receive most of the hardware during that time.

◆ Did you know Bill Skowron and Yogi Berra share the career mark for the most home runs (three) in Game Seven World Series action? Aside from the grand slam in the 1956 World Series, Skowron also homered in the 1958 series and the 1960 classic. Berra homered twice in the 1956 series and once in the 1960 thriller.

58. *During a 13-inning battle on September 9, 1998, Blue Jays shortstop Alex Gonzalez matched the dubious one-game mark for strikeouts with six, striking out six consecutive times. Although six others have fanned a half-dozen times in a game, only one other player has done so in consecutive at-bats. Select him.*

A Carl Weilman
B Don Hoak
C Rick Reichardt
D Billy Cowan
E Cecil Cooper

ANSWER: A

Weilman, a pitcher for the Browns, whiffed over and over again during a wild, 15-inning marathon against the Senators on July 25, 1913. No wonder; fireballing Walter Johnson pitched for Washington that day. Hoak, Reichardt, Cowan, Cooper, and Sam Horn were the others who whiffed six times in a game. Many batters share the nine-inning record of five strikeouts in a game.

Fellow SABR member Skip McAfee directed me to a 1991 *Sports Illustrated* article in which Horn's teammate Mike Flanagan introduced the term "Horn" into baseball's lexicon, for a batter who struck out six times in a game. The players' lexicon for strikeouts in a game includes "hat trick" for three whiffs, "golden sombrero" for four strikeouts, and the ever-so-elaborate "Olympic rings" for those who go down on strikes five times.

◆ Did you know Randy Johnson in 2001 broke Walter Johnson's 88-year-old record for most strikeouts in a relief appearance? On July 19 of the 2001 campaign, Johnson dominated Padre hitters with 16 strikeouts over the final seven innings of a combined one-hit shutout. The Big Unit took over that day to begin the third inning, a day after teammate Curt Schilling started a game that was suspended following stadium light problems. On July 25, 1913, Big Train whiffed 15 over the final 11⅓ innings of a 15-inning marathon against the Browns. The previous NL mark belonged to Rube Marquard, who struck out 14 on May 13, 1911.

59. *On July 28, 1991, Montreal's Dennis Martinez pitched baseball's 13th perfect game in Dodger Stadium, beating Los Angeles by a 2-0* *score. His catcher, Ron Hassey, became the first to catch two perfect games. Can you name the other perfect pitcher Hassey caught?*

ANSWER: Len Barker

Hassey called the signals as Len Barker of Cleveland set the Toronto Blue Jays down in order on May 15, 1981, in Municipal Stadium. The left-handed-hitting catcher caught for 14 years, batting .266. Hassey split time with Terry Steinbach for the 1988–90 Oakland teams that won three straight AL pennants.

60. *Which of the following is false?*

A Pitchers were awarded an assist on a strikeout before 1889.
B Walks, passed balls, wild pitches, balks, and hit batsmen counted as errors before 1889.
C In order to be retired on a strikeout, the batter has to swing and miss on the final strike.
D In 1887 walks were scored as hits.
E Before 1898 a stolen base also was awarded any time a runner advanced an extra base on a hit or out.
F Before 1920 a ball hit over the fence in the bottom of the ninth or the bottom of an extra inning with the winning run on was not counted as a home run.

ANSWER: C

Through 1919, a batter who belted a walk-off hit over the fence with the go-ahead runner on base was only credited with "the number of bases necessary to score the winning run," according to the rules section of *The Baseball Encyclopedia*. Among other interesting notes in this section is the 1931 rule change that stipulated batted balls bouncing over the fence were no longer to be credited as home runs. That's right; they were before.

◆ Did you know Harry Stovey was credited with 156 stolen bases for Philadelphia of the American Association in 1888, yet is not considered the all-time single-season record holder? Instead, Rickey Henderson's total of 130 swipes in 1982 is recognized as the standard. Most discredit Stovey's mark because a stolen base was awarded any time a runner advanced an extra base on a hit or out. But then again, Major League Baseball includes Cap Anson as a member of the 3,000-hit club because he totaled 3,000 hits "by the rule of the time," even though his total included walks. By the same criterion, Stovey's stolen base total in 1888 would be the standard.

The same question must be posed for the single-season strikeout record and the single-season hits mark. Nolan Ryan's 383 whiffs in 1973 are recognized as the record. However, Matt Kilroy struck out 513 batters (over 583 innings) in 1886, pitching for Baltimore of the American Association. The reason the league does not recognize Kilroy's single-season record of 513 Ks is that the pitcher's mound was then only 45 feet away from home plate, and it took seven balls to walk a batter. The same goes for the hits record, which is recognized as 257, set by George Sisler. The 275 hits by Tip O'Neill and Pete Browning in 1887 are not considered the record, because walks counted as hits that year.

To resolve inconsistencies such as these, Major League Baseball should create a committee that sets forth consistent policies and reconciles all the record books and encyclopedias, so that there is one undisputed set of stats.

◆ Did you know that home teams were granted the choice of batting first or second through the 1949 season? According to SABR, it wasn't that rare in the early 1900s for home teams to bat first.

61. *In the first contest of a three-game set in 1991, during which Dennis Martinez would later pitch a perfect game, Expos teammate Mark Gardner allowed no hits through nine innings of a scoreless duel against the Dodgers. Gardner lost his no-hit bid to Lenny Harris leading off the 10th, and lost the contest later in the inning as Darryl Strawberry drove Harris home with a game-winning single. Had Gardner completed his gem, it would have marked the fourth time in history that two no-hitters were thrown in one series. Can you name the two pitchers involved the last time this happened?*

ANSWER: Jim Maloney and Don Wilson

Jim Maloney of the Reds no-hit the Astros, 10-0, on April 30, 1969, in Crosley Field, only to see fireballer Don Wilson of the Astros return the favor the very next day by no-hitting Cincinnati, 4-0. A year earlier, San Francisco's Gaylord Perry no-hit the Cardinals, 1-0, on September 17 in Candlestick Park, and in the same series

St. Louis' Ray Washburn no-hit the Giants, 18 hours later, the next afternoon.

The first time baseball witnessed two no-hitters in the same series was in 1917. On May 5, Ernie Koob of the St. Louis Browns no-hit the White Sox, 1-0, and teammate Bob Groom duplicated the feat the very next day by hurling a 3-0 gem against the same White Sox. Although the no-hitters were not consecutive, as Groom's gem came in the second game of a doubleheader on May 6, the feat of no-hitters on consecutive days by the same team remains unprecedented.

◆ Did you know Ernie Koob's 1-0 no-hitter on May 5, 1917, was against Chicago's Eddie Cicotte, who had no-hit the Browns by an 11-0 margin three weeks earlier?

62. *The 2001 Indians, 1925 Philadelphia Athletics, and the 1911 Detroit Tigers each overcame a record 12-run deficit to win a game. Can you name one of the three NL teams to overcome an 11-run deficit to win?*

ANSWER: The Phillies, Astros, and Cardinals

On April 17, 1976, the Phillies overcame a 13-2 deficit against the Cubs to win, 18-16, thanks to the heroics of Michael Jack Schmidt. The wild, roller-coaster slugfest was not out of the ordinary for these two clubs. Three years later, the same clubs met in Chicago and combined for 45 runs and 50 hits, tying a then-major league record with 11 home runs and setting a standard with 97 total bases. Philadelphia won that 10-inning battle by the football score of 23-22. Schmidt (also with four walks) hit the game's first home run and its last (a game-winning blast in the 10th) to overcome the efforts of Chicago's Dave Kingman, who hit three monster homers and drove in six. Bill Buckner drove in seven for Chicago, which once trailed 21-9 before knotting the game at 22-22. Bob Boone led the Phillies with five RBI, and Pete Rose drove in four and scored four times.

The Astros on July 18, 1994, overcame an 11-0 deficit to beat the Cardinals, 15-12. St. Louis also rallied from an 11-0 deficit to overcome the N.Y. Giants on June 15, 1952, in the first game of a doubleheader.

On the same date 27 years earlier, the Athletics woke up from a sixth-inning 14-2 hole and scored 13 runs in the bottom of the eighth to register a remarkable 17-15 triumph over the Indians, tying the record for largest deficit overcome, a mark set on June 18, 1911. That's when the Tigers came back from a fifth-inning 13-1 pit to pass by the White Sox, 16-15. The Indians on August 5, 2001, trailed the Mariners 14-2 before starting their comeback in the bottom of the seventh inning en route to a 15-14 triumph in 11 innings.

63. *Match these major leaguers with their background:*

1	Luis Castro	A	the first Australian to play in the majors since 1901
2	Yogi Berra	B	the first Nicaraguan to play in the majors
3	Bobby Chouinard	C	a soldier involved in the June 6, 1944, D-Day invasion of Europe
4	Craig Shipley	D	the first Filipino to play in the majors
5	Dennis Martinez	E	the first Colombian to play in the majors

ANSWER: 1—E, 2—C, 3—D, 4—A, 5—B

Joe Quinn, who played from 1884 to 1901, was the first Australian to play in the majors. . . . Chouinard, who was born in Manila, made his debut with Oakland on May 26, 1996.

64. *This Japanese pitcher was so overworked during a Japanese League season that he decided to protest the boot camp–like spring training by resting and, at times, lying down and sleeping in the field while his teammates were drilled. Select him.*

A Tadashi Sugiura
B Kazuhisa Inao
C Takumi Otomo
D Yutaka Enatsu

ANSWER: D

Enatsu, whose actions succeeded in getting his manager fired, had to become a reliever because of the overwork. He adapted and became Japan's best, with 193 saves to go with his 206 wins and 2,987 strikeouts. Enatsu remains the only player to win the MVP in both the Central League and the Pacific League. . . . Otomo was the Sandy Koufax of Japan as he bottled his best years in a short time span, winning an MVP during a four-year period that featured an ERA of no higher than 1.85.

◆ Did you know Kazuhiro Sasaki, Japan's career and single-season record holder in saves, broke the major league rookie record with 37 saves in 2000 for the Seattle Mariners? Sasaki, who saved 229 games in 10 years for Yokohama of the Central League, broke Todd Worrell's rookie mark of 36. Sasaki didn't come out of nowhere, as he in 1998 had the best year ever for a reliever in Japan. He set a new standard with 45 saves to go with a 0.64 ERA as he led the BayStars to the Japan Series title.

65. *Name one of the two major league game rules other than the ones in place for the premiere 1876 season that have stood the longest and are still followed?*

ANSWER: A baserunner is out if hit by a batted ball (in fair territory), and the catcher must catch (on a fly) a batter's third strike tip (foul) for a strikeout. Both were introduced in 1880, according to *The Baseball Encyclopedia.*

◆ Did you know the current distance of 60 feet and six inches between the mound and the plate was chosen by mistake rather than by design? The original surveyor misread the boundary blueprint, which read: 60'0" (not 60'6"). Actually, the front of home plate is 59 feet and 1 inch from the pitcher's rubber.

66. *The New York Yankees are the only team in World Series history to sweep two consecutive fall classics, having done so three times. The clubs to do so were:*

A 1939 and 1940; 1942 and 1943; 1998 and 1999
B 1938 and 1939; 1941 and 1943; 1998 and 1999
C 1927 and 1928; 1938 and 1939; 1998 and 1999
D 1927 and 1928; 1949 and 1950; 1998 and 1999

ANSWER: C
The 1927 Yanks swept Pittsburgh, and the 1928 Yanks swept St. Louis. The 1938 and 1939 Bombers swept Chicago and Cincinnati, respectively. The 1998 and 1999 Yankees swept San Diego and Atlanta, respectively.

67. *Match these pitchers with their achievements:*

1	Ted Abernathy	A	owns the highest NL single-season win total since 1935
2	Gaylord Perry	B	once won 15 consecutive decisions
3	Robin Roberts	C	was the first reliever to save 40 games in a season
4	Dan Quisenberry	D	was the first reliever to save 30 games in a season

ANSWER: 1—D, 2—B, 3—A, 4—C

Roberts was a remarkable 28-7 in 1952, 17 years after Dizzy Dean enjoyed a 28-12 campaign. . . . Perry finished a streaky 1974 season with a 21-13 record and a 2.52 ERA for Cleveland. Overall, he was as reliable as they came. The crafty righthander, who threw the illegal spitball throughout his career and didn't deny it, won at least 15 games each year from 1966 to 1978. Incredibly, Perry wasn't caught for doctoring a baseball until his 21st season. A Mariner at the time, in his penultimate major league campaign, Perry was ruled to have placed a foreign substance on the baseball and ejected. This happened more than eight years after the humorous Perry wrote an autobiography entitled *Me and the Spitter.* A right-handed version of Eddie Plank in the way he annoyed hitters, Perry went through "an array of rituals" on the mound, as the Baseball Hall of Fame describes. Only Perry's rituals included Vaseline, jelly, and such. Between licking his right hand and repeatedly touching the bill of his cap, his jersey, and his pants, Perry relied on keeping hitters off balance over the second half of his career.

◆ Did you know Dizzy Dean is the last pitcher to lead the league in complete games (28) and saves (11) in one season, doing so in 1936? Dean also pitched out of the bullpen often during his magical 1934 season, earning 4 of his 30 wins in relief in addition to picking up seven saves. The heavy usage caught up with Dean, who won just 29 games after the 1936 season.

68. *Match these hitters with their feats:*

1	Cal McVey	A	totaled a record 14 five-hit games
2	Ty Cobb	B	had the only hit in a record-sharing five one-hitters

3 Cesar Tovar   C won three straight batting crowns

4 Lou Gehrig   D holds the record for the most hits (12) in back-to-back games and shares the record with Willie Keeler for the most hits (15) in three consecutive games

5 Stan Musial   E was the first rookie to hit 20 homers

ANSWER: 1—D, 2—A, 3—B, 4—E, 5—C

Pete Rose holds the NL mark of 10 five-hit games, two ahead of Tony Gwynn (whose four five-hit games in 1993 tied the season record set by Willie Keeler in 1897, later equaled by Ty Cobb in 1922 and Stan Musial in 1948). . . . Mike Benjamin, a career .186 hitter entering the 1995 season, set the modern-day mark with 14 hits in three consecutive games for the Giants in 1995. His 14 hits over an 18-at-bat stretch raised his average from .150 to .447. Benjamin had four hits on June 11, four more on June 13, and went 6-for-7 on June 14. (The June 11 and June 14 contests lasted 13 innings apiece.) He had another hit on June 15 (to break up Cub Frank Castillo's perfect game with two out in the seventh) for his 15th hit in four games, falling just one short of the modern-day mark held by Milt Stock (June 30–July 3, 1925) of Brooklyn. The all-time record for four games is 17, set by McVey (July 22, 25, 27–28, 1876) and equaled by Keeler (September 2-4, 6, 1897). Incidentally, McVey's three-game outburst in 1876 came in the midst of major league history's first 30-game hitting streak. . . . Tovar, Eddie Milner, and Hall of Famer Billy Williams had their team's only hit five times. . . . Musial won the batting crown from 1950 to 1952, a feat not repeated in the National League until Tony Gwynn earned a third consecutive batting title in 1989.

◆ Did you know George Brett established a major league record of six consecutive games with three or more hits in 1976? Brett put that streak together from May 8 to 13.

◆ Did you know Roberto Clemente on August 23, 1970, became the first player in the 20th century with back-to-back five-hit games?

69. *In 1983 Rusty Staub of the Mets had eight consecutive pinch-hits, falling one short of the record. Who holds the record?*

A Bill Stein
B Manny Mota
C Dave Philley
D Jose Morales

ANSWER: C

Dave Philley of the Phillies did it over a two-year span, from 1958 to 1959. A .270 career hitter, Philley switched teams on nine occasions, accumulating 1,700 hits—93 in the pinch. . . . Philadelphia's Del Unser (1979) and Los Angeles' Lee Lacy (1978) share the record of homering in three straight pinch-hit at-bats.

◆ Did you know Cincinnati's Mark Lewis hit the first pinch-hit grand slam in postseason history during Game Three of the 1995 National League Division Series against the Dodgers? With the Reds leading, 3-1, in the bottom of the sixth, Lewis hit for Jeff Branson and deposited a pitch from reliever Mark Guthrie over the left-field wall for a 7-1 lead en route to a three-game sweep. But awaiting Cincinnati in the NL Championship Series were the Braves, who swept the Reds in four straight while holding them to five total runs and a .209 batting average. Atlanta's rotation of Greg Maddux, Tom Glavine, Steve Avery, and John Smoltz anchored a staff that allowed just 28 hits and struck out 32.

70. *Which record do Pinky Higgins and Walt Dropo share?*

ANSWER: Higgins and Dropo each connected for a hit in 12 consecutive at-bats, achieving the feat in 1938 and 1952, respectively. Higgins, who broke the 18-year-old mark of 11 consecutive hits set by Tris Speaker in 1920, was en route to his fourth and last .300 campaign in 1938. Dropo, a rookie sensation who never lived up to lofty expectations, tied the mark 14 years later. Dropo did so a month following his trade to the Tigers, in the midst of a 29-homer, 97-RBI season. Dropo's numbers dropped considerably thereafter.

On September 23, 1992, Bip Roberts tied the NL record with his 10th straight hit, a record shared by eight others—Woody Wilson (1943), Buddy Hassett (1940), Joe Medwick (1936), Chick Hafey (1929), Kiki Cuyler (1925), Ed Konetchy (1919), Jake Gettman (1897), and Ed Delahanty (1897).

◆ Did you know that Hall of Fame outfielder Hazel "Kiki" Cuyler was benched midway through the 1927 season because he refused to bat second in the lineup? New Pirates manager Donie Bush wanted Cuyler (the team's most dangerous and powerful hitter) to bat in the second slot. At first, Cuyler refused, before reluctantly accepting. Cuyler sulked, played uninspired, and was benched for the rest of the season in what became known as "l'affaire de Bush." Luckily for the contending Pirates, the Waner brothers (the sophomore Paul and the rookie Lloyd, who finished first and third, respectively, in batting, and first and second in hits) and Hall of Famer Pie Traynor helped make up the league's best offense despite Cuyler's absence. Pittsburgh finished with a league-high .305 team batting average and a co-leading 817 runs scored. Cuyler's replacement, Clyde Barnhart, hit .319 as the team held off the St. Louis Cardinals by 1½ games to win the NL pennant.

Cuyler remained benched as the Pirates were swept by the awesome 1927 Yankees. Alas for Pittsburgh, Bush couldn't come to terms with Cuyler (who would have formed an impressive outfield trio with the Waner brothers) and traded him and his eventual .321 lifetime batting average to Chicago. The Pirates didn't win another pennant for 33 more years. Cuyler finished with 1,305 runs scored, 1,065 RBI, 394 doubles, and 157 triples en route to Cooperstown.

71. *What was strange about Larry Cheney's shutout on September 14, 1913, and Milt Gaston's on July 10, 1928?*

ANSWER: Cheney and Gaston each allowed a record 14 hits during a nine-inning shutout. Cheney of the Cubs defeated the New York Giants by a margin of 7-0. Gaston of the Washington Senators blanked the Cleveland Indians by a score of 9-0. For Cheney, the shutout was 1 of 20 in his career. The righthander went 116-100 with a 2.70 career ERA spanning nine seasons (1911–19), mostly with the Cubs and Dodgers. Cheney put together three straight 20-win campaigns, from 1912 to 1914, for a combined 67-42 ledger. Gaston, a righthander, finished with 10 career shutouts and compiled a 97-164 career record with five teams over 11 years.

One pitcher, however, did allow more hits during the course of an extra-inning whitewash. Hall of Famer Walter Johnson on July 3, 1913, yielded 15 safeties in hurling a 15-inning shutout—his 9th of 11 on the season—for a one-run victory over the host Boston Red Sox.

Big Train walked one and struck out four for the Senators. Ray Collins for the Red Sox also went the distance, finally allowing a run in the 15th. The Boston southpaw surrendered nine hits, walked two, and struck out five. Collins won 19 that year and 20 in 1914.

72. *On November 19, 1979, the Astros signed Nolan Ryan to a four-year, $4.5 million contract, making Ryan the first player to earn a million dollars a year. Three years later, George Foster became the first two million-dollar-a-year player by signing a five-year, $10.2 million contract with the Mets on February 7, 1982. On December 11, 2000, Alex Rodriguez signed a staggering $252 million contract for 10 years with the Texas Rangers, becoming baseball's first $25 million-a-year player. Later that night, Manny Ramirez signed a $160 million deal for eight years with the Boston Red Sox. Below, you'll find nine salary milestones. For a correct answer, fill in six correctly.*

A _____ became baseball's first $3 million-a-year player
B _____ became baseball's first $4 million-a-year player
C _____ became baseball's first $5 million-a-year player
D _____ became baseball's first $7 million-a-year player
E _____ became baseball's first $8 million-a-year player
F _____ became baseball's first $11 million-a-year player
G _____ became baseball's first $12 million-a-year player
H _____ became baseball's first $13 million-a-year player
I _____ became baseball's first $15 million-a-year player

ANSWER: (A) Kirby Puckett signed for $9 million over three years on November 22, 1989. (B) Jose Canseco signed for $23.5 million over five years on June 27, 1990. (C) Roger Clemens signed for $21.521 million over four years on February 8, 1991. (D) Ryne Sandberg signed for $28.4 million over four years on March 2, 1992. (E) Ken Griffey Jr. signed for $34 million over four years on January 31, 1996. (F) Albert Belle signed for $55 million over five years on November 19, 1996. (G) Pedro Martinez signed a $75 million deal over six years. (H) Mike Piazza signed a seven-year, $91 million deal. (I) Kevin Brown signed a seven-year, $105 million deal.

Ken Griffey Jr. had a chance to appear on this list for a second time but rejected an eight-year, $148 million deal from Seattle that would have averaged $18.5 million a year. Instead, he chose to return to his roots in Cincinnati for fewer than $13 million a year. Now that's admirable—so admirable the Reds in 2000 became the first team in the history of the game to reach three million in road attendance. That was no doubt attributed to NL fans wanting to see this stud they call "Junior." All he cares about is having fun, and it shows in his wide smile and turned-around hat. He told me he never worries about numbers, because he knows they will come about as long as he's having fun. He plays like a left-handed Willie Mays. And like Mays, his statistics don't do justice to his grace on the field. "Junior," like Mays, was born to play this beautiful game of baseball, and it shows every time he effortlessly chases down a drive over his head or in the gap, and every time he meets a pitched ball with the sweet spot of his bat. Injuries have slowed him during the past two years, but a healthy offseason should help Junior return to his customary form.

◆ Did you know the 1986 Mets are the last team to carry the majors' highest paid player on their opening day roster and make the postseason? That year, catcher Gary Carter earned $1.96 million.

◆ Did you know salary caps were first imposed in 1889, when Indianapolis owner John T. Brush put a limit on the salaries certain players can make? Brush waited until the first Players Union organizer Monte Ward left the country on a tour to sneak in a rule to cap players' salaries depending on their talent. Players were graded from "A" to "E" according to their talent, with "A" players limited to $2,500 and "E" players limited to $1,500.

73. *Match these pitchers with their outstanding feats:*

1 Ellis Kinder	A registered a 20th-century record 48 complete games
2 Jack Coombs	B won a record 13 consecutive starts
3 Jack Chesbro	C went 31-9 with a 1.30 ERA in his best season
4 Vic Willis	D recorded 45 complete games in a season

ANSWER: 1—B (1949), 2—C (1910), 3—A (1904), 4—D (1902)

Kinder's 1949 mark for the Boston Red Sox was challenged in 1997, when Minnesota's Brad Radke won 12 straight starts to tie Bob Gibson (1968) and Pat Dobson (1971) for the second best stretch. Kinder was 23-6 that season, his only campaign with more than 14 wins. . . .

Chesbro completed 48 of 51 starts in 1904. Overall, "Happy Jack" finished 260 of 332 starting assignments over an 11-year career that featured 198 victories, 153 of which were accrued from 1901 to 1906.

74. *Name the only rookie to play with three different major league teams before winning the Rookie of the Year Award?*

ANSWER: Lou Piniella

Piniella won the award in 1969 for the expansion Kansas City Royals, his third major league team and fifth organization. Originally signed by the Cleveland Indians in 1962, Piniella was drafted away by the Washington Senators the following year. Then, he was traded in 1964 to the Baltimore Orioles, for whom he made his major league debut in September and went 0-for-1 in four games. In 1966, Piniella was traded back to the Indians, for whom he played six games and went 0-for-5 in 1968. After being chosen by the Seattle Pilots in the AL expansion draft following the 1968 season, Piniella was traded to Kansas City in time for spring training of 1969.

On opening day, Piniella finally collected his first major league hit, four years and seven months after his debut. The sweet-swinging, right-handed Piniella went 4-for-5 to open a .282 campaign that included 11 homers, 21 doubles, six triples, and 68 RBI. In left field, Piniella showed good range and a good arm, with 13 assists. From there, he went on to a solid career. The intense and emotional Piniella enjoyed a pair of .300 seasons over the next four years in a Royals uniform, including an All-Star campaign in 1972 during which he finished second in the league in batting and led the junior circuit in doubles. Following an off-year in 1973, Piniella was traded to the Yankees and excelled in the spotlight. "Sweet Lou," who retired with a .291 career batting average, reached that mark in all but 4 of his 11 seasons in the Bronx, helping the Yankees win four pennants and two world championships with many clutch hits. A tremendous competitor, Piniella elevated his game in postseason action, batting .305 in 44 postseason games, including a .319 mark in 22 World Series games. With the game tied at 3-3 in the 10th inning during Game Four of the 1978 World Series, Piniella drove in Roy White with a walk-off single that tied the series, helping the Yankees to a second straight title.

Yankee owner George Steinbrenner saw in Piniella a passionate nature he then fancied in his managers, hiring "Sweet Lou" to guide the Yankees in 1986, just two years after his final year as player. Piniella responded, carrying his competitiveness into his managerial duties and winning 90 and 89 games his first two years. After Steinbrenner hastily fired Piniella a little past the halfway point of the 1988 season, Piniella went to the Cincinnati Reds in 1990 and managed them to a world championship his first year. In 1993 Piniella traveled to Seattle, and he has made the Mariners a contender every year since. Piniella has led the Mariners to three AL West titles, including a remarkable 116-win campaign in 2001, and their only four postseason appearances. For his efforts, Piniella has earned a pair of Manager of the Year Awards and should merit consideration for the Hall of Fame for his dual contribution to the game.

◆ Did you know Lou Piniella holds the unheralded mark for most career home runs (102) without a multi-homer game?

75. *Match these players with their feats, dubious or noteworthy:*

1	Don Baylor	A	is the only player to win the Rookie of the Year Award and Triple Crown
2	Ozzie Smith	B	is the only player other than Ty Cobb to lead his league in hits and triples during the same season three times
3	Frank Robinson	C	was the first player to get caught stealing twice in one inning
4	George Brett	D	is the last non-pitching Hall of Famer to have played every career game at one position

ANSWER: 1—C, 2—D, 3—A, 4—B

Baylor was twice thrown out in 1974. Jim Morrison, Paul Noce, Donell Nixon, Jeff King, and Tony Fernandez have since joined the list. . . . Before Ozzie, Aparicio played all 2,581 of his games in the field at shortstop over an 18-year career (1956–73) with the White Sox, Orioles, and Red Sox. Other Hall of Famers to do so are Frank Baker (1,548 games at third base), Bobby Doerr (1,852 games at second), and catchers Rick Ferrell, Ray Schalk, Bill Dickey, Ernie Lombardi, and Roy Campanella. . . . Brett first led the league in triples and hits in 1975, then in 1976 and in his spectacular 1979 season, during which he hit .329 with 212 hits, 42 doubles, 20 triples, 23 homers, and 107 RBI. In 1979 Brett fell three steals shy of joining Willie Mays as the only players in history with at least 20 doubles, triples, homers, and stolen bases in a single season.

◆ Did you know the 1966 season marked the fifth and last time both a batter and a pitcher won a Triple Crown in the same year? That season, Baltimore's Frank Robinson and Dodgers southpaw Sandy Koufax each earned the honor. It first happened in 1894, when Hugh Duffy and righthander Amos Rusie achieved that level of supremacy, and Nap Lajoie and Cy Young followed in 1901. In 1934 a pair of Yankees, Lou Gehrig and Lefty Gomez, took home Triple Crowns (nonetheless, the team finished seven games behind the AL champion Detroit Tigers). Three years later, Joe "Ducky" Medwick and Gomez accomplished the feat.

76. *Babe Ruth and Lou Gehrig hit a record 783 combined home runs while playing for the same team. Which duo of teammates finished second with 702?*

A Mickey Mantle and Elston Howard
B Norm Cash and Al Kaline
C Mickey Mantle and Yogi Berra
D Ted Williams and Bobby Doerr
E Mickey Mantle and Roger Maris

ANSWER: C

Mantle hit 419 homers and Berra hit 283 from 1951 to 1965. The Mantle-Berra duo won a combined 4 home run titles, compared to the 15 by Ruth and Gehrig.

◆ Did you know Ty Cobb and Sam Crawford are the only teammates to place first and second in RBI in their league for four consecutive seasons? The duo accomplished the great feat from 1908 to 1911, with Detroit.

77. *Match these negro league stars with their unrewarded heroics:*

1 Norman "Turkey"   A was the second most prolific home run
   Stearnes   hitter

2 Mule Suttles   B was revered by black fans the way whites revered Babe Ruth

3 John Henry "Pop" Lloyd C his .368 lifetime average is the best ever

4 Oscar Charleston D was the all-time negro league home run leader with 185 (39 more than Josh Gibson), excluding competition outside the negro leagues

5 Spottswood "Spot" Poles E was nicknamed "The Black Ty Cobb"

ANSWER: 1—D, 2—A, 3—C, 4—B, 5—E

Stearnes, a left-handed home run threat who also hit for average, won seven home run titles and retired with a .359 career mark. Josh Gibson won nine Negro National League home run titles. . . . Suttles, a big right-handed slugger who used a 50-ounce bat, hit 183 homers and batted .338 in the negro leagues. Charleston hit 151. . . . Lloyd was considered the best all-around player during the Dead Ball Era. . . . The left-handed Charleston hit .434 in 1921 with league-leading totals in home runs, triples, doubles, and stolen bases. . . . The speedy and intense Poles is credited with a .400 lifetime batting over a 15-year negro league career, although Lloyd is recognized as the leading hitter because Poles' statistical ledger is incomplete.

◆ Did you know Spottswood "Spot" Poles earned five battle stars and a Purple Heart in War World I?

78. *On September 20, 1981, three Twins marked their major league debut with a home run. Identify the trio that accomplished this feat.*

A Gary Gaetti, Kent Hrbek, and Tim Laudner
B Kirby Puckett, Gary Gaetti, and Mickey Hatcher
C Kent Hrbek, Gary Ward, and Gary Gaetti
D Tom Brunansky, Tim Laudner, and Kirby Puckett

ANSWER: A

Gaetti's first major league home run came in his very first at-bat. The trio of Gaetti, Hrbek, and Laudner was joined on the Twins roster that year by Brunansky, making up the foundation for a franchise that won the World Series six years later.

A huge piece of the puzzle was Puckett, who made his debut in 1984 and launched a dramatic home run in the 1991 World Series to force a Game Seven. Built like Hack Wilson and displaying the enthusiasm and popularity of a late night talk-show host, the five-foot-eight, 215-pound Puckett quickly became one of the league's very best players. An aggressive batter who often chose to swing rather than take a walk, Puckett accrued 2,040 hits over his first 10 seasons—no player in the 20th century had more over his first decade. He led his team to a pair of World Series, during which he excelled, batting .357 with 10 hits in the 1987 fall classic and helping the Twins win their second world championship four years later. After struggling through the first five games of the 1991 World Series, Puckett walked into the team clubhouse before Game Six and proclaimed, "Jump on; I'm driving this bus." And he did precisely so that night, with spectacular defense, a triple, a single, a stolen base, two runs scored, and three RBI, including a dome-moving, walk-off home run in the 11th inning off Atlanta's Charlie Leibrandt.

The 10-time All-Star and six-time Gold Glover was forced to retire in 1996 due to glaucoma. Thus came to an abrupt end a highlight-filled, 12-year career that included 2,304 hits, a batting title, four hit crowns, 207 home runs, and 1,085 RBI. The .318 career hitter is remembered as much for his constant smile as his spectacular plays and heroic hits.

◆ Did you know Gary Gaetti is the only player to homer in his first regular-season at-bat and first postseason at-bat? In fact, Gaetti also became the first player to homer in his first two postseason at-bats. In the 1987 AL Championship Series, Gaetti homered twice in Game One en route to capturing series MVP honors.

◆ Did you know Tim Raines was the last player in the majors allowed to wear a batting helmet with no earflap? As a major leaguer before the rule was set in 1983, Raines had the option of not wearing the earflap.

79. *In the history of the Rookie of the Year Award voting, each league has had co-winners once. In 1979 the American League split its award between Alfredo Griffin and _____, and the 1976 season featured*

National Leaguers Pat Zachry and _____ sharing the Jackie Robin-son Award.

ANSWER: John Castino and Butch Metzger

John Castino shared the award with Griffin, and Butch Metzger shared it with Zachry. Castino, a sure-handed Twins third baseman, batted .285 with little pop in 148 games. Griffin, a shortstop with good range for the Blue Jays, batted .287 with 10 triples and 21 steals in 153 games. Metzger, a right-handed reliever for the Padres, started the season 10-0 (giving him a 12-0 career start) en route to an im-pressive pitching ledger of 11-4, with 16 saves and a 2.92 ERA span-ning 123⅓ innings. Zachry, a right-handed starter for Cincinnati, went 14-7 with a 2.74 ERA (fifth best in the National League) over 204 innings pitched.

◆ Did you know New York Giants lefthander Hooks Wiltse set a record for starting pitchers by winning his first 12 career decisions in 1904? That re-mains the standard among starters, despite the recent efforts of Kirk Reuter and Livan Hernandez and the not-so-recent challenge by Hall of Famer Whitey Ford. Hernandez won his first nine decisions in 1997 for the Marlins. Reuter won his first 10 decisions as a starter over the 1993–94 seasons with the Expos. Ford went 9-0 for the Yankees in 1950 before suffering his first loss. Butch Metzger holds the record for relievers, also winning his first dozen career decisions from 1974 to 1976 for the Giants and Padres. The Rangers' Jeff Zimmerman, who made the All-Star team as a middle reliever during his 1999 rookie year, won his first nine decisions in said season. In 1926, Joe Pate won his first nine career decisions, all in relief, for the Athletics. He never won again. Wiltse and Metzger share the major league record, and Pate, Ford, and Zimmerman share the AL mark.

80. *Which team holds the dubious distinction of being the worst club in history over a single season?*

ANSWER: The 1899 Cleveland Spiders

The 1899 Cleveland Spiders of the National League won just 20 of their 154 games for an ugly .130 winning percentage, finishing 84 games behind Brooklyn. The 20th-century mark for futility belongs to the 1916 Philadelphia Athletics, whose 36-117 mark (.235 winning pct.) left them 54 games behind the pennant-winning Red Sox. The 1962 New York Mets are frequently but erroneously mentioned as the worst team of all time. They hold the dubious mark for most losses (120), but their winning percentage of .250 is the worst neither of all time or of the 20th century. The Spiders suffered so because their multi-team owner Frank DeHaas decided to "transfer" his best players—pitchers Cy Young and Jack Powell, third baseman Bobby Wallace, and outfielder Jesse Burkett—to his St. Louis Cardinals franchise, to give the latter team a better chance of competing. While DeHaas' Cardinals went 84-67 in 1899 for a fifth-place finish, his Spiders fell into a hole, losing 40 of their last 41 games.

◆ Did you know Hall of Famer Jesse Burkett was so disliked by his teammates and opponents he was nicknamed "Crab" for his contemptuous nature? Burkett, who constantly complained and often challenged those in his company to fights, even insulted fans.

81. *Of the following 10 Hall of Famers, only 2 have appeared in a World Series: Nolan Ryan, Ernie Banks, Ralph Kiner, Harry Heilmann, Luke Appling, George Kell, Rod Carew, Ted Lyons, Max Carey, and George Sisler. Select the pair from this list.*

ANSWER: Ryan and Carey

Ryan pitched 2⅓ scoreless innings in earning a save of Game Three of the famed 1969 World Series. Carey, a Hall of Fame outfielder with a .285 career mark and 738 stolen bases, played for the victorious Pirates in the 1925 World Series, batting .458 in the seven-game set with a .625 slugging average and three stolen bases.

A total of 44 major league Hall of Famers did not appear in the World Series, and 23 of them played at least five years during the World Series era. Joining those listed above are: Rick Ferrell, Jake Beckley, Nap Lajoie, Bobby Wallace, Joe Kelley, Billy Williams, Elmer Flick, Willie Keeler, Jim Bunning, Jack Chesbro, Ferguson Jenkins, Addie Joss, Phil Niekro, Gaylord Perry, and Rube Waddell.

◆ Did you know the Cubs' Ernie Banks played the most games (2,528) without ever participating in postseason action? The White Sox's Luke Appling, who like Banks played his entire career in Chicago, played 2,422 games without seeing postseason action. Third on the list is Mickey Vernon, who played 2,409 career games for the Senators, Indians, Braves, and Pirates. As far as World Series action is concerned, Andre Dawson holds that unenviable mark by playing 2,627 games without making an appearance in the fall classic. Bobby Wallace played the longest in terms of years (25, although 9 of those seasons included 53 games or fewer) without appearing in the postseason.

82. *The 1996 Orioles and 2000 Blue Jays share the mark of the most players with at least 20 home runs, each boasting seven. Previously, four teams had six players hit that many homers for them. The four teams are:*

A 1977 Red Sox, 1962 Tigers, 1963 Twins, 1961 Yankees
B 1964 Twins, 1963 Twins, 1984 Tigers, 1975 Reds
C 1961 Yankees, 1965 Braves, 1964 Twins, 1986 Tigers
D 1974 Braves, 1986 Tigers, 1984 Tigers, 1976 Reds

ANSWER: C

The 1961 Yankees were thugs with bats, or so opposing pitchers must have thought. The 1961 Yankees squad was the only team among this group to win more than 88 games and finish first, as they won 100 games and the World Series. Roger Maris hit 61, Mickey Mantle clubbed 54, Bill Skowron hit 28, Yogi Berra hit 22, Elston Howard hit 21, and Johnny Blanchard, 21. Amazingly, Blanchard was a reserve catcher who only played 63 games.

The 1964 Twins had Harmon Killebrew (49), Bobby Allison (32), Tony Oliva (32), Jimmie Hall (25), Don Mincher (23), and Zoilo Versalles (20) all reach the 20 home run mark.

The 1965 Braves had Henry Aaron (32), Eddie Mathews (32), Mack Jones (31), Joe Torre (27), Felipe Alou (23), and Gene Oliver (21) on the list.

The 1986 Tigers featured Darrell Evans (29), Kirk Gibson (28), Lance Parrish (22), Alan Trammell (21), Darnell Coles (20), and Lou Whitaker (20), in becoming the fourth team with six 20-homer players and the only club to have each member of its starting infield hit at least 20 home runs.

The 1996 Orioles were led by Brady Anderson's 50 and supported by Rafael Palmeiro's 39, Bobby Bonilla's 28, Cal Ripken Jr.'s 26, Chris Hoiles' 25, Roberto Alomar's 22, and B. J. Surhoff's 21.

Carlos Delgado and Tony Batista of the 2000 Blue Jays hit 41 apiece, and Brad Fullmer connected for 32, Jose Cruz Jr., 31, Raul Mondesi, 24, Shannon Stewart, 21, and Darrin Fletcher, 20. The team also became the first team to boast four 20-homer players by the All-Star break.

◆ Did you know the 1982 world champion St. Louis Cardinals were the last team to win a World Series without a 20-homer player? George Hendrick's 19 home runs and 104 RBI led the team in both categories, and Lonnie Smith led with a .307 batting average. Keith Hernandez drove in 94 runs and led the squad with a .397 on-base percentage. Catcher Darrell Porter was the only other Cardinal with more than eight home runs, hitting 12 for a lineup that mostly relied on singles, doubles, triples, and stolen bases. Joaquin Andujar and Bob Forsch each won 15 games, and closer Bruce Sutter saved 36. Carrying the team to a 92-win season was its top-notch and best-ranked defense, anchored by a solid infield of Hernandez at first, Tommie Herr at second, the spectacular Ozzie Smith at short, and Ken Oberkfell at third.

◆ Did you know the 1979 Houston Astros are the last team to hit more triples (52) than homers (49)?

83. *The 1885 Chicago White Stockings (the franchise that became the Cubs) were arguably the best 19th-century major league squad, going 87-25. Fill in the blanks to complete the alignment, and name the team's winningest pitcher:*

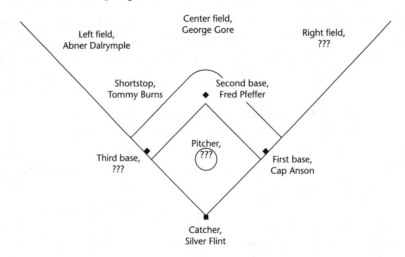

ANSWER: Right field, King Kelly; Third base, Ned Williamson; Pitcher, John Clarkson

The team's player-manager, Cap Anson, handled first-base duties and guided the White Stockings with a tremendous season at the plate. Anson led the National League by a comfortable margin with 108 RBI and paced the circuit with 35 doubles. The three-time batting champion also finished in the top five in home runs, on-base percentage, slugging, hits, total bases, and games played.

Anson, Kelly, Pfeffer, Burns, and Williamson occupied or shared the top five NL spots in RBI. Kelly led the league with 124 runs scored, and Gore, Dalrymple, and Anson all reached triple digits. Dalrymple led the National League in homers with 11, and Kelly, Anson, and Burns followed to occupy or share the league's top four spots. Gore finished fifth in batting and third in on-base percentage.

On the mound, Clarkson comfortably led the league with 53 wins, 623 innings, 10 shutouts, and 308 strikeouts, also finishing with a 1.85 ERA (third). Clarkson's magnificent 1885 performance marked the first of five straight seasons in which he had at least 33 victories. A curveball specialist who loved throwing a drop that fell off the table, Clarkson twice eclipsed the 600-inning mark and twice threw 68 complete games. The overuse didn't start affecting his arm until 1890, when his win total "dipped" to 26. Clarkson retired with an impressive 328-175 mark for a .648 winning percentage, with 485 complete games during an era of two-man starting rotations. The respected Al Spalding was the team's owner.

◆ Did you know Old Hoss Radbourn holds the single-season major league record with 59 wins? The five-foot-nine, 165-pound righthander wasn't a big fella but he pitched like one, mixing hard fastballs with good changeups past slap hitters and sluggers alike. Radbourn set the victory mark in 1884 for the Providence Grays, for whom he won 193 games over five seasons. A workhorse if there ever was one, Radbourn pitched in each of the last 27 games for Providence that year, winning 26 of them en route to a pitcher's Triple Crown. Radbourn took his services to Boston for the next five years before a final campaign with Cincinnati in 1891. Understandably, his arm was shot by then, as with many 19th-century hurlers whose star shone brightly for a brief period before fizzling suddenly from overuse. Radbourn, who actually lasted more than most pitchers during his era, retired with a 309-195 ledger and a

2.67 ERA. Aside from Radbourn, only John Clarkson (53) and Guy Hecker (52) ever reached the 50-win mark. Each did so once.

84. *Three teams in history have hit four consecutive home runs in an inning. Name one of the teams (team and year).*

ANSWER: The 1961 Milwaukee Braves, 1963 Cleveland Indians, and 1964 Minnesota Twins

The 1961 Milwaukee Braves were the first to do it. On June 8, Eddie Mathews, Hank Aaron, Joe Adcock, and Frank Thomas homered in consecutive at-bats during the seventh inning. On July 31 two years later, the Cleveland Indians' Woodie Held, Pedro Ramos, Tito Francona, and Larry Brown did it in the sixth inning off California's Paul Foytack—the only pitcher to yield four consecutive homers. On May 2, 1964, Tony Oliva, Bob Allison, Jimmie Hall, and Harmon Killebrew of the Minnesota Twins hit home runs in consecutive turns at the plate in the 11th inning.

◆ Did you know Joe Adcock, Lou Brock, and Hank Aaron were the only three major leaguers to ever reach the Polo Grounds' center-field bleachers? Luke Easter also accomplished the feat, in a 1948 negro league game. Adcock became the first major leaguer to do so five years later. Then, on consecutive days during the 1962 season, Brock and Aaron joined Adcock and Easter. Although shallow in distance down the lines (280 down left, and 258 down right), the horseshoe-shaped Polo Grounds measured a prodigious 450 feet to its center-field bleachers, located on either side of a cutout square in dead center that measured between 480 to 505 feet from the plate (depending on the year). No player ever homered over the wall in dead center. In fact, no player ever even reached that wall, which ranged from 30 to 60 feet high.

85. *During the 1942 season, many questioned baseball's importance and value during the events of World War II, and there was some sentiment in favor of suspending play. The president, however, was not in agreement, citing reasons such as the role the sport played in increasing the national morale. Can you name this president?*

ANSWER: Franklin D. Roosevelt

Franklin D. Roosevelt made clear his feelings to Commissioner

Kenesaw Landis through a letter (most notably known as the "Green Light" letter) dated January 15, 1942, and stamped THE WHITE HOUSE:

> Thank you for yours of January fourteenth. As you will, of course, realize, the final decision about the baseball season must rest with you and the Baseball Club owners—so what I am going to say is solely a personal and not an official point of view.
>
> I honestly feel that it would be best for the country to keep baseball going. There will be fewer people unemployed and everybody will work longer hours and harder than ever before.
>
> And that means that they ought to have a chance for recreation and for taking their minds off their work even more than before.
>
> Baseball provides a recreation which does not last over two hours or two hours and a half, and which can be got for very little cost. And, incidentally, I hope that night games can be extended because it gives an opportunity to the day shift to see a game occasionally.
>
> As to the players themselves, I know you agree with me that individual players who are of active military or naval age should go, without question, into the services. Even if the actual quality of the teams is lowered by the greater use of older players, this will not dampen the popularity of the sport. Of course, if any individual has some particular aptitude in a trade or profession, he ought to serve the government. That, however, is a matter which I know you can handle with complete justice.
>
> Here is another way of looking at it—if 300 teams use 5,000 or 6,000 players, these players are a definite recreational asset to at least 20,000,000 of their fellow citizens—and that in my judgment is thoroughly worthwhile.

For that letter, many consider Roosevelt a baseball savior.

86. *What was so special about the 1981 minor league game that began on April 18 between the Rochester Red Wings and the Pawtucket Red Sox?*

ANSWER: The game turned out to be the longest game in professional baseball history, lasting 33 innings. The game, played at McCoy Stadium in Pawtucket, Rhode Island, was suspended after 32 innings at 4:07 A.M. on April 19 with the score tied, 2-2, and the temperature below freezing. On June 23, it took Pawtucket 18 minutes to end the 8-hour and 25-minute marathon with a run in the bottom of the 33rd inning for a 3-2 triumph. Bob Ojeda was the winning pitcher, and other notables included second baseman Marty Barrett, third bagger Wade Boggs, catcher Rich Gedman, and Rochester third bagger Cal Ripken Jr. Barrett scored the winning run.

87. _____ *hit the longest home run officially measured, at 618 feet, during a minor league game at Emeryville Ball Park, California:*

A   Roy Carlyle
B   Mickey Mantle
C   Babe Ruth
D   Charlie Keller
E   Joe Bauman
F   Luke Elster

ANSWER: A

Carlyle did it on July 4, 1929, while playing for the Oakland Oaks of the Pacific Coast League. The left-handed-hitting Carlyle, who had hit nine homers in 494 at-bats spanning his only two major league seasons of 1925 and 1926, played for three big league clubs, including the pennant-winning 1926 Yankees. Although a good hitter (.318), Carlyle was a horrible outfielder.

Mickey Mantle on April 17, 1953, connected off southpaw Chuck Stobbs at Griffith Stadium, sending a towering drive well over the left–center field bleachers, a shot reportedly measured at 565 feet. But William Jenkinson of the Society for American Baseball Research estimates the shot at 510 feet instead, since Yankees Public Relations Director Red Patterson's measurement took into account where the ball was found, not where it first landed.

◆ Did you know that Babe Ruth hit a 587-foot home run for the Red Sox versus the New York Giants during a 1919 exhibition game at Tampa, Florida? And on September 10, 1960, Mickey Mantle hit a drive that carried well over Detroit's right-field roof and that, as measured trigonometrically in 1985, would have traveled 643 feet had its flight not been impeded.

88. *True or False? Richie Ashburn of the Phillies once fouled off 14 straight pitches from Cincinnati pitcher Corky Valentine, in a 1954 game, before drawing a walk.*

ANSWER: True

Hall of Famer Richie Ashburn did indeed have great control with his bat, retiring after the 1962 season with a .308 career batting average and 2,574 hits. He twice led the league in batting and three times led in hits. During a sound 15-year career, Ashburn also led the senior circuit in walks four times and triples twice.

◆ Did you know that Richie Ashburn on August 17, 1957, once injured a fan with a foul ball, breaking her nose, and hit her again on the next pitch while she was being carried away on a stretcher? According to *The Baseball Chronology*, her name was Alice Roth, wife of Earl Roth, the sports editor for the Philadelphia Bulletin.

89. *Match these teams with a notable event from their history:*

1 Cardinals A was the franchise that originally inked Tom Seaver before Commissioner William Eckert ruled the signing represented a violation

2 Mets B had all eight starting position players bat at least .300

3 Phillies C scored 16 unearned runs in a 16-4 contest during the 1985 season

4 Braves D this team's manager resigned after opening day in 1960

ANSWER: 1—B, 2—C, 3—D, 4—A

Every regular on the 1930 Cardinals squad hit at least .303. First baseman Jim Bottomley hit .304, second baseman Frankie Frisch hit .346, shortstop Charlie Gelbert hit .304, third baseman Sparky Adams hit .314, rookie right fielder George Watkins hit .373, center fielder Taylor Douthit hit .303, left fielder Chick Hafey hit .336, and catcher Jimmie Wilson hit .318. . . . In the first game of a July 27, 1985, doubleheader against the Astros, the Mets scored six unearned runs in the bottom of the seventh inning and six more unearned runs in the bottom of the eighth inning, on top of four earlier unearned runs. The 16 unearned runs in a game are not a record in themselves, but they are the record for a team that scored no earned runs. . . . Eddie Sawyer resigned from his post as Phillies manager after a loss on opening day. . . . The Braves drafted Seaver and eventually signed him, but not until the college season had started, violating the draft rules of the time. And since Seaver signed a professional contract, he was ruled ineligible to pitch for his college team, USC, again. So Eckert set up a special draft for Seaver, forbidding the Braves from participating and inviting clubs interested in matching Atlanta's $40,000 offer to place their name in a hat. Only three teams took part, and the Mets won the drawing, changing their fortunes forever.

90. *Name the only player in history to hold the single-season club record in batting average for three different franchises.*

ANSWER: Rogers Hornsby

Hornsby hit .424 in 1924 for the Cardinals, .387 for the Boston Braves in 1928, and .380 for the Cubs in 1929. "Rajah" also held the second highest single-season average for the New York Giants, with a .361 mark in 1927, and is one of just two players to collect 200 hits in a season for three teams (Paul Molitor is the other). Hornsby went 2-for-5 on opening day in 1924 and actually improved on that average over the course of the season. Think about that for a moment.

◆ Did you know Rogers Hornsby remains the only player in history to hit .300 over a full season for four different teams? Hornsby hit .300 for the Cardinals, his first team, 10 times. In his lone season (1927) with the Giants, he hit .361, and he then batted .387 the following season as a Brave. The right-handed hitter also hit .300 in each of his two full campaigns with the Cubs.

91. *Who was the first player to hit a home run during the regular season, the All-Star Game, the Division Series, a League Championship Series, and the World Series in the same year?*

ANSWER: Sandy Alomar Jr.

In 1997 Cleveland catcher Sandy Alomar Jr. accomplished this amazing feat, since equaled by Barry Bonds. During that magical 1997 season, Alomar Jr. hit 21 regular-season home runs, won All-Star Game MVP honors in his hometown with a two-run homer, hit a pair

of dingers in the AL Division Series, one in the AL Championship Series, and two more in the fall classic against Florida. Alomar Jr.'s 1997
season remains his best offensively, as he posted career-best figures in
home runs, RBI, batting average, on-base percentage, slugging average, runs, hits, doubles, and total bases.

In 2002 Bonds hit 46 regular-season homers, hit 1 in the All-Star
game, and then went on to club 3 in the NL Division Series, 1 in the
NL Championship Series, and 4 more in the World Series.

◆ Did you know Sandy Alomar Jr. in 1997 also became the first player to
homer in his home park during the All-Star Game and World Series in the
same year?

92. *Nolan Ryan and Randy Johnson are two of only four pitchers in his-
    tory to lead each league in strikeouts. The others are:*

   A Tom Seaver and Rube Waddell
   B Jim Bunning and Cy Young
   C Jim Perry and Cy Young
   D Ferguson Jenkins and Pedro Martinez

   ANSWER: B

Bunning, while with the Tigers, led the American League in
strikeouts with 201 in 1959 and 1960. As a Phillie, Bunning struck out
a league-leading 253 batters in 1967. Young led the league in strikeouts only twice, yet did so in each league. Young whiffed 140 in 1896
for Cleveland of the National League, and 158 five years later for
Boston of the AL. Both figures were produced in the days of contact
baseball.

Johnson enters the 2003 season with eight strikeout crowns: four
with Seattle, from 1992 to 1995, and the last four with Arizona. The
Big Unit also led the major leagues in strikeouts in 1998, when he was
traded from Seattle to Houston on July 31.

◆ Did you know Hideo Nomo in 2001 became the fifth pitcher in history
to throw a no-hitter in two different major leagues, joining Ted Breitenstein,
Cy Young, Jim Bunning, and Nolan Ryan? Breitenstein threw his in the American Association and the National League, and the other four threw theirs in
the American League and National League.

93. *In 1998 Roger Clemens became the first American Leaguer since Ron Guidry (1978–79) to lead his circuit in ERA two years in a row. Can you choose the last NL hurler before Greg Maddux and Randy Johnson to do so?*

A Bob Gibson
B Steve Carlton
C Tom Seaver
D Sandy Koufax

ANSWER: C

Seaver won the crown in 1970 with a 2.81 ERA and in 1971 with a 1.76 ERA. Maddux had the National League's best ERA in 1993 (2.76), 1994 (1.56), and 1995 (1.63)—a far cry from his 8-18 record and 5.59 ERA over his first 36 major league appearances. Clemens has six ERA titles to his credit, more than any other righthander. Johnson has led his league in ERA four times, through 2002.

◆ Did you know Greg Maddux became the first pitcher to post an ERA lower than 1.80 in consecutive seasons since Walter Johnson did it in 1918 and 1919? In fact, Maddux has the third and fifth best single-season ERA figures since the Dead Ball Era ended with the conclusion of the 1919 campaign. Johnson, regarded by many as the best pitcher in history, was 23-13 with an ERA of 1.27 in 1918 and 20-14 with a 1.49 mark in 1919. His career winning percentage of .599 is all the more impressive considering that he didn't have much offensive support.

◆ Did you know Greg Maddux's composite ERA of 1.98 from 1992 to 1995 is the second best four-year stretch since 1956? The 1.86 ERA Sandy Koufax compiled from 1963 to 1966 is the best, and Bob Gibson's combined ERA of 2.08 from 1966 to 1969 is third best.

◆ Did you know that from 1992 through 1998 Greg Maddux compiled the best ERA over any seven-year stretch since World War II? His 2.15 ERA (401 earned runs in 1,675⅓ innings) over that span is ahead of Juan Marichal's best stretch (2.34 from 1963 to 1969), Sandy Koufax's best stretch (2.36 from 1960 to 1966), and Tom Seaver's best stretch (2.38 from 1967 to 1973).

94. *Only two players in history have amassed at least 500 doubles, 500 home runs, and 100 triples. Willie Mays is one. The other is:*

A Lou Gehrig
B Hank Aaron
C Ted Williams
D Babe Ruth

ANSWER: D

Ruth hit 714 home runs, 506 doubles, and 136 triples. Mays hit 660 home runs, 523 doubles, and 140 triples. That's a lot of extra-base hits—2,679 for the two combined. Amazingly, their totals could easily have been higher. Ruth served as a pitcher for his first six years, and Mays played through the 1960s, when many elements heavily favored the pitchers.

◆ Did you know that Hank Aaron (1,477) and Stan Musial (1,377) rank first and second in extra-base hits, while Babe Ruth and Willie Mays rank third and fourth, respectively?

95. *This right-handed Hall of Fame pitcher won 101 more games than he lost, struck out 2,303 batters, completed more than half his starts, and posted 52 shutouts. In addition, this giant of a man is the only NL pitcher to win 25 games in a season and not win the Cy Young Award. Can you name this usually mild-mannered hurler?*

ANSWER: Juan Marichal

Marichal posted a 25-8 mark in 1963 and a 25-6 mark in 1966, only to see Sandy Koufax win the Cy Young Award, unanimously, each year. The Dominican was even unable to challenge Bob Gibson's unanimous selection in 1968, a year in which he went 26-9. Marichal earned 191 victories during the 1960s, more than anyone, without an MVP or Cy Young Award to show for it. Ironically, the only first-place vote Marichal ever received came following an 18-11 season in 1971. Marichal concluded his 16-year career in 1975 with 243 career wins, a .631 lifetime winning percentage, and 244 complete games. Only Dennis Martinez (245) has more victories among Latin American players.

Marichal made a splashing debut on July 19, 1960. The high leg-kicker began his career with a one-hit shutout, yielding only a two-out single in the eighth to Phillies pinch-hitter Clay Dalrymple. Marichal also struck out 12 and walked one.

◆ Did you know Marichal was once fined a then–NL record of $1,750 for throwing his bat and striking Dodgers' catcher Johnny Roseboro with it in 1965? After being brushed back by a Sandy Koufax pitch, Marichal thought Roseboro threw too close to his head in returning the ball to Koufax. After a few words, Marichal connected with Roseboro's head, for which league president Warren Giles fined him and suspended him for eight games. Marichal was also ordered not to make a scheduled trip for a series in Los Angeles toward the end of the season. The August 22, 1965, incident probably cost the Giants the pennant, as they finished two games behind the first-place Dodgers.

96. *Match these players with their unheralded feats:*

1	Herman Schaefer	A	hit 823 home runs in his North American career
2	Josh Gibson	B	holds the record for the longest throw of a regulation (5-5¼ ounce) baseball
3	Glen Gorbous	C	once played 10 positions in a single minor league game
4	Mike Ashman	D	was last man in history to steal first base

ANSWER: 1—D, 2—A, 3—B, 4—C

Here's how Herman "Germany" Schaefer once stole first base. With teammate Davy Jones on third base, Schaefer, on first, stole second, hoping to draw a throw and allow a double-steal opportunity. But the steal was uncontested. In another attempt to draw a throw, Schaefer then "stole," or returned to, first base, to no avail. On the next pitch, Schaefer's plan worked, as he finally drew a throw in his attempt of second, allowing Jones to score a Senator run in a 1910 contest. Since then, a rule has been instituted prohibiting players from stealing first base. . . . According to historian John Coates, Gibson hit 823 home runs against all levels of competition, including the Negro National League, Mexican leagues, and Caribbean leagues. Considering that he played most of his games at spacious Forbes Field and Griffith Stadium, Gibson's performance is even more mind-boggling. (To give you an idea of how difficult it was to homer in Griffith Stadium, an inside-the-park homer on the last day of the 1945 major league season was the only homer in that park that year.) Gibson's prodigious blasts were as much the talk of the country's black population then as Mark McGwire's tape-measure shots were the talk of the overall fan base not too long ago. In July of 1934, Gibson almost hit a ball completely out of Yankee Stadium. Although often and mistakenly reported otherwise, Gibson's 580-foot clout just missed clearing the outside center-field wall by a few feet. Legends are unnecessary when describing Gibson, so why perpetuate them. His feats were awesome in and of themselves. A dozen years later Gibson launched a 550-foot shot in St. Louis. According to James Riley, the pioneering author of *The Biographical Encyclopedia of the Negro Leagues*, Gibson was a .354 career hitter in the Negro National Leagues. He also hit .373 for his career in Mexico, .357 in Cuba, .412 against major leaguers, and .479 in his lone season in Puerto Rico. . . . Gorbous, a Phillies outfielder, threw the ball 445 feet and 10 inches on August 1, 1957, sending the ball out of Connie Mack Stadium. Gorbous broke the record of 445 feet and 1 inch, set a year earlier by Don Grate. Pitching in the minor leagues at the time, Grate accomplished the feat 10 years after a brief two-year stint in the majors, also as a Phillie. . . . Ashman played all nine positions in the field and even served as the designated hitter on June 4, 1983, for the Albany/Colonie A's of the Eastern League.

◆ Did you know Joe Sprinz, a Pacific Coast League catcher, attempted in 1939 to catch a baseball dropped from a blimp at a height of 800 feet? The force of the ball slamming into his mitt caused the mitt to smash into his face, breaking his jaw and at least four teeth. To add insult to injury, the ball fell out of his glove. Earlier, in 1908, Gabby Street caught a baseball dropped from near the top of the Washington Monument, 504 feet high. Catching a baseball falling out of the sky was a publicity stunt born in the late 1800s.

97. *In which year did the Gold Glove Award make its debut?*

    A 1957
    B 1953
    C 1963
    D 1960

ANSWER: A

In 1957 Rawlings Sporting Goods decided to reward the best defensive players at each position with a leather, gold-laced glove on an engraved plaque, much as Hillerich and Bradsby award silver bats to each of the league's top hitters at each position. The year before, a survey revealed that 83 percent of all major leaguers used Rawlings gloves. The Gold Glove voting today is done by managers and coaches, who are not permitted to choose their own players.

◆ Did you know the measurements of a glove cannot exceed 38 inches in circumference and 15 inches in width?

98. *Match these Gold Glovers with their feats of wizardry:*

1	Wes Parker	A	ended Brooks Robinson's incredible Gold-Glove streak with his first
2	Aurelio Rodriguez	B	won the award in 1957
3	Bill White	C	won 10 straight behind the plate
4	Sherman Lollar	D	won seven straight
5	Johnny Bench	E	won the award in his last season

ANSWER: 1—E, 2—A, 3—D, 4—B, 5—C

Parker and Roberto Clemente (who co-owns the outfield record of 12 Gold Gloves) were the only two everyday players to win a Gold Glove in their final season. For Parker, the award was his sixth. . . . Ivan Rodriguez tied Bench's mark of ten consecutive Gold Gloves, earning the hardware from 1992 to 2001. The Angels' Bengie Molina won the award in 2002, becoming the first AL catcher other than Rodriguez to earn the honor since Tony Pena.

◆ Did you know Rocky Colavito is still the only player to field a perfect 1.000 and win a triple crown category (108 RBI in 1965) during the same season? Brett Butler led the National League with 112 runs scored and 108 walks during his perfect (no errors in 380 chances) 1991 season.

99. *Match these Gold Glovers with their defensive achievements:*

1	Phil Niekro	A	was one of three outfielders given the award in its inaugural campaign
2	Willie Mays	B	won a gold glove in each league
3	Ken Griffey Jr.	C	won the award five times
4	Minnie Minoso	D	won the award 10 straight years

5 Jim Kaat   E earned a Gold Glove in each of the
                                  award's first 12 years

ANSWER: 1—C, 2—E, 3—D, 4—A, 5—B

Mays would have won two or three more Gold Gloves had the award existed before 1957. . . . In 1999 Griffey Jr. tied Kaline's AL outfield record with 10 Gold Gloves, but he has yet to win one in the National League. . . . Minoso, Mays, and Kaline (who had a powerful arm and once went 242 straight games without an error) were the first three Gold Glove outfielders. . . . In 2002 Greg Maddux won his 13th Gold Glove, four more than the previous record holder for an NL pitcher, Bob Gibson. Maddux was the only NL pitcher to win a Gold Glove in the 1990s. In the American League, southpaw Mark Langston won seven Gold Gloves. . . . Kaat won 16 gold gloves from 1962 to 1977.

◆ Did you know only one player at each position was awarded a Gold Glove in the award's first season, instead of a representative from each league? The format was changed the very next season.

◆ Did you know Jim Kaat and Brooks Robinson were the first two players inducted into the Rawlings Gold Glove Hall of Fame in 1991? Willie Mays and Roberto Clemente became the third and fourth inductees, respectively, in 1992.

◆ Did you know Brooks Robinson did everything left-handed except throwing a baseball and batting?

100. *Match these negro league stars with their reputations:*

1 Louis Santop   A the top slugger of the Dead Ball Era
2 Biz Mackey   B the best defensive catcher
3 Ted Radcliffe   C was called "Double Duty" for his versatility
4 Bingo DeMoss   D was perhaps the greatest all-around
                           second baseman

ANSWER: 1—A, 2—B, 3—C, 4—D

A stalwart catcher, the left-handed-hitting Santop was the Dead Ball Era's top drawing card, attracting negro league fans with called shots and other brazen claims. . . . Radcliffe earned the nickname "Double Duty" for catching the first game of a doubleheader at Yankee Stadium and pitching a shutout in the second game. At times,

Radcliffe added to his duties by managing. . . . DeMoss, a defensive stalwart, learned so much about the game while playing that he later became a manager. . . . Although there were better-hitting catchers, none was better defensively than Mackey, who was renowned for his incredible throwing arm. Mackey was no slouch at the plate either, hitting for a .335 career average.

101. *Which one of the following is not true about arguably the greatest baseball team ever assembled, the 1927 Yankees?*

A their .489 slugging percentage remains the highest single-season mark

B they led the majors in homers, runs, triples, batting average, and ERA

C they weren't even predicted to win the pennant

D they had a winning record against every team except the Washington Senators

ANSWER: D

The Senators had a tough time (lost 14 of 22) with the Yankees. Washington, the team most experts predicted to beat New York (which supposedly had questionable pitching) and the Philadelphia Athletics, rode a 10-game winning streak into Yankee Stadium on the Fourth of July. A holiday crowd of 74,641 witnessed the doubleheader in which the Yankees dismantled the Senators, 12-1 and 21-1, to strengthen their hold on first place. Washington first baseman Joe Judge confirmed the feeling that many a foe shared when he said, "Those fellows not only beat you, but they tear your heart out. I wish the season was over."

In the eyes of some, the 1998 Yankees were as good as the 1927 juggernaut because the former won an American League record 114 regular-season games and 11 more in the postseason, for a record total of 125. But don't be fooled by the numbers. The 1998 Yankees played a 162-game schedule and had the pleasure of playing the expansion Tampa Bay Devil Rays. Also, the 1998 Yankees had a chance to win more postseason games, since the current postseason has three rounds, whereas the 1927 Yankees only had the World Series. And not only did the 1927 Yankees compile an impressive 110-44 ledger; they outscored their opponents by 376 runs, or an average of 2.4 runs per game. In comparison, the 1998 version outscored its opponents by 1.9 runs per game.

Baseball historian Jerome Holtzman told me he ranked the 1998 Yankees as the "fourth or fifth best team," behind the 1927 and 1961 Yankees, the Big Red Machine of 1975–76, and "maybe even the 1919 Black Sox." The 1970 Orioles were pretty good too, averaging 7.5 runs per game in winning seven of their eight postseason games.

Other record achievements by the 1998 Yankee team include a .700 winning percentage in each of the first four months and getting win number 100 on September 4, the earliest ever. Combining the regular season and the postseason, the 1998 Yankees rank fourth in terms of the best overall winning percentage (.714). Only the 1906 Cubs (.763), 1927 Yankees (.722), and 1909 Pirates (.717) rank ahead.

◆ Did you know the 1906 Chicago Cubs, after posting 116 regular-season wins, were shocked in the World Series by the White Sox? The Cubs were defeated in six games after compiling a magnificent ledger of 116-36 (with two ties) for a record winning percentage of .763. Before the Seattle Mariners in 2001 tied the Cubs' mark of 116 wins, with a winning percentage of .716, the American League's best winning percentage belonged to the 1954 Indians (111-43). Those Indians, who won at a .721 clip, were also stunned in the World Series—in fact, swept. The 2001 Mariners, of course, entered the postseason as favorites but suffered a cruel fate, losing in the AL Championship Series to the Yankees, four games to one.

◆ Did you know the 1998 New York Yankees set a record by playing .753 ball before the All-Star break? The 1998 Yankees went an astounding 61-20 before the break, surpassing the 52-21 mark of the 1942 Brooklyn Dodgers. The 2001 Mariners were 63-24.

◆ Did you know the 1998 Yankees are the only team between 1990 and 2002 to boast the best record in the major leagues and follow through by winning the World Series that year? Great regular-season teams such as the 1990 Athletics, 1993 Braves, 1995 Indians, 1999 Braves, and 2001 Mariners fell short.

102. *Name the Hall of Famer who hit 50 home runs in a season with two different franchises.*

A Willie Mays
B Jimmie Foxx
C Babe Ruth
D Hack Wilson

ANSWER: B

"The Beast" Foxx hit 58 for the Philadelphia Athletics in 1932 and 50 in 1938 for the Boston Red Sox. Mays hit 51 for the New York Giants in 1955 and 52 for the 1962 San Francisco Giants, but that was for the same franchise. Of course, power legend Mark McGwire hit more than 50 with Oakland (in 1996) and St. Louis (in 1998 and 1999). McGwire, who retired following the 2001 season with 583 homers, 1,414 RBI, a .394 on-base percentage, and a .588 slugging percentage, is sure to be a first-ballot Hall of Famer in 2007.

◆ Did you know Jimmie Foxx hit at least 30 home runs in a record 12 consecutive seasons? From 1929 to 1940, Foxx hit 484 of his 534 roundtrippers. His home run totals during that stretch read like this: 33, 37, 30, 58, 48, 44, 36, 41, 36, 50, 35, and 36, respectively. Barry Bonds in 2002 extended his own NL record with an 11th straight 30-homer campaign.

103. *What happened during the 1927 season after Babe Ruth gave Wilcy Moore (a thirty-year-old rookie pitcher) three-to-one odds on a $100 bet that Moore couldn't get three hits in the entire season?*

ANSWER: Moore got six hits (albeit in 75 at-bats for an .080 mark), including a home run, to win $300. With the winnings, the Oklahoma farm boy bought two mules. He named one "Babe" and the other "Ruth." On the mound in 1927, Moore won 19 of his 26 decisions and had 13 saves as a reliever and occasional starter. For Moore, who pitched 213 innings en route to an ERA crown, the 1927 campaign was by far his best.

104. *Match these Negro National and American League championship teams with their history:*

| 1 Pittsburgh Crawfords | A this squad boasted the "million-dollar infield" of Mule Suttles, Dick Seay, Willie Wells, and Ray Dandridge in the early 1940s |

2 Homestead Grays   B the 1935 squad, owned by Gus
                               Greenlee, was one of the best black
                               teams, with five Hall of Famers

3 Newark Eagles   C the club with whom Satchel Paige
                               rediscovered his arm

4 Kansas City Monarchs   D owner Cumberland "Cum" Posey
                               repurchased the services of Josh Gibson
                               just in time for this 1937 squad, which
                               rolled off a 152-11 ledger

ANSWER: 1—B, 2—D, 3—A, 4—C

The Crawfords' five inductees were Paige, Gibson, Oscar Charleston, James "Cool Papa" Bell, and Judy Johnson. Greenlee organized the Negro National League in 1933 and also served as the circuit's president, declaring his Crawfords the inaugural champs despite an incomplete schedule. Greenlee's exciting team saved the negro leagues from the Great Depression. In 1937 the Negro American League was formed, and it coexisted with the NNL through 1948. In 1949 the NAL absorbed the NNL, lasting through 1960. . . . The Grays in 1937 won the first of their nine consecutive Negro National League championships. Six years earlier, the Grays won 136 of their 153 games, with Gibson, Charleston, "Smokey" Joe Williams, and Ted "Double Duty" Radcliffe leading the way. . . . Paige overcame a "dead arm" to revitalize his career and help the Monarchs to four negro league World Series appearances. Paige was the negro league's biggest gate attraction. Only Gibson came close in terms of fan appeal and interest. Together, Paige and Gibson served to boost negro league popularity and attendance to new heights.

◆ Did you know the Pittsburgh Crawfords were named after owner Gus Greenlee's "Crawford Bar and Grill"?

105. *Match these negro league players with their backgrounds:*

1 Joe Williams   A this shortstop was called "the black Honus
                               Wagner," prompting the Pirate Hall of
                               Famer to state he was "proud and honored"
                               to be compared with the African American
                               legend

2	Martin Dihigo	B	caught Satchel Paige to form the best negro league battery
3	John Henry "Pop" Lloyd	C	started out as a teenage pitcher for the St. Louis Stars (a semi-pro team)
4	Josh Gibson	D	became the first Cuban ever elected into the Hall of Fame
5	James "Cool Papa" Bell	E	his fastball was said to be even faster than Walter Johnson's

ANSWER: 1—E, 2—D, 3—A, 4—B, 5—C

Williams was 19-7 against major league teams (in exhibitions), defeating six Hall of Famers: Walter Johnson, Grover Alexander, Chief Bender, Rube Marquard, Waite Hoyt, and Satchel Paige. Williams once threw a 10-inning no-hitter with 20 Ks versus the 1917 Giants, who won, 1-0, on an error. . . . Dihigo was so talented he led the Cuban League in hitting (.358) and pitching (11-2) during the 1936 season with Santa Clara. Dihigo was perhaps the most versatile baseball player (negro leaguer, major leaguer, or what have you) to ever wear spikes. He was nicknamed "El Maestro," Spanish for "The Teacher." . . . Like Babe Ruth, Stan Musial, George Sisler, Sam Rice, Bobby Wallace, and Monte Ward, Bell started out as a pitcher. He was a left-handed knuckleballer who also had a screwball and a curve. An arm injury forced him into the outfield.

◆ Did you know the negro leaguers defeated the major leaguers in 268 of the 436 off-season exhibitions they played? And as former negro leaguer Buck O'Neil explains, a few players enjoyed more success in the major leagues than they were able to in the richly talented negro leagues.

◆ Did you know Martin Dihigo is the only man ever inducted in three Baseball Halls of Fame, as he was enshrined in the Cuban Hall of Fame, the Mexican Hall of Fame, and the Major League Baseball Hall of Fame?

◆ Did you know Ted Williams is a member of four different Halls of Fame? Williams is a member of the Fishing Hall of Fame, the Florida Sports Hall of Fame, the N.Y. State Aviation Hall of Fame, and, of course, the Baseball Hall of Fame.

106. *Match these players with their accomplishments:*

1	Ty Cobb	A	remains the only player to win batting crowns his first two full years
2	Tony Oliva	B	holds the major league record of eight straight 200-hit seasons
3	Willie Keeler	C	registered 640 plate appearances for 16 straight years
4	Pete Rose	D	holds the record of 68 hits in one month
5	Lenny Dykstra	E	is the last player to lead his league in runs, walks, and hits in the same season

ANSWER: 1—D, 2—A, 3—B, 4—C, 5—E

Cobb had 68 hits and batted .535 in July 1912, and he collected 67 hits exactly 10 years later in July 1922. . . . Oliva and Ichiro Suzuki are the only rookies to win an AL batting title. . . . Keeler put together his stretch of 200-hit years from 1894 to 1901, using his "Hit 'em where they ain't" philosophy. He batted at least .362 in all but one year during that span and averaged 140 runs scored during those eight seasons. Keeler did not bat lower than .300 until his 16th season, his 14th full season. . . . Rose's 1974 mark of 771 plate appearances stood until Lenny Dykstra stepped up to the plate 773 times in 1993. The durable and energetic Rose played more games than anyone. He felt it was his duty. Then again, what do you expect from a guy who once said, "With the money I'm making, I should be playing two positions." . . . Willie Wilson's 705 official at-bats in 1980 remains the single-season high, an abundance of opportunities the speedy switch-hitting outfielder used to total 230 hits for a .326 batting average as well as 133 runs scored for the pennant-winning Royals. . . . In 1993 Dykstra became only the third player in history to lead his league in runs (143), walks (129), and hits (194) during the same season. Billy Hamilton (1891) and Rogers Hornsby (1924) were the other two.

◆ Did you know Pete Rose reached base more times than any other player in the history of the game? Not counting reaching on a fielder's choice, as a pinch-runner, as a courtesy runner, or on an error, wild-pitch strikeout, or catcher's interference, Rose reached base 5,929 times. Ty Cobb is second, getting aboard on 5,534 occasions under the same guidelines. Rickey Henderson has reached base 5,316 times through 2002. Carl Yastrzemski reached base 5,304 times, and Stan Musial is fifth at 5,282.

◆ Did you know Ichiro Suzuki in 2001 became the first player since Jackie Robinson 52 years earlier to lead the league in batting average and stolen bases in the same season? In 1949, Robinson batted .342 and swiped 37 bases to win the MVP, as did Suzuki.

107. *True or False? No retired player (with a minimum of 4,000 at-bats) batted .300 in every one of his major league seasons.*

ANSWER: True

Unbelievably, however, Ty Cobb and Tony Gwynn came pretty darn close. Cobb batted .316 or better in each of his major league campaigns except for his abbreviated first one in 1905 (.240). Gwynn batted .309 or higher each season except for his abbreviated first one in 1982 (.289). Ted Williams batted at least .316 in 18 of his 19 major league seasons; in his penultimate campaign of 1959, he hit an uncharacteristic .254. Many hitters have appeared well on their way until something happened to derail them, whether it be an injury, a problem with technique, or just a prolonged slump.

Wade Boggs was one of those guys, well on his way to that elite accomplishment after having played 10 years of major league ball (not to mention his last five years of minor league ball) with a .300-plus average across the board. However, the third baseman slumped to .259 in 1992, as personal problems may have affected his concentration. Boggs recovered to bat .300 in five of his last seven campaigns and retired with 3,010 hits and a .328 lifetime batting average.

108. *Match these greats with their accomplishments:*

1	Jesse Burkett	A	the first hitter to have two straight .400 seasons
2	Sam Thompson	B	is the only non-teammate to beat Babe Ruth for the home run title from 1918 to 1931
3	Hank Aaron	C	is the only man to lead the league in home runs without homering over the fence
4	Ken Williams	D	hit 16 grand slams
5	Ty Cobb	E	his ratio of RBI to games played (.93 to 1.00) is the best of all time

ANSWER: 1—A, 2—E, 3—D, 4—B, 5—C

In 1895 and 1896 Burkett batted .409 and .410, respectively, for the Cleveland Spiders. The line-drive, left-handed hitter won his third batting title in 1901, again leading the National League in hits, as he had while capturing his first two batting crowns. Only Cobb and Rogers Hornsby have duplicated Burkett's feat of back-to-back .400 seasons. . . . Lou Gehrig and Hank Greenberg follow Thompson with .92 RBI per game, while Ruth is at .88. Ruth averaged one RBI every 3.79 at-bats, the best RBI to at-bat ratio ever. . . . Williams' 39 home runs led the American League in 1922, with Ruth's total of 35 ranking third (also trailing the Athletics' Tilly Walker). . . . All nine of Cobb's 1909 home runs were inside-the-park.

◆ Did you know Pete Rose has the most walks drawn (1,556) without leading the league in that department? Rose's total is 12th on the all-time list.

109. *Can you name the major league team that clinched the pennant or division on the earliest date?*

ANSWER: The 1941 Yankees

The 1941 Yankees clinched the AL pennant on September 4 and finished 17 games ahead of the Red Sox with a 101-53 record. In the World Series, the Yankees beat the Dodgers in five games. Charlie Keller had his finest season with 33 homers and 122 RBI. Joe DiMaggio, who captivated the nation with a 56-game hitting streak, led the league with 125 RBI and hit 30 homers. The Yankees, who allowed the fewest runs in the league and scored the second most, benefited from an unspectacular but stable pitching staff that featured Lefty Gomez, Red Ruffing, Marius Russo, and Spud Chandler. None won more than 15 games, yet none lost more than 10. Right-handed reliever Johnny Murphy posted a 1.98 ERA while winning 8 of 11 decisions and saving 15.

110. *Why did the Brooklyn Dodgers decide to sign Jackie Robinson instead of other negro league stars such as Josh Gibson and Satchel Paige, who were more famous and had had more productive careers?*

ANSWER: Dodgers General Manager Branch Rickey decided on Robinson because he was well educated and had already played with (as opposed to just against) Caucasians. Paige was bitter, as was Gibson, who had waited his entire career for such an opportunity and strongly believed he had earned it. Gibson would most likely have followed, but he died of a brain tumor in January 1947. On April 18, 1946, Robinson began play for the Dodgers' AAA farm team (the Montreal Royals). Then, on April 15, 1947, Robinson broke the Major League Baseball color barrier for Brooklyn in a game versus the Boston Braves, who started righthander Johnny Sain on the mound. Robinson went hitless but scored the winning run and played flawless defense at first base. Robinson didn't get a hit until his 21st major league at-bat. Then, he got in a groove and ended the season with a .297 batting average, 125 runs scored, and a league-leading 29 stolen bases.

Robinson's demeanor and positive example made it possible for the American League to integrate less than three months later, when Larry Doby on July 5 broke the junior circuit's color barrier as a member of Bill Veeck's Indians club. Doby, though, wasn't as productive as Robinson in his first season, collecting just five hits in 32 at-bats. Once Doby received the necessary playing time and got comfortable, however, his bat spoke volumes. In 1949 he began a string of eight consecutive seasons with at least 20 homers, a stretch that featured two home run titles and five 100-RBI campaigns. Doby, the first African American to win a home run crown, was inducted into the Hall of Fame in 1998.

◆ Did you know that Jackie Robinson was not the first black to play Major League Baseball? Up to eight blacks played Major League Baseball in the 1800s. Moses Fleetwood Walker on May 1, 1884, became the first black to play in the majors. He and his brother Welday Walker played a combined 47 games for Toledo of the American Association that season. Fleetwood Walker, who drew some jeers from the start by committing five errors in a loss during his first game, lasted the entire 1884 season in the majors despite protests from Cap Anson of the Chicago White Stockings. He hit .263 over 42 games. In 1885 Toledo folded, and the Walkers never returned to the majors. Sandy Nava, a black Cuban, played for Providence from 1882 through 1884 and played briefly for Baltimore of the American Association in 1885 and 1886. Nava was permitted to play since he said he was Cuban, not black. But some began to wonder about Nava's true origin, and he never returned after 1886. William Higgins, George Stovey, Bud Fowler (the first black minor leaguer in

1872), James Jackson, and Frank Grant were also prevented from playing. On July 14, 1887, after Anson again refused to play against integrated teams, the International League voted to not allow any more "colored men" to play.

111. *Who was the first African American to pitch in the majors?*

A Dan Bankhead
B Satchel Paige
C Joe Black
D Sam Jones

ANSWER: A

Bankhead on August 26, 1947, was belted in his debut, allowing six earned runs and 10 hits in 3⅓ innings, but he homered in his first at-bat. After a decision-less season in 1947, Bankhead didn't pitch again at the major league level until 1950. That's when he went 9-4 with three saves despite a 5.50 ERA. Bankhead's uneventful 1951 campaign was his last.

◆ Did you know Eddie Klepp is recognized as the only white man to play in the negro leagues? Klepp, who never played in the majors, pitched for the Cleveland Buckeyes in 1946. He too was isolated, and many establishments his black teammates attended refused to serve him. His skills on the field were not deserving of further opportunity, but his courage was admirable. A song by folk singer Chuck Brodsky titled *The Ballad of Eddie Klepp* ends:

> So while Jackie played for Brooklyn and wore the Dodger blue
> Eddie crossed the line, the one without a queue
>
> . . . .
>
> Now you mention the name of Eddie Klepp and most everyone
>   says "Who?"

112. *Match these brave pioneers with their major league feats:*

1 Dan Bankhead	A	became the first black pitcher to play in a World Series (he pinch-ran)
2 Satchel Paige	B	became the first black pitcher to pitch in a World Series
3 Joe Black	C	became the first black pitcher to throw a no-hitter

4 Sam Jones   D became the first black pitcher to win a
                                   World Series game

ANSWER: 1—A, 2—B, 3—D, 4—C

Paige also became the first black pitcher to win a game and hurl a shutout during the regular season, blanking the White Sox in his second major league start. . . . Black, a bullpen specialist during the season, won Game One of the 1952 World Series for the Dodgers, six-hitting the Yankees, 4-2. Black, a rookie, then lost Game Four, 2-0, and Game Seven, 4-2, although he pitched well (2.53 ERA in 21⅓ innings). . . . The hard to hit, yet wild Jones of the Cubs no-hit the Pirates, 4-0, on May 12, 1955. Jones walked the bases loaded in the ninth but came back to strike out the final three batters to complete the seven-walk no-hitter. The righthander, nicknamed "Toothpick Sam" (not to be confused with "Sad Sam"), struck out 198 and walked 185 that year en route to a 14-20 record. He led the league in walks and strikeouts in the same season three times, piling on repeated high pitch counts, no doubt the cause of later arm trouble that limited a once-promising career to an ordinary 102-101 major league ledger. Known as "Red" in the negro leagues, Jones began his major league career in 1951, at the age of 25.

◆ Did you know that opening day on April 9, 1968, was postponed due to the assassination of Rev. Dr. Martin Luther King Jr. five days earlier? Dr. King, buried on the 9th, was fatally shot in Memphis, Tennessee, after giving his famous "Mountaintop" speech.

113. *The first free agent amateur draft in major league history was held in 1965. The first ever pick was:*

A Johnny Bench
B Tom Seaver
C Rick Monday
D Rod Carew

ANSWER: C

The Kansas City Athletics made Monday, whose 19-year career featured 241 home runs and two All-Star appearances as an outfielder, the first player chosen. Other All-Stars from that inaugural draft included righthander Joe Coleman (two-time 20-game winner), catcher Ray Fosse (two-time Gold Glove winner), reliever John Wyatt (who reached the 20-save mark three times), and first baseman Jim Spencer (who earned a pair of Gold Gloves). Steve Chilcott, who never played in the majors, was drafted first in 1966 by the Mets. Reggie Jackson was selected with the second pick by the Athletics.

114. *Match these one-time superstars with their feats:*

1	Wade Boggs	A	remains the last switch-hitter to win a home run title
2	Joe Carter	B	became the first player in history with 100 RBI for three different teams in three consecutive years
3	Howard Johnson	C	set a record by driving in all nine of his team's runs in a game
4	Mike Greenwell	D	became the first AL player with seven straight 40-double seasons

ANSWER: 1—D, 2—B, 3—A, 4—C

Medwick is the only other player in history to hit at least 40 doubles in seven straight seasons (1933–39, including an NL high of 64 in 1936). . . . Joe Carter drove in 105 runs for Cleveland in 1989, 115 for San Diego in 1990, and 108 for the division-winning Toronto Blue Jays in 1991. . . . "HoJo" hit 38 homers in 1991 for the New York Mets. The first five switch-hitters to win home run titles were Walt Wilmot (with 13 round trippers in 1890), Duke Farrell (12 the following year in the American Association), Rip Collins (35 in 1934), Mickey Mantle (four home run titles), and Eddie Murray, who shared the home run crown (22) with three others during the strike-shortened 1981 season. . . . On September 2, 1996, Greenwell drove in every Red Sox run as Boston defeated Seattle, 9-8, in 10 innings. The previous record of eight was shared by George Kelly of the 1924 Giants and Bob Johnson of the 1938 Athletics.

♦ Did you know Johnny Damon and Shannon Stewart in 2000 became the 41st and 42nd major leaguers to double four times in a game? In doing so, remarkably, on the same day (July 18), they gave the American League 22 such performances, two more than the National League. The only player with four doubles in a World Series game is Frank Isbell, who accomplished the feat for the Chicago White Sox in Game Five of the 1906 fall classic.

115. *When the St. Louis Cardinals objected to playing the Dodgers with Jackie Robinson, and voted to boycott the game, this NL president intervened and stood up for Robinson. He said, "If you do this [speaking to the Cardinals organization], you will be suspended from the league. You will find that the friends that you think you have in the press box will not support you, that you will be outcasts. I do not care if half the league strikes. Those who do it will encounter quick retribution. They will be suspended and I don't care if it wrecks the National League for five years. This is the United States of America, and one citizen has as much right to play as another. The National League will go down the line with Robinson whatever the consequence." Who was this NL president?*

ANSWER: Ford Frick

Ford Frick was the righteous and principled man who stood in the way of this prejudiced act. Frick (NL president from 1934 to 1951) was also the commissioner from 1951 to 1968 and a Hall of Fame inductee (1970). That the Cardinals objected to playing Robinson's Dodgers was most ironic, since retired Cardinal ace Dizzy Dean and his teammates had enjoyed playing the negro league players so much that they staged numerous exhibition games during the season, promoted as the "Dizzy Dean All-Stars" versus the "Satchel Paige All-Stars."

◆ Did you know former player Bill White in 1989 became baseball's first black president, taking over the helm of the National League? The dignified White resigned after five years and a month at his post. A six-time All-Star and a winner of seven Gold Gloves at first base, White retired in 1969 from a 13-year playing career, mostly spent in the Cardinals organization. The line-drive, left-handed hitter posted a lifetime .286 batting average, reaching the 20-homer mark seven times and topping 100 RBI on four occasions.

116. *Match these African Americans with their historic achievements in the major leagues:*

1	Emmett Ashford	A	became the first black pitcher to win 20 games in a season
2	Frank Robinson	B	became the first black pitcher to lead the league in ERA
3	Don Newcombe	C	became the first black umpire
4	Monte Irvin	D	became the first black player to lead the league in RBI
5	Sam Jones	E	became the first black manager to win a pennant
6	Cito Gaston	F	became the first black manager in NL history

ANSWER: 1—C, 2—F, 3—A, 4—D, 5—B, 6—E

In addition to becoming the AL's first black manager, Robinson later became the NL's first black manager, taking the helm for the 1981 San Francisco Giants. He managed three different teams between 1975 and 1991 and won a Manager of the Year Award for Baltimore in 1989. To help remedy the Montreal Expos' financial instability, Robinson left his post as Major League Baseball's vice president of on-field operations to manage the MLB-controlled club for the 2002 season. . . . In 1992 Gaston guided the Blue Jays to the AL pennant and world championship—a feat he repeated in 1993. When Gaston's Blue Jays faced Robinson's Orioles on June 27, 1989, the confrontation marked the first in major league history between two African American managers. . . . Jones led the National League in ERA (2.83) for the Giants in 1959. . . . Irvin drove in a league-leading 121 runs for the 1951 Giants.

◆ Did you know that John "Buck" O'Neil became the first black coach in the major leagues when he was hired by the Chicago Cubs in 1962? A former negro leaguer, O'Neil played in the negro leagues from 1937 to 1955 and player-managed the last 8 of his 19 years on the field.

117. *Two American League pitchers have won 25 games in a season only to fall short of a Cy Young Award. Can you name these two southpaws?*

ANSWER: Jim Kaat and Mickey Lolich

Minnesota's Jim Kaat and Detroit's Mickey Lolich are the two members of this disappointed junior circuit club. Kaat was 25-13 and sported a 2.75 ERA, with league-highs in complete games (19) and innings pitched (304⅔) during the 1966 season. Alas for Kaat, Sandy Koufax won more votes in this season, the last to feature just one Cy Young Award for both leagues combined. Lolich in 1971 posted a 25-14 ledger, with a 2.92 ERA, 376 innings, 29 complete games, and 308 strikeouts (the latter three figures were best in the league, as was his victory total). However, Vida Blue topped Lolich with a 24-8 mark, a league-leading ERA of 1.82, eight shutouts to pace the league, 24 complete games, and 301 strikeouts in 312 innings.

♦ Did you know Mickey Lolich is one of only three pitchers from the 20th century on to strike out 300 batters in a season and not lead the league? The 301 Ks by Detroit's Lolich in 1971 were surpassed by Oakland's Vida Blue, who struck out 308. In 1997 Montreal's Pedro Martinez whiffed 305 batters, 14 fewer than Philadelphia's Curt Schilling. And in 2002 Schilling's 316 Ks were 18 behind teammate Randy Johnson's total. This happened often in the 19th century, and in fact a pair of pitchers failed to win the crown despite recording 400 strikeouts. In the 1886 American Association season, left-hander Toad Ramsey struck out 499 batters and still failed to lead the circuit. That was the year southpaw Matt Kilroy set his all-time mark of 513. Two years earlier in the National League, Charlie Buffington's 417 Ks were 24 shy of Old Hoss Radbourn.

118. *What happened after young club owner Bill Veeck arranged to buy the Philadelphia Phillies and field, mostly, an All-Star team from the negro leagues in the 1943 season to secure a pennant?*

ANSWER: The prejudiced commissioner Kenesaw Landis learned of Veeck's plans and aborted them to prevent the possibility of integration, saying, "The colored ball players have their own League." When Landis died the following year, Branch Rickey almost immediately signed Jackie Robinson. Veeck, who owned three different American League clubs, never did buy the Phillies.

♦ Did you know Jackie Robinson in 1982 became the first African American on a U.S. stamp?

119. *One of the most overlooked men in the establishment of integration was a black sportswriter named Sam Lacey. What did Lacey do to help the process along?*

Lacey urged Leslie O'Conner (the Chairman-Secretary of the Major League Advisory Council) to put together a Major League Committee on Baseball Integration. O'Conner had been Kenesaw Landis' secretary and assistant for 24 years, and after Landis died he had taken over the commissioner's administrative functions, without the title or power. He acted upon Lacey's suggestion, and in April of 1945 the committee was established. Then, new commissioner Albert B. "Happy" Chandler (a former Kentucky Governor) made it known he stood behind the integration ideas, saying, "If a black boy can make it on Okinawa and Guadalcanal, hell, he can make it in baseball."

The only negative consequence of the major leagues' integration was the gradual termination of the negro leagues. The fans of the negro leagues soon started attending major league games instead, to see their black heroes in major league uniforms. By 1951 only six teams remained, and by 1953 only four negro league clubs stood. The league formally folded after the 1960 season. In 1963 the last East-West All-Star Game (a huge black baseball tradition that saw as many whites as blacks in the stands) was played, and the Indianapolis Clowns team was the only squad in existence by 1965. The Clowns played exhibition games against other semi-pro teams for another decade.

120. *Match these negro league characters with their roles:*

1	Bill Lucas	A	hit .564 and led the Negro National Leagues in homers at age 44
2	Ray Dandridge	B	this left-handed first baseman led the Grays to championships in 1940 and 1941, when Josh Gibson went to Mexico for more money
3	John Henry Lloyd	C	was the first black general manager (for the Braves)
4	Buck Leonard	D	never played a major league game

ANSWER: 1—C, 2—D, 3—A, 4—B

Dandridge was great defensively at third base and a consistent .300 hitter. . . . Lloyd was Babe Ruth's choice as best player ever, regardless of color. The left-handed hitting Lloyd concluded a 27-year career with a .368 mark. . . . Leonard, a stable fellow, played all 17 years of his career with the Grays, helping them win nine straight

Negro National League pennants from 1937 through 1945 and three titles. Leonard was a smooth-fielding first baseman whose beautiful swing consistently produced line drives, to the tune of three NNL batting crowns and a .341 lifetime batting average (a mark that excludes a .382 average in exhibitions against major leaguers).

◆ Did you know that Hall of Famers Bill Foster and Andy Cooper actually won more negro league games than Satchel Paige? Foster, considered the best southpaw in the annals of the negro leagues, and Cooper won 137 games apiece, and Paige's total of 123 was third in negro league history. Incidentally, Bill Foster was the younger half-brother of Hall of Famer Rube Foster, "The Father of Black Baseball."

121. *Satchel Paige in 1965 became the oldest player (at least 59 years of age) to appear in a major league game, pitching for the Kansas City Athletics. Can you name the second oldest player to appear in a major league game?*

ANSWER: Minnie Minoso

The 57-year-old Minoso, a seven-time All-Star outfielder, came out of retirement for two pinch-hit at-bats as a member of the 1980 White Sox. After originally retiring in 1964, the .298 career hitter came back in 1976 to play three games as a designated hitter. Among his eight at-bats was a single, making the 53-year-old the oldest player to get a hit. Minoso attempted a third "comeback" in 1992 and 1993 but was refused by the Players Association, after the White Sox front office originally agreed. Had he been permitted to play, Minoso would have tied Nick Altrock's record of most decades played in, five. (Altrock was a left-handed pitcher who won a combined 62 games for the White Sox from 1904 to 1906. He made his debut in 1898 and his last appearance, a gift pinch-hit opportunity, at the age of 57 in 1933. In between, he became a coach for the Senators, who allowed him to make token appearances as well as perform comedy skits.)

Paige on September 25, 1965, made his first appearance in 12 years (for publicity purposes), throwing three shutout innings and allowing just one hit against the Red Sox. To help Paige accrue the required time to receive a pension, the Braves in 1968 hired the former fireballer to serve as pitching coach.

◆ Did you know Satchel Paige threw a 12-inning shutout at the age of 46? On August 6, 1952, Paige of the St. Louis Browns blanked Detroit, yielding seven hits, walking two, and whiffing nine Tigers. The righthander went on to a 12-10 season with a 3.07 ERA for a 64-90 squad, earning his first of two straight All-Star Game appearances. Paige remains the oldest to participate in a mid-summer classic. According to records guru Lyle Spatz of the Society for American Baseball Research, Phil Niekro is the oldest to throw a shutout, doing so in 1985 at the age of 46 years and six months. That's five months older than Paige, if you believe Paige's listed date of birth, July 7, 1906.

122. *Match these superstars with their feats:*

1 Vladimir Guerrero and Alfonso Soriano — A hit 335 career home runs

2 Ron Gant — B had consecutive 30-30 seasons in 1990 and 1991

3 Howard Johnson — C missed a 40-40 season by one home run

4 Darryl Strawberry — D became only the fifth player in history with at least 30 home runs and 30 errors in the same season

ANSWER: 1—C, 2—B, 3—D, 4—A

Both Guerrero and Soriano entered the final day of the 2002 season with a 40-40 season one swing away, and both failed to reach the mark. Soriano did become the first second baseman ever to achieve a 30-30. And Guerrero became the fifth ever with back-to-back 30-30 seasons, joining Willie Mays, Gant, and Bobby and Barry Bonds. . . . HoJo stole 30 bases, hit 38 home runs, and committed 31 errors during the 1991 campaign, becoming the first 30-30-30 man. The first to reach 30 home runs and 30 errors in a season was Rogers Hornsby, who hit 42 homers and committed 30 errors in 1922 and slammed 39 home runs with 34 errors in 1924. Eddie Mathews followed with a 47-homer, 30-error season in 1953. Ernie Banks hit 47 roundtrippers and committed 32 miscues in 1958. Tony Perez of Cincinnati, the fourth Hall of Famer on this list, did it in successive seasons, while playing third base (1969, 37 homers, 32 errors; 1970, 40 homers, 35 errors).

◆ Did you know Jim Gentile's 75 home runs over his first 1,000 career at-bats remains the record over that span? The journeyman first baseman added

104 homers in his next, and last, 1,922 at-bats. Gentile played for six teams in his nine years.

123. *On October 4, 1999, the New York Mets defeated the Cincinnati Reds, 5-0, in the 10th tie-breaking playoff to decide a postseason berth. Up until 1946, a tie had never happened. No two teams had ever finished the regular season schedule with identical records in the same league. That is, until the St. Louis Cardinals and Brooklyn Dodgers found themselves tied with a 96-58 record, facing a best-of-three league playoff. The Cardinals swept the Dodgers and proceeded to beat the Boston Red Sox in seven World Series games. In 1948 the American League had its first deadlock to force a one-game playoff (the American League has always had a one-game playoff system whereas the National League used a three-game system through 1979).*

Match these four one-game playoff results with the year in which they took place:

1	1998	A	the Mariners defeated the Angels, 9-1
2	1959	B	the Astros defeated the Dodgers, 7-1
3	1995	C	the Dodgers defeated the Braves, two games to none
4	1980	D	the Cubs defeated the Giants, 5-3

ANSWER: 1—D, 2—C, 3—A, 4—B

The Cubs defeated the Giants almost 90 years to the day after winning the infamous Merkle game, which was a makeup game and not a playoff. . . . The Dodgers were involved in the first five NL playoffs and lost four of them. In 1946 the Cardinals beat the Dodgers by scores of 4-2 and 8-4. In 1951 the Giants won 3-1 and lost, 10-0, before dramatically winning that unforgettable third game, 5-4. In 1959 the Dodgers beat the Braves by scores of 3-2 and 6-5. Three years afterward, San Francisco again ousted Los Angeles by winning the first game, 8-0, losing the second contest, 8-7, and heroically winning the deciding match, 6-4.

In the National League's first one-game playoff, the Astros clubbed the Dodgers behind the hitting of Art Howe. . . . The last AL playoff took place in Seattle on October 2, 1995, when the Mariners routed the Angels by a score of 9-1 for the AL West title. Incidentally, the Red Sox were involved in the first two AL playoff games and lost each at home.

◆ Did you know the five teams that forced a one-game playoff by winning their last scheduled game all lost? The 1999 Cincinnati Reds, the 1995 California Angels, the 1980 Los Angeles Dodgers, and the 1948 and 1978 Boston Red Sox all suffered that fate.

124. *Match these pitchers with their distinctions:*

1	Ferguson Jenkins	A	the only pitcher to lead both leagues in winning percentage before 2002
2	Larry Benton	B	the only pitcher to allow home runs to all three Alou brothers
3	Jack Chesbro	C	the first pitcher to win 200 games without a 20-win season
4	Milt Pappas	D	the only pitcher to twice lead the league in winning percentage but still end up with a career record under .500

ANSWER: 1—B, 2—D, 3—A, 4—C

As a member of the Pirates, Chesbro led the National League in winning percentage in 1901 (.677, 21-10) and 1902 (.842, 28-6). As a member of the N.Y. Highlanders, Chesbro led the American League in 1904 (41-12) with a .774 winning percentage. Randy Johnson became the second in 2002, with an .828 winning percentage for Arizona, after twice leading the American League in that category. . . . Larry Benton led the National League in winning percentage in 1927 (17-7, .708) and 1928 (25-9, .735) only to finish with a losing career record of 127-128. . . . Charlie Hough (216), Frank Tanana (240), Jerry Reuss (220), Dennis Martinez (245), and Chuck Finley (200) have joined Pappas (209) as the only 200-game winners without a 20-win season.

◆ Did you know Charlie Hough's 216-216 career record represents the highest decision total for any pitcher who finished with a winning percentage of exactly .500? According to the Society for American Baseball Research, Howard Ehmke's 166-166 ledger comes the closest to Hough. Nap Rucker (134-134) is the only other .500 pitcher with at least 200 decisions.

125. *After their loss in the 1960 World Series, the Yankees flabbergasted the baseball world by firing the sport's best manager, Casey Stengel,* *and best general manager, George Weiss, making Stengel the first manager to get the ax after a World Series appearance. The Hall of Fame duo had taken over a third-place team and transformed the Yankees into a championship franchise (with 10 pennants and 7 world championships in 12 years!). Can you name the manager that co-owners Del Webb and Dan Topping replaced Stengel with?*

ANSWER: Ralph Houk

Soon after Houk was hired, he made it known that things were going to be different. The platoon system that Stengel had so brilliantly employed to keep the best possible talent on the field (and help team camaraderie) would be tossed aside. The result: the 1961 Yankees became, arguably, the second best team in baseball history.

Following the Yankees' 1963 World Series loss to the Dodgers, Houk moved up to general manager, and Yogi Berra replaced Houk in the dugout.

After their loss to St. Louis in the 1964 World Series, the Yankees again reacted harshly, firing Berra. Again, Webb was involved in the firing, although there was a new owner in town—the television company CBS, which had purchased 80 percent of the franchise for $11.2 million. The Yankees in 1965 suffered their first losing season since 1925 and fell to the cellar in 1966, for the first time since 1912. Attendance dropped off, and the Yankees lost their aura. That year, Webb sold his remaining 20 percent share of the team, leaving CBS as the sole owner.

In a few years, the team unity and champion aura encompassing the Yankees had vanished. The new owners had taken over the best franchise in sports (a record 39 straight years, from 1926 to 1964, with a first division finish) and treated the dynasty as a Wall Street stock rather than the well-organized gem it represented.

Incidentally, George Weiss became the president of the Mets in 1961 and again hired Stengel as a manager.

◆ Did you know Hall of Famer George Weiss won 15 World Series and 19 AL pennants in 29 years as Yankees general manager? After firing Bucky Harris following the 1948 season, Weiss hired Casey Stengel—a move very few thought was wise. Weiss proved himself a genius, as Stengel piloted the Yankees to 7 world championships and 10 pennants in 12 years. Among Weiss' best player decisions were signing Joe DiMaggio, whom almost every executive had backed away from following an injury, and trading for Roger Maris.

◆ Did you the New York Yankees are Major League Baseball's most valuable team, with an estimated value of $730 million, according to *Forbes* magazine?

126. *Match these sluggers with their accomplishments:*

1	Stan Musial	A	holds the NL record of 369 total bases for a switch-hitter
2	Howard Johnson	B	is the only NL player to lead the league in triples, doubles, and singles in the same season
3	Ripper Collins	C	holds the NL switch-hitting record of 140 runs scored
4	Max Carey	D	is the only NL switch-hitter to lead the league in RBI (with 117)

ANSWER: 1—B, 2—D, 3—A, 4—C

Musial, who led the National League in triples (20), doubles (50), and singles (142) in 1946, also paced the senior circuit in doubles, triples, and hits in the same season four times. Until Colorado's Larry Walker accomplished the feat in 1999, Musial was the last NL player to lead his league in batting average, on-base percentage, and slugging percentage in one season.

Walker's teammate Todd Helton duplicated the latter feat in 2000, as did Barry Bonds in 2002. Helton had the kind of season players fantasize about, batting .372 with 42 homers, 147 RBI, 59 doubles, and 103 extra-base hits. His 103 extra-base hits tied him for the fourth highest single-season figure in history.

◆ Did you know Tris Speaker and Stan Musial share the record of leading a league in doubles eight times? Speaker, who had a major league record 792 two-baggers, led the American League in doubles in 1912, 1914, 1916, 1918, and 1920–23. Musial, who hit 725 doubles, led the National League in that category in 1943–44, 1946, 1948–49, and 1952–54.

◆ Did you know Nellie Fox holds the major league record of leading a league in singles eight times? San Diego's Tony Gwynn led the National League in singles seven times (1984, 1986–87, 1989, 1994–95, and 1997). Fox achieved that record exclusively in the American League. Of his 2,663 career hits, 2,161 were singles. Of Gwynn's 3,141 hits, 2,378 were singles. Pete Rose holds the career singles mark with 3,215.

127. *This solid left-handed starter came up with the California Angels in 1973 and possessed one of the best fastballs in baseball (as his strike-out and ERA title will attest) until shoulder problems made him a "junk-ball" pitcher by the end of the decade. He also owns the distinction of winning the first game in the Kingdome, the first game in New Comiskey Park, and the last game in Memorial Park. Can you name this 240-game winner?*

ANSWER: Frank Tanana

The six-foot-three Tanana went 16-9 in 1975, his second full season, finishing fourth in ERA (2.62) and leading the major leagues with 269 strikeouts, almost a strikeout per nine innings more than teammate Nolan Ryan. He went 19-10 the following year, improving on his ERA and almost duplicating his strikeout total. In 1977 the tough-luck Tanana led the American League in ERA, tied for the major league lead with seven shutouts, and enjoyed his third straight 200-strikeout campaign, yet he had a 15-9 record to show for it. Relying less on strikeouts, Tanana won 18 games in 1978 despite an ERA that soared by more than a run. A sore shoulder sidelined Tanana for all but 90 innings in 1979. He returned to pitch 204 innings in 1980, his final with the Angels, and realized he was going to have to completely reinvent his style of pitching. This task began paying fruit in 1984, when he won 15 for the Texas Rangers. He was traded during the 1985 season to the Tigers, for whom he won a division-clinching game on the last day of the season. He went on to enjoy six more double-digit-win campaigns for the Tigers before retiring after the 1993 season with 2,773 strikeouts in 4,188 innings, 34 shutouts, and a 3.66 ERA.

Tanana beat the expansion Mariners on Opening Day 1977, the White Sox in 1991, and the Orioles in their last game at Memorial Stadium on the last day of the 1991 season.

128. *These brothers were the only brothers to win batting titles:*

    A Joe DiMaggio and Dom DiMaggio
    B Matty Alou and Felipe Alou
    C Paul Waner and Lloyd Waner
    D Irish Meusel and Bob Meusel

E Harry Walker and Dixie Walker
F Ed Delahanty and Jim Delahanty

ANSWER: E

Dixie Walker (Brooklyn outfielder with a .306 lifetime average) led the National League with a .357 batting average in 1944, and brother Harry (a .296 lifetime hitter) won the batting title in 1947 with a .363 mark. Harry played 130 of his 140 games with the Philadelphia Phillies in 1947. . . . Lloyd Waner never won a batting title, but he finished as high as third in his rookie year (1927, the year in which Paul won the first of his three) and among the top ten a total of six times.

◆ Did you know Vince DiMaggio and Dom DiMaggio had a better fielding mark than their more famous brother Joe? Vince retired with a .981 fielding percentage, Dom with a .9783 mark, and Joe with a figure of .9780. Although Joe averaged 2.6 putouts per game and an assist every 11.3 games, Dom averaged 2.81 putouts per game and an assist every 9.3 games, and Vince averaged 2.63 putouts per game and an assist every 8.27 games. Dom's 2.99 total chances per game remains the AL career record by an outfielder.

129. *Match these hitters with their record achievements:*

1	Honus Wagner	A	tied a major league record with a pair of bases-loaded triples in one game
2	Greg Gagne	B	had eight 200-hit campaigns
3	Lou Gehrig	C	tied a modern record with two inside-the-park homers in one game
4	Duane Kuiper	D	hit at least two grand slams with five different teams
5	Walker Cooper	E	was the oldest NL batting champ before Barry Bonds in 2002
6	Dave Kingman	F	hit at least one grand slam with five different clubs

ANSWER: 1—E, 2—C, 3—B, 4—A, 5—F, 6—D

Wagner won his last batting title in 1911 with a .344 mark at the age of 37 years and seven months, or seven months younger than Bonds. Wagner's eight batting crowns are a big reason the Pirates franchise boasts more batting titles (24) than any other organization. The nine other Pirates to win a batting title are: Roberto Clemente (four), Paul Waner (three), Dave Parker (two), Bill Madlock (two), Arky Vaughan, Matty Alou, Dick Groat, Ginger Beaumont, and Ed Swartwood. . . . Gagne, who accomplished the feat on October 4, 1986, for the Twins, remains the last player to hit a pair of inside-the-park home runs in a game. The last NL player was New York's Hank Thompson, who hit two on August 16, 1950, in the Giants' 16-7 rout of the Brooklyn Dodgers at the Polo Grounds. Tom McCreery of Louisville set the all-time record of three inside-the-park home runs in a single game on July 12, 1897. . . . Kuiper remains the last player to have hit two bases-loaded triples in one game. Sam Thompson of the Detroit Wolverines was the first to accomplish that feat, doing so on May 7, 1887. Heinie Reitz of the National League's Baltimore Orioles became the second on June 4, 1894. Willie Clark of the Pirates followed on September 17, 1898. Elmer Valo of the Athletics was the first in the modern era to achieve the feat, doing so on May 1, 1949. Bill Bruton of the Milwaukee Braves, the last before Kuiper, did so on August 2, 1959.

◆ Did you know Toby Harrah and Bump Wills hit inside-the-park home runs on consecutive pitches? Harrah and Wills performed their feats on August 27, 1977, off Yankees' pitcher Ken Clay.

130. *Match these players with their feats:*

1	Johnny Mize	A	shares the major league record of six three-homer contests
2	Jeromy Burnitz	B	is the only player to hit two grand slams in one inning
3	Fernando Tatis	C	twice hit three homers in a game versus Steve Carlton
4	Robin Ventura	D	is the only player to twice hit two grand slams in one day
5	Johnny Bench	E	was part of the only team duo in history that each hit three home runs in the same game

ANSWER: 1—A, 2—E, 3—B, 4—D, 5—C

Mize hit three homers in a game four times for the Cardinals, once for the Giants, and once in Yankee pinstripes. Sammy Sosa matched Mize's career total on August 10, 2002. Mark McGwire, Joe Carter (the AL record-holder), and Dave Kingman have had five such performances. Three of Sosa's power performances came about in 2001, a record for a single season. The active Carlos Delgado of Toronto is among six players with four career three-homer performances. . . . Burnitz and Brewers teammate Richie Sexson made history on September 25, 2001, when each belted a trio of homers in a 9-4 victory over the Diamondbacks. (Babe Ruth and Lou Gehrig in May of 1930 enjoyed three-homer games one day apart.) Never before had two opponents accomplished the feat, much less two teammates. . . . Hank Sauer preceded Bench by two decades in becoming the first player to connect for three homers in a game twice off the same pitcher. Sauer victimized the Phillies' Curt Simmons during the 1950 season and again two years later. . . . Tatis on April 23, 1999, set a record by twice homering with the bases loaded in one inning, taking the Dodgers' Chan Ho Park deep each time. (Park joined Pittsburgh's Bill Phillips in 1890 as the only pitchers to yield two grand slams in one inning.) Tatis' eight RBI in one inning is also a record. Boston's Nomar Garciaparra 17 days later became the 11th player to hit a pair of grand slams in one game and, amazingly, the first to accomplish the feat at home. . . . Ventura, who had already hit a pair of grand slams in one game for the White Sox on September 4, 1995, hit one in each game of a twinbill for the New York Mets on May 20, 1999. He thus became the first to hit two slams in one day on two separate occasions. The other eight to belt two grand slams in one game are: Frank Robinson, Chris Hoiles, Jim Northrup, Tony Cloninger, Jim Gentile, Rudy York, Jim Tabor, and Tony Lazzeri.

◆ Did you know baseball Hall of Famer Dave Winfield is the only athlete ever drafted by the National Football League, the National Basketball Association, and Major League Baseball? Coming out of the University of Minnesota he was a wanted man, as the Utah Stars of the American Basketball Association also drafted him. The NFL's Minnesota Vikings and the NBA's Atlanta Hawks selected the gifted athlete, who chose baseball instead and reported to the San Diego Padres. The Baltimore Orioles also drafted Winfield—out of high school.

◆ Did you know Dick Groat balanced professional basketball and baseball one year? Groat played in the NBA during the 1952–53 season, between his first and second baseball season. Groat played college basketball at Duke, leading the nation in scoring the last two years. He averaged 12 points for the Fort Wayne Pistons.

◆ Did you know Gene Conley won a World Series ring in 1957 and an NBA championship two years later? The six-foot-eight righthander helped the Milwaukee Braves win the 1957 world championship with a 9-9 record and a 3.16 ERA. Eighteen months later, Conley helped the Boston Celtics win the first of their eight straight NBA titles. The dual-talented Conley earned his third NL All-Star selection in 1959, going 12-7 with a 3.00 ERA for the Philadelphia Phillies. He became a 15-game winner for the Boston Red Sox in 1962, during which year Conley and teammate Pumpsie Green mysteriously went AWOL for four days. Without informing the team, Conley and Green left, kept the club in suspense, and even tried to board a plane headed overseas. Refused tickets because they didn't have visas, they soon returned, Green after two days and Conley after four days. Both were fined. Conley's only explanation was that he felt tired and needed time away from the club, to attend to "other plans." Very strange.

131. *Match these players with their accomplishments or distinctions:*

1	Carson Bigbee	A	is the only player to hit a home run out of Memorial Stadium
2	Don Kessinger	B	set a major league record, since tied, with 11 at-bats in a (22-inning) game
3	Gene Woodling	C	was one of the last player-managers
4	Frank Robinson	D	became the first NL switch-hitter to hit a home run from both sides of the plate
5	Augie Galan	E	was platooned with Hank Bauer in Casey Stengel's alignment for the Yankees during their dynasty years

ANSWER: 1—B, 2—C, 3—E, 4—A, 5—D

Stengel, who was routinely platooned as a player in the 1910s and early 1920s, repopularized the strategy after a period when it was rarely employed, because it was considered confidence-deflating. . . . Robinson's memorable homer was measured at 541 feet. . . . Bigbee's standard has since been tied 13 times, including by a quartet of players on May 8–9, 1984. Completing a marathon from the day before, Carlton Fisk, Rudy Law, and Julio Cruz of the White Sox and Cecil

Cooper of the Brewers all finished a 25-inning contest on May 9 with 11 official at-bats. Bigbee was a Pirate outfielder who batted .287 over an 11-year career that started in 1916.

◆ Did you know Craig Biggio in 1997 became only the third player in major league history to go through an entire season (minimum 150 games) without grounding into a double play? Biggio came to bat 619 times in 1997 while playing every game. The Houston Astro second baseman matched a feat first accomplished by Augie Galan, who came to bat 646 times over 154 games for the Cubs in 1935, and later equaled by Detroit's Dick McAuliffe 33 years later, over 151 games and 570 at-bats. Galan (a .287 lifetime hitter), interestingly enough, lined into a triple play that same season.

132. *Babe Ruth hit 40 or more home runs 7 years in a row and in 11 years during a 13-year stretch. No one has duplicated either stretch, but five other players have hit 40 or more homers five years in a row. They are:*

A Ralph Kiner, Duke Snider, Ken Griffey Jr., Sammy Sosa, and Alex Rodriguez

B Lou Gehrig, Jimmie Foxx, Mark McGwire, Barry Bonds, and Sammy Sosa

C Hank Aaron, Willie Mays, Sammy Sosa, Barry Bonds, and Alex Rodriguez

D Mickey Mantle, Frank Robinson, Ralph Kiner, Barry Bonds, and Mark McGwire

ANSWER: A

Kiner did it for the Pirates from 1947 to 1951, Snider for the Dodgers from 1953 to 1957, and Griffey for the Mariners and Reds from 1996 to 2000. Sosa and Rodriguez's streaks are active.

Snider's 43 homers in 1956 won him his only home run crown. Overshadowed by Willie Mays, Mickey Mantle, Ted Williams, and Stan Musial, Snider was a complete player. The left-handed slugger exploited the cozy dimensions of Ebbets Field to great advantage, and he was a great defensive center fielder as well. Snider's speed enabled him to track down fly balls and line drives and finish among the top 10 in steals five times from 1949 to 1955. His 42 homers and career-best 136 RBI in 1955 helped the Dodgers finally break through for their first world championship. In the victorious World Series against the hated Yankees, Snider took matters into his own hands with four homers, seven RBI, and an .840 slugging percentage.

◆ Did you know Willie Mays, Mickey Mantle, and Duke Snider were immortalized in Terry Cashman's song "Talkin Baseball (Willie, Mickey, and The Duke)"? Cashman in 1981 released the song and others about our national pastime, helping to fill the void during the strike.

133. *Choose the Senators' player whose head-on collision at home plate almost crushed Yankee catcher Bill Dickey, provoking the otherwise quiet and well-mannered Hall of Fame receiver to break this right fielder's jaw with a devastating punch that set off one of the wildest brawls in baseball history.*

   A Carl Reynolds
   B Heinie Manush
   C Sam Rice
   D Sammy West

ANSWER: A

William Malcolm Dickey received a $1,000 fine and a 30-day suspension for his part in the 1932 Independence Day brawl. Outside the ballpark, Dickey was as reticent as Lou Gehrig. So perhaps it was fitting that he and Gehrig roomed on the road and became best of friends. (Dickey was the first teammate to find out about Gehrig's fatal disease.)

That brawl, however, doesn't hold a candle to the altercation that took place in Atlanta on August 12, 1984. After Braves right-hander Pascual Perez hit Padres lead-off hitter Alan Wiggins in the back to start off the game, San Diego pitchers retaliated by throwing at Perez during all four of his plate appearances. A pair of nasty brawls ensued, and eventually even fans became involved. Managers Dick Williams of the Padres and Joe Torre of the Braves were among the 19 men ejected. Heck, even the managers' replacements were ejected! Williams was handed a 10-game suspension, and Torre was suspended for 3 games.

◆ Did you know Philadelphia Phillie Frank Thomas started a fight with his teammate Dick Allen, which ended when Thomas swung a bat at Allen? The

July 3, 1965, incident was the last Thomas saw as a Phillie, as he got his release after the game.

134. *In 2001 Ichiro Suzuki got a hit in 135 games, matching a major league record shared by four others. Choose the quartet Suzuki joined:*

A Pete Rose, Rod Carew, Tony Gwynn, and Derek Jeter
B Rogers Hornsby, Ty Cobb, Wade Boggs, and Derek Jeter
C Rogers Hornsby, Chuck Klein, Wade Boggs, and Derek Jeter
D George Sisler, George Brett, Tony Gwynn, and Derek Jeter

ANSWER: C
It took "Rajah" 154 games to achieve the mark in 1922, Klein 156 in 1930, Boggs 161 in 1985, Jeter 158 in 1999, and Suzuki 157. All but Klein led their league in hits that year.

◆ Did you know Chuck Klein is the only major league player with a pair of 420–total base seasons? Klein had 445 total bases in 1930 and 420 in 1932.

◆ Did you know it took Chuck Klein 128 days to hit his 300th and final home run? It took Gary Carter 266 at-bats to reach the same milestone, and it took Jimmie Foxx 66 at-bats to hit his 500th home run.

135. *With Will Clark finishing one short of the RBI title in 1991, the Giants just missed becoming only the second team in history to have a player lead the league in RBI for four straight seasons. Can you name the only team to accomplish the feat?*

ANSWER: The New York Yankees
The Yankees' Bob Meusel led the league in 1925 (138), Babe Ruth in 1926 (145), Lou Gehrig in 1927 (175), and Ruth and Gehrig (142 apiece) shared the title in 1928. The Giants' Clark led the National League in RBI (109) in 1988, Kevin Mitchell led the league in 1989 (125), and Matt Williams led with 122 in 1990, before Clark just missed making history.

136. *During his 1991 MVP season, Cal Ripken Jr. hit 34 home runs for Baltimore. For the future Hall of Fame shortstop, 1991 marked his*

10th consecutive season with at least 20 home runs. Do you know whose record Ripken broke in 1989 for the most consecutive 20-homer seasons by a shortstop?

ANSWER: Ernie Banks

Banks did it for seven years in a row as a shortstop for the Cubs, from 1955 to 1961. Although Banks hit 37 homers in 1962, in that season he was playing his first season at first base. Ripken passed Banks for the most home runs hit as a shortstop in 1993 (Banks had 277 at short). Ripken retired following the 2001 season with 431 homers, 345 as a shortstop. It wasn't until the 2001 season that Banks' single-season shortstop record of 47 homers (in 1958) was surpassed, when Alex Rodriguez clubbed 52. Rodriguez broke his own mark with 57 home runs in 2002.

◆ Did you know in 1969 Boston's Rico Petrocelli set the AL shortstop home run record (40) and the position standard for fewest errors (14) over a full season? The right-handed Petrocelli also drove in 97 runs to earn his second All-Star appearance. Previously, he was best recognized for clubbing two homers in Game Six of the 1967 World Series, forcing a seventh game against the Cardinals.

◆ Did you know Ernie Banks became, technically, the first black manager in major league history when he managed one game in 1973 (May 8) for the ejected Cubs manager Whitey Lockman?

◆ Did you know Ernie Banks is a cousin of NFL Hall of Famer O. J. Simpson?

137. *Which father-son duo has combined for the most home runs ever?*

ANSWER: Bobby and Barry Bonds

Bobby Bonds (332) and his son, five-time MVP Barry Bonds (613), have a combined 945 home runs entering the 2003 season. The Griffeys, Ken Sr. and Ken Jr., have combined for 620 homers (Jr. has 468). Yogi Berra (358) and son Dale Berra (49) combined for 407 home runs, as did Gus Bell (206) and Buddy Bell (201).

Barry Bonds' 9 stolen bases in 2002 gave him (493) and his father (461) a combined 954 steals, 172 more than Maury Wills (586) and his son Bump Wills (196). George Sisler (375) and his son Dick combined for 381, and the Griffeys have combined for 376. The Bonds family, with 2,676 RBI, stands 459 ahead of the Griffeys' total of 2,217. The Bells have 2,048 RBI. Buddy had 1,106 RBI to lead the Bells, Barry has 1,652 to lead the Bonds, and Ken Jr. has 1,358 to lead the Griffeys.

◆ Did you know Barry Bonds defeated Ken Griffey Jr. as Player of the Decade for the 1990s, as determined in a poll conducted by *The Sporting News?* Mike Schmidt won the honor for the 1980s, Pete Rose for the 1970s, and Willie Mays won for the 1960s. Ted Williams won the honor for the 1950s, with Stan Musial earning the inaugural award for the decade from 1946 to 1955.

138. *The Texas Rangers, who began as the Washington Senators in 1961 and moved to Texas in 1972, made the postseason for the first time in 1996, the franchise's 36th year. By winning the AL Western Division, the Rangers snapped a 35-year postseason drought. Which franchise had the longest postseason drought?*

ANSWER: The St. Louis Browns

The Browns, who were born in 1903, did not participate in the postseason until their 1944 World Series appearance, in their 42nd year. That was the only postseason drought from inception longer than that of the Washington-Texas franchise. Overall, there were five other droughts as long or longer than theirs.

The Indians did not appear in the postseason between 1954 and 1995. The Philadelphia–Kansas City–Oakland Athletics' franchise did not earn a postseason berth between 1931 and 1971. In between their 1919 and 1959 World Series berths, the White Sox did not appear in the postseason. The Phillies did not enjoy the fruits of victory between the 1915 and 1950 World Series. The Cubs failed to reach the postseason every year in between 1945 and 1984 and have not won the World Series since 1908. The Cubs will continue to have a difficult time in ending this drought, since they play most of their games during the day. According to several former players, playing in the day takes its toll on a player's endurance and stamina for two reasons: the summer heat wears on a player, and many players habitually stay up past midnight and are unable to get enough sleep before the next day's matinee.

It took 5,690 regular-season games for the Rangers' franchise to reach the postseason. Including the franchise's first 11 years (as the Washington Senators from 1961 to 1971), the Rangers never seriously challenged for a title. Their best finishes were second in 1974 (five games behind), second in 1977 (eight games back), tied for second in 1978 (five games off the pace), second in the first half of the strike-divided 1981 season (one and a half games behind Oakland, which played five more games), and second in 1986 (five games worse than the Angels). The Rangers were in first place at the time of the 1994 strike, albeit struggling with a losing record. In all, the Rangers have had 15 winning seasons since 1961.

◆ Did you know the 1944 AL champion St. Louis Browns had nary a player on their roster with previous World Series experience? The Browns at one point in the season had right fielder Frank Demaree, who had played in four World Series, and righthander Steve Sundra, who pitched in the 1939 World Series for the Yankees, but not on their final regular-season roster. Since then, only the 1961 NL champion Cincinnati Reds entered the World Series that wet behind the ears. They had third baseman Willie "Puddin' Head" Jones, with nine games of postseason experience, briefly to open the season, but not at the end.

139. *The Cincinnati Reds registered the majors' best record of 66-42 (.611) during the strike-shortened season of 1981 but didn't earn a playoff berth. The Dodgers notched a 36-21 mark in the first half (which included all games prior to the 50-day strike), edging the Reds' 35-21 record for the first-half title and the right to play the winner of the second half for the division flag. Which team went 33-20 in the second half to oust the Reds and face the Dodgers in the best-of-five NL West Division Series?*

ANSWER: The Houston Astros

The Astros, who were 28-29 in the first half, won the second half by a game and a half and beat the eventual world champion Los Angeles Dodgers in Game One and Game Two before losing the final three games of the bizarre NL West Division Series. Oddly enough, the St. Louis Cardinals posted the major league's third best total record and the National League's second best at 59-43 (.578) but also failed to make the postseason. The Philadelphia Phillies won the first half (34-21) by one and a half games, and the Expos edged the Cardinals by a mere half game in the second half. As with the Reds, the Cardinals' half-game deficit was of no fault of theirs, because the Expos (30-23) played one more game than them (29-23). A playoff or additional scheduled games would have evened things out, but Commissioner Bowie Kuhn opted not to add such games. Montreal defeated Philadelphia in five games in the NL East Division Series.

The Oakland A's sported the American League's best total record, winning 64 of their 109 games (.587) to win the first half (37-23) by one and a half games over Texas and lose the second half by only one game to Kansas City. Oakland swept the Royals in the AL West Division Series. According to the AL office, Oakland would have received a division playoff bye had it won both halves. The eventual pennant-winning Yankees won the AL East's first half with a 34-22 record (a full two games over Baltimore), as Milwaukee won the second half by a game and a half over Boston and Detroit. It took the Yankees a full five games to dispose of the Brewers before they swept Oakland in the AL Championship Series for the right to represent the American League in the World Series.

Toronto's 37-69 record (.349) was the worst in the majors, and the Cubs' 38-65 mark (.369) was the senior circuit's worst.

◆ Did you know Bill Madlock beat out Pete Rose for the 1981 batting title, preventing the all-time hits leader from becoming the first player to win a batting title in three decades? A winner of three batting titles (1968, 1969, 1973), Rose hit .325 in that strike-shortened season. Although Madlock batted .341, he didn't have enough plate appearances to qualify for the title. So, a rarely invoked rule was used, adding hitless at-bats to Madlock's total to reach the required minimum plate appearances (3.1 per game played by the team). Since Madlock's total still topped Rose's, using this method, Madlock was declared the batting champ. Nine years later, George Brett became the first to win a batting title in three decades.

◆ Did you know Bill Madlock's third of four batting titles, won in 1981 for Pittsburgh, made him the sixth player to win a batting title for two different teams? The others were Nap Lajoie (Athletics, Indians), Rogers Hornsby (Cardinals, Braves), Lefty O'Doul (Phillies, Dodgers), Jimmie Foxx (Athletics, Red

Sox), and Ernie Lombardi (Reds, Braves). Madlock won his 1975 and 1976 batting titles for the Cubs and his 1981 and 1983 titles in a Pirates uniform.

140. *Match these former little leaguers with their big league feats:*

1 Carney Lansford   A was the first Little League graduate to make the Hall of Fame
2 Carl Yastrzemski   B hit five home runs in five at-bats in the 1971 Little League World Series in Gary, Indiana
3 Boog Powell   C is among eight players who have played in a Little League World Series and a major league World Series
4 Bill Connors   D was the first member of a Little League world championship team to make the majors
5 Lloyd McClendon
6 Rick Wise

ANSWER: 1—C, 2—A, 3—C, 4—D, 5—B, 6—C

McClendon's mark of five home runs was broken by Lin Chih-Hsiung, who hit six for Far East champion Shan-Hua of Chinese Taipei in the 1995 Little League World Series. That record didn't last long, however, as Hsieh Chin-Hsiung broke his countryman's year-old standard with seven homers in the Little League World Series' 50th year. . . . Jim Barbieri, Derek Bell, Charlie Hayes, Ed Vosberg, and Gary Sheffield are the five others to play in the Little League and major league World Series, according to the Little League Media Guide. Of that group, Vosberg is the only player to also have played in the College World Series. Barbieri, incidentally, reached the major league World Series in his lone season in the majors (1966). . . . Connors was a little-used reliever for the Cubs and Mets in the late 1960s. Hector Torres, a shortstop for five big league teams, played on the Mexican champs from Monterrey in 1958. In fact, Torres' three-hitter clinched the title for Mexico, which has been crowned three times through 2002.

Chinese Taipei has won a record 17 Little League World Series titles, including 9 over an 11-year stretch starting in 1971. California and Japan are next with 5 championships. Connecticut, New Jersey, and Pennsylvania have won 4 times each.

◆ Did you know Sean Burroughs, son of former major leaguer Jeff Burroughs, threw two no-hitters, slugged three homers, and batted .536 in the 1993 Little League World Series? Burroughs' production helped Long Beach, California, win its second straight Little League World Series title. Jeff, a former American League MVP, served as the team's coach. Sean is a third baseman for the San Diego Padres organization today.

◆ Did you know Angel Macias and Fred Shapiro have pitched the only perfect games in Little League World Series history? Macias hurled his (a 12-inning gem over La Mesa) in the championship game, giving Monterrey, Mexico, the 1957 title. Shapiro threw his in the opening round the year before for Delaware Township, N.J.

◆ Did you know Belgium's Victoria Roche in 1984 became the first girl to play in a Little League World Series game, and Betty Speziale five years later became the first woman to umpire a Little League World Series game? Also in 1989, American first baseman Victoria Brucker became the first girl to start a Little League World Series game.

◆ Did you know Carl Stotz conceived of and in 1939 founded the first league for kids, naming it the Little League and organizing it in his hometown of Williamsport, Pennsylvania? Within 10 years, 307 Little Leagues formed, according to Little League headquarters. The first Little League World Series was played in 1947 at Williamsport, where it has since crowned a champion every August.

141. *Match these teams with their histories:*

1	Detroit Tigers	A	had a 9½-game lead on August 14, 1969, and finished 8 games out of first
2	St. Louis Cardinals	B	was first team to hit 200 home runs in four different seasons (1962, 1985, 1987, 1991)
3	Chicago Cubs	C	lost a record 21 straight games at the outset of a season
4	Baltimore Orioles	D	had never hit more than 144 homers in a season before 1998
5	Philadelphia Phillies	E	hold the modern major league record with 23 consecutive losses

ANSWER: 1—B, 2—D, 3—A, 4—C, 5—E

The Orioles lost 21 straight to begin the 1988 campaign and finished in last place with a 54-107 record. . . . St. Louis in 1955 hit 143 homers, broke that mark by one in 1997, with the late arrival of Mark McGwire, and shattered the new club standard in 1998 with 223. . . . The 1961 Phillies lost 23 straight games en route to a dismal 47-107 record. The Phillies ended 46 games out of first, finishing dead last in the standings, in runs scored (584), and in ERA (4.61). . . . The dubious all-time record for most consecutive losses is 26, suffered by the 1889 Louisville Colonels of the American Association. The 1899 Cleveland Spiders lost 24 straight for the all-time National League record.

◆ Did you know the 1935 Boston Braves were a major league record–worst 7-31 in one-run games? As a result, those Braves finished dead last in the National League with an atrocious 38-115 mark, the worst in franchise history.

142. *Match these superstars with their feats:*

1	Joe Morgan	A	compiled a record 119 extra-base hits in one season
2	Eddie Collins	B	has twice reached 40 homers and 200 hits
3	Alex Rodriguez	C	has stolen the most bases (689) without ever leading the league in that department in a single season
4	Babe Ruth	D	is one of only four 3,000-hit club members who never led the league in hits

ANSWER: 1—C, 2—D, 3—B, 4—A

Lou Brock, Dave Winfield, and Eddie Murray are the other 3,000-hit club members who never led the league in hits. . . . In 1995 Cleveland's Albert Belle became the eighth player in history to total 100 extra-base hits in a season. In doing so, Belle became the first such player with 50 home runs and 50 doubles in the same season, an abbreviated season at that. In 2001 Todd Helton fell a home run shy of duplicating Belle's feat. Only Lou Gehrig, Chuck Klein, and Helton have amassed 100 extra-base hits twice. . . . Ruth's 59 homers, 44 doubles, and 16 triples in 1921 accounted for his extra-base hit record. Six years later Lou Gehrig came close, with 117 such hits. In case you're wondering, Barry Bonds had 107 in 2001, tying Chuck Klein's NL mark, set in 1930.

◆ Did you know Eddie Collins is the only player to hit over .400 during three different World Series? Playing in the World Series for the Athletics in 1910, 1911, 1913, and 1914 and for the White Sox in 1917 and 1919, Collins hit a combined .328. He was also a member of the 1929 and 1930 Athletics' championship teams but did not play.

143. *Match these pinch-hitters with their timely offensive production:*

1	Smokey Burgess	A	had a record 20 career pinch-hit home runs, surpassing Jerry Lynch in 1985
2	Cliff Johnson	B	was the first to hit three grand slams as a pinch-hitter (a record later tied by Rich Reese and Willie McCovey)
3	Yogi Berra	C	was the first to hit a pinch-hit home run in a World Series
4	Ron Northey	D	held the career mark of 145 pinch-hits before Manny Mota broke it in 1979

ANSWER: 1—D, 2—A, 3—C, 4—B

Burgess remains the only man with a pair of 20 pinch-hit seasons. Jerry Lynch's 18 career pinch-hit home runs are second, and his 116 pinch-hits rank sixth all time. These are two of the reasons why baseball historian Bill James chose Lynch as the best pinch-hitter ever. Log-jammed in third place on the all-time career pinch-hit home run list with 16 are: Gates Brown, Smokey Burgess, and Willie McCovey. In 1998 the Yankees' Darryl Strawberry set an AL record and tied the major league record with two pinch-hit grand slams in a season. Strawberry joined the Phillies' Gene Freese (in 1959) and Davey Johnson (1978) and the Giants' Mike Ivie (1978) on that list. . . . Although Mota batted .297 for his career as a pinch-hitter, he hit a remarkable .342 (54-for-158) in that capacity from the age of 38 through the age of 42. Mota, who retired with 150 pinch-hits, came to the plate only once more after that torrid stretch. Lenny Harris in 2001 surpassed Burgess and broke Mota's mark of 150 pinch-hits. He has 173 entering the 2003 season. Greg Gross is fourth on the all-time pinch-hit list with 130.

◆ Did you know Harold Baines is the all-time leader in hits by a designated hitter, the all-time leader in home runs by a DH, the all-time leader in RBI by a DH, and owner of the second highest career pinch-hitting batting average? Baines has accomplished a lot with the bat, getting recognized as a most "professional hitter." His 236 home runs as a DH are 17 more than Don Baylor's total. Baines' 1,689 hits as a DH are 133 more than Hal McRae's. Baines' total of 978 RBI as a DH leads everyone. And his .317 career mark as a pinch-hitter (59-for-186) has him just behind Tommy Davis' .320 mark, among those with at least 150 at-bats in that role.

According to home run researcher David Vincent, Edgar Martinez (208), Jose Canseco (207), and Chili Davis (200) are third through fifth on the designated hitter home run list.

144. *Match these pitchers with their distinctions:*

1	Red Ruffing	A	started a record 82 double plays by a pitcher
2	Lefty Gomez	B	was a prankster who recommended a revolving goldfish bowl to save the fish from having to swim in circles
3	Warren Spahn	C	has the highest career ERA of any Hall of Fame pitcher (excluding managers who were pitchers)
4	Early Wynn	D	has the highest career ERA of any 300-game winner

ANSWER: 1—C, 2—B, 3—A, 4—D

Ruffing's lifetime ERA is 3.80. A pitcher who basically experienced two different careers—a lowly one in a Red Sox uniform and a triumphant one in Yankee pinstripes—Ruffing finished among the top 10 in ERA eight times. All eight of his solid ERA finishes and all six of his All-Star selections came as a Yankee. . . . Wynn's career ERA is 3.54. . . . Vernon "Lefty" Gomez, an eccentric jokester, was as good at making others laugh as he was successful on the mound. And as loose as he was, Gomez wasn't afraid of making cracks on the mound, either. Once when facing slugger Jimmie Foxx, Gomez shook off every sign given by his catcher, Bill Dickey. When his batterymate walked to the plate to find out the cause for the southpaw's uncertainty, Gomez replied, "Let's just stall around and maybe [Foxx will] get mad and walk away." When NASA landed on the moon, Gomez joked the astronauts were baffled to find a baseball there, one hit off him by Foxx. Early in Joe DiMaggio's career, the center fielder was eager to make an impression and told his road roommate Gomez he wanted to excel by playing shallow and make people forget about Tris Speaker. After a fly ball sailed over DiMaggio's head for a game-deciding triple off Gomez one day, the lefthander, while dining with DiMaggio, told the rookie if he doesn't move back a bit he's "going to make them forget about Lefty Gomez."

◆ Did you know Yankees catcher Bill Dickey formed a Hall of Fame battery with a record four inducted pitchers? The Hall of Famer caught Lefty Gomez, Waite Hoyt, Red Ruffing, and Herb Pennock. Three esteemed catchers caught a trio of Hall of Famers. The great Ray Schalk caught Ed Walsh, Ted Lyons, and Red Faber. Roger Bresnahan formed a Hall of Fame battery with Christy Mathewson, Joe McGinnity, and Rube Marquard. And versatile receiver Buck Ewing called pitches for Tim Keefe, Mickey Welch, and Amos Rusie.

145. *Match these venerable broadcasters with their affiliations:*

1	Red Barber	A	the voice of the Phillies
2	Mel Allen	B	the voice of the Brooklyn Dodgers
3	Harry Caray	C	the voice of NBC Game of the Week
4	Ernie Harwell	D	"The Voice of Baseball" and a long-time Yankees announcer before Phil Rizzuto
5	Richie Ashburn	E	the voice of the Detroit Tigers
6	Joe Garagiola	F	the voice of the Seattle Mariners
7	Dave Niehaus	G	the voice of the Cubs and previously of the Cardinals

ANSWER: 1—B, 2—D, 3—G, 4—E, 5—A, 6—C, 7—F

Caray passed away on February 18, 1998, dealing Major League Baseball and the Chicago Cubs a great loss. Caray was more than just a broadcaster; he was an ambassador for the game. Late in his career he chose to become a "fan's broadcaster"—one who cheered and booed, and who was not afraid to get on an umpire, celebrate a Cubs win, or talk about the good old days while drinking beer during the telecast. Most admired Caray that way and will remember him that way. But he wasn't always like that. He was as professional as they came throughout most of his 53-year broadcasting career, which began in 1945 with the Cardinals. But when he joined the Cubs in 1982, he adopted a new free-wheeling style that catered to the fan, becoming a colorful celebrity who will long be remembered for his seventh-inning renditions of "Take Me Out To The Ball Game." His birth name was Harry Carabini. . . . As broadcaster for the Yankees, late in his 34-year career, Barber (the most venerable and admirable broadcaster baseball had seen or heard through 1966) was dismissed from his duties, after 13 years with the Yankees, by the Yankees' over-involved front office for instructing the camera man to show the empty stands of a Yankee home game that was witnessed by a mere 413 fans. The integral broadcaster described the picture by saying, "friends, today's story is the empty seats, not the game." Walter Lanier Barber is most famous for his signature phrases "Oh Doctor," "Catbird Seat" (describing his booth), and "rhubarb" (a slang for heated arguments). He died in 1992 at the age of 84. . . . If Barber is the Babe Ruth of broadcasting, Allen is the Lou Gehrig. Born as Melvin Israel, Allen is the only man to broadcast major league base-ball games in seven decades. He popularized the phrase "How about that?" Allen, who broadcasted 20 World Series and 24 All-Star Games, also made his mark as the voice of *This Week in Baseball,* a position he held until his death on June 16, 1996. . . . Harwell retired in 2002, completing his 43rd season with the Tigers, 55th in Major League Baseball, and 64th overall in broadcasting. . . . Niehaus, who popu-larized phrases such as "bring out the rye bread grandma; it's grand salami time" and "this ball will be flying away" during Seattle's mag-ical season in 1995, has been with the Mariners ever since the team joined the American League in 1977. Niehaus had missed just 17 of the 2,957 games in Mariners' history prior to the 1996 campaign, when he was plagued by illness. . . . Sadly, Cardinals voice Jack Buck passed away in 2002, after broadcasting Cardinals baseball for 47 years. Buck, who enjoyed radio broadcasting more than television, was frequently chosen to broadcast postseason games. A statue of Buck stands outside Busch Stadium.

◆ Did you know Red Barber and Mel Allen were the first two broadcasters inducted into the broadcaster's wing of the Hall of Fame in 1978? Since then, one broadcaster is given the Ford C. Frick Award for broadcasting excellence over a career and is inducted each year. Russ Hodges, Ernie Harwell, Vin

Scully, Jack Brickhouse, Curt Gowdy, Bob Prince, Jack Buck, Lindsey Nelson, Harry Caray, Joe Garagiola, Milo Hamilton, Bob Murphy, and Bob Wolff are among those who followed Barber and Allen. Barber was the first to dedicate his work "to the fans, not the team."

◆ Did you know it was Frankie Frisch, the Hall of Fame second baseman turned broadcaster, who made famous the line, "Ohhhh, those bases on balls"? Frisch made a name for himself with that saying as a television broadcaster for the Giants in 1947.

146. *Match these families with their notable achievements:*

1 Sandy, Sandy Jr., and Roberto Alomar
2 Bob and Ted Kennedy
3 Felipe, Matty, and Jesus Alou
4 Vince, Dom, and Joe DiMaggio
5 Earl Averill Sr. and Earl Averill Jr.

A played in the outfield at the same time for one inning
B followed the DiMaggios and Alous as family trios to play in All-Star competition
C combined for 282 home runs
D combined for 2,927 runs
E the first father and son duo with a World Series RBI

ANSWER: 1—B, 2—E, 3—A, 4—D, 5—C

Ray Boone, Bob Boone, and Bret Boone have joined the DiMaggios, the Alous, and the Alomars as All-Star family trios. Felipe and Matty Alou were All-Stars, but Jesus never was. Felipe's son Moises was the third Alou All-Star. . . . Sandy Alomar Jr. and Roberto Alomar also became the only brothers to each win the All-Star Game MVP, with Sandy earning the honor in 1997 and Roberto the following year. . . . After Willie Mays was given a rest during a 13-5 rout over the Pirates on September 15, 1963, the Alous made history.

◆ Did you know that Ken Griffey Sr. and Ken Griffey Jr. became the first father and son to play on the same team, doing so for the Mariners during the 1990 season? They each got a hit in their first turn at bat together for Seattle on August 31 that year, and then, on September 14, they hit back-to-back home runs in the first inning off California's Kirk McCaskill. In 2001 Tim Raines Sr. and Tim Raines Jr. became the second father and son to play on the same team, doing so on October 3 for the Baltimore Orioles. The Raines duo played four games together but didn't hit safely in the same game.

◆ Did you know Nolan Ryan struck out eight father-son combinations during his illustrious and lengthy career? The eight duos are: Ken Griffey and Ken Griffey Jr.; Hal and Brian McRae; Bobby and Barry Bonds; Sandy Alomar Sr., Sandy Alomar Jr., and Roberto Alomar; Edwardo and Tony Perez; Tito and Terry Francona; Maury and Bump Wills; and Dick "Ducky" Schofield and Dick Schofield.

◆ Did you know Nolan Ryan is the only pitcher to strike out Roger Maris, Barry Bonds, Mark McGwire, and Sammy Sosa?

147. *Match these players with their distinctions:*

1	Lou Gehrig	A	has the lowest career batting average (.253) of any non-pitching Hall of Famer inducted for his playing days
2	Norm Cash	B	hit three grand slams in a five-day span
3	William "Scrappy" Joyce	C	hit an all-time record four triples in one game
4	Jim Northrup	D	was a 13th-round NFL draft pick
5	Ray Schalk	E	hit three grand slams in four days

ANSWER: 1—E, 2—D, 3—C, 4—B, 5—A

Joyce's record feat occurred on May 18, 1897. Lou Gehrig, during a June 30, 1934, contest at Washington, had three triples through four and a half innings wiped away by a rainout. According to Ray Robinson, author of *Iron Horse*, Gehrig on that day was playing with a severe headache and a lump on his head, the result of a beaning suffered the day before during an exhibition game in Virginia. . . . Cash was drafted by the Chicago Bears but decided to sign with the Chicago White Sox, for whom he played parts of two seasons before moving on to Detroit. . . . Schalk's defense more than made up for his .340 career on-base percentage and weakly .316 slugging average. In the 1919 World Series, he threw out a series record 10 runners among 17 who attempted to steal. On the opposite end of the spectrum, Detroit catcher Boss Schmidt allowed seven Cubs to steal in Game One of the 1907 World Series. Also, Schmidt holds a dubious record for catchers with seven World Series errors. He didn't have much luck with the bat either, making the last out of the 1907 and 1908 classics for the Tigers.

♦ Did you know shortstop Art Fletcher holds the career World Series record of 12 errors? The Giants infielder committed a series-high four errors in the 1911 World Series against the Athletics. His 11th inning fumble of a grounder enabled the go-ahead run to score in a 3-2 loss in Game Three. He committed four errors the following October against the Red Sox, a trio of which enabled four unearned runs to score in Game Two, which ended in a 6-6 tie after 11 innings (due to darkness). He committed one miscue in 1913, against the Athletics again, and three more against the White Sox in 1917.

148. *Can you name the team that failed to win the AL pennant despite boasting an incredible 61-16 home record?*

ANSWER: The 1949 Boston Red Sox

The 1949 Boston Red Sox lost the pennant on the last day of the season to the New York Yankees. The Red Sox were only 35-40 on the road entering a season-ending, two-game series in Yankee Stadium, leading by one game. The Yanks won each game, 5-4 (after trailing 4-0) and 5-3, over their former manager Joe McCarthy's club.

During that season, the heart and determination of team leader Joe DiMaggio revealed itself, as DiMaggio overcame a heel injury that forced him to miss the first 69 games of the season and carried the club the rest of the way, batting .346 and slugging .596. DiMaggio returned to the Yankee lineup June 28, just in time for a series at Fenway Park, and, oh, what a return it was. "Joltin' Joe" went 5-for-11 with four homers and nine RBI in the three-game set, helping the first-place Yankees push the Red Sox eight games back in the standings with a sweep, 5-4, 9-7, and 6-2.

DiMaggio also helped New York take both games of a July 4 doubleheader against Boston the following week, stiff-arming the reeling Red Sox to a 12-game deficit. But Boston made a furious comeback, winning 37 of their next 47 games through August 21 and taking over first place with a red-hot stretch in September that featured 12 wins in 13 games.

As the Yankees faced elimination in the penultimate game of the season, the "Yankee Clipper" came down with a viral pneumonia that left him weak and 18 pounds lighter. Yet he played anyway and delivered two big hits on "Joe DiMaggio Day," pulling New York even with Boston atop the AL standings. In the pennant-deciding season finale, the Yankees' Vic Raschi outdueled Boston's Ellis Kinder.

◆ Did you know Joe DiMaggio's much publicized marriage to Hollywood megastar Marilyn Monroe lasted just nine months? The pair divorced on October 27, 1954, because, some sources say, DiMaggio didn't feel comfortable with Monroe's revealing outfits and acts on camera. Eight years later, Monroe either committed suicide or erroneously mixed medications (depending on which account you want to believe). DiMaggio, who never stopped loving Monroe, left flowers by her grave three times a week for 20 years, until the act started receiving public attention. DiMaggio had such admiration for Monroe that he remained faithful to her until her death in 1962. He never remarried, and he never talked about her in public after their marriage ended.

149. *Which Yankee pointed out to manager Billy Martin the excessive amount of pine tar used by George Brett during the 1983 "Pine Tar" incident?*

ANSWER: Graig Nettles

The observant Yankee third baseman Graig Nettles, early during that July 24 contest, warned Martin about the amount of pine tar on Brett's bat. Of course, Martin didn't complain until the Royals' All-Star third baseman belted a pitch from Rich "Goose" Gossage into the upper-deck for a two-run blast and a 5-4 Royals lead in the top of the ninth inning. That's when the whole mess began. Martin showed the umpiring crew that Brett's bat had too much pine tar (above the allowed mark on the handle) and convinced home plate umpire Tim McClelland to cite rule 1.10(b) and judge Brett out, negating the go-ahead home run. (Rule 1.10[b] reads "a bat may not be covered by such a substance more than 18 inches from the tip of the handle.") Well, Brett exploded into a rare display of rage, and the entire Royals team yelled in protest as the Yankees appeared to have been awarded a bizarre 4-3 win.

Two days later, though, AL president Lee MacPhail overruled the umpiring crew's decision and allowed the controversial home run to stand. MacPhail stated that the Yankees should have pointed out the infraction before Brett's plate appearance, and that the excess pine tar didn't aid the home run.

On August 18, the game was resumed from the point of Brett's home run before 1,245 fans. As a result of previous lineup arrangements, and because of second baseman Bert Campaneris' injury and center fielder Jerry Mumphrey's trade to Houston in between the two dates, pitcher Ron Guidry was in center field, the left-handed Don Mattingly was at second base, and George Frazier was on the mound (players not on the roster on July 24 were not eligible to play in the game's resumption on August 18). Frazier struck out Hal McRae to end the top of the ninth inning. In the bottom half, Royals closer Dan Quisenberry retired the Yankees in order for the 5-4 win. The completion of the "Pine Tar" game took just nine minutes and 41 seconds.

150. *Chicago Cubs Ernie Banks and Andre Dawson were the first two MVP winners from a losing team. Name the only other.*

ANSWER: Cal Ripken Jr.

Baltimore's Cal Ripken Jr. earned the award in 1991 as the Orioles were slumping toward a gloomy 67-95 ledger. Ripken was head and shoulders above every other American Leaguer that year, finishing in the top six in homers, RBI, batting average, slugging, total bases, doubles, and hits. He also enjoyed another outstanding defensive performance at shortstop.

Banks' Cubs weren't that bad in 1958 and 1959, winning 72 and 74 games, respectively, in a 154-game schedule. In those two years, Banks homered a combined 92 times and drove in 272 runners. Dawson in 1987 played for a last-place Cubs team that was 76-85, making him the only winner from a cellar dweller. After having signed a blank contract and handed it to the Cubs before the season, telling them to fill it out with whatever amount they thought he deserved, Dawson hit 49 homers and drove in 137.

151. *Match these seasons with their historical importance:*

1 1939   A the first moving picture of a baseball game is shown
2 1925   B the use of resin bags began
3 1903   C a policy making home teams wear white uniforms and the road team dark ones is instituted

4 1911   D the player limit was upped from 23 to 25
5 1933   E by this season every team had adopted the practice
                of stitching numbers on the back of players'
                uniforms

ANSWER: 1—D, 2—B, 3—A, 4—C, 5—E

For about half of the 1986 season, the owners reduced the player limit to 24. To compensate for the strike-shortened spring training, the 1995 season (which began on April 26) featured a roster expansion to 28 players until May 15, when the teams were required to reduce their roster to 25 players. . . . The 1929 Yankees were the first team to wear uniform numbers for an entire season.

◆ Did you know a Princeton professor named Hinton invented the first mechanical pitching machine in 1896? It was first used as a practice device in a major league field in 1908, by the Chicago Cubs.

◆ Did you know that in 1928 NL president John Heydler was the first to suggest the designated hitter rule? Ironically, the NL owners were for it but couldn't convince the AL owners to support the idea.

152. *In the strike-shortened 1981 season, Eddie Murray, Dwight Evans, Tony Armas, and Bobby Grich shared the AL lead in home runs with 22 apiece. During the same season, four AL pitchers tied for the league lead with 14 wins. Jack Morris and Pete Vuckovich were two. Choose the other two:*

A Dennis Martinez and Steve McCatty
B Dennis Martinez and Ron Guidry
C Steve McCatty and Bert Blyleven
D Rick Langford and Ron Guidry

ANSWER: A

Martinez went 14-5 for Baltimore, and McCatty went 14-7 for Oakland, with a league-best 2.32 ERA. Vuckovich was 14-4 for Milwaukee, and Morris posted a 14-7 mark with Detroit. Morris went on to win more games (162) in the 1980s than any other pitcher in the major leagues. Morris also led all pitchers with 133 complete games and 2,443 innings.

153. *Since 1969, the Oakland A's and Atlanta Braves share the mark of 10 League Championship Series appearances. Can you choose the three teams next on the list with nine:*

A The Baltimore Orioles, Cincinnati Reds, and Los Angeles Dodgers
B The Pittsburgh Pirates, Philadelphia Phillies, and Cincinnati Reds
C The New York Yankees, Pittsburgh Pirates, and Baltimore Orioles
D The New York Yankees, Cincinnati Reds, and Los Angeles Dodgers

ANSWER: C

The Yankees, Pirates, and Orioles have made the League Championship Series nine times apiece. The Yankees have advanced to the World Series in eight of those years, winning six world championships. Although Pittsburgh advanced to the World Series only twice in that span, the Pirates were victorious each time. Baltimore reached the fall classic five times, losing three times. Oakland won six pennants and four World Series. Atlanta has lost four of its five trips to the World Series since 1969. The Reds have made eight trips to the League Championship Series.

◆ Did you know the Atlanta Braves in 2002 extended their professional sports record with their 11th consecutive division title? Atlanta won the NL West Division from 1991 to 1993 and, after the strike-aborted 1994 season, won the NL East from 1995 to 2002 (the divisions were realigned after the 1993 season, and Atlanta moved to the NL East). The NBA's Boston Celtics and Los Angeles Lakers each won 9 straight division titles.

154. *What do these 10 Hall of Famers all have in common: Jackie Robinson, Willie Mays, Luis Aparicio, Frank Robinson, Willie McCovey, Billy Williams, Rod Carew, Tom Seaver, Johnny Bench, and Carlton Fisk?*

ANSWER: They are the only 10 Rookies of the Year who have been inducted into Cooperstown. Jackie Robinson won the Rookie of the Year Award in 1947, Mays won in 1951, Aparicio and Frank Robinson in 1956, McCovey in 1959, Williams in 1961, Carew in 1967, Seaver also in 1967, Bench in 1968, and Carlton Fisk in 1972. Fisk also finished fourth in MVP balloting the year he took home the Rookie of the Year Award, preceding by three years the high MVP placing of teammates Fred Lynn and Jim Rice.

Incidentally, Vada Pinson finished runner-up to McCovey in the

1959 NL Rookie of the Year balloting. Over an 18-year career, Pinson batted .286 with 2,757 hits, 256 home runs, 1,170 RBI, and 305 stolen bases. Pinson, who passed away in 1996, certainly deserves consideration for the Hall of Fame.

◆ Did you know Rod Carew was born on a train in the Panama Canal Zone? The Panamanian Hall of Famer retired with 3,053 hits and a .328 career batting average. Carew hit a major league–best .343 during the 1970s.

155. *From 1918 through 1937, this minor leaguer almost mirrored Babe Ruth's major league career, beginning as a good-hitting pitcher who was converted to an outfielder after reaching a high standard of success on the mound. His batting was even better, as he developed into a power-hitting threat the likes of which the Pacific Coast League had never seen. He is considered by many to be the best player in minor league history. Who is he?*

ANSWER: Buzz Arlett

The switch-hitting Buzz Arlett became a full-time outfielder in 1923 after winning a combined 108 games over his first five years, during which he also began experiencing pain in his right (throwing) arm. The six-foot-two Arlett began pummeling the ball on a regular basis for the Oakland Oaks of the Pacific Coast League, winning home run titles and captivating minor league audiences the way Ruth was in the major leagues. In January of 1931, Oakland finally sold the coveted Arlett off to the major leagues, sending him to the Philadelphia Phillies. Offensively, the 32-year-old Arlett had a stellar season, batting .313 and slugging .538 with 18 homers and 72 RBI in just 121 games. But the Phillies weren't happy with Arlett's defense in right field, where the inadequate fielder committed 10 errors and fielded just .955.

Incredibly, Arlett never played again in the majors. He returned to the minor leagues in 1932, and for Baltimore of the International League that year he went about doing what he did best—knock the stuffing out of a baseball. Arlett belted four home runs in a single game twice over a five-week period, spanning June and July of 1932, en route to a 54-homer season. Arlett retired following the 1937 campaign with 432 minor league home runs and a .341 career batting average. For his dual efforts and hitting success on all levels, Arlett was named the most outstanding player in minor league history in a poll conducted by the Society for American Baseball Research.

In terms of hitting and fielding, Ike Boone had a similar career, batting .370 over his minor league career and .321 with a .475 slugging percentage in the majors. But poor fielding in right field limited the left-handed batter's time in the majors, despite an excellent offensive showing for the Red Sox in 1924 and good production in scattered appearances over seven other seasons for three other big league clubs. He would have greatly benefited from the designated hitter rule. In between major league campaigns, Boone enjoyed a monster year for the Pacific Coast League's Mission Reds in 1929, setting an organized baseball record with 553 total bases while batting .407 with 55 homers and 218 RBI, albeit over a 198-game schedule.

156. *Match these pitchers with their achievements:*

1	Jim Barr	A	pitched for 25 years
2	Preacher Roe	B	had 1,503 assists, second on the all-time list for pitchers behind Cy Young
3	Christy Mathewson	C	retired a record 41 straight batters
4	Jim Kaat	D	led the league in strikeouts for four consecutive years without reaching 200
5	Dizzy Dean	E	owns the best single-season NL win percentage in the 1900s among 20-game winners

ANSWER: 1—C, 2—E, 3—B, 4—A, 5—D

In 1972 Barr retired the last 21 Pirates during an August 23 game and the first 20 batters in a game against the Cardinals six days later. The 21st batter to face Barr on August 29 was Bernie Carbo, who doubled to end the perfect game and the streak. The Giants' righthander had his best season in 1974, winning 13 of his 22 decisions, posting the league's seventh best ERA (2.74) in 240 innings, completing 11 starts, and hurling five shutouts. The old mark of 38 consecutive batters retired was set by Pittsburgh's Harvey Haddix in 1959. David Wells set the AL record in 1999 for consecutive batters retired with 38, surpassing the previous mark of 33, shared by Kansas City's Steve Busby and Seattle's John Montague. . . . Roe went 22-3 (an .880 winning percentage) for the Dodgers in 1951, exactly matching the record of Chicago's Fred Goldsmith in 1880. In 1995 Greg Maddux posted the best-ever winning percentage over a single season among those with 20 decisions, .905 (19-2). Randy Johnson's .900 (18-2) mark in the same season is the best in AL history among those with 20 decisions. . . . Cy Young leads all pitchers with 2,013 assists. . . . Kaat, a three-time 20-game winner, pitched 4,530⅓ innings over his 25 years in the majors. . . . Dean's four strikeout titles in his first four years (from 1932 to 1935) included totals of 191, 199, 195, and 190. But Dean never again led the league, and he never amassed 200 strike-outs in a season. Dean pitched one game (a three-hitter) on September 28 in the 1930 season before his 1932 rookie campaign.

♦ Did you know Greg Maddux's 443 putouts is the all-time record for pitch-ers? Maddux in 2000 surpassed Jack Morris' mark of 387 putouts. Phil Niekro is third on the career list, just one behind Morris. Ferguson Jenkins is fourth with 363.

157. *The 1986 Mets were a team of destiny, winning 108 of their 162 games and overcoming seemingly insurmountable obstacles in the postseason for their second world championship. Complete the alignment of this heroic club and include the team's winningest pitcher during that magical season:*

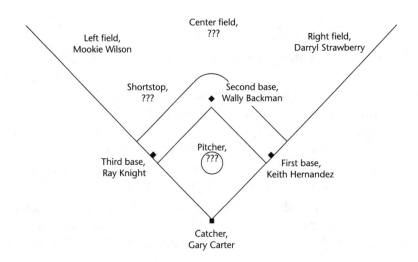

ANSWER: Center field, Lenny Dykstra; Shortstop, Rafael Santana; southpaw Bob Ojeda was the winningest pitcher at 18-5

Ojeda led a solid starting staff that included Dwight Gooden (17-6), Sid Fernandez (16-6), Ron Darling (15-6), and Rick Aguilera (10-7). Keith Hernandez and Gary Carter were the clear-cut leaders of this buoyant ballclub that bordered on arrogant. Both were intense, and Hernandez was one of the best prepared and most analytical players who ever donned a uniform. An on-field manager if there ever was one, the perceptive lefthander often arranged the infield and even advised pitchers in key situations. Arguably the greatest defensive first baseman in the game's history, Hernandez played the position differently than any other first bagger before him. Relying on great instincts, his memory bank of opposing batters' tendencies, and a brand of aggressiveness that always seemed to position him in just the right spot, Hernandez easily stood out. Five times he averaged more than a chance and a half per game above the league average (once he averaged more than three chances above). Aside from having great range, Hernandez (the son of a minor league first baseman) had a gun for an arm, as he led the National League in assists five times. Hernandez retired with more assists than any other first baseman.

◆ Did you know the 1986 Mets had a record four pitchers who received at least one point in the voting for the Cy Young Award that year? Bob Ojeda received nine points, Ron Darling two, and Sid Fernandez and Dwight Gooden got a point apiece. Mike Scott, an ex-Met, garnered the award.

158. *By now, you should know each member of the 1927 Yankees' starting lineup (and the club's defensive alignment). But do you know the 1927 Yankees' most common batting order? Given are Earle Combs batting first and Pat Collins batting eighth. Fill in the rest:*

1 CF Earle Combs
2 _____   A RF Babe Ruth
3 _____   B 2B Tony Lazzeri
4 _____   C 1B Lou Gehrig
5 _____   D LF Bob Meusel
6 _____   E SS Mark Koenig
7 _____   F 3B Joe Dugan
8 C Pat Collins

ANSWER: 2—E, 3—A, 4—C, 5—D, 6—B, 7—F

Within the Yankees' lineup, Ruth, Gehrig, Meusel, and Lazzeri—slots three through six—constituted "Murderer's Row," a moniker at times attributed to the entire batting order. The trio of Ruth, Gehrig, and Combs was especially effective over a prolonged stretch. Ruth, Gehrig, and Combs each scored at least 100 runs every year from 1926 to 1932. (Combs also reached that mark in 1925, when neither Ruth nor Gehrig did, and Gehrig continued his streak of consecutive 100-run seasons through 1938.) Currently, the Yankees duo of Derek Jeter and Bernie Williams take a stretch of seven straight 100-run campaigns into the 2003 season.

◆ Did you know the 1927 Yankees were the first team to amass 100 home runs and 100 triples in a season?

159. *What is the record for the most runs scored in an inning on just one hit? (Name either the team that scored the bunch or the number of runs scored.)*

ANSWER: 11, by the Chicago White Sox

On April 22, 1959, the Chicago White Sox scored 11 runs in a seventh inning that included only one hit. The stunned Comiskey Park audience watched in disbelief as the Kansas City Athletics walked 10 White Sox batters and committed three errors in that inning, which lasted 45 minutes. They lost, 20-6.

By comparison, the quickest major league game in history lasted just 51 minutes, as the Giants beat the Phillies, 6-1, in the season finale on September 28, 1919. The Giants' Jesse Barnes pitched a five-hitter for his 25th win, throwing just 64 pitches.

◆ Did you know the New York Giants scored a record 10 runs off the St. Louis Cardinals before the first out was made during their May 3, 1911, contest?

160. *On May 29, 2000, Oakland Athletics second baseman Randy Velarde turned the 12th unassisted triple play in history, the 11th in regular-season play. On July 8, 1994, Red Sox shortstop John Valentin turned the 11th unassisted triple play (10th in the 1900s) as he tripled up the*

Mariners. Can you name the last National League player to turn an unassisted triple play?

ANSWER: Mickey Morandini

Philadelphia Phillies second baseman Mickey Morandini turned the 10th unassisted triple play on September 20, 1992, in a game against the Pittsburgh Pirates, the first in the National League since 1927. Washington Senators' shortstop Ron Hansen turned the ninth unassisted triple play on July 29, 1968, versus the Indians, the first in 41 years. All but the first unassisted triple play included runners on first and second. Six of the dozen unassisted triple plays occurred in the 1920s, and the most famous unassisted triple play was turned by Bill Wambsganss in the 1920 World Series.

First baseman George Henry Burns and shortstop Ernie Padgett, each a member of the Red Sox, turned their triple plays within a month of each other (September 14 and October 6, respectively) during the 1923 season. Pirate shortstop Glenn Wright turned the sixth unassisted triple play in history on May 7, 1925. Jimmy Cooney (the Cubs shortstop) turned the next one on May 30, 1927, versus the Pirates' Paul Waner, whose brother Lloyd was among the victims. The very next day in the American League, Tiger first baseman Johnny Neun (having read about the exposure Cooney received) caught a line drive on a hit-and-run play, tagged the runner off first base (with shortstop Jackie Tavener beckoning his throw) and waived off his shortstop for the foot race to second base, yelling "I'm running into the Hall of Fame," as legend has it, before stepping on the bag. Paul Hines (May 8, 1878) and Neal Ball (July 19, 1909) turned the first two unassisted triple plays in history.

◆ Did you know Paul Hines' unassisted triple play on May 8, 1878, versus Boston would not have been scored as unassisted by today's rules? The Providence Grays center fielder's feat is sometimes ignored for the following reason. With runners on second and third, Hines caught a Jack Burdock blooper, to the surprise of both runners, who had already approached the plate. In fact, the runner on second (Ezra Sutton) was right behind the runner on third, Jack Manning. Hines kept on running in with the ball to step on third base, retiring both Manning and Sutton, since the latter would have had to touch third en route to his base. But by today's rules, touching third base would have retired only Manning, and Hines would have to touch or throw to second base to retire Sutton. The play became confusing right after Hines touched third. He then threw the ball to the beckoning second baseman Charles Sweasy. The throw was unnecessary, since all three outs had already been made; however, it confused many into thinking it was needed—hence the play's "questionable" status in some record books. None of these facts about Hines' unassisted triple play could have been ascertained had Grays' sportswriter Bill Perin not described the events before his death over 50 years afterward.

◆ Did you know John Valentin and Neal Ball are the only players to homer and turn an unassisted triple play in the same inning?

161. *Major League Baseball has been sending its players to compete against Japanese teams since 1908, and MLB teams have toured Japan 31 times, usually following the World Series. But after Japan's first victory over a touring team, Nippon Professional Baseball All-Star manager Tetsuharu Kawakami claimed "the Americans have nothing more to teach us," issuing a bold challenge. Upon which, Major League Baseball sent this particular American League pennant winner overseas the following year. Choose this club that avenged Major League Baseball's first tour loss to Japan:*

A The 1963 Yankees
B The 1966 Orioles
C The 1965 Twins
D The 1971 Orioles

ANSWER: D

Twenty months after the Japanese NPB All-Stars won six of nine games from the 1970 San Francisco Giants in a specially arranged tour during spring training, the 1971 World Series contestant Baltimore Orioles promptly taught the Japanese yet another baseball lesson in a much-anticipated matchup. The Orioles won 12 of the 14 games played to a decision, including all 8 against the Yomiuri Giants. Baltimore pitcher Pat Dobson (one of four Orioles coming off a 20-win major league season) pitched three shutouts, including a no-hitter against Yomiuri, to help hold Sadaharu Oh to a .111 tour batting average and Shigeo Nagashima to a .258 mark. As indicated by the 1971 world champion Pittsburgh Pirates' non-participation, the Japanese teams (often made up of the Yomiuri club) didn't always play the major league team they wanted.

Japan's only other tour victory came about in 1990, when it beat a squad of major league All-Stars four games to three, with a tie. Since 1986, MLB has sent a squad of All-Stars from various teams to Japan every two years. The closest the Japanese came to beating a major league pennant winner came when the 1966 Los Angeles Dodgers won 9 of the 17 games played to a decision and tied 1. When the 1979 major league All-Stars headed to Japan for a two-game series, they split. The tours are a lot more competitive today than they were over the first 14 series, when major league squads won 195 of the 213 games played to a decision, through 1962.

◆ Did you know that Commissioner Bowie Kuhn threw out the first pitch for the aforementioned 1971 Baltimore-Japan series?

162. *A year after finishing in ninth place, the 1967 Boston Red Sox surprised many by winning the American League pennant in an "Impossible Dream" season that featured Carl Yastrzemski's mighty left-handed swing and Jim Lonborg's strong right arm. Yastrzemski, the league's MVP, won the Triple Crown with an impressive display of clutch hitting down the stretch, and Lonborg tied for the league lead in wins and paced the circuit in strikeouts to earn the Cy Young Award. Name the team's second-leading RBI man and either of the team's 12-game winners.*

ANSWER: George Scott drove in 82 runs, and Gary Bell and Jose Santiago each won a dozen games for the 1967 American League champion Red Sox. Scott, a big and popular first baseman nicknamed "Boomer," also had the team's second highest batting average and on-base percentage, with marks of .303 and .373, respectively. Bell, a hard-throwing righthander who was acquired from the Indians early in the season, went 12-8 with a 3.16 ERA, eight complete games, and three saves for the Red Sox in 24 starts and 5 relief appearances. Santiago, a reliever and spot starter, made 50 appearances, notched five saves, and went 12-4, including a 5-0 record in September, to help the Red Sox edge the Tigers and Twins by one game and the White Sox by three in one of the closest pennant races ever.

Yastrzemski, who batted .326 with 121 RBI and a co-leading 44 homers, dominated the leaderboard, also pacing the junior circuit in on-base percentage, slugging, runs, hits, extra-base hits, and total bases. Lonborg won 22 games and struck out 246 batters over 273⅓ innings, with 15 complete games, a .710 winning percentage, and a 3.16 ERA. Other pitching contributors included closer John Wyatt, who won 10 games and saved 20, and left-handed middle reliever Sparky Lyle, who saved five games and posted a team-best 2.28 ERA. Offensively, right fielder Tony Conigliaro belted 20 homers with 67 RBI and a .287 batting average before suffering season-ending facial injuries in a hideous beaning on August 18. Also, shortstop Rico Petrocelli hit 17 homers, third baseman Joe Foy (who committed 27 errors) hit 16 homers, and switch-hitting center fielder Reggie Smith connected for 15.

The league's best scoring lineup helped the Red Sox compensate for the second worst defense and third worst pitching staff and win 92 games, a 20-game improvement from 1966, under new manager Dick Williams. Yastrzemski, Lonborg, Conigliaro, and Petrocelli earned All-Star selections. Scott won his first of eight Gold Gloves that year, and "Yaz" earned his third of seven.

◆ Did you know Dick Williams remains the only manager in major league history to win a pennant with three different teams as well as finish in first place in all four divisions? Following a 13-year major league career as a .260-hitting outfielder and infielder for Brooklyn, Baltimore, Cleveland, Kansas City, and Boston, Williams tried his hand at managing. He was an immediate success, taking the 1967 Red Sox to the World Series in his first campaign as a big league manager. From 1971 to 1973, Williams guided the Oakland A's to three straight AL West titles, including two world championships. In 1981 Williams managed the Expos to their first and only postseason berth. Three years later, Williams guided the San Diego Padres to their first taste of the postseason, leading them to the World Series. In all, Williams managed six first-place teams and two second-place teams. His is a resume worthy of election into the Hall of Fame.

FIRST POSTSEASON

Best-of-Seven League Championship Series

Game One Question:

San Francisco's Benito Santiago earned the 2002 NL Championship Series MVP Award, becoming only the fourth catcher to garner a League Championship Series MVP award. Atlanta's Eddie Perez was the third in 1999. Can you name the other two?

ANSWER: Darrell Porter and Javier Lopez

Porter, the Cardinals catcher, called three good games (in which St. Louis pitchers allowed only five runs on 15 hits) and hit .556 with three doubles, three runs scored, and five walks as St. Louis swept Atlanta in the 1982 NL Championship Series. Lopez helped the Braves overcome a three games to one deficit in the 1996 series against St. Louis with great hitting. Lopez hit .542, tying the League Championship Series record of 13 hits, with two homers, five doubles, and six RBI. Perez hit .500 with five RBI against the Mets in 1999, collecting 10 hits in six games, including two homers, for a slugging percentage of .900. Santiago drove in five key runs and played outstanding defense.

Game Two Question:

Can you name the only shortstop to garner a League Championship Series MVP award?

ANSWER: Ozzie Smith

Ozzie Smith, another Cardinal, was the star of the 1985 NL Championship Series as he smoked Dodger pitching at a .435 clip with 10 hits, four runs scored, and three RBI. His biggest swing came at the end of Game Five. With the series tied up and the score even at 2-2, the switch-hitting shortstop stepped to the plate to face Los Angeles closer Tom Niedenfuer with one out in the bottom of the ninth inning and delivered the first left-handed home run of his career. (It was this dramatic home run that prompted the late Jack Buck to say, "Go crazy, folks, go crazy!") Niedenfuer was so shaken up that he yielded Jack Clark's pennant-clinching three-run homer in Game Six for his second straight defeat. Leading, 5-4, with two out in the top of the ninth at Dodger Stadium, Los Angeles manager Tommy Lasorda and Niedenfuer elected not to walk Clark with first base open and paid the price.

Game Three Question:

Who was the first player to steal home in an American League Championship Series game?

ANSWER: Reggie Jackson

Jackson's steal of home (on the front end of a double steal) during Game Five of the 1972 AL Championship Series versus Detroit came in the second inning, tying the game at 1-1. The A's won the game, 2-1, and their first pennant in 41 years. Jackson was a quiet 5-for-18 in his second postseason series after hitting .333 with two homers in the 1971 AL Championship Series. Alas, Jackson pulled a hamstring during his steal of home and was forced to miss what would have been his first World Series. The 1972 World Series was one of the most thrilling ever played.

Jeff Branson became the first to steal home in an NL Championship Series, for the Reds (on the front-end of a double steal) in Game Two against Atlanta. The Reds were swept.

Game Four Question:

Which player holds the career League Championship Series record for most hits?

ANSWER: Pete Rose

Rose's 45 hits are the most in League Championship Series history. Rose played in a record seven League Championship Series, winning six of them. Ironically, Rose hit only .269 in World Series play, as opposed to his .381 mark in League Championship Series play. Rose won three World Series rings (in 1975 and 1976 for the Reds, and in 1980 for the Phillies).

The AL Championship Series record holder is Reggie Jackson, who had 37 hits over a record 11 League Championship Series (which amounted to an average of only .227). George Brett's 35 hits over six League Championship Series and 103 at-bats give him a .340 batting average to go with his record nine home runs. Brett won the 1985 AL Championship Series MVP. Steve Garvey hit a record eight NL Championship Series home runs for the Dodgers and Padres. Garvey's 21 League Championship Series RBI were the record until David Justice (27) passed him in 2000.

◆ Did you know only Richie Hebner played in more National League Championship Series than Pete Rose? Appearing in eight NL Championship Series, Hebner represented Pittsburgh in 1970–72, 1974, and 1975, Philadelphia in 1977 and 1978, and the Cubs in 1984.

Game Five Question (if necessary):

With four wins in the 1991 and 1992 NL Championship Series, John Smoltz became the second pitcher in League Championship Series history to record victories in four consecutive starts. Can you name the other?

ANSWER: Jim Palmer

Palmer won his only AL Championship Series starts in 1969, 1970, and 1971, and his first start in the 1973 AL Championship Series (the Birds needed Palmer only once in 1969, 1970, and 1971, sweeping Minnesota twice and then Oakland in 1971). All four starts were complete games. Smoltz won both of his starts in the 1991 NL Championship Series, including Game Seven in Pittsburgh, and his first two of the 1992 NL Championship Series (Game One and Game Four) before his Game Seven no-decision. Smoltz, who owns a 6-2 career record in League Championship Series competition, won twice more in 1996 but has not won since. Only Dave Stewart (8-0, 2.03 ERA) has notched more LCS victories than Smoltz. The other three pitchers with five LCS wins are Juan Guzman (5-0, 2.27 ERA), Andy Pettitte (5-1), and Tom Glavine (5-9).

Game Six Question (if necessary):

Can you name the pitcher who won the 1983 AL Championship Series MVP despite only one appearance?

ANSWER: Mike Boddicker

Baltimore rookie Mike Boddicker pitched a gem in Game Two, hurling a five-hit shutout against Chicago with 14 strikeouts. The Orioles won Game Four by the score of 3-0 in 10 innings for the pennant. The White Sox's Brett Burns had pitched 9⅓ innings of five-hit, shutout ball before yielding a solo home run to Tito Landrum in the top of the 10th inning.

◆ Did you know the AL Championship Series MVP Award is officially known as the "Leyland S. MacPhail Jr. Award"? The following words are inscribed on the trophy: "Championship Series, Leyland S. MacPhail Jr. Award."

Game Seven Question (if necessary):

Can you name the years of the Blue Jays' five division titles?

ANSWER: 1985, 1989, 1991, 1992, and 1993

Probably the most successful expansion team (although the Royals and Mets may argue), Toronto posted a winning record each year from 1983 to 1993 with five division titles to its credit. The 1985 Blue Jays blew a three games to one lead (it just so happened that 1985 was the first year the best-of-seven format was used for the League Championship Series) to Kansas City. The 1989 Blue Jays were smothered by Oakland in five games. The 1991 Blue Jays were beaten by Minnesota, the third straight time the Jays lost to the eventual world champions.

The 1992 Blue Jays finally brought home the Canadian bacon, thanks to their General Manager Pat Gillick, who acquired free agents Jack Morris and Dave Winfield and traded for former Mets ace David Cone on August 27 of the 1992 season. Morris responded with a 21-win season, Toronto's first-ever. Winfield hit .290 with 26 home runs and 108 RBI, and David Cone won four games (2.55 ERA) in September and pitched brilliantly to win Game Two of the AL Championship Series versus Oakland. Series MVP Roberto Alomar and right fielder

Joe Carter led the Blue Jays to their first pennant and made possible the first World Series outside of the United States.

In 1993 the Blue Jays became the first team since the 1977–78 Yankees to repeat.

If you have won four League Championship Series games, you advance to the World Series.

FIRST WORLD SERIES

Best-of-Seven World Series

Game One Question:

Can you name the MVP of four of the following World Series?

A 1966
B 1969
C 1970
D 1976
E 1989

ANSWER: (A) Frank Robinson hit two game-winning home runs versus Los Angeles. (B) Donn Clendenon hit .357 with three home runs versus Baltimore. (C) Brooks Robinson hit .429 with two home runs and six RBI and played spectacular defense. (D) Johnny Bench hit .533, including two homers and five RBI in Game Four alone. (E) Dave Stewart won both his starts (1.69 ERA) in the A's sweep over San Francisco.

   Clendenon slugged 1.071 in the 1969 World Series, during which more than a few Mets turned in outstanding and unforgettable performances. Southpaw Jerry Koosman (2.04 ERA) won both his starts, going 8⅔ innings to win Game Two by a score of 2-1 and going the distance to win the clinching Game Five, 5-3. Right fielder Ron Swoboda batted .400 and made a spectacular, completely out-stretched diving catch with the bases loaded in the ninth inning of Game Four to preserve Tom Seaver's 2-1, complete game triumph. Tommie Agee, who made 19 putouts in a flawless five-game series and homered in Game Three, made a slew of breathtaking grabs in center field, including a pair of gems to save five runs in that third game. In debt to Agee for his great catches that day were starter Gary Gentry and reliever Nolan Ryan, who combined for a four-hit, 5-0 shutout. . . . Stewart in 1989 was the third of five straight pitchers to win the World Series MVP award. Frank Viola (2-1, 3.72) began the streak with Minnesota in 1987, and Jack Morris (2-0, 1.17 ERA) capped it with Minnesota in 1991. That marked the third time that pitchers ran up a five-year streak since the advent of the World Series MVP Award in 1955. The hitters ran up a streak of 10 straight years, from 1975 to 1984. Reliever Mariano Rivera won the award in 1999 and, after his teammate Derek Jeter took home the honor in 2000, Arizona's Randy Johnson and Curt Schilling shared the trophy in 2001, giving pitchers the award in 24 different World Series—one more than the hitters.

◆ Did you know Derek Jeter in 2000 became the first player to win the All-Star Game MVP and the World Series MVP awards in the same year? Jeter has repeatedly proven he is a spotlight performer. In his first six full seasons as the Yankees' starting shortstop, Jeter helped New York win five pennants and four world championships with an array of clutch hitting, acrobatic fielding, and uncanny leadership that can only be described as extraordinary. Jeter has batted .291 with a .360 on-base percentage and a .427 slugging average in his five World Series, including a .409 batting average and an .864 slugging average in the 2000 fall classic, during which he set a five-game series record with 19 total bases. His 22 World Series runs scored puts him in the top 10, as he enters the 2003 season just 28 years of age. And after just seven full seasons, Jeter is already the all-time postseason hits leader (with 101). In terms of talent, drive, youth, maturity, and diplomacy, Jeter is Major League Baseball's version of Tiger Woods.

Game Two Question:

Who said, "Sparky, don't worry; we'll win tomorrow. But wasn't that the greatest game you ever saw in your life?"

ANSWER: Pete Rose

Pete Rose, MVP of the 1975 World Series, was the gutsy player telling his Reds manager Sparky Anderson his thoughts on the dramatic and unforgettable Game Six, to which the losing manager responded, "Pete, you're crazy."

Sure enough, the Reds won Game Seven to bring Cincinnati its first world title since the Paul Derringer and Bucky Walters days of 1940. It wasn't easy, though, as the Reds trailed, 3-0, through five innings of play. Tony Perez's third home run of the series in the sixth pulled the Reds within 3-2, before Rose's single (his 10th hit of the series) in the top of the seventh knotted the game at 3-3. Joe Morgan, whose Game Three–winning RBI single in the bottom of the 10th gave the Reds a two games to one advantage, blooped an RBI base hit in the top of the ninth off rookie reliever Jim Burton for a 4-3 lead that proved decisive.

Rose batted .370 with a double, triple, and two RBI. Perez pushed in six of his seven RBI during the last three games to break an 0-for-15 slump (hence the first baseman's .179 series average is deceiving).

◆ Did you know Hall of Famer Joe Morgan struggled in postseason play, batting just .182 over 11 series? Morgan hit .235 over four World Series and an anemic .135 (13-for-96) with an uncharacteristic on-base percentage of .303 in League Championship Series action.

Game Three Question:

Who saved the Reds' Game Seven win in the 1975 World Series?

ANSWER: Will McEnaney

Southpaw Will McEnaney came in to relieve Clay Carroll (the winner in relief) to open the bottom of the ninth against the mighty Red Sox. McEnaney retired pinch-hitter Juan Beniquez (flied out to right) and pinch-hitter Bob Montgomery (grounded out to short) and induced the pernicious Carl Yastrzemski (.310 with four RBI in the series) to fly out to center fielder Cesar Geronimo for the final out. McEnaney also saved two games for the Reds during the 1976 World Series.

◆ Did you know Boston's Carl Yastrzemski also made the final out in the 1978 American League East division playoff game against the New York Yankees? Another Hall of Fame Red Sox left fielder, Ted Williams, made the final out in two no-hitters: Allie Reynolds' pennant-clinching gem in 1951 and Jim Bunning's masterpiece seven years later.

Game Four Question:

This Red Sox outfielder in the 1986 World Series hit a lead-off home run off the Mets Rick Aguilera in the top of the 10th inning to ignite a two-run frame that preceded the Mets' miraculous Game Six comeback. Can you name this timely Red Sox hitter?

ANSWER: Dave Henderson

Henderson's homer drove in the first run, and Marty Barrett's single drove in the second, giving the Red Sox a 5-3 lead in the top of the 10th inning. Henderson batted .400 with two homers and five RBI in the series, and Barrett had four RBI. The Red Sox, however, had to watch in agony as the Mets came back in the bottom half of the inning to win the game and even the series.

After Wally Backman and Keith Hernandez each flied out, Gary Carter lined Calvin Schiraldi's two-strike offering to left field for a base hit. Pinch-hitting for Aguilera, Kevin Mitchell singled to center field. Up next was Ray Knight, who singled to shallow center, driving in Carter and sending Mitchell to third. Boston reliever Bob Stanley took over on the mound to face Mookie Wilson with the tying run 90 feet away, Howard Johnson on deck, and a Red Sox world championship still one out away. With two strikes, Stanley uncorked a game-tying wild pitch, sending Knight over to second base. Then came Mookie's grounder, which scooted under Bill Buckner's glove to score Knight and send America into disbelief. For his blunder, Buckner has been unjustly blamed for the series loss. Many unforgiving souls have forgotten that the game had already been tied, and that the series still had a Game Seven to be played. Buckner did not lose the series; the Red Sox lost the series.

The hobbled Buckner, whose weak ankles usually prompted manager John McNamara to replace him in the late innings with Dave Stapleton, was left in to field first base on this occasion. (McNamara has since stated that he wanted to reward Buckner by leaving him on the field for the final out.) The saddest part of the story is that Buckner's otherwise excellent and courageous career will always take a back seat to the error. Buckner, who played in parts of four decades (from 1969 to 1990), retired in 1990 with 2,517 hits, a .289 lifetime batting average, more than 1,200 RBI, the 1980 batting title, a pair of league-best performances in doubles, and a few defensive records along the way. Among many other things, the rally rendered Henderson's home run forgotten.

◆ Did you know the Shea Stadium scoreboard operator prematurely wished the Red Sox congratulations on winning the 1986 World Series in the bottom of the 10th inning of Game Six? The media was equally as hasty, having already voted Red Sox pitcher Bruce Hurst the series MVP. The left-handed Hurst went 2-0 with a 1.96 ERA over 23 innings. Of course, that MVP honor was scratched with the Mets' improbable comeback and given to New York third bagger Ray Knight, who batted .391 with five RBI in the classic.

Game Five Question (if necessary):

Can you run off all 26 world championship seasons for the New York Yankees?

ANSWER: 1923, 1927, 1928, 1932, 1936, 1937, 1938, 1939, 1941, 1943, 1947, 1949, 1950, 1951, 1952, 1953, 1956, 1958, 1961, 1962, 1977, 1978, 1996, 1998, 1999, and 2000.

◆ Did you know the New York Yankees' 26 world championships are more than any other franchise among the four major sports leagues? The Montreal Canadiens of the National Hockey League have been crowned 24 times (23 times by winning the Stanley Cup), the Boston Celtics have won 16 National Basketball Association titles, and the Green Bay Packers have won 14 National Football League championships.

Game Six Question (if necessary):

When Atlanta's David Justice homered off Cleveland's Jim Poole in Game Six of the 1995 World Series, Braves southpaw Tom Glavine made it stand up for a series-clinching 1-0 victory. There have been four other instances where a 1-0 World Series victory was decided by a home run. Name either the four winning pitchers or the four players who homered for the game's only run. (Clue: the years are 1923, 1949, and 1966.)

ANSWER: The four home runs were hit by Casey Stengel, Tom Henrich, Paul Blair, and Frank Robinson. The four winning pitchers, respectively, were Art Nehf, Allie Reynolds, Wally Bunker, and Dave McNally.

On October 12, 1923, Stengel homered in the seventh inning as Nehf and the New York Giants outdueled Sam Jones and the New York Yankees for a Game Three win. On October 5, 1949, Henrich homered in the ninth inning as Reynolds and the New York Yankees edged Don Newcombe and the Brooklyn Dodgers in Game One. On October 8, 1966, Blair belted a home run in the fifth inning as Bunker and the Baltimore Orioles blanked Claude Osteen and the Los Angeles Dodgers in Game Three. The very next afternoon, Robinson slugged a fourth-inning homer as McNally and the Orioles beat Don Drysdale and the Dodgers to complete a sweep.

◆ Did you know Yankee hurler Allie Reynolds is the only pitcher to record a World Series win in five consecutive years? Reynolds, who posted a 7-2 career World Series mark and a 182-107 lifetime ledger, won his first World Series decision in 1949. Reynolds went on to go 1-0 in 1950, 1-1 in 1951, 2-1 in 1952, and 1-0 in 1953. Three other pitchers have had the good fortune and skill to win a World Series game in four consecutive years: Art Nehf, Monte Pearson, and Vic Raschi.

Nehf, a southpaw who pitched for the Braves, Giants, Reds, and Cubs over his 15-year career, won a World Series game for the Giants in 1921, 1922, 1923, and 1924. The 184-game winner went 4-4 over those four World Series and had no record in his 1929 World Series appearance for Chicago. Pearson, a righthander who pitched for the Indians, Yankees, and Reds over his 10-year career, posted a 1-0 record in each World Series from 1936 to 1939, for a perfect 4-0 series mark. Pearson concluded his career with a 100-61 record. Raschi posted a 132-66 career record and a 5-3 World Series mark, going 1-1 in 1949, 1-0 in 1950, 1-1 in 1951, and a sparkling 2-0 in 1952.

Game Seven Question (if necessary):

Fill in the starting pitching matchups for any three of the following Game Sevens involving the Cardinals:

A 1926 World Series: St. Louis (_____) versus Yankees (_____)
B 1931 World Series: St. Louis (_____) versus Athletics (_____)

C 1934 World Series: St. Louis (_____) versus Tigers (_____)

D 1982 World Series: St. Louis (_____) versus Brewers (_____)

ANSWER: (A) Jesse Haines (2-0, 1.08) defeated the Yankees' Waite Hoyt, 3-2. (B) Bob Grimes (2-0, 2.04) defeated the Athletics' George Earnshaw, 4-2. (C) Dizzy Dean (2-1, 1.73) defeated the Tigers' Eldon Aucker, 11-0. (D) Joaquin Andujar (2-0, 1.35) defeated Pete Vuckovich's Brewers, 6-3 (Bob McClure lost the game in relief for Milwaukee).

The Haines-Hoyt matchup remains the only World Series Game Seven duel between two Hall of Fame pitchers. If Jim Kaat or Mickey Lolich ever get in, that would change.

◆ Did you know the Cardinals have won seven Game Sevens in World Series play, more than any other team? St. Louis won the deciding game in 1926, 1931, 1934, 1946, 1964, 1967, and 1982. By comparison, the Yankees have won five Game Sevens. Each franchise has played in 10.

◆ Did you know the home team has won Game Seven 18 of 35 times? That total is close to even, but the home team has won the last eight Game Sevens.

Allow me to congratulate you on your world championship if you answered four questions correctly!!!!

Second Season

◆ Did you know the Boston Red Sox won all five of their world championships in the period from 1903 to 1918? Boston established itself as a dominant club over the century's first two decades, earning six pennants and winning each of the five World Series it played in (there was no series in its other pennant-winning season, 1904). But the phrase "postseason woes" has been synonymous with the Red Sox ever since. They lost the 1946 World Series, the 1967 World Series, the 1975 World Series, and the 1986 World Series, not to mention dropping a one-game playoff in 1948 and 1978. When they won the opener of the 1998 AL Division Series, they snapped the longest-ever postseason losing streak (13 games), which had begun after they won Game Five of the 1986 World Series. The Red Sox then dropped the final two games of that set, were swept in four by Oakland in the 1988 and 1990 AL Championship Series, and were swept in three by the Indians in the 1995 AL Division Series. Interestingly enough, star pitcher Roger Clemens started 5 of those 13 games.

◆ Did you know four different World Series used a best-of-nine format, although none of them ever required a Game Nine? The 1903, 1919, 1920, and 1921 fall classics each required five wins for the title, with all but the seven-game 1920 series ending after eight games.

◆ Did you know the 1987 Detroit Tigers are the only team (before the advent of the wild-card format) to trail by as many as eight games in April and still make the postseason? The veteran club, led by the fiery Kirk Gibson, well-rounded shortstop Alan Trammell, and sluggers Darrell Evans and Matt Nokes, as well as by the hard-working pitching trio of Jack Morris, Walt Terrell, and Frank Tanana, came back to finally overtake the Blue Jays on the penultimate day of the season and beat them out on the final day for the AL East title.

163. *In honor of Cal Ripken Jr.'s accomplishment-filled career, this fourth season will open with a question about the Hall of Fame–destined baseball ambassador. In his swan-song 2001 campaign, Ripken played in his 3,000th game, becoming only the seventh major leaguer in history to play in that many contests. (An eighth followed in 2002.) Below is a list of eight players, seven of whom played in at least 3,000 major league games. Choose the man who did not play in 3,000 major league games:*

A Babe Ruth
B Hank Aaron
C Ty Cobb
D Stan Musial
E Pete Rose
F Eddie Murray
G Carl Yastrzemski
H Rickey Henderson

ANSWER: A

Ruth, who opened his career as a pitcher and played in the days of 154-game schedules, participated in 2,503 major league games. Ruth was born in Baltimore, the city Ripken played in for 21 major league seasons. In order of games played, the 3,000-game club includes Rose, Yastrzemski, Aaron, Henderson, Cobb, Murray, Musial, and Ripken. (Willie Mays finished eight games shy.) In his 3,001 games, Ripken achieved many great feats. Some of the lesser-known numbers and facts are as follows:

—Ripken played in 502 consecutive games after tying Lou Gehrig's streak of 2,130 in setting his unreachable standard of 2,632 straight games played.
—Before Ripken, the Orioles' previous record of consecutive games played was 463, held by Brooks Robinson.
—Ripken's streak was so long that eight managers guided the Orioles during the course of it (Earl Weaver, Joe Altobelli, Cal Ripken Sr., Frank Robinson, Johnny Oates, Phil Regan, Davey Johnson, and Ray Miller).
—Major leaguers went on the disabled list an astounding total of 5,045 times during Ripken's streak.

—The Orioles drafted three players (Larry Sheets, Bob Boyce, and Edwin Hook) ahead of Ripken in 1978, a trio that combined to play 748 major league games—less than a fourth as many games as Ripken logged by himself, and 28.4 percent as many games as Ripken logged solely during the Streak.

—Six shortstops (Nick Esasky, Rex Hudler, Buddy Biancalana, Lenny Faedo, Phil Lansford, and Glenn Franklin) were drafted ahead of Ripken in 1978, and that group combined to play 2,069 major league games—two-thirds as many games as Ripken logged in an Orioles uniform, and 563 games fewer than Ripken logged during the Streak.

—A grand total of 44,351,211 fans (a number that includes myself a few times) went to see Ripken play in Baltimore during the Streak.

164. *Gregarious batsman extraordinaire Tony Gwynn also retired in 2001, bringing to an end a tremendous career heavy with accomplishment. The left-handed lumber guru simply hit 'em where they weren't, piling up hits with an alarming frequency. In doing so, Gwynn tagged the very best pitchers hard and often. With a .300 batting average being the meter stick, who got the best of whom: eight-time batting champion Tony Gwynn or four-time Cy Young Award winner Greg Maddux?*

ANSWER: Gwynn

Gwynn batted a whopping .429 off Maddux, tagging the righthander for 39 career hits, more than he enjoyed off any other pitcher. Gwynn told me that his success off Maddux was in part a consequence indicative of Maddux's great control: "he's always around the plate and I'm a contact hitter." Of course, if that's all there was too it, then every contact hitter would average well against Maddux. To me, the key stats in this Hall of Fame matchup are the zero strikeouts and 10 walks in 91 at-bats. The strikeout number of course stands out, but the walks are especially intriguing, given that Maddux doesn't walk many and Gwynn didn't walk often. This means that Maddux was extra careful with Gwynn, who slugged .538 against the future Hall of Famer despite never homering off him.

The modest Gwynn was plenty good with the bat against all types of pitchers, getting hits off the hard-throwing Tom Seaver and

Nolan Ryan, the slider-throwing Steve Carlton, and knuckleballer Phil Niekro, all Hall of Famers.

Gwynn's .338 career average is at least seven points better than any hitter whose career started after Ted Williams' began in 1939. Stan Musial batted .331, and Wade Boggs and Rod Carew hit .328. Only Ty Cobb and Nap Lajoie reached the 3,000-hit plateau faster than Gwynn, who accomplished the feat in 2000 off rookie Dan Smith at Montreal in his 2,284th game and 8,874th at-bat.

◆ Did you know Tony Gwynn struck out just 434 times in his illustrious 20-year career, for an average of 21.7 whiffs per season or a strikeout every 21.5 official at-bats? Gwynn was so hard to strike out, Pedro Martinez failed to ring him up in 35 official career at-bats.

165. *Match these prolific sluggers with their marks:*

1	Babe Ruth	A	won an NL record five RBI crowns
2	Honus Wagner	B	hit the most homers (45) in a season without reaching 100 RBI
3	Paul Waner	C	struck out 150 times a record five years in a row
4	Sammy Sosa	D	led his league in RBI more often (six times) than any other player
5	Harmon Killebrew	E	holds the major league record of 14 straight games with an extra-base hit

ANSWER: 1—D, 2—A, 3—E, 4—C, 5—B

Ruth won his first three RBI titles in back to back seasons, leading the American League from 1919 to 1921. . . . Wagner led the senior circuit in runs batted in more often than Hank Aaron, Rogers Hornsby, and Mike Schmidt, each of whom did it four times. . . . Waner had 12 doubles, five triples, and three home runs from June 3 to 19, 1927, according to the Society for American Baseball Research. . . . Sosa struck out 174 times in 1997, 171 times in 1998 and 1999, 168 times in 2000, and 153 times in 2001. Sosa carries a dubious streak of eight seasons with at least 134 whiffs into 2003, and he is 763 whiffs behind the all-time leader, Reggie Jackson. Bobby Bonds' dubious single-season strikeout mark of 189 in 1970 was challenged in 2000 by Florida's Preston Wilson, who whiffed 187 times, and by

Milwaukee's Jose Hernandez, who whiffed 185 times in 2001 and 188 times in 2002. . . . Killebrew was able to drive in just 96 runs for the Twins in 1963, when he homered an AL-leading 45 times. For Killebrew, the 1963 campaign was a fluke, as he eclipsed the 100-RBI mark nine times and led the circuit three times in that category.

◆ Did you know Dave Nicholson owns the worst career at-bat to strikeout ratio for a non-pitcher? According to the Elias Sports Bureau, Nicholson's ratio of 1 strikeout per 2.48 at-bats is the worst among non-pitchers with at least 1,000 at-bats. Nicholson, an all-or-nothing outfielder who played during the 1960s, whiffed 573 times in 1,419 at-bats. Melvin Nieves (1:2.54), Rob Deer (1:2.75), and Bo Jackson (1:2.85) round out the top four.

166. *Match these players with their feats:*

1	Red Schoendienst	A	is the only player in the live ball era to win a batting title without homering
2	Marty Marion	B	became the first shortstop to win a league MVP Award, doing so while splitting time between the seventh and eighth slots in the lineup
3	Rod Carew	C	holds the all-time shortstop record of 5,133 putouts
4	Joe Tinker	D	led NL second basemen in fielding percentage seven times
5	Rabbit Maranville	E	became the first man ever to steal home twice in one game

ANSWER: 1—D, 2—B, 3—A, 4—E, 5—C

Marion, whose offensive numbers (.267, 63 RBI, 50 runs) are arguably worse than those of any other non-pitching MVP, was honored in 1944 for his defensive ability and his importance to his team's success. Marion is not in the Hall of Fame, even though contemporary shortstops such as the Yankees' Phil Rizzuto and the Dodgers' Pee Wee Reese are in. Marion, a seven-time All-Star, helped lead the Cardinals to three world championships with stellar range and sure-handed glove work. However, Rizzuto collected seven rings, and Reese soundly led Marion and Rizzuto in career homers, RBI, runs, and World Series batting average. . . . Carew batted .318 in his homerless season of 1972, and he won the 1977 MVP over an additional 10 players receiving first-place votes. Zack Wheat, who won the 1918 NL batting title (.335), and Ginger Beaumont, who paced the NL with a .357 average in 1902, were the only others to pace their league in batting without homering. . . . Tinker accomplished the feat on June 28, 1910.

◆ Did you know Hugh Jennings holds the distinction of having driven in the most runs during the course of a season without the benefit of a home run? It happened in 1896, when Jennings drove home 121 runs for the Baltimore Orioles. Lave Cross of the Philadelphia Athletics drove in 108 runners in 1902, the best figure without a home run in the 20th century. Don't misunderstand, however. Cross wasn't a punch-and-Judy hitter, as he drove in 1,345 runs over a 21-year career that featured 411 doubles and a .292 lifetime batting average. Cross had a knack for coming through with runners aboard, finishing in the top ten in RBI six times

◆ Did you know Nap Lajoie, Milt Stock, and Johnny Pesky are the only three players in the modern era to accrue 200 hits in a season without homering? Lajoie collected 214 hits in 1906, Stock 204 in 1920, and Pesky 207 in 1947. Sam Rice reached the 200-hit plateau with just one homer three times, and Matty Alou did twice.

167. *In 1990 the pennant-winning Oakland A's boasted Bob Welch (27-6) and Dave Stewart (22-11). The All-Star pitchers combined for 49 wins—the most by a team duo since 1944. Which two pitchers combined for 56 wins in 1944?*

ANSWER: Hal Newhouser and Dizzy Trout
MVP Hal Newhouser (29-9) and MVP runner-up Dizzy Trout (27-14) won a combined 64 percent of the Tigers' 88 victories in 1944. Their efforts were not enough to lead the Tigers to the pennant, as the club finished one game short of the pennant-winning St. Louis Browns. With major league rosters depleted due to the war, the 1944 AL champion Browns may have been the worst pennant winner ever. Ironically, the Browns didn't have a 20-game winner, as Nels Potter (a career 92-game winner) led the team with 19 victories, and Jack Kramer won 17 for the eventual World Series losers. Luke Sewell managed the club, which was led by Vern Stephens' bat (109 RBI).

168. *Eight different sluggers have hit 50 home runs in a season yet failed to lead their league in that department. Name any five of the seven unfortunate sluggers.*

ANSWER: Sammy Sosa, Mark McGwire, Luis Gonzalez, Mickey Mantle, Jimmie Foxx, Jim Thome, Brady Anderson, and Greg Vaughn

Sosa leads the way with three such seasons. Gonzalez smashed 57 home runs in 2001 yet still finished 16 behind Barry Bonds. In 1997 McGwire staged a fearsome assault on Roger Maris' standard of 61 homers by belting 58. But McGwire didn't get a chance to lead a league in that department, since he was traded from the American League's Oakland Athletics to the National League's St. Louis Cardinals on July 31. (In hitting 24 homers for St. Louis, McGwire also became the first player to hit at least 20 for two different teams in the same season.)

Of course, in 1998 McGwire smashed an unbelievable total of 70 homers, eclipsing Sosa's 66, the most ever hit without leading a league. Finishing third in 1998 with a "meager" total of 50 was Greg Vaughn of San Diego. In 1999 Sosa was once again denied a home run title despite hitting 63 (McGwire hit 65). In 2002 Thome homered 52 times, finishing 5 behind AL leader Alex Rodriguez. In 1996 Baltimore lead-off hitter Brady Anderson shocked the baseball world by becoming the 14th player in history to hit 50 home runs, reaching the plateau during the season finale. But McGwire won the crown with 52. Mickey Mantle's 1961 total of 54 was second to Maris' 61, and Jimmie Foxx's total of 50 was second to Hank Greenberg's 58 in 1938. McGwire, Foxx, and Greenberg shared the mark for most home runs by a right-handed hitter (58) before McGwire and Sosa each surpassed that mark more than once.

◆ Did you know Sammy Sosa in his spectacular 1998 campaign tied a major league record with 11 multi-homer games? Sosa tied Hank Greenberg's major league mark, set in 1938, and broke Ralph Kiner's NL mark of 10, set in 1947.

169. *With 6 saves over the 2001 and 2002 postseasons, the Yankees' Mariano Rivera extended his all-time postseason saves record to 25 and his career World Series saves record to 8. Whose mark of 15 career postseason saves did Rivera break?*

ANSWER: Dennis Eckersley

Eckersley's 15 postseason saves were passed in 2000 by Rivera, who also owns the record for saves in Division Series action (11). Eckersley's 11 saves in League Championship Series play remain a record. Rivera's 8 career World Series saves broke the previous mark of 6, set by Rollie Fingers. John Wetteland, Johnny Murphy, and Allie Reynolds each recorded 4 saves in fall classic play.

Of course, Rivera wasted a golden opportunity in Game Seven of the 2001 World Series, blowing a 2-1 lead for a heart-breaking 3-2 loss. Rivera had established such an aura of dominance in fall classic action that his rare blown save was shocking; it marked his first postseason blown save after 23 straight conversions. Even with that defeat, Rivera's career World Series numbers are impressive. The smooth, right-handed speed-baller owns a 2-1 ledger with eight saves in nine opportunities and a 1.67 ERA over 27 innings, during which he struck out 25 and yielded just 22 hits. The greatest closer in postseason history had allowed only one earned run in 15⅔ innings entering that ninth inning of Game Seven of the 2001 World Series.

◆ Did you know the Yankees were 155-1 when leading after eight innings of play in postseason action prior to Mariano Rivera's blown save in Game Seven of the 2001 World Series? The franchise's only other such defeat occurred on October 3, 1947. That's when the Yankees' Bill Bevens took a no-hitter into the ninth but gave up two runs and lost, 3-2, to the Brooklyn Dodgers.

170. *Match these teams with their performances:*

1	1991 Reds	A	broke the major league record for most consecutive seasons leading their league in batting average
2	2000 Rockies	B	held the NL record for attendance (3,608,881) before Colorado drew a standard of 4,483,350 in its inaugural 1993 season
3	1961 Tigers	C	won 101 games but still finished in second place—eight games back
4	1982 Dodgers	D	were successful in stealing a base a record 82 percent of the time
5	1975 Reds	E	tied a modern record with their ninth straight opening day win

ANSWER: 1—E, 2—A, 3—C, 4—B, 5—D

From 1983 to 1991 the Reds won each opening day, tying a mark set by the Brooklyn Dodgers from 1919 to 1927 and later equaled by the St. Louis Browns from 1937 to 1945 and by the New York Mets from 1975 to 1983. For the Mets, their streak marked a reversal of their first eight opening days—a loss each year from 1962 to 1969. The all-time record for most consecutive opening day wins is 10 by the Boston Beaneaters (1887–96), according to researcher Lyle Spatz. . . . Colorado, which has led the National League in batting each year since 1995, broke the previous mark of five straight league-leading averages set by Connie Mack's Athletics from 1910 to 1914. . . . The 1975 Reds were successful in 168 of their 204 attempts. Although it's no surprise that Joe Morgan was 67 of 77 and Dave Concepcion 33 of 39, Johnny Bench was 11 of 11, and Dan Driessen was 10 of 13. Talk about stereotype-breakers. . . . The 1993 Blue Jays re-set the American League record for attendance with 4,057,947, surpassing the four million mark for the fourth time in the Sky Dome. In 2002 Dodger Stadium drew more than three million for the 17th time, extending its record.

171. *En route to their 1991 World Series confrontation, the Twins and the Braves each won three road games in their League Championship Series, becoming the first two teams in history to do so in LCS action. In World Series play, 20 teams have won three road games in a single series. Can you choose the last club to do so?*

A The 1968 Tigers
B The 1972 A's
C The 1979 Pirates
D The 1983 Orioles
E The 1996 Yankees

ANSWER: E

The five choices are the last five teams to achieve this feat. Of course, each of the teams won its series: the 1968 Tigers, 1972 A's, and 1979 Pirates in seven games; the 1983 Orioles in five; and the 1996 Yankees in six. The 1996 Yankees, who lost the first two games at home, won all three in Atlanta before wrapping up the series with a Game Six victory at Yankee Stadium.

◆ Did you know the 1979 Pittsburgh Pirates are the only world championship team, outside the strike-shortened 1981 season, without a 15-game winner? The top winner for that united Pirates team was southpaw John Candelaria, who earned 14 victories. Bruce Kison won 13, and Bert Blyleven and Jim Bibby each won a dozen games. Relievers Kent Tekulve, who also had 31 saves, and Enrique Romo each won 10.

172. *In only two World Series has the home team won every game. Choose them:*

    A The 1947 and 1987 World Series
    B The 1924 and 1956 World Series
    C The 1955 and 1991 World Series
    D The 1987 and 1991 World Series

ANSWER: D

The Twins won Game One, Game Two, Game Six, and Game Seven in 1987 over St. Louis and 1991 over Atlanta, losing their three road games each time. Many other series have come close, and the rivalry between the New York Yankees and the Brooklyn Dodgers is one to note. The 1955 and 1956 World Series featured the home team winning in each of the first six games. However, the Dodgers won Game Seven, 2-0, in Yankee Stadium for the 1955 world championship, and the Yankees crushed the Dodgers, 9-0, in Ebbets Field for the 1956 title. By the way, in no series has the road team won all the games, although the Yankees-Braves set in 1996 came close. The road club won the first five contests before the Yankees put Atlanta away with a 3-2 victory in Game Six at the Stadium.

◆ Did you know Terry Pendleton (1991 MVP Award winner) played for the 1987 Cardinals and 1991 Braves against the Twins in the World Series, and thus was winless in Minnesota in eight World Series games?

173. *Match these World Series underachievers with their slumps:*

    1 Gil Hodges   A hit only .217 in seven World Series
    2 Dave Winfield   B was great in his first World Series but only 1-for-20 without an RBI or a run scored in his second

3 Roger Maris   C was 1-for-22 with one RBI in his first appearance in the World Series

4 Mike Schmidt   D although he did well in his seven World Series appearances, some never let him forget his 0-for-21 performance in 1952

5 Orlando Cepeda   E batted .171 and slugged .289 in three World Series

ANSWER: 1—D, 2—C, 3—A, 4—B, 5—E

Hodges' 0-for-21 snooze cost Brooklyn the title in the 1952 fall classic. . . . Winfield's woeful performance in the 1981 postseason may have prompted Yankee owner George Steinbrenner to call his outfielder "Mr. May" following a 1985 regular-season game, to contrast "Mr. October," Reggie Jackson's well-earned moniker. . . . Schmidt won MVP honors for his efforts in the 1980 fall classic but suffered three years later. . . . Cepeda was 6-for-48 with no homers, three RBI, and eight strikeouts in his first two World Series before a two-homer, six-RBI performance for the 1968 Cardinals. He did bat .455 and slug .909 for the Braves in the 1969 NL Championship Series.

◆ Did you know Willie Mays, baseball's third leading home run hitter, failed to homer in 20 World Series games, a span covering 71 at-bats and four separate fall classics? Mays didn't hit for average either, batting an uncharacteristic .239 with a mere three extra-base hits and six RBI.

◆ Did you know the 1961 Yankees were so deep that they defeated the Cincinnati Reds, four games to one, in the World Series despite a combined .120 average by Roger Maris (.105) and Mickey Mantle (.167)? Maris and the injured Mantle combined for just two extra-base hits and two RBI. So talented were the Yankees that unheralded Hector Lopez stepped in for the ailing Mantle, whose injured hip made it impossible for him to play, and drove home seven runs in nine at-bats. Lopez homered and tripled, slugging .889.

174. *The Dodgers, who had lost all of the franchise's seven World Series until 1955, exploded out of the gates in 1955 with a 10-0 start and with a nine-game lead 24 games (22-2) into the season. Their newfound tough and "cocky" attitude paid off with a 98-55 regular season and their first world championship. Fill in the 1955 Dodgers alignment, and name their winningest pitcher:*

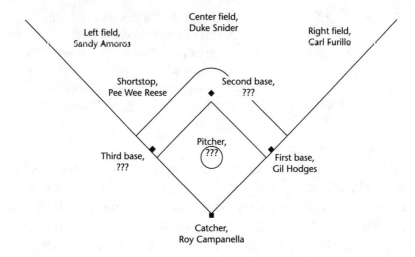

ANSWER: Second base, Jim Gilliam; Third base, Jackie Robinson; Pitcher, Don Newcombe

Robinson played mostly at third base his final two years (1955-56), after playing at first base in 1947, mostly second base from 1948 to 1952, and mostly in the outfield from 1953 to 1954. Newcombe was 20-5; no other Dodger won more than 13 games. Reliever and spot starter Clem Labine went 13-5. Carl Erskine won 11, Billy Loes earned 10 victories, and Johnny Podres, nine.

The lovable Don Zimmer played second and third base for five teams from 1954 to 1965, struggling to a .235 career average before deciding to manage. Zimmer was the player who last wore uniform number 14 for the Cincinnati Reds before Pete Rose.

◆ Did you know Brooklyn traded Jackie Robinson to the rival Giants for Dick Littlefield and $30,000 on December 13, 1956? Rather than cross over to the hated Giants, Robinson retired. Now that's a rivalry, not to speak of loyalty!

175. *Match these seasons with their importance:*

1	1978	A	the year in which the major leagues suffered their first collective strike, which delayed opening day and forced the cancellation of 86 games
2	1972	B	major league umpires refused to call this year's League Championship Series in order to obtain a raise in salary and benefits

3 1976 C was the first and only year in which all four division
             winners repeated
4 1970 D was the year in which baseball's second strike of note
             occurred (no regular-season games were canceled, but
             all of spring training was lost)

ANSWER: 1—C, 2—A, 3—D, 4—B

The 1972 season, set to open on April 6, didn't begin until the
15th. The 13-day strike, which began at a minute past midnight on
April 1, was primarily over the lack of a pension plan for the players.
. . . The 12 umpires assigned to the 1970 playoffs went on strike and
missed the first two playoff games in each league before a settlement
was reached. . . . The umpiring staff was denied a 60 percent raise in
December of 1994 (talk about bad timing) and was locked out for 120
days by the owners. According to the Umpire Union Chief, Richie
Phillips, the owners ceased paying umpires (who are paid over 12
months, rather than only during the regular season) as of January 1,
1995. Before they received a raise of between 25 and 37.5 percent one
week into the 1995 season, major league umpires were earning about
25 percent less than National Basketball Association and National
Hockey League officials despite working twice the amount of games.
Arguably, MLB's greatest umpire strife occurred in 1999, when a total
of 22 umpires had their services terminated after issuing the league
an ultimatum. Thirteen NL and nine AL umpires lost their jobs as the
result of a ploy gone awry by the union, whose intention was to get
baseball officials to the negotiating table. With a collective bargain-
ing agreement set to expire on the last day of 1999, Phillips urged the
umpires to submit their resignations in August. The strategy failed
when many of the umpires refused to step down, thus dividing the
umpires union. Phillips obviously had overestimated his support.
Among the issues dividing the umpires and baseball's central offices
were the supervision of umpires and the strike zone. The umpires ex-
pressed frustration over the questioning of their integrity and approach. Baseball unsuccessfully tried to centralize the duties of umpires, who have continued to enforce arbitrary guidelines, such as the
strike zone, to their own taste. Before the season, MLB Executive Vice
President Sandy Alderson had handed down an edict ordering umpires to call higher strikes, but it was widely ignored.

◆ Did you know crew chiefs Frank Pulli and Terry Tata, who have a combined 55 years of major league experience, were among the umpires whose resignations were accepted by major league baseball in 1999? Jim Evans, Eric Gregg, Greg Kosc, and Joe West, each with at least two decades of experience, also had their resignations accepted. The list of departing umpires also included highly rated umpires such as Pulli and Richie Garcia. Drew Coble, a highly rated AL umpire, lost his job while his wife was dying of cancer.

176. *Match these lesser-known, courageous players with the obstacles they conquered:*

1 William Hoy   A survived a heart attack to become a bullpen ace

2 John Hiller   B pitched 10 years in the majors despite a malformed right arm, the result of polio

3 Bert Shepard   C after losing a leg in a World War II battle, he signed as a coach and made a relief stint

4 Buddy Daley   D enjoyed a successful major league career despite being a deaf-mute

5 Monty Stratton   E returned to play in the minors after a leg amputation

ANSWER: 1—D, 2—A, 3—C, 4—B, 5—E

Hoy, whose handicap, according to some historians, triggered the umpires' custom of raising their right hand to signal a strike, collected 2,044 hits over a 14-year career for six teams. The left-handed-hitting outfielder swiped 594 bases in his career and posted a .287 batting average and .386 on-base percentage. . . . Having never won more than nine games or saved more than four in the six years prior to his 1971 heart attack, the southpaw Hiller went an amazing 10-5 with a 1.44 ERA and league-highs of 38 saves and 65 appearances for Detroit in 1973. . . . With an artificial leg, Shepard pitched 5⅓ strong innings for the Senators on August 14, 1945, yielding just one earned run and three hits against the Red Sox. Shepard also batted three times in the no-decision. . . . The southpaw Daley went 60-64 with a World Series win for the Yankees in 1961 and posted a 7-5 mark for the Yankees in 1962—each a championship season. . . . After consecutive 15-win seasons for the White Sox, Stratton had his right leg amputated following a hunting accident in November of 1938. Refusing to give up hopes of playing again, the righthander continued training and eventually made a comeback for Sherman of the Eastern League in 1946. He won 18 games that year.

♦ Did you know migraine headaches curtailed the career of Indians left-handed slugger Hal Trosky? A powerful first baseman, Trosky was headed toward the Hall of Fame when excruciating headaches debilitated him to such an extent that he decided to retire before the 1942 season. From 1934 to 1940, Trosky belted AL pitching, accruing six straight seasons with at least 100 RBI and 25 homers. In 1936 Trosky hit 42 homers, had 216 hits, and led the circuit with a whopping 162 RBI. Trosky, who came back to play two more seasons but was never able to post similar numbers, retired in 1946 with a slugging percentage of .522.

177. *Match these Japanese superstars with their achievements:*

1	Sadaharu Oh	A	hit 657 home runs and became known as the greatest ever Japanese catcher
2	Katsuya Nomura	B	was known as "The God of Batting," retiring with a .313 lifetime batting average
3	Tetsuharu Kawakami	C	stole 1,065 bases in his illustrious career, with a high of 106 in his 122-game 1972 season
4	Shigeo Nagashima	D	Japan's most popular player ever, who won five MVPs while playing for the famous Yomiuri Giants
5	Yutaka Fukumoto	E	depended on his mastery of martial arts for his physical, spiritual, and mental edge

ANSWER: 1—E, 2—A, 3—B, 4—D, 5—C

Oh started out as a pitcher, hitting only .161 in his 1959 rookie season, before turning things around. . . . Nomura, who caught a record 2,918 games, at one time was Japan's all-time home run and RBI leader as well, before Oh surpassed him en route to his record totals of 868 and 2,170, respectively. Oh is also number one in runs scored, with 1,967. Nomura and Oh retired in 1980. . . . Kawakami, who won five batting titles, later became a manager and led the Yomiuri Giants to nine consecutive Japan Series championships from 1965 to 1973. . . . Fukumoto's team, the Hankyu Braves, took out a half-million dollar insurance policy on his legs, because he was such a big part of the team's six pennants in his first 13 years. On June 16, 1993, Rickey Henderson stole his 1,066th base, passing Fukumoto for the world lead. Fukumoto also holds Japan's career record of 115 triples. . . . Nagashima, the Yomiuri third baseman who was renowned as "Mr. Giant," hit 444 home runs, drove in 1,522 runners, and batted .305 during a 17-year career. Nagashima's popularity led to such high expectations for his son, Kazushige Nagashima, that he was unable to handle the pressure of playing in Japan and instead tried to make it in the United States. He was unable to climb the Dodgers' minor league ladder.

◆ Did you know former major leaguer Nigel Wilson became the fourth (and last) player to hit four home runs in a Japanese League game? Wilson, a left-handed outfielder and designated hitter who totaled just 35 at-bats for three major league teams from 1993 to 1996, accomplished the feat for the Nippon Ham Fighters in 1997. The first to do so in the Japanese League was Yoshiyuki Iwamoto of the Shochiku Robins, in 1951. Sadaharu Oh duplicated the feat 13 years later for the Yomiuri Giants. Tony Solaita of the Nippon Ham Fighters became the third in 1980.

178. *Match these truly dedicated and talented superstars with their heroics in Japanese baseball:*

1	Sachio Kinugasa	A	is the only member of the 3,000-hit club, and also won seven batting titles
2	Hiromitsu Ochiai	B	broke Lou Gehrig's all-time consecutive-game streak in 1987, and hit 504 homers in his career
3	Sadaharu Oh	C	won three Triple Crowns and became the first Japanese player to make $600,000 a year
4	Isao Harimoto	D	won back-to-back Triple Crowns
5	Ichiro Suzuki	E	hit over .340 for seven straight years

ANSWER: 1—B, 2—C, 3—D, 4—A, 5—E

Kinugasa's streak ended at 2,215 consecutive games, a mark that Cal Ripken Jr. surpassed on June 14, 1996, with Kinugasa on hand in Kansas City. . . . Ochiai (a Wade Boggs with power) led the league in batting, homers, RBI, and runs five times for each category. He also hit 52 home runs in 1985, in only 130 games. . . . Harimoto accumulated 3,085 hits and retired with a .319 career batting average, and he also had power, belting 504 home runs. Harimoto, whose .31915 career batting average is bettered only by Tsutomu Wakamatsu's .31918 and Leron Lee's .320 (among those with at least 4,000 at-bats), also set the single-season mark for highest batting average (.383) in 1970 before Randy Bass hit .389 in 1986. Bass' mark still stands, although Ichiro Suzuki came quite close a few times. . . . Suzuki compiled the following batting averages over his last seven years in Japan: .385 (in 1994), .358, .356, .345, .358, .343, and .387. His seven consecutive batting crowns eclipsed the four straight won by Harimoto, from 1967 to 1970. His .353 career batting average would easily be the highest, but he is 381 at-bats shy of qualifying. I did the math and figured if he was charged a hitless at-bat the 381 times he would need to qualify, his average would still be a stout .3195.

179. *Who was the last American League switch-hitter to win the MVP?*

ANSWER: Vida Blue

Pitcher Vida Blue won the MVP in 1971. (I'm allowed one trick question, aren't I?) For what it's worth, Blue batted .118 in 1971 and just .104 for his career. Mickey Mantle is the American League's only other switch-hitter to earn MVP honors, winning in 1956, 1957, and 1962. In 1999 Atlanta's Chipper Jones became the fourth switch-hitter in 14 years to win the NL MVP, following St. Louis' Willie McGee in 1985, Atlanta's Terry Pendleton in 1991, and San Diego's Ken Caminiti in 1996. The switch-hitting Pete Rose also walked home with baseball's top individual honor for the National League in 1973, and Frankie Frisch won the National League's first award in 1931. Although Frisch's 1931 MVP campaign was by no means his best statistically (.311, 96 runs scored, 82 RBI, and 28 steals), the writers recognized his strong leadership and his knack for clutch hitting during a season in which the Cardinals won 101 regular-season games and the world championship.

180. *In addition to being the losing pitcher in Nolan Ryan's fifth no-hitter, _____ was professional baseball's lone 20-game winner during the 1981 season.*

ANSWER: Ted Power

Ted Power reached the 20-win plateau in the Dodgers' farm system during the major league's strike-shortened campaign. Power made his major league debut late in the season, making five appearances for Los Angeles. He served as a reliever for his first six seasons, leading the National League with 78 appearances as a member of the Reds in 1984 and recording 27 saves (third in the National League) the following year. His second career, as a starter, wasn't as successful.

181. *Of the teams that have thrown a no-hitter, which club has since waited the longest for another?*

A The Baltimore Orioles
B The Atlanta Braves
C The Chicago Cubs
D The Boston Red Sox

ANSWER: C

Milt Pappas hurled the Cubs' last no-hitter, an 8-0 win against the San Diego Padres on September 2, 1972. The Giants haven't thrown a no-no since September 29, 1976, when John Montefusco blanked the Braves.

◆ Did you know the New York Yankees have avoided being no-hit for 44 consecutive years, a major league record? The Yankees, despite playing in the same division as Boston's Pedro Martinez, were last no-hit on September 20, 1958, by Baltimore's Hoyt Wilhelm.

182. *Who was the celebrated Phillies catcher who lost a grand slam on the nation's Bicentennial holiday (July 4, 1976), when he passed the hesitant Garry Maddox on the basepaths?*

ANSWER: Tim McCarver

McCarver, who was credited with a three-run single, talks about that incident yearly as he broadcasts San Francisco Giants games and nationally televised contests, including the postseason. He passed Maddox, who stood near first determining the ball's fate, and was called out for passing a teammate on the basepaths. To my ears, McCarver is the most insightful and knowledgeable broadcaster in the business.

◆ Did you know Tim McCarver became the first catcher in the modern era to lead the league in triples when he hit 13 in 1966 for the Cardinals? Carlton Fisk, who hit a league-best nine three-baggers in his 1972 rookie season with the Red Sox, is the only other.

◆ Did you know the broadcaster who analyzed Brad Fullmer's steal of home in Game Two of the 2002 World Series was the previous player to steal home in World Series competition? Doing so as part of a double steal in Game Seven of the 1964 fall classic, Tim McCarver helped the Cardinals defeat the Yankees for the title. McCarver played above his head in that series, hitting .478 with a slugging percentage of .739. Bill Dahlen was the first to steal home, doing so in the 1905 World Series for the victorious New York Giants. With Dahlen on third base and teammate Art Devlin on first, aggressive manager John McGraw called for a double steal, which worked perfectly in the fifth inning of Game Three, won by the Giants, 9-0. In between Dahlen and McCarver, 10 others have stolen home in World Series play. You already know Bob Meusel accomplished the feat twice. The others are: George Davis (1906), Jimmy Slagle (1907), Ty Cobb (1909), Buck Herzog (1912), Butch Schmidt (1914), Mike McNally (1921), Hank Greenberg (1934), Monte Irvin (1951), and Jackie Robinson (1955). Fullmer, who slid safely on the back end on a double steal, became the 13th to do so in the fall classic.

183. *Match these Japanese pitchers with their feats:*

1 Eiji Sawamura — A perhaps the greatest Japanese pitcher ever, this rubber-armed lefthander earned a still-standing Japanese record 400 victories

2 Masaichi Kaneda — B won 350 games and pitched in 949 games

3 Kazuhisa Inao — C went 317-238 with 3,061 strikeouts

4 Tetsuya Yoneda — D won a record five ERA crowns and back-to-back MVPs

5 Keishi Suzuki — E still a true legend, is best known for whiffing major leaguers Charlie Gehringer, Babe Ruth, Lou Gehrig, and Jimmie Foxx consecutively during a 1934 All-Star Game (between major league and Japanese stars) at 18 years of age

6 Yutaka Enatsu — F struck out 401 batters in 329 innings at the age of 20

ANSWER: 1—E, 2—A, 3—D, 4—B, 5—C, 6—F

Kaneda holds many other career records, including strikeouts (4,490), complete games (365), and innings pitched (5,526⅔). He also hurled a record 64 consecutive scoreless innings and hit 36 home runs, a record for pitchers. Known as the "God of Pitching," Kaneda also threw two no-hitters, including a perfect game. A free-thinker, Kaneda made some enemies among traditionalists by training on his own and declaring himself a free agent. . . . Sawamura also pitched three no-hitters before dying in battle for his country in 1944. Sawamura left behind a 63-22 career record, a 1.74 ERA, and 554 strikeouts. . . . Inao would have undoubtedly been the best pitcher in Japanese history had his arm not been so badly overworked. Inao's 1.98 career ERA remains the third best in Japanese history, behind Hideo Fujimoto's 1.90 and Jiro Noguchi's 1.96. In 1961 Inao tied the league record of 42 wins and set the league mark with 353 strikeouts. . . . Enatsu once pitched an 11-inning no-hitter—on one day's rest! He also once retired 33 straight batters en route to a 14-inning one-hitter.

184. *Identify the 1952 National League MVP.*

A Hank Sauer
B Willie Mays
C Roy Campanella
D Jim Konstanty

ANSWER: A

Sauer of the Chicago Cubs hit 37 home runs to tie for the NL lead and boasted a league-best 121 RBI to accompany the league's second highest slugging percentage. For the Cubs left fielder, the 1952 season marked his fifth straight campaign of at least 31 homers. Two years later Sauer hit a career-high 41 home runs, en route to a career total of 288 over 15 years.

◆ Did you know Hank Sauer in 1952 became the first player to ever win an MVP while playing for a team that finished in the second division? Carrying the offensive load, Sauer was only able to help the Cubs finish as high as fifth place, with a 77-77 ledger.

185. *Describe the outcome in the final major league game at JFK Stadium.*

ANSWER: On September 30, 1971, the Washington Senators were forced to forfeit a game to the New York Yankees despite leading, 7-5, with two out in the ninth inning. That's when the fans, knowing their team was moving to Texas for the 1972 season, rushed the field looking for souvenirs. The umpires had no option but to award the Yankees a standard 9-0 (a run for each inning) forfeit win.

186. *On August 6, 1986, Texas and Baltimore set a major league record by combining for three grand slams in a 13-11 Rangers victory. Texas' Toby Harrah hit one in the second inning. Which two Orioles hit grand slams in a nine-run fourth inning?*

A Larry Sheets and Jim Dwyer
B Cal Ripken Jr. and Jim Dwyer
C Eddie Murray and Larry Sheets
D Mike Young and Eddie Murray

ANSWER: A

Sheets and Dwyer became the fifth teammates to hit grand slams in the same inning. Cecil Cooper and Don Money of Milwaukee hit grand slams in the same inning six years earlier, and Jimmy Wynn and Denis Menke accomplished the feat during the 1969 season. Bob Allison and Harmon Killebrew of the Twins did it in 1962. Tom Burns and Malachi Kittridge were the first teammates to perform the feat, doing so in 1890 for the Chicago White Stockings.

The record of three grand slams in a game was equaled the following year during a Chicago Cubs–Houston Astros tilt at Wrigley Field. Propelling the Cubs to a 22-7 rout, Keith Moreland and Brian Dayett belted bases-loaded homers, overcoming that of the Astros' Billy Hatcher on June 3.

187. *A 44-year-old Fred "Deacon" Johnson in 1938 earned his first win since 1923, a record span of 15 years between victories. Can you name the controversial pitcher who went eight seasons in between victories during the 1970s?*

ANSWER: Jim Bouton

In 1978, Jim Bouton came out of retirement to win one game in four decisions for the Atlanta Braves following a seven-year hiatus. A one-time fastball pitcher who played a big role for the pennant-winning 1963 and 1964 Yankee teams, Bouton reinvented himself as a knuckleballer in 1969 after injuries robbed him of his arm strength. It was during the 1969 season that Bouton wrote *Ball Four,* the controversial, best-selling diary of life as a major leaguer, as he pitched for the expansion Seattle Pilots and the Houston Astros. His revealing accounts of teammates and fellow players broke an unwritten rule among the brotherhood of major leaguers, leaving the outcast Bouton more isolated than before. After enduring a 4-6 campaign with the Astros in 1970, he called it quits for the first time. Bouton, who pitched for the Yankees from 1962 to 1968, earned his only All-Star appearance in 1963 during a 21-7 season and the next season won 18 games—one more than Whitey Ford—to lead the Yankees' staff. Bouton won two games in the 1964 World Series, with a 1.56 ERA in 17⅓ innings.

According to Lee Sinins of the Society for American Baseball Research, 55 pitchers have gone seven or more years in between victories, including Babe Ruth (1921–30).

188. *Which Hall of Famer made millions of dollars by investing in Coca-Cola stock?*

ANSWER: Ty Cobb

Cobb, a shrewd businessman, became a millionaire by age 35 in an era of few millionaires, largely because of investments in Coca-Cola. Cobb also invested wisely in General Motors, cotton, and real estate. After being approached on a golf course in 1914 by Coca-Cola marketer Robert Woodruff, Cobb originally hesitated, because Coca-Cola was "unlisted on the Big Board of the New York Stock Exchange," according to Al Stump, author of *Cobb.* After conducting further research and picking Woodruff's brain, Cobb made a $10,800 initial investment following the war. Pleased with the outcome, Cobb continued buying shares as the years went by. At one point, Cobb owned 22,000 shares at $181 per (that's $3,982,000 worth). Aside from his interests in automobiles, cotton, real estate, Coca-Cola, and other stocks, Cobb by 1921 also owned two minor league teams, managed a Pacific Coast League team in the winter, and, of course, served as player-manager for his Tigers team. How did Coca-Cola hold up during the Great Depression, you ask? Despite the difficult times, Coca-Cola declared three major stock dividends. It seemed everything Cobb touched turned to gold.

189. *In 1953 Cleveland Indians third baseman Al Rosen won the home run title, led the league in RBI, and finished second in batting average, losing out in that department by only one point. Name the 1953 AL batting champion who prevented Rosen from winning the Triple Crown.*

ANSWER: Mickey Vernon

Vernon won the batting title that year with a .337 mark, edging out Rosen, who smashed 43 homers and had a major league–best 145 RBI. Rosen also led the league in runs, slugging percentage, total bases, and OPS (on-base plus slugging percentage). For his efforts, Rosen won the 1953 MVP Award in the seventh season of a ten-year career that featured five straight 100-RBI campaigns. The four-time All-Star, who abruptly retired in 1956 because of nagging injuries and an unwillingness to cope with booing, homered 192 times in just 3,725 at-bats and slugged .495.

The left-handed Vernon won two batting titles over a 20-year career, spent mostly in a Washington Senators uniform. The seven-time All-Star, who also won the 1946 batting title and led the league in doubles three times, batted .286 with 2,495 hits and 490 two-baggers over a career that bridged four decades, from 1939 to 1960.

190. *Only two of the following dozen players failed to capture the Jackie Robinson Award for the best rookie. Choose them:*

A Harry Byrd
B Herb Score
C Albie Pearson
D Bob Allison
E Del Unser
F Ron Hansen
G Don Schwall

H Rico Carty
I Wally Moon
J Bill Virdon
K Tony Kubek
L Tom Tresh

ANSWER: E and H

Unser lost out to the Yankees' Stan Bahnsen in 1968, and Carty lost out to Dick Allen in 1964. . . . Byrd (1952, Athletics), Score (1955, Indians), and Schwall (1961, Red Sox) were pitchers. Pearson (1958, Senators), Allison (1959, Senators), Moon (1954, Cardinals), and Virdon (1955, Cardinals) were center fielders. Hansen (1960, Orioles), Kubek (1957, Yankees), and Tresh (1962, Yankees) were shortstops. Other obscure Rookie of the Year winners include Carl Morton (1970, Braves), Earl Williams (1971, Braves), Tommy Helms (1966, Reds), and Gary Peters (1963, White Sox).

191. *Match these managers with their accomplishments:*

1	Bobby Cox	A	became the first manager to win a pennant in both current leagues
2	Joe McCarthy	B	managed a record four clubs to division crowns
3	Tony LaRussa	C	this winner of three straight pennants was the first to win three straight All-Star Games
4	Leo Durocher	D	was the first manager to win the Manager of the Year Award in both leagues
5	Billy Martin	E	was the first manager to win 500 games for three different franchises

ANSWER: 1—D, 2—A, 3—C, 4—E, 5—B

Cox won the AL award in 1985 with Toronto and the NL award in 1991 with Atlanta. . . . McCarthy, owner of the highest career winning percentage (.614; 2,126 wins and 1,335 losses), led the Cubs to the NL pennant in 1929 and the Yankees to a pennant in 1932. The 1932 flag was his first of eight in New York. McCarthy and Casey Stengel each won a record seven world championships. Stengel managed the American League in five consecutive mid-summer classics twice, losing four of five the first time and winning three the next. . . .

Durocher was 738-565 for the Dodgers, 637-523 for the Giants, 535-526 for the Cubs, and 98-95 for the Astros. LaRussa has joined Durocher, leading the Cardinals to a 604-529 record after going 522-510 at the helm of the White Sox and 798-673 in Oakland. . . . Martin led the 1969 Twins, the 1972 Tigers, the 1976 and 1977 Yankees, and the 1981 A's to division titles. He remains the only manager to take four different teams into the postseason. Martin brought into his managerial duties the same fiery intensity he displayed as a player, the same attitude Stengel respected when he managed the young Martin in the Pacific Coast League. When Stengel was made manager of the Yankees in 1949, he sought out Martin, who debuted as a player the following year. One of Stengel's favorite players, Martin solidified a deep bench his first two seasons, playing second base and filling in wherever needed—third base, shortstop, the outfield. He was all about winning from the get-go. Martin earned the starting second base role in 1952 and, although he batted a career-best .267, made his greatest impact with his excellent defense. Playing in his first World Series that October, Martin made his mark in helping the Yankees defend their title. In a foreshadowing of his heightened ability during critical situations, Martin had a homer among his five World Series hits, drove in four runs, and alertly made a great catch in Game Seven of the 1952 fall classic. With the Yankees leading, 4-2, in the bottom of the seventh inning at Ebbets Field, the Dodgers' Jackie Robinson stepped to the plate with two out and the bases loaded. Robinson mustered just a low pop fly to the infield between first base and the mound, but for some reason neither relief pitcher Bob Kuzava nor first baseman Joe Collins (each of whom had entered the game that inning) reacted. Realizing this, Martin raced from his position toward the mound and made a lunging grab to end the threat and keep the Dodgers from tying the game. Two innings later, the Yankees celebrated their fourth straight world championship. In 1953 Martin enjoyed perhaps his finest season, playing solid defense and posting career bests of 15 homers, 24 doubles, six triples, 75 RBI, and 151 hits. In the subsequent World Series Martin put on a show with two homers and series-best figures of eight RBI, 12 hits, two triples, a .500 batting average, a .520 on-base percentage, and a .958 slugging average; it was a performance that comfortably earned him the Babe Ruth Award as World Series MVP. He went on to bat .320 in the 1955 World

Series and slug .519 with two homers in a victorious cause in the 1956 fall classic.

Martin became one of the most popular Yankees, befriending Mickey Mantle and Whitey Ford, with whom the second baseman frequently partied. After earning his lone All-Star appearance in 1956, Martin was traded during the 1957 season to the Kansas City Athletics for supposedly being a bad influence on Mantle, whose own nightlife activity is well documented. Devastated by the trade, Martin spent the last four and a half years in relative obscurity, lending his reliable services to six teams over that span. His 11-year career came to an end following the 1961 season with the Twins, who would later give him his first major league managerial position, in 1969. Martin responded immediately by leading a team that had won only 79 games the previous year to a 97-65 ledger, to grab the inaugural AL West Division title.

◆ Did you know Hall of Fame manager Joe McCarthy didn't allow his players to smoke a pipe, because he believed such a vice would make them complacent?

192. *Match these men with their managerial history:*

1 Sparky Anderson	A won his second Manager of the Year Award in 1992
2 Charlie Grimm	B with 863 wins as an NL manager and 1,331 wins as an AL manager, he is the only man with as many as 700 victories in both leagues
3 Jimmy Dykes	C managed a 20th-century record-sharing six teams
4 Jim Leyland	D won the Manager of the Year award a record four times
5 Tony LaRussa	E lost all four World Series he managed

ANSWER: 1—B, 2—E, 3—C, 4—A, 5—D

Anderson, a Hall of Famer, remains the only manager to win 100 games during a season in both leagues. He led the Reds to 102 wins in 1970, 108 in 1975, and 102 in 1976, and then won 104 for the 1984 Tigers. He retired with 2,194 regular-season wins after the 1995 campaign, having passed Bucky Harris' total of 2,157 for third on the all-time list. Anderson in 1994 passed Joe McCarthy's total of 2,125. Only Connie Mack and John McGraw won more. Mack holds the unreachable record of 3,731 wins, and McGraw is second with 2,763. . . . The Giants' Dusty Baker in 2000 joined LaRussa as the only field generals to earn three Manager of the Year Awards. Baker won his first in 1993 and added his second in 1997, both for the Giants. In 2002 LaRussa won his fourth, guiding the Cardinals to a division title amidst tragedy. LaRussa won his first three in the American League, his first for the White Sox in 1983 and his next two with the Athletics in 1988 and 1992. LaRussa and Tom Lasorda were the recipients of the award in its first year, 1983. Besides LaRussa, Baker, and Leyland, five others have won the award more than once: Anderson, Lasorda, Bobby Cox, Lou Piniella, and Joe Torre. . . . Grimm and Hughie Jennings are the only managers to go winless in four trips to the fall classic. . . . Dykes never won a pennant (or even finished second) in his 21 years, a record until Gene Mauch posted 26 such tearful years. Mauch still holds the dubious distinction of playing or managing the longest (35 years) without appearing in a World Series. Joe Torre was not far behind before ending his drought in his 32nd year. Torre played and managed 4,272 regular-season games before managing the Yankees to the 1996 World Series. Mauch's total is 4,246.

◆ Did you know Gene Mauch managed the 1964 Phillies as well as the 1982 and 1986 Angels? The 1964 Phillies blew a 6½-game lead (and the pennant) with 12 games left. The 1982 Angels blew a two games to none lead in the best-of-five AL Championship Series versus Milwaukee. The 1986 Angels blew a three games to one advantage in the AL Championship Series versus Boston (one strike away from clinching in Game Five). That's as heartbreaking as you can get.

◆ Did you know six teams have overcome a two games to none deficit to win a best-of-five postseason series, and the last two have done so by winning Game Five on the road? The 2001 Yankees won the AL Division Series by winning Game Five in Oakland, thanks to the defensive alertness of Derek Jeter, and the 1999 Red Sox won the AL Division Series by winning Game Five in Cleveland, thanks to the heroics of the injured Pedro Martinez, who came on to pitch six hitless innings of relief. Previously, the 1981 Dodgers (against Houston in the NL Western Division Playoffs), 1982 Brewers (against the Angels in the AL Championship Series), 1984 Padres (against the Cubs in the NL

Championship Series), and 1995 Mariners (against the Yankees in the AL Division Series) had pulled off the improbable, each winning Game Five at home.

193. *Match these nine well-known and successful managers with their real names (the right column has the managers' given first and middle names only):*

1	Mickey Cochrane	A	Stanley Raymond
2	Bucky Harris	B	Alfred Manuel
3	Whitey Herzog	C	Gordon Stanley
4	Billy Martin	D	Dorrel Norman Elvert
5	Bucky Rodgers	E	Charles Dillon
6	Casey Stengel	F	Robert Leroy
7	Gabby Street	G	Charles Evard
8	Sparky Anderson	H	George Lee
9	Connie Mack	I	Cornelius McGillicuddy

ANSWER: 1—C, 2—A, 3—D, 4—B, 5—F, 6—E, 7—G, 8—H, 9—I

Street managed five seasons and one game of another. He marched the Cardinals to consecutive pennants in 1930 and 1931, winning the World Series the second time around. As a player, Street spent all of eight seasons behind the plate. From 1908 to 1911 he served as Walter Johnson's personal catcher.

◆ Did you know Max Carey, who was born Maximilian Carnarius, completed a six-year ministerial program in 1909 before switching course and becoming a major leaguer? About to join the ministry, the religious Carey impressed in a specially arranged tryout with the Pirates. He then played a few games in 1910, using the name Max Carey to protect his amateur status, before joining the major league club for good in 1911.

◆ Did you know Frenchy Bordagaray's birth name is Stanley George Bordagaray? Frenchy is better known for his pinch-hitting exploits—a .312 career mark in the pinch—than his frequent bonehead plays. His .465 pinch-hitting average (20-for-43) in 1938 remains the highest single-season mark among those with at least 40 pinch-hit at-bats.

◆ Did you know Charles Leo Hartnett was nicknamed "Gabby" as an ironic commentary on his shy personality? Hartnett became more personable as the years passed.

194. *During the final three weeks of the 1992 season, Seattle's six-foot-ten Randy Johnson came into his own thanks to a two-hour meeting on the art of pitching with his hero, Nolan Ryan. Soon after, Johnson showed no mercy and took no prisoners in striking out 45 batters over a three-game span. Who holds the record for most Ks in three successive starts?*

ANSWER: Ryan

Ryan punched out 47 batters in 27⅓ innings (August 12–20) during the 1974 season. Although Johnson couldn't match Ryan's three-game mark, after he switched leagues he tied Dwight Gooden's 1984 NL mark of 43 Ks over three starts, in 1999. Johnson's three-game stretch in 1992 included an 18-strikeout (eight-inning) performance in Texas on September 27th to tie Ron Guidry's AL mark for left-handers. The Big Unit later broke that record, registering a pair of 19-strikeout performances in 1997.

Since the talk with Ryan and Rangers' pitching coach Tom House, Johnson is 180-60 entering the 2003 season, having taken his game to a new level. Johnson was advised to land on his right toes—not on his right heel—to add further velocity to his pitches and leave him in better defensive position. Johnson earned his first of five Cy Young Awards in 1995, and had his first 20-win season two years later. In 2000 Johnson became the 12th pitcher to reach the 3,000-strikeout plateau. In 2001 he earned a share of the World Series MVP Award for helping carry the Diamondbacks to a world championship. And in 2002 he won a career-high 24 games and the pitcher's Triple Crown.

◆ Did you know Kerry Wood broke a major league record previously shared by four pitchers when he struck out 33 batters in consecutive starts in May of 1998? Wood followed his 20-strikeout performance on May 6 by whiffing 13 in seven innings at Arizona five days later. Randy Johnson in 1997 had tied the previous mark of 32, which was first set by Luis Tiant in 1968 and later equaled by Nolan Ryan in 1974 and Dwight Gooden 10 years later. Since then, Pedro Martinez whiffed 32 batters over two straight starts in 2000.

195. *Match these teams with their associations:*

1 Brooklyn Dodgers   A have boasted a record nine eventual Hall of Famers on their roster more than once

2	Minnesota Twins	B	had the worst road record (29-52) of any pennant winner and the worst regular-season mark of any world champion
3	New York Yankees	C	once went a record 165 consecutive innings without scoring more than two runs in a single inning in World Series action
4	Chicago Cubs	D	once went 40 straight seasons without a pennant
5	Oakland Athletics	E	have won more regular-season games (9,579) than any other team in sports

ANSWER: 1—C, 2—B, 3—A, 4—E, 5—D

The Dodgers' World Series scoring drought lasted from 1916 to 1947. . . . The 1987 Twins, who were 85-77 during the regular season, became world champs despite their woes away from home. . . . The Yankees featured 9 future Hall of Fame players each year from 1930 to 1933. In 1932, 13 Hall of Famers played for the Bronx Bombers and the Cubs in the fall classic (still the most in any World Series). The Yankee list includes Babe Ruth (1936 inductee), Lou Gehrig (1939), Bill Dickey (1954), Herb Pennock (1948), Red Ruffing (1967), Earle Combs (1970), Lefty Gomez (1972), Joe Sewell (1977), and Tony Lazzeri (1991). The Cubs' list includes Gabby Hartnett (1955), Burleigh Grimes (1964), Kiki Cuyler (1968), and Billy Herman (1975). Including manager Joe McCarthy, the 1931–33 Yankees had the best Hall of Fame representation (10). Among the Yankee position players from that team, only shortstop Frank Crosetti and left fielder Ben Chapman are not enshrined in Cooperstown. Sewell, a shortstop through most of his career, played at third for this Yankee squad.

A May 24, 1928, game played between the Yankees and Athletics is the game most heavily decorated with Hall of Famers. Ruth, Gehrig, Combs, Lazzeri, Waite Hoyt, and Leo Durocher played for the Yankees. Ty Cobb, Tris Speaker, Mickey Cochrane, Al Simmons, Eddie Collins, Jimmie Foxx, Lefty Grove, and Jimmy Dykes played for the Athletics. Aside from the 14 players, Hall of Famers Miller Huggins and Connie Mack managed. Even two of the umpires—Bill McGowan and Tom Connolly—were Hall of Famers. Three Yankee Hall of Fame players didn't get in the game: Dickey, Pennock, and Stan Coveleski. The visiting Yankees, by the way, won by a score of 9-7. Lazzeri drove in six runs, and Grove was tagged with the loss.

◆ Did you know the Chicago Cubs are the only team that has been around continuously from the time of the National League's inception, 1876? They were then called the White Stockings.

196. *Can you name the first catcher to wear a protective helmet in a game? This Hall of Fame receiver caught 100 or more games in each of his first 13 full seasons to set an NL record.*

ANSWER: Johnny Bench

Bench also adopted and popularized the one-handed catching style introduced by Randy Hundley. Bench's father from the time of his childhood trained him to be a major league catcher. In fact, his father was so determined to ready Bench for the majors that he trained his son to throw 254 feet from a crouch. That measurement is twice the distance from home plate to second base.

◆ Did you know the Cincinnati Reds of 1975–76 outstole their postseason foes (the Pirates, Phillies, Red Sox, and Yankees) by a 32-1 margin over the four series? Only the Yankees' Mickey Rivers was able to steal on "The Arm" of Johnny Bench, doing so in Game Four of the 1976 World Series.

197. *Who was the first umpire ever?*

ANSWER: Bill McLean

The sport needed an honest game, and McLean, an ex–prize fighter who was honest and knowledgeable, was the perfect choice in 1876. NL umpires began getting paid in 1884, as John Gaffney became the first to receive money for his game-calling. Gaffney came up with the idea of umpiring behind the catcher with nobody on base, and by 1888 he was paid $2,500 plus expenses for a season. The $2,500 salary was more than that of most players. In 1885 it became a custom for the visiting team to pay the umpire $5 a game and the home team to pay the expenses. As early as 1883, the American Association was paying its umpires $140 a month plus expenses. Ben Young was the American Association's leading umpire, and he initiated the code of ethics for umpires. Until 1908 the National League and the American League each had only six umpires. Today, the major leagues have 70 umpires under salary. Tom Connolly umpired the first AL game in 1901.

198. *Place these events or decisions in chronological order:*

A The American League began its policy of issuing every player two passes to any park.
B Teams began allowing fans to keep foul balls.
C The National League began making all its clubs carry a tarp for the field in the event of rain so as to be able to resume play as soon as possible afterward.
D William Taft became the first president to throw out the first pitch on opening day.

ANSWER: D (1910), C (1915), A (1915), B (1916)

President Taft threw out the first pitch for the first time on April 14, 1910, before the Washington Senators' opening day win over the Philadelphia Athletics. According to *The Sporting Life*, umpire Billy Evans walked up to Taft in his box seat, handed him the ball, and asked him to throw the ball over the plate to usher in a new season. A curious President Taft agreed and hurled it to Walter Johnson, who caught the tradition-starting first pitch and later had Taft sign it, which itself became a tradition. President Franklin D. Roosevelt tossed a record eight opening day first pitches. Presidents Dwight Eisenhower and Harry Truman each threw out the first pitch on opening day seven times. . . . On April 29, 1916, Cubs owner Charles Weeghman became the first to allow his fans to keep foul balls.

◆ Did you know Benjamin Harrison on June 6, 1892, became the first sitting president to see a major league game? Cincinnati beat Washington in the game, 7-4, in 11 innings.

◆ Did you know that a Yankee fan sued his favorite team and won $7,500 for being pummelled by ushers and Yankee stadium guards while attempting to retrieve a foul ball lodged in the screen behind home plate during the 1937 season? David Levy, who suffered a fractured skull as a result of the beating, convinced all teams to allow their fans to keep the foul balls hit into the stands. Until then, only a few clubs had permitted their fans to keep foul balls.

199. *Match these umpires with their histories:*

1 Bob Emslie   A this former National League umpire became the league president but was soon fired

			because he favored the umpires on too many occasions
2	Cy Rigler	B	started the custom of raising his right arm to call a strike, according to some
3	Tom Lynch	C	called all three games of the major league's only triple-header in the 20th century
4	Peter Harrison	D	was first player to retire and become an umpire for a lengthy time

ANSWER: 1—D, 2—B, 3—A, 4—C

Emslie received a ton of abuse, mostly from manager John Mc-Graw, for wearing a hairpiece. If Emslie made a call McGraw didn't agree with, the Giants manager would get under Emslie's skin by telling him to buy a box of hairpins. It was a psychological maneuver by Mc-Graw to make Emslie think twice about making a judgment against the Giants. McGraw's salty mouth earned him a record 118 ejections during his career, according to the Umpires and Rules Committee of the Society for American Baseball Research. Second on the list with 98 is Earl Weaver, another argumentative Hall of Fame manager.

200. *The best team of the 1890s was clearly the 1896 Baltimore Orioles. For that matter, you could have taken the Orioles' 1894 or 1895 team as well. They were that good. They compiled an 89-39 record in 1894, an 87-43 record in 1895, and a 90-39 record in 1896. In winning three straight pennants, the Orioles won the Temple Cup in 1895 and 1896. Can you name this team's manager?*

ANSWER: Ned Hanlon

Hall of Famer Ned Hanlon won 1,313 games over 19 years, during which he led his squad to five first-place finishes. In winning the pennant by $9\frac{1}{2}$ games, the 1896 Orioles led the league in runs scored (995), triples (100), batting average (.328), slugging (.429), and stolen bases (441). In addition, they had the second best ERA (3.67) and the third best fielding percentage (.948). They were so dominant, they outscored the opposition by a staggering 333 runs, or by more than $2\frac{1}{2}$ runs per game. Whew!

The Orioles were led by shortstop Hughie Jennings, who hit .401 with 121 RBI—each mark was second in the league—and led all shortstops in fielding. Right fielder Willie Keeler hit .386 with 210 hits (one more than Jennings), 153 runs scored, and 82 RBI. Left fielder Joe Kelley hit .364 with 100 RBI. Catcher Wilbert Robinson, or "Uncle Robbie" as he was affectionately called, hit .347 while providing the team with solid leadership. First baseman Jack Doyle hit .339 with 101 RBI. Heinie Reitz, who batted .287, had the team's second highest RBI total (108). At third base, Jim Donnelly filled in admirably for the injured John McGraw and hit .328. Center fielder Steve Brodie hit .297 while leading all outfielders in putouts.

On the mound, ace Bill Hoffer went 25-7 for the best winning percentage (.781) in the league. Arlie Pond won 16 of his 24 decisions, George Hemming was 15-6, Duke Esper went 14-5, and Sadie McMahon 11-9. Notably, a young and fresh righthander by the name of Joe Corbett made an impression on Hanlon by winning three complete-game victories and registering an impressive 2.20 ERA late in the season. So impressed was Hanlon by this 20-year-old rookie that he made Corbett his other starter for the Temple Cup, behind Hoffer.

In the Temple Cup, Baltimore obliterated the second-place Cleveland Spiders. The Orioles outscored them 25-5 in sweeping the four-game series by scores of 7-1, 7-2, 6-2, and 5-0. Choosing Corbett turned out to be a wise choice, as the youngster pitched even better than Hoffer. Corbett won both his starts, including a Game Four shutout, and registered a minuscule ERA of 0.50. He even hit .500 in six at-bats. Hoffer also won both his starts (Game One against Cy Young and Game Three), with a 1.50 ERA. Hoffer wasn't bad with the bat either, getting two triples in seven at-bats. Among the position players, Keeler and Kelley each hit .471 with four RBI. Jennings hit .333 with five runs scored and three runs driven in. A healthy McGraw started all four games at third and had 4 of the team's 11 thefts. Keeler, Kelley, and Jennings were a part of five pennant winners from 1894 to 1900, for Baltimore and Brooklyn.

201. *Match these old timers with their histories:*

1	Clyde McCullough	A	baseball's first designated runner
2	Heinie Zimmerman	B	set a season record of 672 at-bats without homering
3	Rabbit Maranville	C	was banned for life (along with Hal Chase)

4 Herb Washington

in 1919 for offering several teammates bribes if they would throw a game

D remains the only player to play in a post-season but not the preceding regular season

ANSWER: 1—D, 2—C, 3—B, 4—A

Zimmerman, Chase, and Lee Magee were banned for life from professional baseball following the 1919 season for fixing games and conspiring to fix games. According to Bill James, author of *The Bill James Historical Baseball Abstract,* Chase and Zimmerman went so far as to attempt to bribe others, including Magee, to throw games. Suspected for quite some time, Chase finally upset the wrong people. In 1918 his manager on the Reds, the respected Christy Mathewson, voiced his suspicions. During the subsequent offseason, NL President John Heydler dismissed official league accusations brought by Mathewson and Reds owner Garry Herrmann, chalking up Chase's erratic play to "carelessness." Still convinced of Chase's guilt, the Reds traded him to the Giants soon thereafter. In New York, manager John McGraw kept a close eye on Chase and, after some more questionable play by the first baseman, refused to play him down the stretch in 1919. In the offseason, the league charge against Chase that was earlier dismissed was brought back, thus producing his banishment. So it was no surprise when rumors abounded during the Black Sox scandal that he had served as a liaison between certain members of the White Sox and the gamblers. Zimmerman was a teammate of Chase's on the 1919 New York Giants and was also said to have been giving less than his best effort.

Given that Zimmerman struggled at the plate and on the field in the 1917 World Series, one might suspect that he threw the 1917 fall classic as a member of the losing Giants club. A .297 batter throughout the regular season, Zimmerman went a dismal 3-for-25 in the series with one run scored and zero RBI, while the rest of the team batted .276 with 17 runs scored. With the series tied, Zimmerman committed a throwing error in Game Five in a three-run eighth inning for the victorious White Sox, who won 8-5. Zimmerman earned permanent goat horns the following contest. Besides going hitless again, Zimmerman was less than solid defensively during a sloppy fourth inning, during which the White Sox scored a trio of unearned runs for a series-clinching 4-2 victory in Game Six. Chicago's Eddie Collins opened the inning with a grounder to third, where Zimmerman fielded the ball and overthrew first base, allowing Collins to scamper to second base. The next White Sox batter, Joe Jackson, also reached via an error as Giants right fielder Dave Robertson dropped a fly ball, putting runners on the corners without an out. Then Oscar "Happy" Felsch grounded back to the mound, where Giants pitcher Rube Benton fielded the ball and threw to Zimmerman in an attempt to get Collins, who had advanced a little too far off the bag between third and home. Zimmerman threw the ball to catcher Bill Rariden, who caught the ball, chased Collins back toward third before throwing back to Zimmerman. Anticipating this, Collins took off for home, but no Giant player covered home—a costly team breakdown. Zimmerman, well behind Collins, inexplicably raced after the White Sox speedster while the other Chicago baserunners moved up to second and third without opposition. Those two runners (Jackson and Felsch) came around to score on a single by Chick Gandil, providing the margin of victory. . . . A long-time catcher, McCullough didn't play during the 1945 regular season due to war action and came back in time to strike out as a pinch-hitter in Game Seven of the World Series versus the victorious Detroit Tigers. . . . Oakland A's owner Charley Finley hired world-class sprinter Herb Washington to pinch run. Considering that Washington (who held the world indoor record in the 50-yard and 60-yard dash) had no previous baseball experience, the six-foot, 170-pounder performed decently. He was sent in to pinch run 93 times and stole 29 bases in 45 attempts, with 29 runs scored, in 1974. The 1975 season was a brief one for Washington, who scored four runs with two stolen bases in three attempts in his 13 appearances and then was released. Washington never batted. For what it's worth, Washington is listed as a right-handed hitter and thrower. Washington may have spelled his own doom by getting picked off during the ninth inning in Game Two of the 1974 World Series. Before Washington, Finley experimented with Allan Lewis, who totaled 23 official at-bats in an A's uniform from 1968 to 1973 yet appeared in nine World Series games and scored a combined three runs in the 1972 and 1973 fall classics. (Lewis was successful in 44 of 61 career steal attempts.) In 1975 Finley acquired Matt Alexander (a rarely used but fast utility player and pinch-hitter from the Cubs the previous two years) to replace Washington. In Alexander's three years with Oakland, the switch-hitting speedster stole 63 bases while collecting only 12 hits in 82 at-bats. In that same 1975 season Finley also brought in Don Hopkins, who stole 21 bases in 30 attempts and scored 25 times in 82 contests, a stretch that included but eight plate appearances and his only major league hit. Finley, for reasons only he could explain, thought it would be a good idea to have more than one designated pinch-runner at a time, thus occupying two spots on his roster with players who could neither hit well, field well, or pitch. In 1976 Finley thanked Hopkins for his services and welcomed Larry Lintz, who turned in an even better performance, with 31 steals in 42 attempts and 21 runs scored in 68 games, a stretch that included four plate appearances. Following the 1977 season, Alexander caught on with the Pirates, who used him in the same capacity from 1978 to 1980. Alexander, who made an appearance in the 1979 World Series, retired with 103 steals in 145 attempts, 111 runs scored, and only 36 hits.

◆ Did you know Billy Maharg, the gambler mentioned as a central figure in the Black Sox scandal, is the same man who played for Detroit as a replacement player on May 18, 1912? If you'll recall, it was on that day that Tiger players went on strike to protest AL president Ban Johnson's indefinite suspension of Ty Cobb for hitting a fan. Maharg (whose real name is Graham, spelled backward as Maharg, some historians believe) went 0-for-1 in that 1912 game for the Tigers with two flawless chances at third base. He also came to bat once for the Phillies in 1916. Maharg, a prize fighter as well, was 31 at the time of his debut and 38 during the Black Sox scandal.

202. *From the year (1967) when the Major League Baseball Players Association started keeping track of players' salaries, the minimum salary has skyrocketed from $6,000 to $300,000. The average salary for the 2002 season was $2,345,920—a far cry from 1967. The average salary then was:*

A $25,000
B $19,000
C $34,608
D $24,909

ANSWER: B

The average salary was up to $40,839 by 1974, $76,066 by 1977, $143,756 by 1980, $241,497 by 1982, $371,571 by 1985, $497,254 by 1989, and $578,930 by 1990. It rose to $1,153,343 in 1994 before falling to $1,053,793 the following year, marking its first drop since the collusion years. The average salary in 1942 was less than $6,000.

◆ Did you know the 2001 average salary of a Japanese League player was only $465,000?

203. *Although only one no-hitter has been thrown in World Series play, four pitchers have hurled one-hitters. Can you name the last pitcher to achieve this feat of a near no-no?*

ANSWER: Jim Lonborg

In Game Two of the 1967 World Series, Boston's Jim Lonborg retired the first 19 Cardinals and 23 of the first 24 before yielding a double to Julian Javier with two out in the eighth inning. Lonborg won that game, 5-0, walking only one and striking out four. He also three-hit the Cardinals in Game Five, 3-1, before losing Game Seven to Bob Gibson.

The Cubs' Ed Reulbach threw the first World Series one-hitter in Game Two of the 1906 fall classic, which the ChiSox won in six games. Reulbach allowed a single with none out in the seventh inning to Jiggs Donahue. He walked six. Claude Passeau, another Cub, allowed only a second-inning single to Rudy York in the third game of the 1945 World Series, which the Tigers won in seven games. Passeau walked just one.

Bill Bevens' one-hitter in 1947 remains the most famous in World Series history. An out away from a no-hitter, the Yankee righthander yielded a game-winning two-run double to Brooklyn's Cookie Lavagetto, which gave the Dodgers a 3-2 victory in Game Four.

Three other complete-game one-hitters have been hurled in postseason play, although they came outside the World Series. Incredibly, all three occurred in the 1999 and 2000 postseasons. Atlanta's Kevin Millwood allowed only a second-inning homer to Houston's Ken Caminiti in winning Game Two of the 1999 NL Division Series. The Mets' Bobby Jones threw a one-hitter in a 4-0 shutout of the Giants to close out the 2000 NL Division Series, allowing only a fifth-inning double to Jeff Kent. The Yankees' Roger Clemens was simply awesome in his one-hit shutout of the Seattle Mariners, winning Game Four of the 2000 AL Championship Series with the help of 15 strikeouts (a nine-inning AL Championship Series game record). The only hit off Clemens was a seventh-inning double by Al Martin that grazed the glove of first baseman Tino Martinez.

204. *The 1991 World Series was a historic masterpiece, an unforgettable event that featured five one-run contests, each of which was won in the winning team's final at-bat, and a trio of extra-inning thrillers. Its unbelievable drama made the world stop to watch and forget its economic pressures, if only for a few weeks. Those seven nail-biting and exhilarating games made baseball enthusiasts out of everyone. The 1991 fall classic ranks up there among the best ever, with the World Series of 2001, 1975, 1972, 1967, 1962, 1926, 1924, and 1912. Match these records with their World Series:*

1 The Giants and Angels combined for 21 home runs in this series, breaking the previous combined mark of 17	A 2001 World Series	
2 The last 1-0 game occurred in this series	B 1972 World Series	
3 This series featured a quartet of one-run games that included a trio of walk-off hits	C 2002 World Series	
4 Five one-run games were played in this seven-game thriller	D 1996 World Series	
5 Six one-run games were played in this seven-game thriller	E 1975 World Series	

ANSWER: 1—C, 2—D, 3—A, 4—E, 5—B

The Dodgers and Yankees were the opposing teams in all three fall classics that included 17 home runs. Both teams set the standard in 1953, tied it two Octobers later (when Duke Snider hit four homers), and combined for 17 once more in 1977 (as Reggie Jackson clobbered five). The Yankees hit nine roundtrippers in the 1953 series, and the Dodgers hit nine in the other two. The Marlins and Indians in 1997 combined for 16, 8 apiece. . . . Andy Pettitte outdueled John Smoltz as the Yankees beat the Braves, 1-0, in Game Five of the

1996 fall classic to unlock a series tie en route to a Yankee title. The previous year, Atlanta blanked Cleveland, 1-0, in Game Six to clinch its 1995 world championship. The Twins blanked the Braves, 1-0, in 10 innings in Game Seven to capture the 1991 world championship, and the Red Sox opened the 1986 classic with a 1-0 shutout in New York, which won in seven games. . . . The 2001 World Series featured a barrage of dramatic finishes that began in Game Four, when the Yankees' Tino Martinez forced extra innings with a two-run homer to straight-away center in the ninth and teammate Derek Jeter drilled a walk-off shot to right in the 10th, tying the series. In Game Five the Yankees' Scott Brosius sent the game into extra innings with a two-run homer in the bottom of the ninth, and rookie Alfonso Soriano ended the game three innings later with a walk-off single. Then in Game Seven, the Diamondbacks turned the tables on the Yankees, scoring twice in the bottom of the ninth to win the finale, 3-2, in sensational fashion. Arizona's Tony Womack tied the game with a double down the right-field line, and Luis Gonzalez blooped a single over the shortstop for a walk-off RBI to end the series. . . . The 1972 World Series was the most closely played and definitely one of the most exciting in the annals of the fall classic. Playing without the injured Reggie Jackson, the A's came out on top in the first two games, each a one-run decision at Cincinnati. Series MVP Gene Tenace homered twice, and the bullpen pitched four scoreless innings, as Ken Holtzman and the A's won the opener by a 3-2 score. Joe Rudi's third-inning homer and tremendous ninth-inning catch against the left-field wall the following day was enough to support the splendid pitching of Catfish Hunter, who won 2-1.

The series then shifted to Oakland, where Jack Billingham out-dueled Blue Moon Odom in Game Three, and Cesar Geronimo singled in the only run of the contest. In Game Four, consecutive RBI singles by pinch-hitters Don Mincher and Angel Mangual gave the A's a walk-off 3-2 victory and a three games to one series lead. In comparison to the first four games, Game Five was a high-scoring affair, won by the Reds. Bobby Tolan's RBI single in the eighth tied the game and Pete Rose's single in the ninth won it, 5-4. Back home at Riverfront Stadium, the Reds forced Game Seven by routing the A's, 8-1, in the only contest not decided by one run. Johnny Bench homered, and Geronimo and Tolan each drove in two runs. The A's regrouped for the finale, though. RBI doubles by Tenace and Sal Bando vaulted the A's to a 3-2 lead, and Rollie Fingers—in his sixth appearance—nailed down his second save as well as the franchise's first world championship in 42 years.

◆ Did you know Tino Martinez's ninth-inning home run and Derek Jeter's 10th-inning home run in Game Four of the 2001 World Series marked the first time in World Series history that a team tied a game with a ninth-inning homer and won it with a homer in extra innings?

◆ Did you know the 1905, 1906, 1907, and 1918 World Series included no home runs? Pitchers such as Christy Mathewson, Ed Walsh, Mordecai Brown, Orval Overall, Carl Mays, and Babe Ruth had a little something to do with that.

205. *Only two shortstops in history have led the major leagues in RBI two years in a row. Ernie Banks accomplished the feat in 1958 and 1959, earning the MVP award each year. The other was a Red Sox star whose 159 and 144 RBI over consecutive seasons tied for the major league lead each season, though he didn't earn a league MVP either year. Name this man.*

ANSWER: Vern Stephens

The Alex Rodriguez of his day, Stephens enjoyed those two monster RBI campaigns in 1949 and 1950. The three-time RBI champion spent 12 of his first 15 years with the Browns and the Red Sox, earning seven All-Star invitations. The right-handed slugger drove in 1,174 runs during a career played exclusively in the American League, homering 247 times and batting .286. The 1945 AL home run champion hit a career-high 39 homers in 1949, a figure that accompanied his 159 RBI, the latter total a single-season record for shortstops.

Stephens' mark of 159 RBI is one of the few offensive records for shortstops that Rodriguez has not broken. The Rangers' 27-year-old superstar has rewritten much of the shortstop record-book and has set his eyes on even loftier marks that he appears destined to surpass. He carries into the 2003 season a loaded ledger that already features 298 home runs, 872 RBI, 1,354 hits, 885 runs, 160 stolen bases, a .309 batting average, and a .959 OPS (on-base plus slugging percentage). His 52 home runs in 2001 broke Banks' record for shortstops, and his

57 home runs in 2002 set the bar even higher, also making him one of just five sluggers with consecutive 50-homer campaigns. (Have I mentioned that he's just 27?) A-Rod has only picked up momentum since making a big splash with a spectacular 1996 season for the Mariners. Even in that year, his first full season, Alexander Emmanuel Rodriguez showed signs of greatness. In addition to hitting 36 homers and driving in 123 runs, Rodriguez set shortstop single-season standards with 215 hits, 141 runs, 54 doubles, a .631 slugged percentage, 91 extra-base hits, and a position record–tying 379 total bases. Rodriguez also led the majors with a .358 batting average, the highest figure ever by a player under the age of 22. Rodriguez became the first AL shortstop to win a batting title since Lou Boudreau 52 years earlier, and the first major league shortstop since Dick Groat in 1960. The only other shortstops to win the batting title are Jack Glasscock (1890), Honus Wagner (seven times; 1903–04, 1906–09, 1911), Luke Appling of the White Sox (1936, 1943), Cleveland's Lou Boudreau (1944), Pittsburgh's Arky Vaughan (1935), and Boston's Nomar Garciaparra (1999 and 2000).

◆ Did you know Cecil Fielder's major league–leading 124 RBI in 1992 made him the second player in history, along with Babe Ruth, to lead the majors in RBI for three straight years? Ruth's three years came from 1919 to 1921. Ty Cobb led the American League in RBI from 1907 to 1909. Joe Medwick led the National League in RBI from 1936 to 1938. And George Foster led the National League in RBI from 1976 to 1978.

206. *Match these defensive wizards with their wizardry:*

1	Mike Bordick	A	handled 261 consecutive errorless chances, a record at his position
2	Ryne Sandberg	B	owns the major league record of 110 consecutive errorless games and 543 consecutive errorless chances
3	Don Money	C	played in 193 consecutive errorless games, a record at his position
4	Steve Garvey	D	played in 123 consecutive errorless games, a record at his position

ANSWER: 1—B (SS); 2—D (2B); 3—A (3B); 4—C (1B)

Shortstop Mike Bordick of the Orioles carries his streak into the 2003 season, after surpassing Rey Ordonez's mark of 101 straight games without an error. Ordonez broke Cal Ripken's streak of 95 in 1999. Omar Vizquel in 2000 matched Ripken's AL mark of 95 straight games without an error, almost matching Ripken's mark of 431 straight chances without an error as well, with 428. Ripken, whose errorless-game streak lasted from April 14 to July 27, 1990, broke Kevin Elster's shortstop record of 88 consecutive error-free games. In the first week of April of 1996, Ripken had another string, this one of 74 straight errorless games, snapped. . . . Sandberg in April 1990 surpassed Hall of Famer Joe Morgan's record errorless game streak of 91. Sandberg's streak lasted from June 21, 1989, to May 17, 1990. . . . Garvey's streak lasted from June 26, 1983, to April 14, 1985.

◆ Did you know that when Ryne Sandberg smacked 40 home runs in 1990 (two off the second baseman record), he became the first player ever to hit 40 home runs in one season and steal 50 bases in another (54 in 1985) during his career? Sandberg retired following the 1997 season with 282 homers, hitting a record 277 while playing second base to eclipse the previous mark of 266 set by Joe Morgan. Rogers Hornsby hit 264 while playing second.

Perhaps no game better reflected Sandberg's clutch power abilities than his dramatic performance on June 23, 1984. With his Cubs trailing, 9-8, in the bottom of the ninth inning, Sandberg belted a pitch from great St. Louis closer Bruce Sutter for a game-tying homer that forced extra innings. After the Cardinals scored twice in the top of the 10th, Sandberg again hammered Sutter, this time with two out, for a game-tying two-run shot that extended the thrilling game yet again. The Cubs won the contest in the 11th, thanks to the spectacular offensive display by Sandberg, who went 5-for-6 with seven RBI. Sandberg also fielded nine chances at second base without an error.

207. *Match these sure-handed second basemen with their accomplishments:*

1	Ryne Sandberg	A	broke Bobby Grich's record for best single-season fielding percentage
2	Bret Boone	B	this eight-time Gold-Glover participated in a record 161 double plays one year
3	Eddie Collins	C	led the league in fielding a record nine times and totaled an all-time record of 14,156 career chances

4 Bill Mazeroski	D won a position record 10 Gold Gloves and owns the best career AL fielding percentage, .987
5 Roberto Alomar	E set a major league record by a second baseman with 582 consecutive errorless chances

ANSWER: 1—E, 2—A, 3—C, 4—B, 5—D

Sandberg's defensive artistry at second enabled the Cub to surpass Tom Herr (.9890) as the all-time leading fielder with a .9894 percentage. The winner of nine Gold Gloves, Sandberg broke Manny Trillo's record of 479 consecutive errorless chances. . . . In 1997 Boone sported a magnificent fielding percentage of .99670510 (two errors in 607 total chances), the slightest bit better than the .9966996 mark set by Grich in 1985, when he committed two errors in just one fewer chance for the California Angels. Boone, who in 1998 came within .005 of leading NL second basemen in fielding for an unprecedented fourth straight year, enters the 2003 season with a career fielding percentage of .9864 (87 errors in 6,397 total chances at second). As neither Boone nor Grich played 150 games in their stellar seasons, I'd be remiss if I didn't mention that Jose Oquendo holds the single-season record among those who played 150 games. In 1990 the versatile Oquendo played exactly 150 games at second for the Cardinals, fielding at an unequaled .996 clip. . . . Collins was an outstanding defensive player, always alert. In addition to his record total of fielding titles and total chances, he holds position record totals for games (2,651), putouts (6,526), and assists (7,630). . . . Alomar would be contending for Sandberg's career fielding mark were it not for his early, error-prone days with the San Diego Padres. . . . Mazeroski fielded at a .992 clip during that great 1966 season. He was arguably the greatest fielder of all time. Mazeroski, who perfected the pivot on the double play, still holds the major league career record for double plays turned by a second baseman with 1,706—a number even more astounding when you consider that only three *first* basemen had participated in more twin killings when he retired. Besides leading second basemen in chances an NL record eight times, "Maz" also led second basemen in assists nine times and double plays eight times— the latter two marks being major league records. Mazeroski turned the pivot so quickly he earned the nickname "No Touch," for a release so rapid it seemed he never touched the ball. Broadcaster Joe Garagiola once said of Mazeroski, "Instant replay was no match for the blinding speed of a Mazeroski 6-4-3." All that is even more incredible given that Mazeroski played in Forbes Field, considered to have the worst infield dirt of any era. The field was built over a layer of bedrock, covered by clay soil and sod. No wonder nary a no-hitter was thrown there in its 61 years as the home of the Pirates.

◆ Did you know second baseman Eddie Collins was a member of the famous $100,000 infield of the Philadelphia Athletics, along with Hall of Fame third baseman Frank Baker, first baseman Stuffy McInnis, and shortstop Jack Barry? The quartet played together from 1911 through 1914, a period that included three pennants and two world championships for the Athletics. Thanks to their infield stability, Philadelphia led the league in fielding in each of the four seasons. The quartet combined for 47 hits, a .336 average, and 22 RBI in its two victorious World Series but just 10 hits, a .172 average, and 3 RBI in its 1914 series loss to the Boston Braves. McInnis took over for the aging Harry Davis in 1911.

208. *Match these outfielders with their defensive résumés:*

1	Tris Speaker	A	played a record 2,943 games in the outfield
2	Ty Cobb	B	handled over 520 chances in a season four times, a mark no one else has achieved more than once
3	Richie Ashburn	C	is the last outfielder to throw out three runners at the plate in a single game
4	Jack McCarthy	D	accepted 566 chances in a season, a record that still stands
5	Taylor Douthit	E	accepted 7,459 chances over his career, a record that still stands

ANSWER: 1—E, 2—A, 3—B, 4—C, 5—D

Of the 10 highest single-season putout totals by an outfielder, Ashburn owns six, including 538 in 1951. . . . Despite his heroics on April 26 of the 1905 season, the 36-year-old McCarthy was replaced in the outfield by Frank "Wildfire" Schulte, who hit 93 home runs and 124 triples during the Dead Ball Era. . . . Douthit led the National League in putouts three times and three times batted over .300.

Anaheim's Darin Erstad on July 24, 2000, tied a major league mark for outfielders with 12 putouts in a game, doing so in a 12-inning victory over the Rangers. Erstad was the 14th outfielder but only the 3rd left fielder to record that many putouts in a game, joining Tom McBride and Rickey Henderson. Rolando Roomes remains the only right fielder to total 12 putouts in a game, in a 17-inning contest for the Reds in 1989. Among the 10 center fielders who achieved this feat were Gold Glovers Garry Maddox, Gary Pettis, and Rick Manning. Center fielders Lyman Bostock and Earl Clark were the only outfielders to gather their dozen putouts in a nine-inning game.

◆ Did you know Darryl Hamilton knocked off Terry Puhl as the owner of the highest career fielding percentage among outfielders with at least 1,000 games played? Hamilton retired with a fielding percentage of .9949 (14 errors in 2,777 total chances). Puhl's mark is .9932.

209. *Match these outstanding shortstops with their Gold Glove–worthy feats:*

1	Ozzie Smith	A	won 13 consecutive Gold Gloves
2	Cal Ripken	B	led the league in double plays a record eight times
3	Omar Vizquel	C	owns the best career fielding percentage with a mark of .9835
4	Luis Aparicio	D	won eight Gold Gloves
5	Mark Belanger	E	won nine Gold Gloves

ANSWER: 1—A, 2—B, 3—C, 4—E, 5—D

Vizquel, who has won nine of the last ten AL Gold Gloves, is the leading fielding shortstop (142 errors in 8,631 total chances) of all time among those with 1,000 games played. Larry Bowa (.97968) is second, and Tony Fernandez is third, with a mark of .97956. . . . Ripken's string of defensive wizardry moved him ahead of Alan Trammell and former Orioles shortstop Mark Belanger for the second best career fielding percentage in the American League and into fourth on the all-time list with a .97930 mark. And to think that Orioles manager Earl Weaver was doubted when he decided in 1982 to convert Ripken from a third baseman to a shortstop. Ripken, who retired following the 2001 season, did not play at short over his last four years.

Lost in this tight race is new Hall of Famer Ozzie Smith (fifth), who has a .97868 fielding percentage. However, hardly a soul will argue against Ozzie's status as the best defensive shortstop of all time, considering his unbelievable range and acrobatics. "The Wizard" also holds the major league record for most career assists (8,375) and double plays (1,590) at short. By the way, Osborne Earl Smith also collected 2,460 hits and 580 stolen bases.

◆ Did you know that two of the four players who played all nine positions in a game were or are shortstops? Bert Campaneris, a shortstop for the Kansas City Athletics, was the first to do so in 1965. Cesar Tovar, an outfielder with a lot of infield experience (shortstop included), duplicated the feat three years later for the Twins. In 2000 Rangers shortstop Scott Sheldon and Tigers third baseman Shane Halter doubled the membership to four. No National Leaguer has ever accomplished the feat.

◆ Did you know Rafael Ramirez and Dick Groat led their league in errors six times, sharing the dubious record for shortstops?

◆ Did you know Lou Stringer's four errors on April 15, 1941, remain the most by a shortstop in his major league debut? Stringer was immediately shifted to second base, playing just eight more games throughout his 338-game career at short.

210. *Match these hot-corner guardians with their feats:*

1	Brooks Robinson	A	holds the third baseman single-season record of 412 assists
2	Jeff Cirillo	B	led the league in assists for seven straight seasons
3	Graig Nettles	C	played in a record 99 consecutive errorless games
4	Don Money	D	holds the single-season record of a .989 fielding percentage, among those with 150 games played
5	Ron Santo	E	led the league in assists a record eight times and owns the best career fielding percentage of .971
6	Pie Traynor	F	shares the NL record with seven putout titles

ANSWER: 1—E, 2—C, 3—A, 4—D, 5—B, 6—F

Although Robinson's .971 mark is the best ever, Ken Reitz's NL record .970 mark is not far behind. Robinson, whose quick reflexes, great range, and strong arm enabled him to turn in spectacular defensive play, also owns the records for highest career totals of assists, double plays, and putouts. . . . Cirillo's streak, which bridged the 2001 and 2002 seasons, tied that of John Wehner, which, remarkably, lasted from August 2, 1992, through September 29, 2000. . . . Nettles' defensive prowess wasn't limited to his record-setting 1971 season. Seven years later, Nettles displayed his ability in front of a national audience, as he made four spectacular stops in Game Three of the 1978 World Series. He saved at least six runs in the 5-1 victory. . . . Santo's NL mark of seven assist titles was tied by 10-time Gold Glove winner Mike Schmidt. Only Robinson, with eight, had more. From 1965 to 1969 Santo anchored one of the best infields of all time, playing the hot corner while Don Kessinger played short, Glenn Beckert played second, and Ernie Banks guarded first base. But the Cubs couldn't capitalize, finishing eighth in 1965, last in 1966, and third in each of the next two seasons before their late-season collapse in 1969. Kessinger turned into an outstanding fielder, earning five All-Star invitations based on his performance with the glove. The solid-hitting Beckert, although always overshadowed by Bill Mazeroski, was a fine fielder in his own right, finally winning a Gold Glove in 1971. After an inconsistent tenure at shortstop, Banks led all first basemen in assists five times, also winning a fielding title there. . . . Traynor, Santo, and Willie Jones each led his league in putouts seven times. Jones, a defensive specialist for the Phillies from the late 1940s to the late 1950s, retired with a .963 fielding percentage and a range factor (total chances per nine innings) of 3.09—both marks impressive for that era.

◆ Did you know that Heinie Groh still holds the NL single-season fielding percentage mark (of .983 in 1924) for third basemen with at least 100 games played? This vastly overlooked player was considered a winner by many contemporaries, because of his well-rounded talent. He retired in 1927 with a then-record .967 career fielding percentage. Remarkably, his percentage remains among the top 10 on the third basemen's all-time list despite the advancement of gloves and infields. Groh remains the only player in the top 10 in career fielding percentage to have played in the 1910s. This career .292 hitter (1,774 hits) was on the world champion Reds of 1919, the champion Giants of 1922, the pennant-winning Giants of 1923 and 1924, and the pennant-winning Pirates of 1927. Henry Knight Groh helped make defense an art, but he has not been fully appreciated by the Hall of Fame Committees (neither the BBWAA or Special Veterans Committee granted him more than five votes).

◆ Did you know infielders and outfielders must play 108 games at their position to win a fielding title, but catchers are "only" required to catch 81 games to be eligible? A pitcher must pitch 162 innings to be eligible (unless he fields more chances than the leader).

211. *Match these first basemen with their defensive histories:*

1	Keith Hernandez	A	recorded an amazing 1,700 consecutive errorless chances
2	Eddie Murray	B	led his league in fielding percentage a record nine times
3	Bill Buckner	C	recorded a single-season high of 184 assists
4	Stuffy McInnis	D	once posted a .999 fielding percentage and still owns the record of 2,413 games played at first base
5	Hal Chase	E	never led the league in fielding, although he is considered to have been well ahead of his time
6	Charlie Grimm	F	led his league in double plays a record six times

ANSWER: 1—F, 2—D, 3—C, 4—A, 5—E, 6—B

Buckner's 184 assists came in 1985—the year before. Despite weak knees and ankles, Buckner set a still-standing, single-season assist record for first basemen in 1985. Yet those knees finally let him down in 1986, when he allowed Mookie Wilson's grounder to scoot between his legs. . . . Murray is the all-time first base leader with 1,865 assists, having passed Jake Beckley for the most games at first with the first game he played in 1994. Hernandez is second in career assists with 1,682. . . . McInnis' record errorless streak is even more exceptional considering that he set it from May 31, 1921, through June 2,

1922, an era when first basemen wore gloves that resembled round oven mitts. McInnis' fielding percentage of .99939 in 1921 still stands—after eight decades—as the AL standard. A converted short-stop, McInnis registered a .993 career fielding percentage at first base. . . . Steve Garvey is the all-time leading fielder (.995940) at first base. Don Mattingly is second with a figure of .995821, and Wes Parker is third at .995664. Not far off are the active J. T. Snow, San Francisco's smooth left-handed fielder, who has made but 50 errors over 11 seasons for an average of .995540, and Baltimore's David Segui, who entered the 2001 season as the all-time leader before slipping to .994979. Of this group, Mattingly won 9 Gold Gloves, 2 more than George Scott for the AL career lead, and 2 shy of Hernandez's record total of 11.

◆ Did you know that five first basemen share the record of 22 putouts in a game, last achieved by Seattle's Alvin Davis on May 28, 1988? Don Mattingly did it in 1987, Ernie Banks in 1963, Hal Chase in 1906, and Thomas Jones of the St. Louis Browns in 1906.

212. *Match these catchers with their defensive achievements:*

1	Pat Moran	A	led his league in fielding a record eight times, in addition to turning a career record 226 double plays
2	Buddy Rosar	B	has the all-time high of 1,221 accepted chances in a season
3	Bill Freehan	C	his .993 career fielding average is tops
4	Ray Schalk	D	his 1,859 assists is the highest career total
5	Johnny Edwards	E	his 214 assists is the single-season high
6	Deacon McGuire	F	shares the highest single-season fielding average of 1.000

ANSWER: 1—E, 2—F, 3—C, 4—A, 5—B, 6—D

In 1997 the Florida Marlins' Charles Johnson had perhaps the best defensive season by a catcher in the game's history. Johnson matched Rosar's perfect season and then some, catching a record 123 games without committing an error in 1997 (Rosar caught 117 games for the Athletics in 1946). In addition, Johnson allowed just one passed ball (on September 19) and did not commit a single catcher's interference all year. Johnson set two other major league records, going 1,295 consecutive chances accepted without an error and catching 172 consecutive games without an error (both streaks came to an end as a result of an error on his second chance during the 1998 season opener). . . . Schalk, a diminutive workhorse behind the plate, caught at least 100 games in 11 straight seasons and a dozen overall. . . . Johnny Edwards owes his aforementioned record to his battery-mates on the Astros pitching staff during the 1969 campaign. The Houston staff set a single-season record of 1,221 strikeouts (later surpassed by two staffs in 1996), led by Don Wilson's 235, Larry Dierker's 232, and Tom Griffin's 200. In 1996 the Braves' pitching staff struck out 1,245 batters and the Dodgers' staff struck out 1,212. The 2001 Cubs' staff surpassed the Braves' standard with 1,344 strikeouts. Led by Kerry Wood, the Cubs' staff boasted six pitchers who whiffed at least 100 batters. The other five hurlers were Jason Bere (175), Kevin Tapani (149), Jon Lieber (148), Julian Tavarez (107), and middle reliever Kyle Farnsworth (107). . . . Elston Howard and Jim Sundberg were less than .0008 behind Freehan for best career fielding average. . . . Oscar Stanage's 212 assists in 1911 for the Tigers is the AL record. The poor-hitting yet excellent-fielding receiver helped the Tigers to the 1909 AL pennant and spent 13 of his 14 seasons in a Tiger uniform.

◆ Did you know Hall of Famer Ray Schalk is believed to be the first catcher to back up plays at first and third base? In fact, Schalk is the only catcher to record a putout at every base.

213. *Gabby Hartnett (1,793 games caught and 163 double plays) and Del Crandall (a very solid catcher for the Braves) share the National League record of six assist titles. Which receiver holds the American League honor, also with six?*

A Thurman Munson
B Yogi Berra
C Jim Sundberg
D Ray Schalk

ANSWER: C

Sundberg also caught 1,927 games, won six Gold Gloves, and owns the sixth best putout total of all time with 9,767. Sundberg caught at least 132 games in each of his first seven seasons (1974–80). . . . The rifle-armed Hartnett, whom Hall of Fame manager Joe Mc-Carthy once described as "the perfect catcher, a manager's dream," also led the National League in fielding percentage six times. This string marked a tremendous improvement for a man who led all league catchers in errors during three of his first four seasons. Hartnett, whose alertness and intelligence behind the plate were often lauded by his pitchers, was reliable as well, catching at least 100 games a dozen times. . . . Crandall, a career .254 hitter who never batted .300 or hit more than 26 homers in a season, was selected to eight All-Star Games. That should reveal how good he was behind the plate. He led all NL catchers in fielding four times and earned four Gold Gloves, an award that was born halfway through Crandall's career.

◆ Did you know Johnny Kling, the great defensive catcher for the powerful Cubs teams of the early 1900s, briefly retired after winning the world pocket billiards championship following the 1908 season? Kling returned to the diamond in 1910 after losing his title. The career .272 career was as good as they come defensively, adept at throwing out baserunners and calling games and often leading the National League in various defensive categories. Kling helped the Cubs to four pennants from 1906 to 1910, playing a big role as Chicago defeated Detroit in the 1907 and 1908 World Series.

◆ Did you know pitcher John Burkett has bowled 10 perfect games? The righthander, who enters the 2003 season with a 154-127 career mark, is an avid bowler and seeks to become a professional in that sport as well. Burkett won a league-best 22 games for the 1993 Giants and became an All-Star for the second time in his career in 2001 for the Braves.

214. *Match these players with their feats:*

1	Carlton Fisk	A	recorded 7,095 overall putouts, a record for a non-catcher
2	Ryne Sandberg	B	is the only player to lead the league in batting during three different decades
3	Willie Mays	C	was the all-time leader with 2,225 games caught until 1993
4	George Brett	D	is the AL career leader with 12,417 chances accepted and 11,369 putouts as a catcher

5 Bob Boone   E is the only player to win a Gold Glove in
                            his first year at a new position

ANSWER: 1—D, 2—E, 3—A, 4—B, 5—C

Brett won the batting title in 1976, 1980, and 1990. . . . Seven-time Gold Glove winner Bob Boone was the first to break Al Lopez's mark of 1,918 games caught. In his last game, Fisk passed Boone with 2,226 games caught. Gary Carter caught 2,056 games. Carter is the all-time leader with 13,109 chances accepted and 11,785 putouts behind the plate.

◆ Did you know that when Bret Boone won the Gold Glove in 1998, he and his father Bob Boone became the second father-son duo to win Gold Glove awards? Barry Bonds, who has won eight Gold Gloves, and his father Bobby were the first father-son team to each garner the award. Barry stands as one of the best defensive left fielders of all time.

215. *When Roger Clemens struck out 20 Seattle Mariners for the major league, nine-inning record on April 29, 1986, he helped catcher Rich Gedman tie a major league mark of 20 putouts. Whose record did Gedman tie for the most putouts in a game by a catcher? (Hint: he caught a 19-K game.)*

A Jerry Grote
B Tim McCarver
C Ellie Rodriguez
D Jeff Torborg
E Frankie Pytlak

ANSWER: A

Grote caught Tom Seaver's 19-strikeout game on April 22, 1970, against the Padres. He also caught a pop foul during that game. Dan Wilson (who caught Randy Johnson) and Sandy Martinez (who caught Kerry Wood) have since tied the record. Clemens tied his own record with another 20-strikeout performance 10 years later, on September 18, 1996, in Detroit (a mark since tied by the Cubs' Kerry Wood in 1998 and the Diamondbacks' Randy Johnson in 2001). Remarkably, the 34-year-old walked no one, just as he had on April 29, 1986. In throwing a four-hit shutout in his 1996 masterpiece,

Clemens also tied Cy Young's career Red Sox records of 192 wins and 38 shutouts. Clemens never did surpass those lofty club standards, as he signed a free-agent contract with Toronto after the season.

Clemens, who struck out the side three times in each gem, is so motivated by the strikeout, or "K," that he named his four sons Koby, Kory, Kacy, and Kody. In 1998 Clemens whiffed 18 batters in a 3-0 shutout for Toronto against Kansas City, making him the first pitcher with a trio of nine-inning performances featuring at least 18 strike-outs. In that year, he won his second straight Cy Young Award for the Blue Jays and the fifth in his career, surpassing the four garnered by Steve Carlton and Greg Maddux for a new standard. The Red Sox benefited from Clemens' first three Cy Young Awards, in 1986, 1987, and 1991. Clemens' sixth Cy Young Award in 2001, for the Yankees, extended his own record, also making him the first player to win a Baseball Writers Association of America award for three teams (the BBWAA decides the MVP, the CY Young Award, the Rookie of the Year Award, the Manager of the Year, and the Babe Ruth Award). In 2002 Randy Johnson surpassed Maddux and Carlton with his fifth Cy Young Award.

◆ Did you know that Nolan Ryan had three extra-inning 19-strikeout performances, in addition to his nine-inning gem, giving him a total of four? "The Express" struck out 19 on June 4 of the 1974 season versus Boston in a 12-inning game, then versus Detroit on August 20, 1974, in 11 innings, and then in a 10-inning affair on June 8, 1977, against the expansion Toronto Blue Jays.

216. *In 1930 Baseball in Japan was beginning to challenge Sumo (wrestling) as Japan's favorite sport. Back then, baseball in Japan was known as:*

A Hike and Yoshu
B Yakyu or Beisu Boru
C Beibu Rusu
D Tetsu Wan

ANSWER: B

Yakyu or *Beisu Boru* both translate as *baseball*. . . . *Hike* and *Yoshu* mean *out* and *safe*, respectively. . . . *Beibu Rusu* is the Japanese name for Babe Ruth. . . . *Tetsu Wan* means *Iron Arm*, a moniker given to Kazuhisa Inao, who was a 276-game winner with a career 1.98 ERA and 2,574 strikeouts. Inao was among the very best pitchers Japan ever had, and would have achieved an even higher level of greatness had it not been for the chronic overwork his throwing arm endured. Inao, who once won a record 20 straight games, pitched six times in the 1958 Japan Series versus the Giants, winning the last four games of the seven-game series for his champion Nishitetsu Lions.

217. *Talk about a Tetsu Wan: This Nankai Hawk submarine-style pitcher had arguably the best season by a Japanese hurler. In only his second season in 1959, this unbelievable iron man pitched 371 innings, won 38 of his 42 decisions, struck out 336 batters, and walked only 46 as he posted a minuscule 1.40 ERA. Then, in a tremendous test of courage, he single-handedly beat the Giants in the Japan Series. Who was this masked man?*

ANSWER: Tadashi Sugiura

Tadashi Sugiura not only pitched all four games but won all four games in the 1959 Japan Series over the mighty Giants. That alone was amazing. But considering the workload he took on over the last two months of the regular season, it was quite simply superhuman. While pitching in half his team's games over the last two months, Sugiura won 17 of his final 18 decisions.

From August 1 on, this college teammate of Shigeo Nagashima's pitched 54 straight shutout innings, struck out 95, and walked only four, posting a microscopic ERA of 0.10. It wasn't until his final win that his Hawks clinched the pennant. But Sugiura's work was only beginning, as he then started Game One, despite a bruised elbow, and pitched five innings of relief in Game Two.

After a day off, Sugiura started Game Three and won again, but not before his teammates witnessed his determination. He popped a blister on his middle finger but kept pitching despite the pain, delivering bloody balls to his catcher, according to historian Gary Garland. In the ninth inning he felt as if his arm was about to fall off, with a 2-2 score and runners on second and third with one out, but manager Kazuto Tsuruoka failed to see Sugiura's fatigue and desperate look and, in lieu of taking him out, sent him a good luck charm. Sugiura won the game, 3-2, in 10 innings. He then started Game Four and pitched a shutout! The clincher marked the Hawks' first series win over the Giants, and Sugiura was rewarded with the league's MVP award and a new car (license number 38-4) by his fans. However, because of the brutal overwork his arm suffered, his best days were behind him. Japanese managers believed in a "the future is now" philosophy. It wasn't until the late 1970s that the Japanese adopted the major league's philosophy toward handling pitchers.

218. *Match these players with their Japanese history:*

1	Lefty O'Doul	A	a pitcher who was the victim of overwork
2	Hiroshi Oshita	B	began calling the Yomiuri Giants the "Tokyo" Giants
3	Futoshi Nakanishi	C	an injury cut short his career of 244 homers and a .307 career batting average
4	Hiroshi Gondo	D	won three batting titles and three home run titles and helped inspire a nation that was depressed in the years following World War II

ANSWER: 1—B, 2—D, 3—C, 4—A

After seasons of 35 and 30 wins, Gondo simmered down to 10, 6, and 1 win campaigns. Same story; Gondo was a victim of another manager's win-now philosophy. . . . Nakanishi won five home run titles over a six-year span from 1953 to 1958. . . . Oshita and Nakanishi led the Lions to three Japan Series titles.

219. *Match these major league strikeout kings with their artistry:*

1	Roger Clemens	A	is the only pitcher in the top 10 in strikeouts who played before 1959 (before expansion)
2	Walter Johnson	B	never led the league in strikeouts
3	Jerry Koosman	C	never struck out more than 74 batters in a season during his 21-year career
4	Gaylord Perry	D	his 3,909 strikeouts are third on the all-time list
5	Ted Lyons	E	his 2,556 career Ks rank him 23rd on the all-time list and 7th among lefthanders

ANSWER: 1—D, 2—A, 3—E, 4—B, 5—C

William Roger Clemens, relying on a great fastball, hard-breaking curveball, and troublesome forkball, has surpassed the career strikeout totals of Bert Blyleven, Tom Seaver, Don Sutton, Perry, Johnson, Phil Niekro, Ferguson Jenkins, Bob Gibson, Jim Bunning, Mickey Lolich, Cy Young, Frank Tanana, Warren Spahn, Bob Feller, Tim Keefe, Koosman, and Christy Mathewson over the last seven years. The six-time Cy Young Award winner surpassed Johnson in 2001 to become the American League's all-time strikeout leader.

Another hard-thrower quickly climbing the strikeout chart is Arizona's Randy Johnson, who enters the 2003 season with 3,746 Ks, fourth all time.

◆ Did you know that J. R. Richard tied the major league record of 15 strikeouts in a major league debut on September 5, 1971? The flame-throwing righthander tied Karl Spooner's old mark, set on September 22, 1954. The Brooklyn lefthander also struck out 12 in his second start—four days later—for a total of 27 in his first two starts. Milwaukee's Steve Woodard tied the American League record of 12 strikeouts in his debut on July 28, 1997, matching the total last set by Elmer Myers of the 1915 Philadelphia Athletics.

◆ Did you know Nolan Ryan struck out 2,465 batters after his 35th birthday? Ryan's post-35 strikeout total exceeds the career total of all but 25 pitching artists!

220. *Can you name the only major league player to hit the* ABE STARK *sign in Ebbets Field during a major league game?*

ANSWER: Carl Furillo

Aware of the outstanding defensive ability of Carl Furillo, who played in front of the sign in right field, clothier Abe Stark offered a free suit to any batter that struck the ABE STARK sign, which stood only five feet off the ground, right below the 40-foot scoreboard, on a line during the game. The sign stated, "Hit Sign, Win Suit." Ironically, Furillo himself was the player who finally hit the sign, cheered by the famous Dodger Sym-Phony Band.

Fellow Dodger pitcher Rex Barney offers a different account, claiming that the Phillies' Ron Northey hit a pitch off him directly at Furillo, but that Furillo somehow slipped, allowing the ball to hit the sign. According to Barney, Furillo later told him he allowed the ball to hit the sign on purpose to see if Northey would be given a suit. He was, according to Barney.

The scoreboard also had a great feature. The Schaefer Beer sign illuminated the "h" or the "e" to report the scorer's decision for a hit or error.

◆ Did you know Brooklyn's Carl Furillo remains the only player to hit a pinch-hit home run in the first inning? Following an early pitching change in a game against Philadelphia on May 24, 1947, Furillo was inserted with two on and two out in place of Gene Hermanski. He responded with a three-run homer.

221. *Match these major league teams with their unique achievements:*

1	1930 Cardinals	A	won the pennant without a single player who hit .300, drove in 100 runs, slugged 30 homers, or won 20 games
2	1907 Cubs	B	their pitching staff recorded a major league single-season low ERA of 1.73
3	1973 Mets	C	their .349 batting average is the all-time best
4	1894 Phillies	D	had all eight regulars hit over .300

ANSWER: 1—D, 2—B, 3—A, 4—C

The 1930 NL pennant–winning Cardinals were the only 20th-century squad to feature .300 hitters at all eight positions. First baseman Jim Bottomley hit .304, second baseman Frankie Frisch hit .346, shortstop Charley Gelbert hit .304, third baseman Sparky Adams hit .314, left fielder Chick Hafey hit .336, right fielder Gene Watkins led the club with a .373 mark, and catcher Jimmie Wilson hit .318. As a team, the Cardinals batted .314. The only other club to have all eight regulars hit .300 was the .349-hitting Phillies squad of 1894. Among their regulars were right fielder Sam Thompson (.404), left fielder Ed Delahanty (.400), and center fielder Billy Hamilton (.399), all Hall of Famers. The trio achieved history by collectively batting .401 and just missed becoming the only outfield to feature three .400 hitters. They are also one of three Hall of Fame outfields. The others are Detroit's outfield of Ty Cobb, Sam Crawford, and Harry Heilmann and the Senators' trio of Goose Goslin, Heinie Manush, and Sam Rice. . . . The Mets' top hitter in 1973 was Felix Millan (.290). Rusty Staub's 76 RBI, John Milner's 23 home runs, and Tom Seaver's 19 wins also led this ordinary team. As a matter of fact, almost everything about the 1973 Mets was ordinary. The team won a mere 82 games, scored 608 runs (the second fewest, and just 20 more than they allowed), hit 85 home runs (the second fewest), batted .246 (the second lowest average), slugged a league-low .338, stole a mere 27 bases (the second lowest), were the fourth-best fielding team (.980), and posted the third best ERA (3.27).

◆ Did you know the 82-79 record posted by the 1973 New York Mets is the worst over a full season by a pennant or division champion? In fact, those Mets spent just 20 days in first place.

222. *Match these solid hurlers with their histories:*

1	Mike Torrez	A	won the 1948 American League playoff game
2	Bill Fischer	B	his 18 wins in 1987 were the fewest by an NL leader (excluding the strike-shortened 1981 and 1994 campaigns)
3	Gene Bearden	C	won Game Three and Six of the 1977 World Series
4	Rick Sutcliffe	D	holds the major league record of 84⅓ consecutive innings without issuing a walk

ANSWER: 1—C, 2—D, 3—A, 4—B

Fischer in 1962 broke Christy Mathewson's mark of 68 consecutive frames without a walk. The efficient Randy Jones in 1976 tied Mathewson for the NL standard, but in 2001 the equally quick-working Greg Maddux set the senior circuit record with a streak of 72⅓ innings. Twelve innings shy of Fischer's major league mark, Maddux ended the streak with an intentional walk—valuing his team's priorities over his own. . . . Bearden capped off a tremendous rookie season in 1948 with his 20th victory in the playoff game against the Red Sox. The Indians southpaw knuckleballer, who also won the ERA title that season, threw a five-hit shutout in Game Three of the ensuing World Series versus the Braves and saved the finale without yielding a run. Bearden, who played five more seasons in the majors, never even came close to duplicating his rookie-season feats.

◆ Did you know it was Bill Fischer who yielded Mickey Mantle's prodigious home run in Yankee Stadium on May 22, 1963? Mantle tagged the right-handed Kansas City Athletic for what would have been the longest travelling ball in history, had the ball not hit the upper part of the upper deck facade. Amazingly, the ball was still rising when it hit the facade, and some speculate that it would have cleared the facade had it been three feet shorter. Had it done so, the ball would have traveled at least 630 feet, mathematicians have estimated.

223. *Can you name the only two owners to have their numbers retired?*

ANSWER: Gene Autry and August A. Busch Jr.

Gene Autry (#26), known as "America's Favorite Cowboy," walked away as owner of the brand new Los Angeles Angels in December of 1960 after attending the AL expansion meeting in St. Louis seeking radio rights to his Golden West Broadcasting firm. As owner, he distinguished himself by not interfering with the plans of his general managers, although he was tremendously involved in the team's publicity. Autry became one of Hollywood's first tycoons after selling over 20 million records. Autry, who was awarded the first gold record ever, died in 1998. The Angels won their first world championship four years later, with his widow, Jackie, there to hold the World Series trophy.

The late August A. Busch Jr. (#85), president of Anheuser-Busch, bought the unstable Cardinals franchise in 1953 when owner Fred Saigh was forced to sell after being sentenced to a federal prison for income tax evasion, and kept the club in St. Louis. A master showman and a great marketer who turned a small business into the world's largest brewing company, Busch Jr. is also remembered for riding into Busch Stadium on the Clydesdale wagon. He bought Sportsman's Park in 1953 from Bill Veeck for $800,000 and renamed it Busch Stadium. In 1966 he opened up the current Busch Stadium and destroyed the old one. Busch Jr. passed away in 1989, and the Busches sold the major league franchise after the 1995 season to concentrate on their brewery.

◆ Did you know Fred Saigh, who owned the Cardinals for five years, chose to sell to Anheuser-Busch so that the team would remain in St. Louis, rather than selling for a lot more money to a group that intended to move it to another city? In February 1953, Saigh was sentenced to 15 months in prison and fined $15,000 for owing $19,099 in back taxes.

224. *On July 20, 1916, the Giants traded three Hall of Famers to the Reds for Buck Herzog and Red Killefer. Can you name the three inductees?*

ANSWER: Christy Mathewson, Edd Roush, and Bill McKechnie

Mathewson retired after the season, Roush turned out to be a Giant mistake who greatly benefited the Reds with 10 straight .300 campaigns, and McKechnie later became a great manager. Interestingly, the Giants won the pennant in 1917 without much help from Herzog (.235) or Killefer (waived).

Roush, a solid center fielder, was an integral member of that overlooked Reds world championship squad in 1919. With a 96-44 ledger, the Reds that year won eight more regular-season games than their more publicized and infamous World Series opponents. Roush, who won his second batting title, and Heinie Groh combined to carry Cincinnati's offense. Both of them finished in the top five in batting, on-base percentage, slugging, runs, and RBI. Pitchers Slim Sallee (21 wins), Dutch Ruether, and Hod Eller each placed in the top ten in wins, ERA, and complete games, and, with fourth starter Ray Fisher (14-5), the group won 73 of 100 decisions.

Although the talented but crooked White Sox were giving less than their best effort, a few Reds put up some good numbers in their own right. Among them were a few unrecognized stars. Rookie left fielder Pat Duncan came out of nowhere to lead all series participants with eight RBI. Weak-hitting right fielder Greasy Neale opened eyes with 10 hits. And fifth starter Jimmy Ring surprised all those not involved in the scandal with a three-hit shutout in Game Four, giving the Reds a three games to one advantage. The usual cast also played a role, of course, as Roush made the most of his six hits with seven RBI, and Eller pitched two complete-game victories with 15 strikeouts and two walks—a performance that would have probably merited him the series MVP trophy had the award existed then.

The 1919 Reds club was a good story, as it made a notable improvement from its previous year thanks to shrewd off-season trades that netted the likes of reliable first baseman Jake Daubert, the left arm of Sallee, and the talented but troubled Fisher (a recovering alcoholic the team decided to give a second chance). The return of Ruether and shortstop Larry Kopf from the military helped the Reds' cause as well. Those additions translated into an enhanced pitching staff and an unselfish style of play under new manager Pat Moran, who directed Cincinnati to a nine-game margin over the second-place Giants. Regardless of the Reds' success, however, the 1919 season and subsequent World Series will forever be remembered for its fixed ending.

225. *Can you name the first pair of brothers in baseball history? (Hint: go way back).*

ANSWER: George Wright and William "Harry" Wright

Proclaimed by some as "The Father of Baseball," Harry Wright was elected to the Hall of Fame in 1953 for his role as pioneer. He organized the first professional team, his Cincinnati Red Stockings (the reason the Cincinnati Reds frequently open the National League season), and also played a big part in organizing the first professional league, the National Association. Harry became the player-manager when he decided to pitch in 1867. Harry then recruited his talented brother George, who earned the starting shortstop job and became the superstar field leader of the 1869 Red Stockings squad that went 59-0 and didn't lose until June 4, 1870. However, that performance was not as a member of a league, as the National Association wasn't ready to go until 1871. With George Wright's average consistently hovering around .400, Cincinnati used the league's best offensive and defensive shortstop and most innovative manager to win the National Association title from 1872 to 1875.

In 1876 the National League was formed, and George Wright became the first batter up in National League history, hitting for the Boston Red Caps, managed by Harry. On that team, George and Harry were joined by a third brother, 27-year-old Sam Wright, who played two games and went 1-for-8. (Sam had only 38 more at-bats spread between the 1880 and 1881 seasons.) The Red Caps finished fourth in 1876 behind the Chicago White Stockings (who later became the Cubs), before finishing first in each of the next two seasons with Harry as manager and George at short. Harry continued to manage until 1893. As for George (elected to the Hall of Fame in 1937), he left his brother in 1879 to be a player-manager for the Providence Grays, for whom he won his eighth pennant in nine years. In his only year as manager, George had the privilege of managing the great Paul Hines, who had won baseball's first Triple Crown the year before.

George founded a sporting goods company as well as helping to popularize the sports of hockey, tennis, and golf in the United States. He laid out the first public golf course in this country and eventually made the tennis Hall of Fame. Harry remained with the game (even after his retirement) until his death in 1895. He invented the cork center of the livelier ball and the technique of overhand pitching, reduced the number of balls required for a walk (from nine to six), and increased the distance between the pitcher's mound and home plate from 50 feet to 55 feet.

◆ Did you know the Spalding products company we buy from today was founded by Hall of Famer Al Spalding? The righthander from Illinois first joined the Red Stockings to help manager Harry Wright win four flags in five years with a 207-56 record. (In those days, the season was short and the pitches were delivered underhanded, so a pitcher could afford to pitch that many games.) In 1876 Spalding jumped to Chicago, where, as a player-manager, his 47-13 mark helped the White Stockings to a 52-14 record and the first National League crown. His arm finally gave out as his playing days were simmering down in 1877. That's when Albert Goodwill Spalding opened his sporting goods business, beginning with the first Spalding Baseball Guide in 1877. Hall of Fame writer Henry Chadwick edited the book. In 1882 Spalding (a 1939 Hall of Fame inductee) became the president of the Chicago ballclub, which finished first behind the playing and managing skills of Cap Anson.

Spalding died in 1915, but his name remained on every official National League ball until 1976.

226. *Match these Hall of Famers with their early struggles:*

1	Sandy Koufax	A	hit only .178 with one homer over 118 at-bats in his first year
2	Luke Appling	B	didn't win his first game until he was 31 years of age

3	Dazzy Vance	C	hit a mere .235 with only 11 home runs in his first five years
4	Willie Mays	D	was 0-for-28 to begin his rookie year
5	Reggie Jackson	E	had just one hit in his first 26 career at-bats, even struggling in the field during this time
6	Harmon Killebrew	F	was demoted to the minors early in his career and seriously considered quitting
7	Mickey Mantle	G	was 36-40 during his first six years

ANSWER: 1—G, 2—D, 3—B, 4—E, 5—A, 6—C, 7—F

Koufax was so unreliable in the first half of his career, his manager didn't use him in either of his first two World Series (in 1955 and 1956). The wild Koufax, who was averaging 5.26 walks per nine innings, would later turn things around, though. "I became a good pitcher," he says, "when I stopped trying to make them miss the ball and started trying to make them hit it." His catcher Norm Sherry, who advised Koufax to "let hitters hit the ball," also advised Koufax to target his body, not his mitt. Pitching coach Joe Becker got Koufax to tighten the windup on his delivery so as to improve his control and hide the ball. With that, Koufax's fastball became literally almost unhittable. . . . After his manager Lew Fonseca reassured him (much as Leo Durocher would assure a rookie named Willie Mays 20 years later), Appling started hitting. The rest is history. . . . Vance, plagued by wildness (and injuries), won his first game seven years after his 1915 debut. From 1922 to 1925, Vance won 86 contests for Brooklyn. He went on to lead the National League in strikeouts seven straight years (from 1922 to 1928) and in ERA three times en route to a 197-win career. Vance enjoyed his best season in 1924, winning the pitcher's Triple Crown with a 28-6 mark, a 2.16 ERA, and 262 strikeouts.

◆ Did you know Reggie Jackson's average of .194 with California in 1983 is the lowest single-season average (during a season of at least 400 plate appearances) for a non-pitching Hall of Famer inducted for his playing ability?

227. *The 1961 Yankees won the AL pennant with an incredible 109-53 record and beat the Reds, four games to one, in the World Series to win the world championship. Fill in the blanks to this great alignment:*

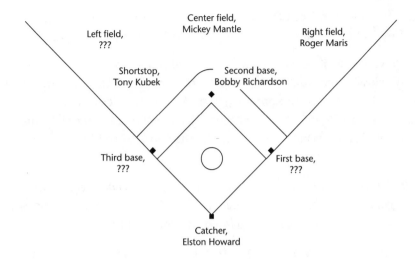

Center field,
Mickey Mantle

Left field,
???

Right field,
Roger Maris

Shortstop,
Tony Kubek

Second base,
Bobby Richardson

Third base,
???

First base,
???

Catcher,
Elston Howard

ANSWER: First base, Bill "Moose" Skowron; Third base, Clete Boyer; Left field, Yogi Berra

The 1961 Yankees scored the second most runs (827) in the majors behind Detroit and hit .263, behind the Tigers' league-leading .266 figure, despite hitting 60 more homers (240-180) and winning eight more games (109-101). Southpaw Whitey Ford was unquestionably the ace of the pitching staff with a dazzling 25-4 record, leading the majors in victories, winning percentage, and innings. Right-handed starters Ralph Terry, Bill Stafford, and Rollie Sheldon contributed by winning a combined 41 of 58 decisions.

228. *Match these recently retired players with their career stats:*

1	Gary Carter	A	2,143 hits and 859 RBI
2	Dave Parker	B	328 homers, 1,434 RBI, and 2,592 hits
3	Ken Griffey Sr.	C	385 homers, 1,384 RBI, and 2,446 hits
4	Dwight Evans	D	324 homers and 1,225 RBI

ANSWER: 1—D, 2—B, 3—A, 4—C

Carter hit 296 of his 324 home runs as a catcher. He began and ended his career with the Expos but will be best remembered for leading the 1986 Mets to a world championship. He has not received enough votes to be inducted into the Hall of Fame in his first five years of eligibility, although Carlton Fisk, who has comparable numbers, was elected in 2000. . . . Parker ended his career in Milwaukee, Griffey in Seattle (alongside his son), and Evans in Baltimore.

◆ Did you know Keith Hernandez holds the single-season and career records for game-winning RBI? In the nine years, from 1980 to 1988, that Major League Baseball used the game-winning RBI as an official statistic, Hernandez collected 129. In 1985 "Mex" compiled a record 24 of them. Hernandez (a career .296 hitter) retired with 2,182 hits and 1,071 RBI.

229. *The memorable words of Jack Buck still linger in our heads: "And it's going to be a home run. Unbelievable, I don't believe what I just saw." What was the venerable broadcaster announcing?*

ANSWER: Buck was broadcasting Kirk Gibson's unforgettable two-run homer in the bottom of the ninth inning, which concluded a dramatic first game of the 1988 World Series between the visiting Oakland A's and the Los Angeles Dodgers. Game One was decided on that one swing, if you can believe it. Leading, 4-3, entering the bottom of the ninth, the A's had the major league's best reliever in Dennis Eckersley on the mound. In true story-book fashion, Eckersley retired the first two batters before issuing a rare walk to pinch-hitter Mike Davis (an ex-teammate). The swinger in the on-deck circle was Dave Anderson, but manager Tommy Lasorda directed the script perfectly. Lasorda called Anderson back to the dugout as the most unexpected, but welcome, figure entered the batter's box to the roar and excitement of a sellout Dodger Stadium audience.

Gibson, the season's NL MVP, had strained his hamstring and seriously injured his knee during Game Seven of the NL Championship Series against the Mets. NBC broadcaster Vince Scully, reacting to an NBC camera shot of Gibson in the training room, announced that the inspirational leader was definitely out of this game and unavailable. Gibson responded by saying, "bull s——." As Kirk geared up to face "The Eck," realization set in that he was indeed hobbled (a term almost synonymous with Gibson during that postseason) and might not be up to the challenge. The situation looked even more bleak when Gibson found himself behind in the count, no balls and two strikes, looking overmatched. Somehow, Gibson managed to work the count full, and then he belted Eckersley's backdoor slider into the right-field seats. The crowd went berserk. Gibson had overcome intense pain to show the world that miracles and Hollywood finishes are still very much possible.

For Gibson, that was his only at-bat of the series, but it served its purpose of inspiring the Dodgers to defeat the A's, four games to one. The A's had taken a 4-2 lead in the second inning of Game One on Jose Canseco's grand slam, but the slam would be Canseco's only hit in 19 series at-bats.

◆ Did you know Dodgers pitcher (and Series MVP) Orel Hershiser went 3-for-3 in Game One of the 1988 World Series to tie a fall classic record for most hits in a game by a pitcher? Only five other hurlers have been able to collect three hits in a series game: Jack Coombs for the Athletics in 1910, Charley Hall for the Red Sox two years later, Rube Foster of the Red Sox in 1915, Dutch Ruether for the Reds in 1919, and the Giants' Art Nehf in 1924. In his 1910 fall classic performance, Coombs collected a total of five hits, still the series standard for a pitcher.

230. *Match these teams with their histories:*

1 Indians A ended Orel Hershiser's major league record of 59 consecutive scoreless innings

2 Athletics B became the first team in history to boast three players who hit three homers in a game during the season

3 Reds C had the best home record in their league during the 1980s (452-330)

4 Astros D have finished last in their league (or division) 29 times, while accumulating another major league record of 16 seasons with 100 losses

ANSWER: 1—B, 2—D, 3—A, 4—C

Joe Carter, Cory Snyder, and Brook Jacoby each hit three home runs in one game for the 1987 Indians. . . . Hershiser ended the 1988 season with six straight shutouts before yielding a first-inning run on opening day, 1989. . . . The Athletics' AL record of 29 last-place finishes spans three cities: Philadelphia (18), Kansas City (6), and Oakland (5).

◆ Did you know the 1987 Indians also became the first team to boast three 30-homer players (Joe Carter, Cory Snyder, and Brook Jacoby) and three 30–stolen base players (Carter, Julio Franco, and Brett Butler) in the same season?

◆ Did you know second baseman Craig Biggio in 1995 became the first Houston Astros position player to start an All-Star Game since 1973? Outfielder Cesar Cedeno started for the NL team 22 years earlier.

◆ Did you know Henry Aaron in 1963 was the first player to hit 40 homers and steal 25 bases in the same season?

231. *On January 7, 1992, Tom Seaver received a record 98.84 percent of the votes by the Baseball Writers Association of America to earn election into the Hall of Fame. In 1999 Nolan Ryan came within a vote of Seaver with an astounding 98.79 percent. Knocked down to third was Ty Cobb's total of 98.23 percent of the vote, gained in 1936. In 1999 George Brett received the fourth highest percentage (98.19 percent), making Henry Aaron's 97.83 percent in 1982 the fifth best in the Hall of Fame's history. Mike Schmidt (96.52 percent), Johnny Bench (96.42 percent), Steve Carlton (95.82 percent), Babe Ruth (95.13 percent), and Honus Wagner (95.13 percent) round out the top ten. Can you choose the player who came the closest to an induction without receiving enough votes? (Clue: this man was eventually elected.)*

A Orlando Cepeda
B Phil Rizzuto
C Richie Ashburn
D Nellie Fox
E Cecil Travis

ANSWER: D

Fox received 295 of the 297 required votes (297 represented 75 percent of the vote that year) in the 1985 BBWAA elections. The stellar second baseman finally made it in 1997, chosen by the Veterans Committee, after just missing again in 1995 and 1996. In 1996 Fox received the required votes to gain election, but Jim Bunning earned one more vote. And since the Veterans Committee was allotted just one selection from the modern major league players' category every year, only Bunning was chosen. Cepeda had a similar fate, falling seven votes shy in the 1994 BBWAA elections before making it via the Veterans Committee in 1999.

Negro National League star Leon Day was fortunate enough to receive the required votes in 1995 after just missing in 1993. With his friend and supporter Roy Campanella ill, unable to attend and cast a ballot (presence was required), Day fell one vote short in 1993.

Bunning came within four votes of election in 1988—the 15th and final year he was eligible to be voted on by the BBWAA. The near miss was hard to take for the current five-term Republican congressman from Kentucky, considering that nine writers sent in signed ballots with no candidates checked. In any event, Bunning collected 3,213 total votes en route to his eventual election by the Veterans Committee. No one has ever received more votes. Gil Hodges' 3,010 total votes are the most by a player not enshrined.

◆ Did you know Joe DiMaggio, Grover Cleveland Alexander, Eddie Collins, Rogers Hornsby, Mel Ott, Roy Campanella, Yogi Berra, Bill Dickey, Whitey Ford, Hank Greenberg, Harmon Killebrew, and Charlie Gehringer were among those not elected to the Hall of Fame on their first ballot? In fact, no player was elected on the first ballot from 1937 to 1961. The guidelines for election were very different in those days. Only a one-year wait was required for a retired player to become eligible between 1946 and 1953, and Ott's 61 percent was the highest first-ballot score during that span. The incumbent five-year wait was imposed in 1955. DiMaggio received just 44 percent on his first ballot.

232. *Match these players with their fielding woes:*

1	Bob Johnson	A	his career error total is the highest in major league history
2	Butch Hobson	B	was the last player to commit 50 errors in a season
3	Herman Long	C	was the last outfielder to commit 20 errors in a season
4	Roy Smalley Sr.	D	became the first regular to post a sub-.900 fielding average since 1916
5	Dick Stuart	E	was nicknamed "Dr. Strangeglove" for his horrible defense

ANSWER: 1—C, 2—D, 3—A, 4—B, 5—E

Johnson committed 20 errors in 1935 for the Philadelphia Athletics. Montreal's Vladimir Guerrero came close to matching his total in 1999, making 19 errors to tie Lou Brock (1966) and Chili Davis (1988) for the most since World War II. Cy Seymour holds the dubious outfield record with 36 errors committed for Cincinnati in 1903. . . . Hobson fielded .899 and made 43 errors in 1978 for the Red Sox. Dodgers' shortstop Jose Offerman committed 42 errors during the 1992 season, the highest total since Hobson. . . . Smalley (not to be confused with his switch-hitting son, who spent 9 of his 13 big league seasons with the Twins) made 51 errors for the 1950 Cubs. . . . Long made an all-time worst 1,096 errors during his career. Long, who played from 1889 to 1904, committed 1,070 of his miscues at shortstop, playing mostly for the National League's Boston Beaneaters. The .278 career hitter, who hit 91 home runs, committed over 100 errors in a year three times, including a dubious record of 122 in 1889. Germany Smith was the only other player to commit at least 1,000 errors, making 1,007 miscues from 1884 to 1898. . . . Stuart led all first basemen in errors during each of his first seven seasons, committing 143 during that stretch. Stuart was just bad at fielding, whereas Long and Smith had an excuse. They were playing in an era of either no gloves or winter-wear gloves that some wore to soften the blow of the drives, which didn't do much to help their fielding. Slowly but surely, glove manufacturers helped along the evolution of the glove with a bigger webbing and softer padding for major leaguers and baseball enthusiasts. You'll find that error totals have decreased with time, coinciding with the glove's gradual advancements, to the tune of about 90 percent fewer errors since the days of Long and Smith.

◆ Did you know Hall of Famer Lou Brock led National League outfielders in errors a record seven times and was second in two other seasons? Brock was definitely not without flaws, especially in the outfield. He committed at least 10 errors each season from 1965 to 1974 and retired with a fielding percentage of .959, poor for that era. Although he was blessed with speed, his range was limited, so limited in fact that he was shifted from center field to right then finally to left.

◆ Did you know Yankees shortstop Tom Tresh once went three consecutive starts without a single chance offered? From July 30 to August 1, 1968, the

30-year-old Tresh failed to get a chance over a stretch spanning 26 innings. By comparison, the record for most chances by a shortstop over a single game—never mind three—is 19, shared by Washington's Danny Richardson (1892) and Cincinnati's Eddie Joost (1941). Tresh, a two-time All-Star earlier in the decade, won a Gold Glove in 1965.

◆ Did you know Bob Brenly on September 14, 1986, tied the modern major league record for most errors in an inning? A catcher asked to play third base for the Giants that day, Brenly committed four errors in the fourth inning. Brenly made up for that awful fourth inning with a pair of home runs and four RBI, including the game-winner in the bottom of the ninth.

233. *Match these players with their MVP season:*

1	Gabby Hartnett	A	1972 AL MVP
2	Dick Allen	B	1942 NL MVP
3	Zoilo Versalles	C	1952 AL MVP
4	Phil Cavarretta	D	1965 AL MVP
5	Bobby Shantz	E	1935 NL MVP
6	Mort Cooper	F	1945 NL MVP

ANSWER: 1—E, 2—A, 3—D, 4—F, 5—C, 6—B

Allen belted 37 home runs, hit .308, slugged .603, and drove in 113 runs, just missing the Triple Crown as he finished behind Carew (.318) in batting. . . . Versalles, who led his league with 39 errors and 122 strikeouts in 1965, never again batted above .249 or drove in more than 50 runners for the remaining five years of his career. . . . Cooper (league-leading 22 wins, 1.78 ERA, and 10 shutouts) and Shantz (24-7, 2.48) each became their league's fifth MVP pitcher.

234. *Long before the "Black Sox" scandal and the days of Judge Kenesaw Landis, this National League president was the man who first stood up for baseball and upheld the integrity of the game. He saw to it that gambling and unsportsmanlike conduct would not be tolerated and succeeded in saving the integrity of the game. Who was this former millionaire coal dealer from Chicago?*

ANSWER: William A. Hulbert

Hulbert, "The Father of The National League," became the cir-

cuit's second president after Morgan G. Bulkeley (the first chief) retired following the inaugural 1876 season. Hulbert quickly established
some solid ground rules that distinguished the National League from
any other league. One of the eight original owners, the Chicago
White Stockings chief executive took over as president after Bulkeley handed down his decision to ban the New York Mutuals and
Philadelphia Athletics (till 1883) for not playing the final week's
schedule after his White Stockings had already won the title in a
league that also included the Louisville Grays, Hartford Dark Blues,
Boston Reds, Cincinnati Red Stockings, and St. Louis Brown Stockings. That set the tone for his administration. He knew that this decision would be criticized, because New York and Philadelphia were
the league's greatest gate attractions. But to Hulbert, finance was not
the issue—the games' integrity was. So Hulbert upheld the penalty for
the purpose of establishing structure and respectability.

Hulbert also helped to preserve the game's virtue by taking a
strong stance against gambling. Toward the end of the 1877 season,
The Louisville Courier accused four Louisville Grays of deliberately losing games for bribes as the club squandered its pennant hopes. Hulbert unleashed an investigation and discovered that ace pitcher Jim
Devlin, outfielder George Hall, shortstop Bill Craver, and reserve infielder Al Nichols had thrown at least three games, gifting Boston the
NL pennant. Hulbert suspended them for life, disregarding the quartet's claim that they were merely attempting to earn money owed
them by the team owner. Hulbert was a hero to many, as the self-pro-
claimed "George Washington of Baseball" had once again upheld the
game's integrity. And the league's first banishment case served as an
important precedent for the major leagues and Judge Landis four
decades later during the "Black Sox" scandal.

Hulbert, who died in 1882, was responsible for many other as-
pects of the game. He made players bound to the team that signed
them, banned Sunday baseball, and played a big role in the signing
of Adrian "Cap" Anson, luring him from the Athletics. It's no wonder that he's in the Hall of Fame.

One decision came back to haunt him, however—his banning
of the sale of beer during games. Capitalizing on the fans' desire to
drink beer during games, a group of brewmeisters in 1882 formed the
American Association, which gave the National League some com-

petition. It all turned out for the better, as the National League put teams back in New York and Philadelphia to compete with the American Association teams and an agreement was made in 1884 (the same year that the Union Association was created to compete with the National League and the American Association) that both leagues would cease "stealing" players from each other and play a postseason series to determine the champion.

The championship series was first given the name "World Series" in its first year, 1884. In that year, the NL's Providence Grays beat the American Association's Metropolitan Club in a best-of-five series to earn recognition as "champions of the world." The title was renamed the "Temple Cup" in 1894 and the "Chronicle-Telegraph Cup" in 1900 (after a two-year postseason hiatus due to the Spanish-American War and financial troubles). The 1903 World Series (regarded as the inaugural series for its official arrangement) was officially called the "World's Championship Series." According to the game programs, the name of the fall classic was changed to "World's Series" in 1912 before it became the more familiar "World Series" in 1936. In some later years, however, such as 1944, the name "World's Series" appeared on the cover. By 1964 the fall classic was unanimously called the "World Series."

◆ Did you know John Tener was the first player to become a president of a major league? He became the NL president in 1914, a post he held until he resigned in 1918. The right-handed pitcher won 25 games from 1885 to 1890.

235. *NCAA (college) Baseball annually honors its best players by presenting them with the Golden Spikes Award. In 1991 Arizona State's Mike Kelly won the award for his unbelievable play as a 19-year-old sophomore. Kelly also achieved All-American status on three occasions, a feat that previous Arizona State students such as Reggie Jackson, Bob Horner, and Barry Bonds couldn't achieve. Match these past Golden Spikes Award winners with their college and the year they won the honor:*

1 Will Clark   A Arizona State, 1984
2 Jim Abbott   B Miami-Dade, 1990

3 Tim Wallach   C Alabama, 1983
4 Dave Magadan   D Michigan, 1987
5 Alex Fernandez   E Cal State Fullerton, 1979
6 Oddibe McDowell   F Mississippi State, 1985

ANSWER: 1—F, 2—D, 3—E, 4—C, 5—B, 6—A

Bob Horner was the award's first winner in 1978, representing Arizona State. . . . The one-armed Jim Abbott was one of the major league's top lefthanders at one point, going 18-11 with a 2.89 ERA for California in 1991. His 87-win total over a 10-year career is impressive, but even more impressive is his total of only nine errors over those 10 years. . . . Another winner was Mark Kotsay, who took the Golden Spikes Award in November 1995. Kotsay, who also earned College World Series MVP honors that year while leading Cal State Fullerton (57-9) to the title, hit .422 with 21 homers, 90 RBI, and 15 stolen bases in addition to posting a 2-1 record with 11 saves and 0.31 ERA on the mound. He enters the 2003 season with six major league years under his belt, batting .284 while showing impressive outfield skills.

◆ Did you know Pete Incaviglia was chosen as college baseball's Player of the Century as well as the best player in College World Series history in separate polls? In a vote conducted by *Baseball America's* readers and media panel, Incaviglia was selected as the best college baseball player of the 1900s. Playing for Oklahoma State in 1985, Incaviglia set NCAA single-season records with 48 home runs, 143 RBI, 285 total bases, and a .915 slugging percentage. Finishing second in the voting was Bob Horner (Arizona State). Robin Ventura (Oklahoma State) finished third, Burt Hooton (Arizona State) placed fourth, and Dave Winfield (Minnesota) fifth. Rounding out the top 10 were Shell Stephenson (Wichita State), John Olerud (Washington State), J. D. Drew (Florida State), Eddie Bain (Arizona State), and Derrick Tatsuno (Hawaii).

Incaviglia also received the most votes in a poll conducted by the *Omaha World Herald* in 1996 to determine the best players in College World Series history. As part of the 50th College World Series celebration, an all-time College World Series team was chosen, with Incaviglia being picked as the best designated hitter. Incaviglia hit .357 with four homers and 16 RBI over 11 College World Series games from 1983 to 1985. His Oklahoma State teammate Mike Day, who never played in the majors, was voted as the best catcher. Will Clark of Mississippi State was voted as the best first baseman, and Todd Walker of Louisiana State earned recognition for his stellar play at second. Texas' Spike Owen was chosen as the shortstop, Robin Ventura as third baseman, and Barry Bonds, Mark Kotsay, and Minnesota's Dave Winfield as outfielders. Ohio State's Steve Arlin and Burt Hooton of Texas were honored as the best pitchers in College World Series play. USC's Rod Dedeaux, who won a record 11 NCAA championships, easily won the balloting for the best coach.

236. *The Colorado Rockies, Florida Marlins, and Arizona Diamondbacks have all established new expansion precedents for swift postseason berths or successes. In 1995 the Rockies became the youngest expansion team ever to gain entry into the postseason, with a wild-card entry in their third season. In 1997 the Marlins shocked the world by becoming the youngest franchise to reach and win the World Series, in their fifth season. The Diamondbacks broke both marks by winning the NL West in 1999, their second season, and the World Series in their fourth. Prior to the 1990s, two teams had earned a postseason berth in their eighth year, the previous mark. Can you name either of these two teams?*

ANSWER: The 1969 New York Mets and 1976 Kansas City Royals

The Mets, who entered the National League in 1962 with the Houston Astros, won the Eastern Division in 1969 before sweeping the Atlanta Braves in the NL Championship Series and beating the overwhelmingly favored Baltimore Orioles, four games to one, in the World Series. The Royals, who entered the American League in 1969 along with the Seattle Pilots (who later became the Milwaukee Brewers), won the Western Division before dramatically losing to the New York Yankees in the AL Championship Series, three games to two.

In 1969 the Montreal Expos and San Diego Padres also began play, joining the National League as each league expanded to 12 teams. Baseball's fifth expansion in 1993 delivered the Rockies into the NL West and the Marlins into the NL East. In 1994 MLB realigned the divisions and created a Central Division in each league. And baseball's sixth expansion became official on opening day 1998, when the Tampa Bay Devil Rays joined the American League East and the Diamondbacks joined the National League West, increasing the number of teams in Major League Baseball to 30.

◆ Did you know the Florida Marlins made even bigger news after winning the 1997 World Series by dumping 12 players in a series of severe cost-cutting moves during the off-season? Owner Wayne Huizenga wanted to sell the team and cut down on player payroll after claiming that he had lost money again. As a result, the Marlins became the first world champions to lose 100 games the following year (finishing 54-108). Kevin Brown, Moises Alou, Robb Nen, and Al Leiter were among those dealt away following the fall classic. Even more remarkable was the inadequate quality of minor league talent the Marlins were settling for in return. The Marlins' 38-game decline the following season was the largest in NL history.

The largest decline ever was that of the 1915 Philadelphia Athletics, who lost 56 more games than they had in 1914. After winning their fourth pennant in five years in 1914, the Athletics were forced to sell off most of their talent. In 1915 they lost 109 games and suffered the first of seven straight last-place finishes.

237. *Match these off-the-field figures with their histories:*

1	Bancroft "Ban" Johnson	A	the great labor negotiator who convinced the players in 1966 they needed a union and gave them bargaining leverage they have enjoyed ever since
2	Henry Chadwick	B	should have been the game's first commissioner and the man who presided over the "Black Sox" scandal
3	William Harridge	C	invented the box score
4	Marvin Miller	D	was AL president from 1931 to 1959

ANSWER: 1—B, 2—C, 3—D, 4—A

Johnson was replaced as a candidate for commissioner after he refused the requests of Charles Comiskey, owner of the White Sox, that he not order an inquiry into the "Black Sox" scandal. To get even, Comiskey headed a vote that passed over Johnson and chose Judge Kenesaw Landis (who was best known for fining John D. Rockefeller's Standard Oil Trust $29 million, and for ruling in favor of the major leagues in the suits brought by the Federal League) as the game's judge. Landis is still considered the most powerful executive in the game's history. . . . Chadwick also invented the scoring system, wrote baseball's first guide in 1860 *(Beadle's Dime Baseball Player)*, wrote the first hardcover book about baseball in 1868 *(The Game of Base Ball)*, and edited many other *Guides.* In *The Game of Base Ball*, Chadwick revealed, among many other things, that he made "K" the symbol for strikeout by taking the strongest letter from the word "struck." . . . Harridge's 27-plus-year tenure as league president remains the longest. . . . Miller helped the players see that, although they were not the lowest paid workers in the country, they were among the most exploited. As Miller told the media, "There was a huge difference in what they were worth and what they were being paid." Miller made the owners repeatedly augment their contributions to the players' pension fund, increase the players' salaries (even the minimum salary), and agree to the creation of a new union, the Major League Players Association (thus allowing agents to accompany players into salary negotiations and also allowing arbitration in salary disputes). Miller was also the force behind the first three major strikes in major league history. In addition to representing the players during the 13-day strike in 1972, the 1976 spring training lockout, the 1980 one-week strike, and the 50-day strike in 1981, Miller also purged the reserve clause in 1975, before retiring in 1984. It is because of Miller that the current head of the union, Donald Fehr, is considered by many involved in MLB to be the most powerful man in baseball.

◆ Did you know the major league owners took out insurance with Lloyds of London before the strike in 1981, and only reached an agreement with the players as the insurance was running out? The strike took place largely because the owners wanted to implement a free-agent penalty that would have handed over an average player to the team losing the free agent. The players felt it was the owners' way of trying to unfairly regain what they had lost fair and square in court. The owners caved in again.

238. *Match these influential men with their histories:*

1	Warren Giles	A although he was elected to the Hall of Fame, his tenure as commissioner wasn't the smoothest, as he banned 18 major leaguers for jumping to the Mexican League for higher salaries (which left

	many wondering whether the reserve clause was in jeopardy)
2 A. B. "Happy" Chandler	B this former part-owner and president of the Yankees had his contract terminated and was bought out for his part in a brawl following his team's world championship celebration
3 Tom Yawkey	C this Hall of Fame NL president (1951–69) witnessed the league expand to the West Coast during his tenure due to lower attendance and Brooklyn's unwillingness to build a new stadium
4 Larry MacPhail	D a Red Sox owner and a 1980 Hall of Fame inductee who was criticized for not integrating his team until 1959

ANSWER: 1—C, 2—A, 3—D, 4—B

Larry MacPhail's son Lee was elected into the Hall of Fame by the Veterans Committee in March of 1998, making the two the first father-son combination in the Hall of Fame. Lee became AL president (1974–83) after serving as player personnel director of the New York Yankees from 1948 to 1958, building a team that won nine American League pennants and seven World Series titles. Larry's grandson Andy is the Cubs' president and CEO following a highly successful reign as vice president and general manager of the Twins, whom he guided to a world title in 1987 and 1991. There's more; Andy's nephew (his name is also Lee) is the director of scouting for the Expos. . . . Chandler also suspended Leo Durocher for associating with gamblers in 1947 but failed to suspend MacPhail (a close friend who chose Chandler as commissioner) for doing the same. At the time, Durocher was a Dodger manager, a rival of Yankees president MacPhail. It sounded as fishy then as it sounds now.

◆ Did you know it was Larry MacPhail who hired Leo Durocher as the Brooklyn Dodgers' player-manager in 1939? Durocher first came up to the majors for two games in 1925 with the Yankees and returned in 1928 as a 23-year-old in awe of his historical surroundings. The good-fielding, decent-hitting shortstop (.247 lifetime batting average) was traded to Cincinnati after the 1929 season (to make way for the good-hitting Mark Koenig), then to the famous "Gas House Gang" in St. Louis, where he won a championship ring with that rambunctious squad, before being traded to Brooklyn in time for the 1938 season, the year before he began his managerial career. His 2,008 managerial victories (seventh on the all-time list) earned "The Lip" a berth in the Hall of Fame in 1994. He passed away in 1991 at the age of 86. Quite a character, Durocher will be missed.

◆ Did you know Lee and Andy MacPhail were one of two father-son teams to win the Sporting News Major League Executive of the Year Award? Lee MacPhail won the award as a member of the commissioner's office in 1966. Andy won it in 1991 as the general manager of the Twins (for whom he engineered two world championships in five years). Clark Griffith won the award in 1943, and his son Cal followed suit in 1965 after he moved the Senators franchise from Washington, D.C., to Minnesota following his father's death.

239. *Which Chicago White Sox owner is recognized as the most stingy in major league history?*

ANSWER: Charles Comiskey

Comiskey paid his players so poorly that many blame him for the "Black Sox" scandal, although his tight-fisted ways were no excuse for what they might have caused. The White Sox owner had the lowest payroll in the majors despite having, without a doubt, the most talented team. He was so cheap that when his ace Eddie Cicotte won his 29th game of the 1919 season, he, fearing that Cicotte would earn a 30th victory and collect on a $5,000 incentive clause he had put in the pitcher's contract, ordered his manager Kid Gleason not to pitch Cicotte for the remaining *three weeks* of the regular season, allegedly so that "he can rest up for the Series." Even the great Joe Jackson was only making $6,000 a year. Dickie Kerr, a blooming star and an honest member of that 1919 White Sox club who won twice with a 1.42 ERA in that scandalous World Series, was also affected by Comiskey's close-fisted ways. This lefthander went 13-7 in his rookie season of 1919, 21-9 in 1920, and 19-7 in 1921. When Kerr asked Comiskey for a raise after the 1921 campaign, the archaic owner refused to augment Kerr's $4,500 salary. Kerr quit the team and played semi-pro for three years, making $5,000 a season. As for Cicotte, he never earned more than $3,500.

Comiskey's treatment of his players was ironic considering that he had supported the Players League in 1890. The Players League was a circuit that was instituted to give players the right to play for the highest bidder, in an attempt to eliminate the reserve clause (which stated a player had to stay with the team that drafted him unless he was traded or waived).

◆ Did you know Charles Comiskey came to be so maligned he handed over a then-record $125,000 to the San Francisco Seals in 1922 for the rights to Willie Kamm? The purchase was obviously an attempt to change his miserly image.

240. *Who was Ed Barrow?*

ANSWER: Ed Barrow was a Hall of Fame general manager and president, best known for putting together the great 1927 and 1939 Yankee clubs and leading the organization to its first 14 pennants and 10 world championships. Barrow's excellence ranks him with pioneer Branch Rickey—and slightly ahead of George Weiss—as one of the very best executives ever. His first managerial experience came with the Detroit Tigers in 1903 and 1904. He didn't manage again until Harry Frazee hired him in the late 1910s to lead his Red Sox. In 1918 Barrow was able to lead Boston to the world championship, in part because of his ingenious idea of switching Babe Ruth over to left field on days when he did not pitch. When Frazee sold Ruth to the Yankees for $125,000 (plus a $300,000 mortgage loan for Fenway Park), Barrow followed Ruth to the Big Apple as a general manager in 1921, helping the Bronx Bombers to six pennants in his first eight years at his new post. Along with his assistant Weiss, Barrow built up a farm system in the mold of Rickey's Cardinals. The two met in one of the best World Series in early history, the 1926 fall classic (comparable to the classics of 1909, 1912, 1924, and 1925). The Cardinals won it in seven games, limiting the Bombers to just 21 runs.

Barrow became the president of the Yankees in 1939 following the death of owner Colonel Jacob Ruppert. In 1945 Dan Topping and Del Webb bought the team and hired Larry MacPhail as president. The Yankees owe a lot to Ed Barrow, who served them for 25 fantastic years. Barrow won the Sporting News Executive of the Year Award twice (1937, 1941), and he could have won the award five more times but it wasn't given out until 1936. Weiss followed Barrow with a record four Executive of the Year Awards (1950–52, 1960). Rickey won the award three times (1936, 1942, 1947).

◆ Did you know that Ed Barrow supported and authorized the playing of Lizzie Arlington, the first woman to pitch in organized baseball? The 20-year-old Arlington played one game in 1898 for Reading, Pa., of the Class A Atlantic League. Barrow also was the first man to paint the distances from home on the outfield fences and to put numbers on players' uniforms, in 1923 and 1929, respectively.

241. *Match these women's leagues with their histories:*

1	All-American Girls Pro Baseball League	A	the first women's professional baseball league (1883)
2	The Young Ladies Baseball Club	B	formed a four-team league in 1988
3	"Blondes" and "Brunettes"	C	played the first women's game for profit (1875)
4	American Women Baseball Association	D	the biggest women's league, lasting from 1943 to 1954

ANSWER: 1—D, 2—A, 3—C, 4—B

The AAGPBL was a baseball league, although it was originally intended to be (and named) the All-American Girls Softball League. The AAGPBL or AAGPBBL (the name varied) served as a means of diversion from the war, as 176,000 fans attended its games in 1943. A total of 910,000 attended in 1948, when it presented a 108-game schedule that featured colorful team names such as the Racine Belles, the South Bend Blue Sox, the Kenosha Comets and, my favorite, the Rockford Peaches. The league folded in 1953. In 1988 the league received Hall of Fame recognition, and it was later portrayed in the hit film *A League of Their Own.* . . . The AWBA was founded by journalist Darlene Mehrer in Illinois. Although the AWBA features only one team today, it had five at one point, according to incumbent president Sue Lukasik.

◆ Did you know on May 31, 1997, Ila Borders became the first woman in the 20th century to pitch in a regular-season professional game? Borders was brought in to pitch in the sixth inning of the St. Paul Saints' Northern League game against Sioux Falls. She gave up three earned runs without retiring a batter, but her contribution to history obviously goes way beyond numbers. When she retired in 2000, she remained the only woman since 1898 to play men's professional baseball.

◆ Did you know the White Sox drafted Carey Schueler in 1993, making her the first woman ever chosen in the Free Agent Amateur Draft? The daughter of White Sox General Manager Ron Schueler was selected in the 43rd round but decided to enroll at DePaul University to play basketball on a scholarship.

242. *Match these heroes with their performances in providing diversion on the field during the World War II years of 1943 to 1945:*

1	Mort Cooper	A	posted a high of 65 wins, the most of any player during this period
2	Dizzy Trout	B	was the only player to record 100 RBI all three years
3	Dixie Walker	C	led his league in hits (twice), triples (twice), runs scored (twice), steals (twice), batting average, and slugging average during the three-year period but never came close in any category thereafter
4	Snuffy Stirnweiss	D	won a league-high 23 games (one-third his career total) in 1945
5	Red Barrett	E	this four-time All-Star registered two of his three 20-win seasons during this era
6	Bob Elliott	F	this career .306 hitter won his only batting title in 1944 and his only RBI title in 1945

ANSWER: 1—E, 2—A, 3—F, 4—C, 5—D, 6—B

Righthander Mort Cooper benefited from the services of his catcher, Walker Cooper—his brother. Teammates on the Cardinals from 1940 to 1945, the Coopers remain the only batterymate brothers in World Series history, teaming up during the fall classics of 1942, 1943, and 1944. Walker Cooper caught soundly and batted .300 over the three series, while Mort went a combined 2-3 with a 3.00 ERA. Mort Cooper would have probably earned series MVP honors in 1944 for posting a minuscule 1.12 ERA and striking out 16 in 16 innings, had the award existed then. . . . Trout's Hall of Fame teammate Hal

Newhouser recorded 62 wins during the three-year period. . . . George Case stole 140 bases during that stretch, more than any other player. . . . Tommy Holmes' 589 hits were the three-year high, as were Bill Nicholson's 75 homers and 338 RBI. A left-handed slugger for the Cubs at the time, Nicholson clubbed 235 home runs and drove in 948 by the time he retired with the Phillies.

◆ Did you know Ralph Kiner's 23 home runs in 1946 marked the last time a home run leader hit fewer than 32 (excluding the strike-shortened 1981 season)? Vern Stephens' 24 home runs in 1945 marked the last time an AL champion hit fewer than 32. George Kelly and Rogers Hornsby shared the NL RBI lead with 94 in 1920 to mark the last time in either league (excluding 1981) an RBI leader drove in fewer than 105 runs. Bobby Veach had 78 RBI in 1918, marking the last time an AL player led in that department with fewer than 105 over a full season. Veach's total of 78 RBI, however, was not the lowest for a league leader in the 20th century. Hy Myers of Brooklyn led the National League with 73 RBI in 1919, a year after Sherry Magee led the National League with 76 for his fourth RBI crown. RBI stats were not kept for most of the 19th century, but researchers have recently been retrieving such numbers for that era. RBI stats are still not available for a few seasons in the 19th century.

243. *More than one thousand foreigners have played Japanese Baseball, many from the United States and Major League Baseball. Some have given their home country a good name, some have not. Match these players with their notable achievements:*

1 Daryl Spencer   A this big Russian pitcher became Japan's first 300-game winner

2 Randy Bass   B once stood in the batter's box holding his bat upside down and still drew a walk, as opposing pitchers preferred that Nomura and not a Gaijan (foreigner) win the home run and batting titles

3 Leron Lee   C this Hawaiian pitcher for the Osaka Tigers, nicknamed "Bozo," won two MVP Awards and finished at 237-144 with a 1.99 ERA

4 Vic Starffin   D a .250 hitter in the majors, he won a Triple Crown in his rookie season in Japan

and also hit 283 home runs during an 11-year career

5 Henry Wakabayashi E became so popular and lovable that he agreed to shave his beard for an advertisement, a sign of his popularity and a gesture of acceptance

ANSWER: 1—B, 2—E, 3—D, 4—A, 5—C

Spencer wound up losing the home run title (42-38) and the batting title (.320–.311) to Nomura. It wasn't rare to see Japanese players go out of their way to prevent an American from winning a title. It happened to Bass and a few others. . . . Leron Lee was treated so well that he brought his brother Leon (268 homers, .308 batting average) over. . . . Starffin, a Japanese Hall of Famer, won a co-record 42 games in a season and fashioned a 1.01 ERA in 1940. His 83 career shutouts are a record, one more than Masaichi Kaneda's total. . . . Wakabayashi, a six-time 20-game winner, was inducted into the Japanese Baseball Hall of Fame in 1964.

244. *These brothers—one a lefthander, the other a righthander—combined for 296 wins and became the first brothers to each record a 20-win season. Name this Indian and this Tiger.*

ANSWER: Stan and Harry Coveleski

Stan and Harry Coveleski combined for seven 20-win campaigns. A Hall of Fame righthander, Stan posted a 215-142 record and an ERA of 2.89 over a 14-year career that ended in 1928. Harry recorded an 81-55 ledger with a 2.39 ERA during a nine-year career. Stan's four 20-win seasons came in consecutive fashion (1918–21) for the Indians, as did Harry's trio of 20-win seasons for the Tigers (1914–16). Stan won all three of his starts (0.67 ERA) in the 1920 World Series, hurling a five-hitter in each one to help the Indians defeat the Dodgers in the best-of-nine series, five games to two. However, he lost both of his starts for the Senators in their 1925 World Series collapse against Pittsburgh.

245. *In 1991 the Texas Rangers promoted a 19-year-old catcher, Ivan Rodriguez, from Double-A. The teenager turned many a head with his*

great defense, poise, and unbelievable arm. Over the years, Ro-
driguez's exploits have prompted many to favorably compare him
with the greats behind the plate. The five-foot-nine, 205-pound
Puerto Rican hit .264 and caught 88 games that first season, placing
him second on the list of most games caught as a teenager. Can you
choose the catcher who caught the most?

A Frankie Hayes
B Johnny Bench
C Benito Santiago
D Jim Sundberg

ANSWER: A

Hayes caught 89 games as a teenager for the 1933 and 1934 Philadelphia Athletics. Rodriguez became the sixth youngest All-Star in history in 1992. He has evolved into one of the best catchers of all time, carrying a .305 career batting average, a .489 slugging percentage, and a .990 career fielding percentage into the 2003 season. The 10-time Gold Glove winner and 10-time All-Star has thrown out at least 48 percent of would-be base stealers seven times in his career, four times reaching 50 percent. (Since this stat became official in 1989, only Ron Karkovice, Gilberto Reyes, and Mike Matheny have also thrown out more than 50 percent in a full season, each doing so once.) Overall, "Pudge" has gunned down 46.9 percent (395) of the 843 baserunners who have attempted to steal on him throughout his career.

En route to winning the 1999 MVP, Rodriguez became the first catcher in history to hit 20 homers and steal 20 bases in the same season. (The closest any catcher had come to a 20-20 season was in 1987, when San Diego's Benito Santiago hit 18 homers and stole 21 bases.) Rodriguez and Jim Sundberg have combined to win 16 Gold Gloves for the Texas Rangers franchise.

◆ Did you know Frankie Hayes, Ray Mueller, and Mike Tresh are the only three receivers since 1895 to catch every game their teams played in one season? Hayes, who also holds the record of 312 consecutive games caught, achieved that mark in 1944 for the Athletics. Mueller also achieved that mark for the Reds in 1944, and Tresh did it in 1945 for the White Sox. Hayes and Mueller caught 155 games, and Tresh caught 150 games. A big reason this trio was asked to catch so many games was World War II, during which many players (among them the trio's backups) were drafted. Teams were often left with no choice but to overuse their talented players, to compensate for their lack of depth.

246. *Match these owners and executives with their achievements:*

1	Clark Griffith	A	was the first female owner and team president
2	Aaron Champion	B	was the first female owner of a World Series champion
3	Helen Britton	C	was a pitcher, manager, and owner
4	Judge Fuchs	D	was the last owner to manage his club for an entire season
5	Marge Schott	E	was first owner in baseball history
6	Joan Whitney Payson	F	was the owner of the 1990 champion Reds

ANSWER: 1—C, 2—E, 3—A, 4—D, 5—F, 6—B

"The Old Fox," as Griffith was known, had a Hall of Fame career packed with adventure. As a diminutive right-handed pitcher, Griffith won 240 of his 381 decisions (with a 3.31 career ERA) over a 20-year career with the Cubs, White Sox, Yankees (then the Highlanders, for whom Griffith became the first manager), Reds, and Senators. The five-foot-six, 156-pound Griffith was also a player-manager for the latter two teams, but he played in only four games during those stops. He managed the Washington Senators from 1912 to 1920, when he took over as president with a controlling interest in the team. He finally won his first World Series in 1924, with subsequent pennants in 1925 and 1933 (in 1901 with the White Sox, he went 24-7 to help win the first American League pennant). Still not profiting enough, Griffith was forced to sell his successful player-manager and uncle-in-law Joe Cronin for $225,000 after the 1934 season just to keep the club in Washington. Griffith died in 1955, and his son Calvin took over the team in Griffith Stadium. . . . Joan Whitney Payson was the original owner of the Mets, presiding over the Amazin' 1969 world champions. She died in 1975. She might just be the first woman elected into the Baseball Hall of Fame.

◆ Did you know Clark Griffith hired a 27-year-old second baseman named Bucky Harris to manage the 1924 Senators? Not only had Harris never managed before; two-thirds of his players were older than he was. But Griffith and Harris knew what they were doing and had the Senators in their first-ever World Series by October. With the help of fellow Hall of Famers Goose Goslin, Sam Rice, and the great Walter Johnson, Harris won the first of his three pennants as a manager and overcame the heavily favored New York Giants, who were in their fourth straight fall classic, to win the title in seven games. Harris' two RBI forced a Game Seven, and Johnson won his first World Series game to clinch it in relief. Harris, a month shy of his 28th birthday, became the youngest manager to win a world title. Thanks to Griffith, Harris—a career .274 hitter—had successfully embarked on a new career. Harris went on to post 2,157 managerial wins, and he also led the 1947 Yankees to a world championship.

◆ Did you know Joe Cronin, the great hitting shortstop, became AL president in 1959? Cronin capped a full career in the majors that included tenures as a general manager (of the Red Sox) and manager by presiding over the American League for 14 years and 11 months. In 1933 Cronin became the youngest player-manager to win the pennant, leading the Senators to the World Series at the age of 26. In 1934 he married owner Clark Griffith's niece, Mildred Robertson, and was traded to the Red Sox for financial reasons. In 1945 he concluded a wonderful 20-year playing career that featured eight 100-RBI seasons and a .301 lifetime batting average. Two years later he retired from managing, after a 15-year managerial career that featured a .540 winning percentage.

247. *Match these pitchers with their feats:*

1	Roger Clemens	A hurled a shutout at least once in a record 21 straight seasons
2	Grover Alexander	B holds the record for strikeouts (35) in a seven-game World Series
3	Bob Gibson	C holds the record for strikeouts (23) in a four-game World Series
4	Walter Johnson	D shares the highest single-season win total since 1968 with Steve Carlton
5	Warren Spahn	E once hurled 52 innings at the start of a season before issuing a walk
6	Bob Welch	F is one of only two pitchers to win 300 games and never strike out 200 in a season

7 Sandy Koufax   G is the last AL Cy Young Award winner to win 20 games the year after receiving the award, and is the only pitcher to win 60 percent of his decisions and strike out 200 batters for seven straight seasons

ANSWER: 1—G, 2—E, 3—B, 4—A, 5—F, 6—D, 7—C

Johnson's 21-year streak helped him accumulate a career record of 110 shutouts, 20 more than runner-up Grover Alexander, 30 more than Christy Mathewson, and 34 more than Cy Young. In *Walter Johnson: A Life*, Jack Kavanagh said, "[Johnson's] already unbreakable lifetime total of 110 shutouts would have been much higher had his team's defense been steadier and he less generous to batters when a game was safely won." . . . Clemens' league-best 2.41 ERA in 1992 was his third straight ERA title and the fourth of six. . . . Randy Johnson is the last NL pitcher to win 20 games the year following a Cy Young Award–winning campaign. . . . Early Wynn is the only other pitcher to win 300 games and not have a single 200-strikeout season. . . . Welch went 27-6 for Oakland in 1990. Not only did that spectacular ledger represent his only 20-win season; it marked his only season of more than 17 wins. . . . Although Gibson's 35 strikeouts in the 1968 fall classic remain the single-series record, his mark over a single post-season has been surpassed a few times. Randy Johnson now holds the record, with 47 in 2001. Johnson took advantage of the current three-tier postseason structure. Gibson's still-standing record of 17 strike-outs in Game One of the 1968 World Series broke the mark of 15, set by Koufax exactly five years earlier. (Koufax broke the mark of 14 set by the Dodgers' Carl Erskine 10 years earlier.) Gibson walked just one in the masterful five-hit shutout to open the 1968 fall classic.

◆ Did you know Roger Clemens in 1986 became the only pitcher to win the MVP Award, the Cy Young Award, and the All-Star Game MVP in one sea-son? Clemens, who went 24-4 with a 2.48 ERA, remains the only starting pitcher since 1971 to win the MVP. Clemens started that season 14-0.

◆ Did you know that Roger Clemens, in his first year away from the Boston Red Sox organization, 1997, became the first American Leaguer to win the pitcher's Triple Crown since Hal Newhouser in 1945? Determined to prove that the Red Sox' decision to not re-sign him following the 1996 season was a mistake, Clemens went 21-7 with a 2.05 ERA and a career-high 292 strikeouts. He then proved it was no fluke by repeating the feat in 1998, joining Lefty Grove, Grover Cleveland Alexander, and Sandy Koufax as the only pitchers to win the pitcher's Triple Crown in consecutive seasons. Newhouser in 1945 went 25-9 with an ERA of 1.81 and 212 punchouts.

248. *Match these pitchers with their histories:*

1	Vean Gregg	A	is the only eligible pitcher in the 3,000-K club not in the Hall of Fame
2	Wes Ferrell	B	pitched the most lopsided no-hitter (15-0) in the 20th century
3	Frank Smith	C	won 20 games in each of his first three seasons
4	Randy Johnson	D	won 20 games in each of his first four full seasons
5	Bert Blyleven	E	tied the modern record for the most wins in April (six)

ANSWER: 1—C, 2—D, 3—B, 4—E, 5—A

Gregg, who combined for 63 victories from 1911 to 1913 for Cleveland, never again won more than 12 games, concluding an eight-year career with a ledger of 92-63 and a 2.70 ERA. . . . Ferrell remains the last pitcher to win 20 games in each of his first three full seasons, adding 23 victories in his fourth full season (sixth overall) for a 20th-century record. Also for the Indians, Ferrell went 21-10 in 1929, 25-13 in 1930, 22-12 in 1931, and 23-13 in 1932. What a start! Ferrell won 20 games twice more in a 15-year career that included 193 wins. . . . Smith of the White Sox no-hit the Tigers on September 6, 1905, in the second game of a doubleheader. Going back to the 1800s, only Pud Galvin's 18-0 gem on August 4, 1882, was more lopsided. . . . Johnson actually accomplished the feat twice for Arizona, in April 2000 and April 2002, tying Dave Stewart (1988) and Vida Blue (1971). The Big Unit was 6-0 with an 0.91 ERA in April 2000, and 6-0 with a 1.37 ERA in April 2002.

◆ Did you know Oakland's Tim Hudson in 2000 became the seventh pitcher in history with 20 wins in his first 24 career decisions? He joined King Cole, Ferdie Schupp, Larry Jansen, Whitey Ford, Vida Blue, and Juan Guzman.

249. *Match these relievers with their histories:*

1	Bobby Thigpen	A	began his career as a starter, completing only 2 games in his first 27 starts
2	Mitch Williams	B	holds the record of eight wins in relief during one month
3	Gregg Olson	C	became the first reliever in history to record 30 saves for three different teams
4	Rollie Fingers	D	did not allow a run in a record 26 straight appearances
5	Jeff Reardon	E	recorded 13 saves in one month during the 1990 season, tying John Franco's feat of July 1988

ANSWER: 1—E, 2—B, 3—D, 4—A, 5—C

Lee Smith broke Thigpen and Franco's mark by registering 15 saves in June 1993. Robb Nen saved 14 games in setting the mark for July, in 2000. . . . Mitch Williams set a reliever's record for most wins in a month. In August of 1991, the "Wild Thing" went 8-1 in relief with five saves and a 1.34 ERA for the Phillies. . . . Aside from the 26 consecutive scoreless appearances, Olson—the 1989 American League Rookie of the Year—also hurled 36 consecutive scoreless innings. Warren Brusstar of the Cubs in 1983 pitched shutout ball in 25 consecutive appearances.

◆ Did you know Toronto's John Frascatore tied a major league record, held by eight others, by earning wins in three consecutive games? The right-handed reliever earned a win on June 29, June 30, and July 1, in 1999. Other American Leaguers to turn the trick are California's Chuck McElroy, three years earlier, Hal White of the Tigers (September 26,* 27, and 28, 1950), Grant Jackson of Baltimore (September 29 and 30, and October 1, 1974), and the Yankees' Sparky Lyle (August 29, 30, and 31, in his Cy Young season of 1977). In the National League, the pitchers who have accomplished the feat are the Dodgers' Mike Marshall (June 21, 22, and 23, also his Cy Young season), Gene Garber of the Phillies (May 15,* 16, and 17, 1975), Al "The Mad Hungarian" Hrabosky of the Cardinals (July 12, 13, and 17, 1975), and Pittsburgh submariner Kent Tekulve (May 6, 7, 9, 1980). Dates with an asterisk represent the second game of a doubleheader.

250. *The Dodgers of the 1960s won primarily on the strength of their pitching, speed, and defense. Scores such as 1-0, 2-1, and 3-2 were common, as the offense was less than spectacular. But then again, it didn't have to carry the load, because the team had pitchers such as Sandy Koufax, Don Drysdale, Claude Osteen, and Ron Perranoski. In fact, the 1965 world champion Dodgers didn't have a single .300 hitter except for this pitcher. Can you name this team's leading hitter?*

ANSWER: Don Drysdale

Drysdale hit .300 (39-for-130) with seven homers and a .508 slugging percentage in 1965. His total of seven homers that season not only was just five fewer than the team's leader but also tied the NL single-season mark for pitchers, which he had already shared with Don Newcombe. Three years after Newcombe's feat in 1955, Drysdale enjoyed the first of a pair of seven-homer campaigns. In 2001 Mike Hampton tied their NL record. Hampton, by the way, also slugged .582, taking advantage of Coors Field's thin air.

251. *Match these great Dodger teams with their memorable achievements:*

1	1955 Dodgers	A	posted a .213 batting average, the worst in NL history
2	1966 Dodgers	B	gave a beautiful tribute to Roy Campanella, as a record 93,103 fans came to the Los Angeles Coliseum on "Roy Campanella Night" to demonstrate their love for the man paralyzed in an auto accident
3	1908 Dodgers	C	used only five starters all year, a record low for the 20th century
4	1956 Dodgers	D	beat the Phillies, 5-4, in 10 innings, at Roosevelt Stadium in the first game ever played in New Jersey
5	1959 Dodgers	E	became the first team to bounce back from a two games to none deficit in a best-of-seven World Series

ANSWER: 1—E, 2—C, 3—A, 4—D, 5—B

In the 1921 fall classic, the Giants also lost the first two games but won the best-of-nine series, five games to three. In 1996 the Yankees became the 11th team—and 10th in a best-of-seven series—to make such a comeback, beating the Braves in six games. . . . The five Dodger starters in 1966 were Sandy Koufax, Don Drysdale, Claude Osteen, Joe Moeller, and rookie Don Sutton. . . . The Dodgers played a total of 15 games in Jersey City over the 1956 and 1957 seasons, going 11-4. . . . Campanella, the three-time MVP and future Hall of Famer, crashed his car on the icy roads of Long Island, New York, on the night of January 28, 1958. The accident left him paralyzed from the chest down. The exhibition game played in his honor, as he watched from his wheel chair, was on May 7, between his Dodgers and the Yankees. Although "Campy" spent the remaining 34 years of his life in a wheel chair, he courageously turned his situation into a positive by helping others, continuing to serve as an ambassador of the Game till his dying day.

◆ Did you know the Dodgers organization held its breath as it endured two more car accidents, following Roy Campanella's, over the next two months in 1958? Jim Gilliam and his family suffered one soon after Campanella's, and Duke Snider, Johnny Podres, and Don Zimmer were involved in a third while trying to beat the team's spring training curfew on March 5. None involved in the two accidents was seriously injured.

◆ Did you know the Los Angeles Coliseum hosted the most attended World Series game ever? In Game Five of the 1959 fall classic between the visiting Chicago White Sox and the Dodgers, a World Series record of 92,706 spectators witnessed the AL champions stave off elimination until the next game with a 1-0 victory, as Bob Shaw outdueled a young Sandy Koufax. Games Three and Four were also witnessed by more than 92,000 fans. The Dodgers wrapped up the series at Comiskey Park in Chicago with a 9-3 rout before 47,653 fans.

252. *Which general manager is responsible for bringing night baseball to the major leagues?*

ANSWER: Larry MacPhail
MacPhail, hired as the Cincinnati Reds general manager in 1933, gained approval from the league and from team owner Powell Crosley Jr. to install arc lights over Crosley Field and play seven night games—

one against each National League opponent—during the course of the 1935 schedule. MacPhail cited an opportunity for increased attendance, because nine-to-five workers would have an opportunity to attend games.

The first night game in major league history was set for May 23, 1935, but it was rained out, so the mega-event had to wait until the following evening. On May 24, following the commemorative button-pressing by President Franklin D. Roosevelt from the White House, the Reds beat the Phillies, 2-1. Critics were silenced as Cincinnati drew more than 61,000 fans over the first three nighttime affairs and averaged more than 18,000 for the seven games. Those figures represented a tremendous improvement over the Reds' customary, day-game totals of less than 5,000. Their success notwithstanding, it took three years for another team to follow the Reds' lead. The Dodgers were the next, adding lights to Ebbets Field and playing under them in 1938.

Ironically enough, the inaugural night game in Wrigley Field (the last established major league stadium to use lights) was also postponed because of rain. The August 8, 1988 (8/8/88), game with the Phillies was postponed in the bottom of the fourth inning, delaying the historic first for one day. So on August 9 the Cubs defeated the Mets, 6-4, in the first official night game at Wrigley Field. Home to the Cubs since 1916, the storied park finally hosted a night game, fifty-three years after Crosley Field. The event made for some talk of broken traditions but also some beautiful images, such as the one in the August 15, 1988, issue of *Sports Illustrated*.

253. *Babe Ruth had the most feared, and one of the most beautiful, swings in the history of the game, a swing that lit up scoreboards with 714 home runs. Ruth was so feared that he drew 2,062 walks, a total that accounted for almost one-fifth of his career plate appearances. Can you name the player whose swing Ruth emulated?*

ANSWER: Joe Jackson

Ruth learned his swing from Joe Jackson, who had 1,774 career hits in 4,981 at-bats, with 785 RBI, 873 runs scored, 168 triples, and 202 stolen bases. As a youngster for the Boston Red Sox, Ruth asked for and received batting tips from Jackson, who obliged with instructions on how to stand in the batter's box. Jackson turned out to be as good a teacher as he was a hitter. In fact, Ruth and Jackson even borrowed each other's bats from time to time, according to Joe Thompson, author of *Growing Up with "Shoeless" Joe.* Thompson also revealed that Jackson used one particular 40-ounce bat, which he endearingly named "Black Betsy," throughout his career without a major break.

◆ Did you know Barry Bonds in 2001 and Mark McGwire in 1998 joined six Hall of Famers in a club of players who led the major leagues in home runs and walks in the same season? Others to accomplish the feat were Babe Ruth, Lou Gehrig, Ted Williams, Hank Greenberg, Mike Schmidt, and Harmon Killebrew.

254. *The 1930 Philadelphia Phillies batted .315 but still finished in last place with a 52-102 record, due to an awful 6.71 ERA. Who was their leading hitter?*

ANSWER: Chuck Klein

Hall of Fame right fielder Chuck Klein hit .386, left fielder Lefty O'Doul hit .383, and third baseman Pinky Whitney hit .342. The Phillies remain the only team to finish in the cellar despite hitting .300. Their starting rotation was horrible, save for ace Phil Collins, who finished with a mighty 16-11 record and a 4.78 ERA. Southpaw Les Sweetland was 7-15 with a 7.71 ERA, Claude Willoughby went an abysmal 4-17 with a 7.59 ERA, Hal Elliott was 6-11 with a 7.67 ERA, and Hap Collard was 6-12 with an ERA of 6.80 ERA. Ray Benge was 11-15 with an ERA of 5.70, decent by comparison.

The Phillies' 6.71 ERA and 1,199 runs allowed that year remain dubious major league records. The Phillies, who had posted a hefty ERA of 6.13 the year before, allowed opposing teams to bat .342 off them in 1930.

255. *Match these ball players with their histories:*

1	Dave Bancroft	A	his career .425 on-base percentage is 15th best on the all-time list
2	Ferris Fain	B	played on five world championship teams
3	Reggie Jackson	C	never led the league in RBI

4 Willie Mays   D holds the single-season shortstop record
                     of 984 total chances

ANSWER: 1—D, 2—A, 3—B, 4—C

Bancroft's 984 chances were achieved for the New York Giants during the 1922 season. . . . From 1971 to 1982, Jackson proved himself as a winner by helping his team win the division 10 times (only his 1976 Orioles and 1979 Yankees teams failed to win the division during that 12-year span) and the pennant 6 times. . . . Mays did finish second twice and third three times. He posted 10 seasons of at least 100 RBI, including a high of 141 in 1962.

◆ Did you know Reggie Jackson became the only player to strike out 100 times for 18 straight years (the strike-shortened 1981 season excluded) with 115 punchouts in 1986? But Reggie still survived. The streak started in 1968 (his second year) and almost would have included the strike-shortened 1981 season, when he struck out 82 times in only 94 contests. His highest single-season strikeout total was 171, in 1968. Jackson retired following the 1987 campaign, in which he whiffed 97 times in 336 at-bats. Reggie's 2,597 career strikeouts head the all-time list. For Jackson, the high totals were merely necessary baggage on the road to 563 career home runs.

◆ Did you know Mark McGwire struck out 155 times and walked 162 times in his record-breaking season of 1998, for a record total of 317 non-contact at-bats?

256. *Match these players with their places in baseball folklore:*

1 Paul School   A succeeded Mickey Mantle in center field
                     and, later on, Ernie Banks at first
2 Joe Pepitone   B was traded from the Orioles to the Reds
                     for Frank Robinson, who won the Triple
                     Crown in his first American League season
3 Manny Sanguillen   C was replaced by George Brett at third base
4 Milt Pappas   D succeeded Thurman Munson behind the
                     plate
5 Jerry Narron   E succeeded Roberto Clemente in right field

ANSWER: 1—C, 2—A, 3—E, 4—B, 5—D

Sanguillen took over right field for his very close friend Clemente but lasted just 59 games in right, committing eight errors during that time. Richie Zisk played in right for the next year and a half in Pittsburgh before giving way to a fellow by the name of David Gene Parker. . . . While the other eight Yankee starters stood at their positions during a pre-game tribute to Munson the day after his tragic plane crash of August 2, 1979, Narron waited on the top step of the Yankee Stadium dugout, leaving home plate vacant in honor of the team's deceased captain.

◆ Did you know the two passengers with Thurman Munson on that plane crash survived but couldn't rescue him amidst the flames? Munson was the pilot of the private jet that crashed just short of the runway at Akron-Canton Airport in Ohio. Munson loved flying, and he often flew on off-days during the season in order to spend time with his family.

257. *This club recorded the highest team batting average in history, led the league in fielding, and had the league's third best ERA, but still finished in third place. Can you name this squad?*

ANSWER: The 1930 New York Giants

The 1930 Giants, who hit an incredible .319, finished a disappointing five games behind St. Louis and three games behind second-place Chicago. The Giants posted a league-leading .974 fielding average and a 4.59 ERA. They were led by Bill Terry's .401 mark, Fred Lindstrom's .379 mark (only fifth in the league when it would have led the circuit in any of the following four years), Mel Ott's .349, and Travis Jackson's .339.

Contributing to these very high batting averages and ERAs was the decision by Judge Kenesaw Landis and the major league owners to liven the ball (by using a thicker and fuller rubber core) so as to create more excitement among the fans, thus increasing attendance figures that had been hurt by the Great Depression.

Also in that year, the Phillies yielded a record 1,199 runs, and the Pirates' pitcher Ray Kremer became the first pitcher in history to win 20 games with an earned run average of greater than five (5.02).

◆ Did you know the lowest batting average of the 160 professional baseball teams (in the majors and minors) during the 1930 season was .258? The National League averaged (yes, averaged) .303, the American League averaged .288, the Central League, .308, the American Association, .307, the Southern Association, .304, the N.Y.-Penn. League, .303, and the Pacific Coast League, .302.

258. *Match these pitchers with their performances:*

1	Dazzy Vance	A	had the highest single-season ERA (of 9.85) among pitchers with at least 89 innings in the 20th century
2	Bobo Newsom	B	once went 18-7 with a 5.27 ERA
3	Steve Blass	C	was one of only two starters in 1930 with an ERA under 3.00
4	Roxie Lawson	D	was one of seven 20-game winners in 1930, and one of the only 20-win duo of teammates that year
5	George Earnshaw	E	posted the highest single-season ERA (5.08) for a 20-game winner (1938), yielding a 20th-century record 186 earned runs

ANSWER: 1—C, 2—E, 3—A, 4—B, 5—D

In 1930 Vance and Lefty Grove were the only starters with an ERA under 3.00. Vance of Brooklyn paced the senior circuit with an ERA of 2.61, while Grove of the Athletics led the American League with an ERA of 2.54. . . . Earnshaw (22 wins) teamed up with Grove (28 wins) to form the only 20-win duo in 1930, a nightmare year for pitchers in which the Cubs' Guy Bush would post an ERA of 6.20 (the worst ever for a 200-inning performer) yet still go 15-10. . . . Lawson's 1937 campaign was by far his best in a nine-year career that featured a 5.37 ERA.

◆ Did you know the National League's composite ERA in 1930 was 4.97, and the American League's ERA was 4.65? The Washington Senators' 3.96 ERA represented the only team figure under 4.28!

259. *Match the following pitchers with their performances:*

1	Jim Merritt	A	once won 16 games in a row
2	Bob Grim	B	won two games in the 1960 World Series

3	Harvey Haddix	C	was the last pitcher to win 20 games with an ERA of over 4.00 prior to Jack Morris in 1992
4	Ewell Blackwell	D	this Dodger faced four batters in his debut and surrendered four straight hits before being taken out, never to return to professional baseball
5	Henry Heitmann	E	once won 20 games with fewer than 200 innings pitched

ANSWER: 1—C, 2—E, 3—B, 4—A, 5—D

Merritt was 20-12 with a 4.08 ERA for the Reds in 1970. Morris went 21-6 with a 4.04 ERA for the world champion Blue Jays in 1992. . . . A pitching paradox of more recent time occurred in 2001, when Roger Clemens became the first starting pitcher to earn the Cy Young Award without a complete game. His 3.51 ERA was the second highest among AL Cy Young Award winners, behind only LaMarr Hoyt's figure of 3.66 in 1983. . . . Grim was 20-6 in 199 innings pitched for the Yankees in 1954. Pedro Martinez was 20-4 in 199⅓ innings pitched in 2002. . . . Heitmann completed the shortest pitching career in history against St. Louis on July 27, 1918.

◆ Did you know Earl Whitehill is the pitcher with the highest career ERA among 200-game winners? The left-handed Whitehill, who pitched for the Tigers, Senators, Indians, and Cubs from 1923 to 1939, retired with a record of 218-185 and an ERA of 4.36. He was able to keep his ERA under 4.00 in only 5 of his 17 seasons.

260. *Match these pitchers with their histories:*

1	Rube Waddell	A	made what is believed to be the worst relief appearance in history
2	Jack Chesbro	B	set an AL record by walking only 29 batters in 380 innings
3	Eddie Rommel	C	his wild pitch cost his team a shot at the pennant, with one game left in the season
4	Cy Young	D	was the last out in Cy Young's perfect game

ANSWER: 1—D, 2—C, 3—A, 4—B

In Cy Young's perfect game, Waddell was not lifted for a pinch-hitter despite a .162 career average and .122 average during that 1904 season. The only other perfect game in which a pitcher made the last out was the gem thrown by Monte Ward, who retired Pud Galvin. . . . After winning 41 games (a 20th-century record) for the Highlanders in 1904, Chesbro uncorked a wild pitch that allowed the Boston Pilgrims—owners of a 1½-game lead entering the penultimate game of the season—to win the game, 3-2, and clinch the pennant on October 10. Chesbro and Ed Walsh stand as the only two pitchers to register 40 wins in the modern era. . . . Rommel took over in the second inning and yielded 14 runs on 29 hits over the final 17 frames during an 18-17 Athletics victory over the Indians. Rommel was not relieved because he and ineffective starter Lew Krause were the only two pitchers manager Connie Mack brought with him for the one-game series at Cleveland. Perhaps Mack reacted too soon after Krause gave up three runs and four hits in the first. Rommel became the lucky winner, anyway, in the wild, 18-inning game on July 10, 1932. (Incidentally, it was during that contest that Johnny Burnett produced a record nine hits.)

As to horrible outings, Cincinnati's Harley "Doc" Parker may have had the worst start of the 20th century. On June 21, 1901, Parker gave up 21 runs—14 earned—and 26 hits in a 21-2 loss to Brooklyn. The eight-inning outing was his only appearance of the season and, not surprisingly, his last major league game. He pitched in 17 games for the Cubs during the 1890s.

◆ Did you know Christy Mathewson's total of 37 wins in 1908 was the highest NL figure of the 20th century? In a campaign that featured a 37-11 record, Mathewson, as did Jack Chesbro, ended the season on a down note. He lost to the Cubs in the "Fred Merkle" game that decided the NL pennant. Mathewson had three other 30-win and seven other 25-win seasons.

◆ Did you know Zip Zabel's 18⅓-inning relief appearance remains the longest in major league history? On June 17, 1915, the Cubs' Zabel entered the game with two out in the first inning and won a 19-inning, 4-3 decision over the Brooklyn Dodgers.

261. *Match these winners with their awards:*

1	Harmon Killebrew	A	1967 NL Cy Young Award
2	Boog Powell	B	1956 AL Rookie of the Year
3	Early Wynn	C	1959 Cy Young Award
4	Mike McCormick	D	1969 AL MVP
5	Luis Aparicio	E	1970 AL MVP

ANSWER: 1—D, 2—E, 3—C, 4—A, 5—B

Killebrew in 1969 hit 45 home runs and drove in 140 runners despite being walked 145 times, for a .430 on-base percentage. . . . In an otherwise ordinary career, the southpaw McCormick won 22 of 32 decisions with a 2.85 ERA in 262⅓ innings for the Giants in 1967.

262. *Can you name the only player to win MVP honors during the 1930s and not gain entry into the Hall of Fame?*

ANSWER: Bucky Walters

In 1939, Cincinnati righthander Bucky Walters led the National League with 27 wins (against 11 losses), a 2.29 ERA, 31 complete games, and 319 innings. He also paced the senior circuit with 137 strikeouts that year, just three seasons after leading the majors with 21 losses. Walters, who pitched for 16 years and registered a 198-160 career record with a 3.30 ERA and 242 complete games, also won each of his two starts in the 1940 World Series with an ERA of 1.50. His standout 1940 series performance came one year after losing both appearances in the 1939 fall classic against the Yankees.

Although Walters and Derringer each won two games in the 1940 classic, it was the performance of little-used outfielder Jimmy Ripple that caught most people off-guard. The left-handed hitter, who spent a good deal of the 1940 season in the Dodgers' minor league system, was picked up as a free agent by the Reds after the Dodgers were penalized for misusing the waiver rule. In 32 games down the stretch that year, Ripple batted .307 for Cincinnati with a .397 on-base percentage and a .525 slugging mark, helping the Reds win the NL pennant. In the subsequent World Series, Ripple put on an offensive show. He helped the Reds tie the series at a game apiece by breaking a 2-2 tie with a third-inning, two-run homer in Game Two. Ripple doubled in the Reds' third run in their 5-2 victory in Game Four, again helping the Reds tie the series, was 2-for-2 with an RBI single in the first inning of a 4-0 win in Game Six, helping the Reds knot the series for the third time. The clutch Ripple came through yet again in Game Seven, during which the Reds trailed 1-0 entering the bottom of the seventh. With Frank McCormick on second base and none out, Ripple drilled a pitch from Tiger starter Bobo Newsom (who had already won two games in the series) off the right-field screen at Crosley Field, plating McCormick with the tying run. After catcher Jimmie Wilson sacrificed Ripple to third and pinch hitter Ernie Lombardi was intentionally walked, shortstop Billy Myers launched a deep sacrifice fly to center, driving in Ripple with the series-deciding run. All told, Ripple slugged .571 in the series, got on board 44 percent of the time, and drove in six runs to carry the Reds' offense, while Walters and Derringer carried the pitching load. For the unheralded Ripple, who batted .282 over a career that spanned parts of seven seasons, the 1940 World Series marked his third classic in five years—and the third classic in which he boasted an on-base percentage of at least .400.

Incidentally, McCormick (the team's first baseman) gave the Reds a second straight MVP season that 1940 campaign, driving home 127 runners with 19 homers, 44 doubles, and a .309 batting average.

The previously retired Wilson wasn't supposed to be laying down any bunts or calling great games for Walters or Derringer. The 40-year-old was a Reds coach when Lombardi, the team's starting catcher, went down with an injury. A solid catcher for the Cardinals in his day, Wilson donned the tools of ignorance during the September stretch run, helped the Reds comfortably defeat the pack, and then shocked the Tigers by batting .353 in the series. He retired (for good) after the series, with a second world championship ring as a player—a well-earned reward for a solid performance in the clutch.

263. *Match these Most Valuable Players with their distinctions:*

1	Rickey Henderson	A	the only winner from a Canadian team
2	Kevin Mitchell	B	the oldest winner in history (39 years old)
3	George Bell	C	the 1990 AL winner
4	Willie Stargell	D	the 1989 NL winner

ANSWER: 1—C, 2—D, 3—A, 4—B

Toronto's George Bell won his MVP in 1987. Bell and Sammy Sosa (1998) are the only Dominican MVP winners. . . . Stargell was a great leader and a father figure to his own teammates as captain of the "We Are Family" 1979 Pirates squad. He was such a respected authority figure, teammates did as he said and looked forward to receiving "Stargell Stars," golden-colored stars he gave out for outstanding plays or hustle. Incredibly, his teammates didn't consider themselves above such a reward and played their hearts out for them.

◆ Did you know the MVP Award is also known as the Landis Plaque, in honor of Kenesaw Mountain Landis? During the 1944 World Series, the BBWAA decided to honor the bed-ridden commissioner, whose health was failing, by giving the Most Valuable Player the Landis Plaque. Previous winners were given the *Sporting News* Trophy.

264. *As a group, Major League Baseball teams were not receptive to the idea of integration. That's no secret. Very few organizations are free of culpability for the ban, and for the slow acceptance of African Americans into their culture afterwards. Which pre-expansion team was the last to integrate and has had the fewest African Americans don its uniform since the color barrier was broken?*

ANSWER: The Boston Red Sox

The Red Sox finally joined the ranks of the integrated major league teams on July 21, 1959, when Elijah "Pumpsie" Green pinch-ran for them. He then started at second base the next day, going 0-for-3. Green, a second baseman whom Boston had cut the day before its season opener that year, was joined by right-handed pitcher Earl Wilson a week later.

Even after they integrated (12 years after the first major league team, and 2 years after the Boston Bruins of the National Hockey League), the Red Sox were known as an organization with few black players. According to a stunning August 4, 1991, report in the *Boston Globe*, the Red Sox had employed only 33 African American major leaguers, "the fewest of any major league club," during the four and a half decades since Jackie Robinson broke the color barrier, and had never had more than 5 African American players on the team at a time. The report also noted that very few African Americans could be found among the fans at recent games at Fenway, citing informal surveys indicating that there were no more than 80 African Americans in attendance at any one.

At least one former player, Tommy Harper, has sued the organization for alleged discrimination, according to Howard Bryant, author of *Shut Out: A Story of Race and Baseball in Boston.* And according to the *Boston Globe,* the Boston chapter of the NAACP filed discrimination charges against the team for originally waiving Green.

265. *Match these players with their lesser-known achievements:*

1	Roger Maris	A	hit 100 home runs for three different teams
2	Darrell Evans	B	hit 35 career lead-off home runs, including 11 in one season
3	Harry Hooper	C	set a national high school football record by returning four kickoffs for touchdowns in one game
4	Bobby Bonds	D	once led off each game of a doubleheader with a home run

ANSWER: 1—C, 2—A, 3—D, 4—B

Evans became the second player to hit 100 homers for three different teams (Atlanta, San Francisco, and Detroit). Reggie Jackson is the only other (Oakland, New York Yankees, and California). . . . Hooper accomplished that feat for the Red Sox on May 13, 1913, versus Washington, a feat not duplicated for another 80 years, when Oakland's Rickey Henderson led off each game of a July 5, 1993, doubleheader against Cleveland with a home run. Hooper, who hit 10 lead-off home runs during a 17-year career played mostly in the Dead Ball Era, is recognized mostly for his defensive abilities (outstanding range, a sure glove, and 344 outfield assists) in right field. But his offensive abilities were considerable, too. The left-handed hitter boasted a .281 career batting average with a .368 on-base percentage, 1,429 runs scored, 375 stolen bases, 1,136 walks, and 160 triples. . . . Bonds' career lead-off home run total is surpassed only by Rickey Henderson, who has 80 through the 2002 season, and Brady Anderson, who hit 44. The retired Devon White had 34 for the fourth best total ever, and Paul Molitor had 33. On September 29, 1996, Baltimore's Brady Anderson reached three milestones with one swing of the bat. He broke Bonds' 1973 mark of 11 lead-off homers in a season by launching his twelfth to start the season finale. The blast also enabled Anderson to tie the single-season home run mark from the top spot of the order (35) as well as register his 50th homer of the campaign. Bonds also hit 35 homers in a season in games in which he batted first, doing so in 1973. Anderson helped his cause earlier in the year by doubling a previous record, shared by many, as he led off four consecutive games with a homer. He performed the incredible feat from April 18 to 21.

◆ Did you know Anaheim Angels left fielder Darin Erstad set a major league record in 2000 by driving in 100 runs as a lead-off hitter? The Yankees' Alfonso Soriano had 99 of his 102 RBI from the lead-off spot in 2002. Boston Red Sox shortstop Nomar Garciaparra held the record of 98 for three years, having shattered the mark of 85 set 41 years earlier by Harvey Kuenn of the Detroit Tigers. Garciaparra also hit 30 home runs, the fifth highest total for a lead-off man, to run away with Rookie of the Year honors. According to researcher Herman Krabbenhoft, Kuenn broke the mark of 84 RBI shared by Taylor Douthit of the 1930 St. Louis Cardinals and Dom DiMaggio of the 1948 Boston Red Sox.

266. *Match these major league parks with their history:*

1 Briggs Stadium — A with the closing of Tiger Stadium, this is the oldest park in the majors, having served as a major league home longer than any other

2 Braves Field — B the site of the 1954 All-Star Game, which saw reliever Dean Stone win the game without facing a batter

3 Fenway Park — C the last AL park to install lights

4 Municipal Stadium — D it took 10 years for someone to hit an over-the-fence home run in this park

ANSWER: 1—C, 2—D, 3—A, 4—B

Fenway Park and Tiger Stadium (then Navin Field) each opened on April 20, 1912, a few days after America learned of the sinking of the Titanic. (Each home team won its opener in 11 innings.) Exactly four years later, on April 20, 1916, the Cubs moved into Wrigley Field, which will be hosting major league games for its 90th campaign in 2003 (it hosted the Federal League's Chicago Whales during its first two years). Fenway Park will be in its 92nd year of hosting major league games in 2003. Tiger Stadium served as home of the Tigers for 88 years. Yankee Stadium will be hosting Yankee games for its 79th season in 2003. . . . . After first viewing Braves Field and its ever-so prodigious dimensions of 402 feet down the lines and 550 feet straight away in 1915, Ty Cobb proclaimed, "no one will ever hit a baseball out of this park." The Giants' Frank Snyder on May 28, 1925, became the first player to hit a ball out. And it wasn't until 1928 that the dimensions were reduced to 353 feet down the lines and 387 feet to center. . . . . Dean Stone threw out Red Schoendienst attempting to steal home in that 1954 All-Star Game for the win.

◆ Did you know Hugh Bradley became the first to homer over the 37-foot, two-inch left-field wall at Fenway Park in 1912? The wall wasn't called "Green Monster" until 1947, when it was painted green to cover billboard ads for Calvert, Lifebuoy Soap, and Gem Blades.

◆ Did you know Ted Williams warned Rip Sewell not to throw his famous "Eephus" pitch during the 1946 All-Star Game at Fenway Park? The serious Williams, wanting no part of that slow-moving floater, especially amidst a ter- rific performance in front of his own fans at Fenway, shook his head in Sewell's direction as he came to bat in the eighth inning of a 9-0 AL rout. With two men on, Williams fell behind Sewell, who sandwiched a fastball be- tween a pair of "Eephus" pitches. Expecting anything with a 1-2 count, Williams timed Sewell's next high-arching bloop just right, sending it over the right-field wall for his second home run and fourth hit of the game. Williams, who reached base in all five plate appearances, drove in four and scored four as well to lead the junior circuit to a 12-0 victory in arguably the greatest individual offensive showcase in All-Star Game history. Sewell, a two- time 20-game winner during the war years, was past his prime and relying on the trick pitch to upset batters' timing.

267. *Match these parks with their histories:*

1 Los Angeles's   A has always raised its 1919 pennant flag at
   Wrigley Field   half-mast

2	Wrigley Field	B	where a flag is raised to signal a win or loss following a game
3	Comiskey Park	C	where 72,086 fans attended an All-Star Game and welcomed back baseball after the 1981 strike
4	Tiger Stadium	D	where Ted Williams' walk-off three-run homer in the 1941 All-Star Game gave the American League a 7-5 win
5	Municipal Stadium	E	home of the Los Angeles Angels in 1961 and where the famous 1959 Home Run Derby took place

ANSWER: 1—E, 2—B, 3—A, 4—D, 5—C

The Home Run Derby was held following the 1959 season and was aired in July of 1960. It included 26 shows, each one pitting two power hitters against each other. The winner was invited to come back for the next show, while the loser had to wait for his next turn. Hank Aaron won the most challenges and took home the most money, $13,500 of the $84,500 in total prize money, according to Dave Gush of the Society for American Baseball Research. Other competitors included the likes of Mickey Mantle (who won the last show in the event's history over Jackie Jensen), Willie Mays, Harmon Killebrew, Rocky Colavito, Ernie Banks, Frank Robinson, Eddie Mathews, Duke Snider, and Dick Stuart. Mantle's 44 total home runs were the most in the tournament. Jensen defeated Banks, 14-11, in the highest scoring contest.

◆ Did you know the Padres hosted the first major league games in Mexico and Hawaii? On April 19, 1997, the Padres hosted the Cardinals for a doubleheader in the opening game of a three-game series billed as the Padres Paradise Series at Honolulu Stadium. The Padres lost the first two games to the Cardinals before salvaging the finale. This came less than a year after they hosted the Mets in a three-game series in Monterrey, Mexico, from August 16 to 18, marketed as La Primera Serie. The Padres won two of three in the first major league games ever played outside the United States or Canada. The Padres in 1999 made history again by hosting the first-ever season-opening game outside the United States or Canada, losing, 8-2, to the Colorado Rockies on April 4 in Monterrey.

The 2000 season began with a series between the Mets and Cubs on March 29 and 30 at the Tokyo Dome in Japan. Those games marked the first major league games outside North America. The teams split the two games, with the Cubs winning the opener and the Mets triumphing the next night.

The Blue Jays and Rangers opened the 2001 season in San Juan, Puerto Rico, marking the third consecutive season that MLB started its regular season outside the continental United States. The game was played at Hiram Bithorn Stadium, where many a major leaguer has played winter ball.

268. *Match these parks with their histories:*

1 Weeghman Park   A was later known as Wrigley Field
2 Shibe Park   B was also known as Connie Mack Stadium
3 Hilltop Park   C was the park for the Highlanders, later known as the Yankees
4 Dodger Stadium   D is located on the real estate known as Chavez Ravine

ANSWER: 1—A, 2—B, 3—C, 4—D

Connie Mack Stadium was the first-ever steel and concrete park. It was also the park where the hosting Athletics invited the cross-town Phillies to play after their home, the Baker Bowl, collapsed twice, causing a total of 13 deaths and about 250 injuries. . . . Dodger Stadium and Chavez Ravine were a part of the sale of the Dodgers in 1998. In 1997 Dodgers owner Peter O'Malley announced that he would sell the Dodgers and the team's property to Fox Television owner and media mogul Rupert Murdoch for $350 million. Murdoch received arguably the best run organization in sports.

◆ Did you know speculation still exists that the Cleveland Indians, leading the 1948 World Series three games to one, lost Game Five at home on purpose so as to avoid the destruction of their field? A record crowd of 86,288 gathered for Game Five, but the Boston Braves untied a 5-5 duel with a six-run seventh inning to stay alive. Before the game there was talk that fans would rush onto the field if the Indians won. The Indians peacefully wrapped up the series in Boston the next day. Owner Bill Veeck made out like a bandit, drawing 238,491 fans for the three games without having to pay for damages.

269. *Who was the pitcher that Athletics manager Connie Mack chose to hold out of the final two weeks of the 1929 season so that he could instead scout the National League's Chicago Cubs in anticipation of a World Series matchup?*

ANSWER: Howard Ehmke

Veteran Howard Ehmke scouted the Cubs' lineup thoroughly, compiling a book each on Rogers Hornsby, Kiki Cuyler, Hack Wilson, Riggs Stephenson, and Charlie Grimm. So impressed was Mack by Ehmke's scouting that he surprised the baseball world by announcing the 35-year-old Ehmke (who went 7-2 with just 55 innings, in his penultimate season) as the starter in Game One, even though he also had Lefty Grove, George Earnshaw, Eddie Rommel, and Rube Walberg to choose from. The side-armer didn't disappoint, striking out a then World Series record 13 batters and going the distance in a 3-1 victory, holding the Cubs scoreless until the bottom of the ninth. The Athletics won the series in five games and held Hornsby (.238), Cuyler, Wilson, Stephenson, and Grimm to a combined five extra base hits, none homers. Remarkably, Mack didn't start Grove or Walberg at all in the series, fearful of the Cubs' heavily right-handed lineup. In fact, Mack started the six-foot-four, right-handed Earnshaw in Game Two and Game Three before going with 46-year-old Jack Quinn in Game Four. Ehmke started Game Five but was replaced by Walberg with two out in the fourth, trailing 2-0. The Athletics won the game, 3-2, with a dramatic ninth inning to wrap up the series.

◆ Did you know the Athletics' George Earnshaw remains the last pitcher to start consecutive games in a single World Series? Earnshaw, who started Games Two and Three in 1929, started Games Five and Six for manager Connie Mack in the 1930 fall classic, further justifying his moniker, "Moose," which reflected his reputation as a workhorse. A 20-game winner in each of the Athletics' pennant-winning seasons from 1929 to 1931, when he was an outstanding 67-28, the hard-throwing Earnshaw was 4-3 with a 1.58 ERA in eight World Series starts.

◆ Did you know that Connie Mack was given the first chance at a 19-year-old minor league pitcher from Baltimore named George Herman Ruth but rejected the "round and slow" youngster bound for Boston? Can you imagine Ruth on the same team as all those Athletics greats?

270. *Match these teams with their feats:*

1 Brewers   A is the last club to have teammates finishing first and second in the MVP voting

2 Indians   B is the only team to sweep the MVP award and Cy Young Award two years in a row

3 White Sox   C once scored nine runs with two outs and nobody on in the ninth to win, 14-13

4 Giants   D registered a major league record 68 saves in one season

ANSWER: 1—B, 2—C, 3—D, 4—A

In 1981 the Brewers' Rollie Fingers took both awards, becoming the first reliever to win the MVP and Cy Young Awards in the same season. The year after, the 1982 Brewers' Pete Vuckovich won the Cy Young Award and Robin Yount won the MVP Award. . . . The Indians' nine runs (still the record for two outs and nobody on) in the ninth came against Washington on May 23, 1901. Trailing by a score of 13-5 with nobody on base, the Tribe put together eight hits, a walk, a hit-batter, and a passed ball off starter Casey Patten and reliever Wally Lee. Two other teams have scored nine runs in the ninth (the 1901 Boston Pilgrims and 1929 Indians), but they both put men on base before two were out, and both won comfortably. . . . In 2000 the Giants' Jeff Kent and Barry Bonds finished one-two in the MVP voting, 10 years after Bonds and Bobby Bonilla finished one-two for the Pirates. In 1989 Kevin Mitchell and Will Clark did the same for the Giants. . . . The ChiSox recorded 68 saves in 1990, due in large part to Bobby Thigpen's record 57 saves. Thigpen's record has stood since then, even in this day of pitching specialization. Starter-turned-closer John Smoltz saved 55 in 2002. Trevor Hoffman's 53 saves in 1998 are tied with Randy Myers' total of five years earlier for the third-highest single-season figure. Eric Gagne saved 52 in 2002. Dennis Eckersley (51 in 1992), Rod Beck (51 in 1998), and Mariano Rivera (50 in 2001) are the only others to reach 50 saves.

◆ Did you know that in their inaugural game as a franchise the Detroit Tigers erased a 13-4 deficit by scoring 10 runs in the bottom of the ninth? The improbable 14-13 victory in 1901 over the Milwaukee Brewers (the Orioles franchise) came at Bennett Park. A century later, it is still believed to be the largest ninth-inning comeback in history.

271. *Match these Hall of Famers with their histories:*

1	Lou Gehrig	A	hit into the most double plays in history (351)
2	Babe Ruth	B	led the league in slugging percentage eight times
3	Ty Cobb	C	led the league in runs scored eight times
4	Cal Ripken Jr.	D	holds the single-season record of 301 runs produced (runs plus RBI minus home runs)

ANSWER: 1—D, 2—C, 3—B, 4—A

During the 1931 season Gehrig led the American League with 163 runs scored and 184 RBI (the league record), and tied for the lead with 46 home runs (with Ruth, of course). . . . Carl Yastrzemski's AL record total of 323 double plays hit into (since World War II, when such records began to be recorded) was surpassed by Cal Ripken Jr. in 1999. In 2000 Ripken broke Hank Aaron's all-time mark of 328 double plays hit into. Behind Ripken, Aaron, and "Yaz" are Dave Winfield, with 319, Eddie Murray, with 316, and Jim Rice, with 315. Rice's 36 double plays hit into in 1984 and his 35 a year later remain the two highest single-season totals. Tampa Bay's Ben Grieve in 2000 set the dubious mark of double plays grounded into by a left-handed batter with 32. So much for having an advantage from the left batter's box.

272. *True or False? Shortstop Joe Tinker and second baseman Johnny Evers once went two years without saying a single word to the other and hardly talked at all from 1905 on.*

ANSWER: True

Unbelievably, the most famous keystone combination and two-thirds of the most famous double-play team in history performed at its best without talking much to each other on the field from 1905 through 1912. Tinker, reportedly upset because Evers once did not ask him to share a taxi ride, withdrew from speaking much to Evers (just as stubborn). In 1907 Tinker fired a ball from just 10 feet away that broke Evers' finger. For two years they reportedly didn't utter a single word to each other. In 1938 both players broke the silence and apologized. Evers died in Albany, New York, on March 28, 1947, and Tinker passed away soon afterward on July 27, 1948, in Orlando, Florida. Frank Chance, the other third of the combination, died on September 15, 1924, in Los Angeles.

◆ Did you know that Lou Gehrig and Babe Ruth didn't talk to each other from 1934 through 1939 (the day of the Speech), because Gehrig's mother had insulted Ruth's wife by saying that she dressed her natural daughters better than she dressed Ruth's daughter from a previous marriage? That explains the numerous film clips of Ruth crossing home plate following a homer while Gehrig (who followed Ruth in the batting order) conveniently looked away, talking to a bat boy or someone else nearby, instead of congratulating him. At the end of Gehrig's speech, Ruth walked up to his former teammate, put his arm around him, and spoke to him for the first time in more than five years.

273. *Match these managers with their histories:*

1	Red Schoendienst	A	managed for 23 years without the benefit of a multiyear contract
2	Jimmy Dykes	B	became one of just the second set of brothers to manage at the same time
3	Walter Alston	C	managed for 23 years without winning a pennant
4	Rene Lachemann	D	won consecutive NL pennants during a 14-year managerial career spent in one city
5	Ted Turner	E	managed for only one game

ANSWER: 1—D, 2—C, 3—A, 4—B, 5—E

Schoendienst managed the 1967 and 1968 St. Louis Cardinals to the World Series, winning in 1967. . . . Dykes, who replaced the legendary Connie Mack in 1951, still holds the dubious record of 2,962 games managed without a first-place finish. Mack had been the Athletics owner and manager over the previous 50 years—since 1901! It's safe to say that Mack had a strangle-hold on his position as manager. . . . In 1994 Rene and Marcel Lachemann joined Harry and George Wright (in 1879 with Providence and Boston, respectively) as the only brothers to manage at the same time. Ironically, Rene and Marcel were both fired in 1996 by Florida and California, respectively. There have been two other sets of brothers to manage in the majors, but not concurrently: Deacon and Will White, and Jack and Dave Rowe. . . . On May 11, 1977, Ted Turner, owner of the Atlanta Braves, fired Dave Bristol (8-21) and took over as manager himself in an attempt to stop a 16-game losing streak. After a 2-1 loss in Pittsburgh, NL president Chub Feeney forced Turner to give up managing the team and return to his owner's box. Dave Bristol resumed the helm and guided the team to a 61-101 (make that 61-100) season, before Bobby Cox took over in 1978 for the first—and least successful—of his two tenures as manager of the Braves. Ever since, persons holding financial interest in a team have been made aware that they will not be allowed to manage it, a little-known restriction that had actually already been in effect. Robert Edwards Turner was officially entered into the books as a manager with an 0-1 record.

274. *On August 10, 1995, the Cardinals were awarded a 2-1 forfeit victory over the Dodgers. Disgruntled by some questionable calls from home plate umpire Jim Quick, Dodger fans peppered the field with give-away baseballs, and Quick declared the first forfeit in 16 major league seasons. Can you name the two major league teams involved in the previous forfeited game, which occurred during the 1979 season?*

ANSWER: The Chicago White Sox and Detroit Tigers

The White Sox were forced to forfeit the second game of a July 12, 1979, doubleheader against the Tigers after more than 5,000 fans swarmed the Comiskey Park field on "Disco Demolition Night," damaging the grounds. A promotion had urged music fans to attend a between-games burning of disco records, to celebrate the end of the era of disco. During the event rampant spectators trespassed onto the field, leaving the grounds in a condition not suitable for play. Following 39 arrests, and more than an hour after the scheduled start of the second game, the umpiring crew decided that the game could not be played. The following day, AL president Lee MacPhail awarded the Tigers the standard 9-0 forfeit win (a run for each inning), giving Detroit a sweep of the twinbill.

On September 15, 1977, Toronto was awarded a 4-0 victory after Baltimore manager Earl Weaver pulled his team off the field, because umpires refused to move a hazardous tarp on the mound at Exhibition Stadium. The last NL game to end in a forfeit before July 1995 was on July 18, 1954, when Philadelphia was awarded a 9-0 win after various antics by Cardinals players obviously aimed at stalling the game until darkness arrived at Busch Stadium. There have been 39 forfeits from the 20th century on but only five since 1954.

◆ Did you know all statistics for games forfeited after four and a half innings are included in the record books, except for the winning or losing pitcher? Also, if losing or tied at the time of the forfeit, the team awarded the win shall be declared 9-0 victors. If ahead, the team given the win shall be awarded the victory by the score at the time of the announcement.

◆ Did you know that before 1912 pinch-hitters, pinch-runners, and defensive substitutes were not credited with a game played?

275. *Match these postseason performers with their ups and downs:*

1	Ryan Klesko	A	was 0-for-22 in one World Series, the worst in a single series
2	Barry Bonds	B	broke Gene Tenace's postseason record of futility with 22 consecutive hitless at-bats with runners on
3	Dal Maxvill	C	became the sixth player to homer in three consecutive World Series games
4	Mickey Mantle	D	struck out a World Series record 54 times

ANSWER: 1—C, 2—B, 3—A, 4—D

Maxvill, who is among 10 players with at least 15 at-bats to go hitless in a single World Series, went hitless in 1968, a big reason for his .117 lifetime postseason batting average. White Sox catcher Billy Sullivan Sr. and Cubs left fielder Jimmy Sheckard suffered through a miserable slump in the 1906 World Series, each going 0-for-21 in that all-Chicago classic. Giants right fielder Red Murray (1911) and the well-known Gil Hodges (1952) also went hitless in 21 official at-bats during the course of a single World Series. . . . Reggie Jackson (in 1977), Lonnie Smith (1991), Klesko, and Barry Bonds (2002) were the last four to homer in three consecutive World Series games. The other three were Lou Gehrig (1928), Johnny Mize (1953), and Hank Bauer (1958). . . . Bonds' slump stretched to 28 at-bats before ending in 1992. In fact, Bonds batted just .196 with a homer and six RBI in 97 postseason at-bats through 2001. Incredibly, Bonds had failed to win a single playoff series over his first 16 major league seasons, losing three times with Pittsburgh and twice with San Francisco. But all that changed in grand style, as Bonds rewrote the postseason record book in 2002 while leading the Giants to the NL pennant and within one win of a world title. In the three rounds, Bonds batted .356, hit a post-season record eight home runs, drove in 16, slugged .978, scored 18 times, and reached base at a .581 rate. The most alarming number, however, was 27, as in the number of walks he drew in the 17 post-season games. Not since Babe Ruth has a batter been so feared. Bonds emphatically shed his reputation for postseason failure.

◆ Did you know George Earnshaw still holds the dubious World Series mark for most career at-bats without a hit? The pitcher had 22 official hitless trips to the plate spanning three World Series (1929–31).

◆ Did you know Johnny Mize in 1949 became the first player to play in an All-Star Game for one league and then play in the World Series for the other league in the same season? Mize earned All-Star recognition as a Giant and then appeared in the fall classic for the victorious Yankees following a mid-season trade. David Cone in 1992 became the second player to do so, helping the Blue Jays win the title after spending most of the regular season with the Mets. With the bevy of All-Star jettisons by faltering teams looking to save money these days, this list is growing by leaps and bounds.

276. *Which Tigers third baseman did Cardinals left fielder Joe Medwick slide into so hard as to provoke a rhubarb during Game Seven of the 1934 World Series?*

ANSWER: Marv Owen

Marv Owen was the third bagger who took umbrage after "Ducky"'s hard slide. When Medwick later took his left-field position in the bottom of the sixth, the entire left-field bleacher section began throwing debris at Medwick at such a dangerous rate that Commissioner Kenesaw Landis requested that Medwick sit out the remainder of the game (his team was already comfortably ahead 9-0 en route to an 11-0 rout). His expulsion from the game (for his own safety) left the outfielder one hit short of the series record of 12 hits. The 11-0 Game Seven clobbering is matched only by the Kansas City Royals' blasting of the Cardinals by the same margin in Game Seven of the 1985 series.

◆ Did you know the Shea Stadium crowd was as rowdy after the Pete Rose–Bud Harrelson fight during the third game of the 1973 NL Championship Series as it was during the 1934 World Series mess? NL president Chub Feeney asked the Mets to quiet the hostile crowd in left field, where Rose played. Rusty Staub (who had already homered twice and been brushed back in his third at-bat prior to the brawl), Yogi Berra, Willie Mays, Tom Seaver, and Cleon Jones marched to left field to quiet the crowd. The Mets won, 9-2, but the game will be remembered primarily for the fifth-inning brawl at second.

277. *Match these games and their importance:*

1	May 9, 1984 (Milwaukee at Chicago)	A	the teams combined for a record 31 strikeouts
2	May 23, 1984 (Detroit at California)	B	Dave Kingman hit a ball that went through the netting of the dome's ceiling (180 feet above) and didn't come down
3	May 4, 1984 (Oakland at Minnesota)	C	marked the first time in history that a game in a dome was called due to rain
4	September 28, 1995 (Houston at Chicago)	D	the teams battled for 25 innings in the longest game ever by time (eight hours, six minutes)
5	July 13, 1997 (Texas at Seattle)	E	the teams tied a record by using 18 pitchers during an 11-inning duel
6	June 16, 1976 (Pittsburgh at Houston)	F	the visiting team won its 16th straight road game

ANSWER: 1—D, 2—F, 3—B, 4—E, 5—A, 6—C

Harold Baines of the White Sox homered off Milwaukee's Chuck Porter (on the game's 753rd pitch) in the bottom of the 25th inning for a 7-6 win. The first 17 innings were played to a deadlock the day before, and the game was resumed before the regularly scheduled game the next day, May 9. In all, the teams battled for 34 innings over two days. On May 11, 2000, the Milwaukee Brewers defeated the Chicago Cubs by a 14-8 margin, matching the major league nine-inning mark of four hours and 22 minutes, set by the Orioles and the Yankees on September 5, 1997. . . . Detroit's 16th straight road win tied the AL record set by Washington in 1912. The team fell one short of the major league mark set by the 1916 Giants. . . . When Kingman's towering fly ball didn't come down, it was ruled a ground-rule double. The ball was sent to the Baseball Hall of Fame after it was retrieved by a groundskeeper. . . . The game at Houston was postponed due to the serious flooding around the Astrodome that prevented the fans, umpires, and stadium laborers from entering. . . . The nine-inning mark for pitchers used is 16, set by the Giants and Astros on September 28, 2002. In 1997 the Mariners and Athletics tied the extra-inning mark of 18 pitchers used—a mark originally set by the Indians and Senators in 1971.

◆ Did you know that Tom Seaver won both games decided on May 9, 1984, between the Brewers and his White Sox? Seaver won the 25-inning marathon in relief (his only career relief victory) and started and won the scheduled contest.

◆ Did you know Carlton Fisk caught all 25 innings (a record for one game) during the marathon between Chicago and Milwaukee that ended on May 9, 1984?

278. *Which of the following teams has thrown the most no-hitters in the history of Major League Baseball?*

    A The New York Yankees
    B The Chicago White Sox
    C The Brooklyn and Los Angeles Dodgers
    D The Philadelphia Phillies

ANSWER: C

Hideo Nomo hurled the Dodgers' 20th no-hitter with a gem in Colorado against the Rockies on September 17, 1996, extending the franchise's record. The White Sox have thrown an AL-high 16 no-hitters and have been a victim 12 times. The Phillies have been no-hit 17 times, the most.

◆ Did you know the San Diego Padres and Houston Astros each lost an opportunity at a no-hitter during separate games in the 1970s when manager Preston Gomez lifted a starting pitcher for a pinch-hitter? Managing the Padres on July 21, 1970, Gomez in the eighth inning lifted Clay Kirby, who despite not allowing a hit had fallen behind, 1-0. Reliever Jack Baldschun gave up three hits as San Diego lost, 3-0. While managing the Astros, Gomez did it again—this time to starter Don Wilson. On September 4, 1974, Wilson was losing a 2-1 no-hitter after eight innings when Gomez pulled him from the game. Wilson was going for his third no-hitter.

279. *Match these Latin ball players with their achievements:*

> 1 Orlando Cepeda   A the first Latin pitcher inducted into the Hall of Fame
>
> 2 Juan Marichal   B the first Latin manager to win a pennant
>
> 3 Al Lopez   C the first Latin player to win the NL Rookie of the Year Award
>
> 4 Dolf Luque   D the first Latin 20-game winner

ANSWER: 1—C, 2—A, 3—B, 4—D

Cepeda, who won the 1958 Rookie of the Year Award, remains the only player to have won both the NL Rookie of the Year Award and the MVP Award (1967) by a unanimous vote. . . . Marichal was inducted to Cooperstown in 1983, following in the steps of Roberto Clemente (1973) and Al Lopez (1977), and preceding Luis Aparicio (1984). . . . Luque, a 193-game winner, enjoyed his only 20-win season for the Reds in 1923 (27-8, 1.93). A short and savvy Cuban righthander, Luque lasted 20 years in the majors, offering his services as a relief pitcher in his final four seasons. Luque pitched till he was 44 years of age, winning the clinching 1933 World Series game for the world champion Giants at the age of 43.

◆ Did you know Fidel Castro, a hard-throwing yet wild Cuban pitcher, was offered a $5,000 signing bonus by the Giants in 1949? However, the right-handed, 22-year-old law student from the University of Havana refused the offer to become a lawyer.

280. *Match these franchises with their successes:*

> 1 Tigers   A posted the highest batting average outside the 1930 season (.316)
>
> 2 Dodgers   B had the highest winning percentage for a second-place finisher (.680)
>
> 3 Cubs   C had the largest margin of victory by a pennant winner or division champion (27½ games) prior to the 1995 Indians

4 Pirates   D avoided last place for 86 straight years (from 1906 through 1991)

ANSWER: 1—A, 2—D, 3—B, 4—C

Every regular on the 1921 Detroit Tigers (managed by Ty Cobb) hit at least .281, and six of them topped the .300 mark. Harry Heilmann (19 home runs, 139 RBI) led the league with a .394 mark, Cobb finished second at .389, Bobby Veach, "the other" outfield great in Detroit (.310 career average), hit .338, and rookie first baseman Lu Blue hit .308. Third bagger Bobby Jones and catcher Johnny Bassler hit .303 and .307, respectively. And if you're wondering, those Tigers finished in sixth place, 27 games behind. . . . The Cubs of 1909 were 104-49 but finished 6½ games behind the 110-42 Pirates. The 1954 New York Yankees would be able to sympathize, going 103-51 (a .669 winning percentage) and finishing a full eight games behind the Indians (111-43). . . . The 1995 Cleveland Indians (100-44) won the AL Central Division by an astounding 30 games over the second-place Kansas City Royals (70-74). The Pirates were an amazing 103-36 (.741) in 1902, finishing 27½ games in front of second-place Brooklyn. The Pirates also dominated the National League in 1901 (7½ games) and 1903 (6½ games). The 1936 Yankees finished 19½ games ahead of Detroit as they posted a 102-51 (.667) mark. The 1983 White Sox (99-63) won the AL Western Division by 20 games over the Royals but were disposed of by the Orioles, three games to one, in the League Championship Series.

◆ Did you know the 1902 Pirates remain the last team to avoid a streak of at least three losses? Not even the 1906 Cubs, the 2001 Mariners, or the great Yankee clubs of 1927, 1961, or 1998 were able to avoid three straight defeats.

281. *Match these teams with their distinctive histories:*

1 1910 White Sox   A the only team from 1900 on that didn't have a player with 100 hits in a full season

2 1996 Mariners   B the "Hitless Wonders" hit only .211 with seven home runs

3 1995 Rockies   C set a record with 19 back-to-back home runs

4 1972 Mets   D set a record low with one complete game

ANSWER: 1—B, 2—C, 3—D, 4—A

Tommie Agee led the Mets with 96 hits in 1972. . . . The 1982 Brewers and 1977 Red Sox jointly held the single-season record of 16 back-to-back homers before the Mariners broke the mark in 1996. The Orioles also matched the previous standard of 16 that year. . . . That 1995 Colorado team also set the record, since broken, of going 110 straight games without a complete game, going back to the 1994 campaign. Over the 2001–02 seasons, Tampa Bay set the existing record of 194 straight games without a complete game. Those marks are a product of an era of pitching specialization and, in the case of Colorado, park altitude. The 1993 Rockies also became the first team in the modern era to not pitch a single shutout.

282. *Match these hitting greats with their feats:*

1	Billy Goodman	A holds the major league record of 17 straight games with an RBI
2	Jim Bottomley	B his 19 sacrifice flies in one season is still a record
3	Ray Grimes	C shares the modern-day record of 18 straight games with a run scored
4	Gil Hodges	D won a batting title despite not being a regular
5	Red Rolfe	E is the only player with two 6-for-6 games

ANSWER: 1—D, 2—E, 3—A, 4—B, 5—C

Ray Grimes of the Cubs drove in a total of 27 runs during those 17 games in 1922, a stretch that ended on July 23. . . . Hodges' record of sacrifice flies was achieved in 1954. . . . Kenny Lofton in 2000 tied Rolfe's mark of scoring in 18 straight games, crossing home in every game between August 15 and September 3. Rolfe accomplished the feat for the 1939 Yankees, scoring 30 runs during that stretch. Billy Hamilton holds the all-time record of 24, set back in 1894. Ted Kluszewski holds the modern NL record, scoring in 17 straight games for the 1954 Cincinnati Reds. . . . Goodman, a .300 hitter over a 16-year career, led the American League in 1950 with a .354 batting average but could not find his way into the Red Sox lineup as a regular. A "one-man bench," Goodman was a member of the last team to hit .300 and the second to last team to score 1,000 runs. The great hitting club scored 1,027 runs (only the 1999 Indians have reached

1,000 runs since), hit .302, and slugged .464, on their way to a third-place finish. Boston boasted rookie first baseman Walt Dropo (.322, 34, 44), second baseman Bobby Doerr (.294, 27, 120), shortstop Vern Stephens (.295, 30, 144), third baseman Johnny Pesky (.312), right fielder Al Zarilla (.325), center fielder Dom DiMaggio (.328), injury-hampered left fielder Ted Williams (.317, 28, 97), and catcher Birdie Tebbetts (.310). Pitching did the Red Sox in (4.88 ERA).

The seven teams to score 1,000 runs since 1900 are: the 1931 Yankees (1,067), 1936 Yankees (1,065), 1930 Yankees (1,062), 1950 Red Sox (1,027), 1999 Indians (1,009), 1930 Cardinals (1,004), and the 1932 Yankees (1,002).

◆ Did you know the 1996 Seattle Mariners, who came within seven runs of 1,000, set major league records for total bases and extra-base hits in a single season? In 1996 the Mariners exploited the league's pitching, thinned by expansion, by pounding 607 extra-base hits for a 2,741 total bases. The old records of 580 extra-base hits and 2,703 total bases were held by the 1936 Yankees. Seattle just missed becoming the first team in 46 years to score 1,000 times.

◆ Did you know Eddie Murray's 128 sacrifice flies are the most since the statistic was introduced in 1954? Murray produced 92 of his 128 sacrifice flies in the American League and 36 in the National League. Cal Ripken is the AL career leader with 127, four more than Robin Yount. Hank Aaron is the NL record holder, having hit 113 of his 121 sacrifice flies in the senior circuit.

283. *Bill Veeck and Charles Finley are undoubtedly the two greatest innovators baseball has known. Some of their antics are famous. However, some have not yet reached the point of notoriety. Can you differentiate between their innovations? Fill in "V" for Veeck or "F" for Finley:*

A began the practice of playing World Series games exclusively, at night _____
B was the first to put players' names on the back of their uniforms
_____
C advocated interleague play _____
D had the fans manage a game by revealing their decisions on giant place cards _____
E this Marines supervisor owned the first team to draw two million fans _____

F this son of a Chicago Cubs general manager learned enough about baseball that he was able to rise from his hot dog–selling days as a youngster in Wrigley Field to eventually own three clubs _____
G this insurance tycoon once put a jackass in his bullpen named after himself _____
H won two Executive of the Year Awards _____

ANSWER: A—F, B—V, C—F, D—V, E—V, F—V, G—F, H—V

Veeck owned the Indians, White Sox, and the St. Louis Browns (which he tried to save). His 1948 world champion Indians team was the first to draw two million fans. . . . Finley will not be confused with the fun-loving Veeck in the minds of many since he continually feuded with his managers and players en route to five consecutive division titles and three straight World Series victories.

◆ Did you know that Charles Finley forced a healthy player to sign a statement indicating that he was physically injured (so that he could be replaced on the roster with an able player) during the 1973 World Series? That player was Mike Andrews, whose two errors in the top of the 12th inning allowed the Mets to even the series with the A's at a game apiece. Furious and apprehensive of his second baseman's abilities (after all, he had been acquired for his glove), Finley forced Andrews to sign the statement of injury "for the good of the team," as the Oakland owner was all but ready to replace Andrews with rookie Manny Trillo. The tactics were so unfair that Andrews' teammates protested and demanded that he be allowed back on the team. Commissioner Bowie Kuhn agreed and disallowed Finley's roster change. Andrews was flown back in from his Massachusetts home to New York, where the Mets were to host Games Three, Four, and Five.

In the midst of Game Four, in which the Mets would tie the series up with a 6-1 win, Andrews was given a pinch-hitting opportunity. Sympathetic to Andrews, the Shea Stadium sellout crowd of 54,817 gave him a standing ovation before and after he grounded out to third base. The Oakland A's won the last two games at home to win their second of three straight titles.

After the series, Kuhn fined Finley $5,000 for the Andrews incident, $1,000 for announcing to the fans that Trillo's absence was the Mets' fault, and another $1,000 for ordering the lights at the Oakland Coliseum turned on in the Athletics' half of the ninth inning of Game Two (without permission from the commissioner). That move (you must admit that Finley knew what he was doing) allowed the A's batters to see the pitchers better and score twice to force the game into extra innings. They lost anyhow, 10-7. Kuhn placed Finley on probation, warning the Oakland owner that more "conduct detrimental to the game" and "not in the best interest of baseball" would result in a suspension. So bothered by his owner's behavior was manager Dick Williams that he resigned rather than continue to be associated with him, despite the opportunity for a third consecutive world championship. Of course, Alvin Dark led Oakland to its third straight title in 1974, anyway.

284. *Match these stadiums with their place in history:*

1	Forbes Field	A	was originally built for a Canadian Football Stadium League team
2	Jack Murphy Stadium	B	had a capacity of fewer than 30,000
3	Crosley Field	C	although built for baseball, hosted football for its first two years
4	Exhibition Stadium	D	had three decks of stands, elevators, telephones, lights, inclined ramps, and even maids in the ladies' restrooms when it first opened
5	Wrigley Field	E	this stadium with natural turf was named for a sportswriter

ANSWER: 1—D, 2—E, 3—B, 4—A, 5—C

Forbes Field opened in 1909. . . . Exhibition Stadium was built in 1975 for the CFL's Toronto Argonauts. . . . Wrigley Field was built in 1914 and first used by the Chicago Cubs in 1916. . . . Since the Sky-Dome opened its doors in the middle of the 1989 season, 15 teams have obtained new parks. Only the expansion Devil Rays' park (Tropicana Field) is not a grass field. The other new parks are: the White Sox's new Comiskey Park (1991), Baltimore's Oriole Park at Camden Yards (1992), Florida's Joe Robbie Stadium (1993), Colorado's temporary home Mile High Stadium (1993) and then Coors Field (1995), the Rangers' The Ball Park in Arlington (1994), Cleveland's Jacobs Field (1994), Atlanta's Turner Field (1997), the expansion Diamondbacks' Bank One Ballpark (1998), the Mariners' Safeco Field (1999), the Giants' Pac Bell Park (2000), the Tigers' Comerica Park (2000), the Astros' Minute Maid Park (2000), the Brewers' Miller Park (2001), and the Pirates' PNC Park (2001).

Also, since the SkyDome opened, the Cardinals' Busch Stadium, the Royals' Kauffman Stadium, and the Reds' Cinergy Field have switched to grass surfaces. Is there a message here? Yes, owners are discovering that artificial turf causes injury and adds wear and tear on their high-priced athletes. New, asymmetrical parks with grass also appeal to fans because the asymmetrical structure re-creates the feel of old ballparks.

Owners have also found that a new stadium rejuvenates communities and peaks tourist interest, and some are even using their stadiums to gross more money by other means, such as lending their name to corporations. Florida's Joe Robbie Stadium is now Pro Player Stadium. The Giants' Candlestick Park was changed to 3Com in its final years before the team moved into Pac Bell Park (named after the famous phone company). Coors Field and the Brewers' new stadium, Miller Park, were named after beer corporations. The Reds renamed Riverfront Stadium as Cinergy Field in 1997, and the Angels renamed Anaheim Stadium as Edison International Field of Anaheim later that same year. Even the 1998 expansion clubs got into the act before playing a single game—the Diamondbacks sold their stadium name to Bank One, and the Tampa Bay Devil Rays didn't wait long before changing the name of their park from the ThunderDome to Tropicana Field 16 months before their first scheduled game. Talk about squeezing opportunity.

◆ Did you know the Diamondbacks' Bank One Ballpark is the first sports facility in the world featuring a retractable roof, air conditioning, and a natural turf playing field? Designed by the firm of Ellerbe Beckett, it is also furnished with a swimming pool behind the center-field wall for its fans. With a capacity of 40, the swimming pool is available at a cost of $4,000 per game. Bank One Ballpark's elevation of 1,117 feet above sea level is the second highest in the majors behind Coors Field, which is an astounding 5,282 feet above sea level.

◆ Did you know the San Diego Padres are the only major league team not to own priority in a shared ballpark? The NFL's San Diego Chargers have the last say in scheduling conflicts with the Padres at Qualcomm Stadium, formerly known as Jack Murphy Stadium—thus the occasional baseball-less Saturday or Sunday in San Diego during football season.

285. *With the election to the Hall of Fame of George Brett in 1999 and Michael Jack Schmidt in 1995, the number of third basemen in Cooperstown grew to 11. Schmidt and Brett became the fourth and fifth third basemen to be elected by the Baseball Writers Association of America (BBWAA). Can you name the other three?*

ANSWER: Pie Traynor (1948), Eddie Mathews (1978), and Brooks Robinson (1983)

The other six third basemen—Jimmy Collins, Frank "Home Run" Baker, Freddie Lindstrom, George Kell, and negro leaguers Ray Dandridge and Judy Johnson—were elected by the Veterans Committee. Schmidt and Brett are among an elite membership of 95 players elected by the BBWAA through 2002.

Of the Hall of Fame's 254 members, 189 earned the honor playing in the majors, 18 players were elected based on their production in the negro leagues, 16 were managers, 8 were umpires, and 23 were pioneers or executives. Of the 207 Hall of Famers, including negro leaguers, who earned their election based on performance on the playing field, 68 were pitchers, 22 were right fielders, 20 were center fielders, 19 were left fielders, 23 were shortstops, 19 were first basemen, 16 were second basemen, 13 were catchers, and, of course, 11 played the hot corner. (The numbers add up to more than 207 because certain players played a significant amount of games at more than one position.)

It has been 42 years since Cooperstown failed to induct a player (in 1960). The BBWAA failed to elect a player in 1996 for the first time since 1971, but the Veterans Committee chose four that year. Ozzie Smith was the lone selection in 2002. There shouldn't be a problem continuing this streak in coming years, with Ryne Sandberg, Lee Smith, and Eddie Murray becoming eligible in 2003; Paul Molitor, Dennis Eckersley, Dennis Martinez, and Joe Carter in 2004; Wade Boggs in 2005; Will Clark, Albert Belle, Gary Gaetti, and Orel Hershiser in 2006; and the great trio of Tony Gwynn, Cal Ripken Jr., and Mark McGwire in 2007. Wow! I know where I want to be in early August of 2007.

◆ Did you know George Brett and Mike Schmidt were drafted 34th and 35th, respectively, in the 1971 Free Agent Amateur Draft? Brett, the only third baseman to reach 3,000 hits, in 1999 became the 11th to be inducted into the Hall of Fame. In 1995 Schmidt, an eight-time home run champion and 12-time All-Star, had become the 10th.

286. *Match these pitchers with their obscure or dubious feats:*

1	Jerry Garvin	A	allowed Ted Williams to become the first player to hit a home run off a father and his son
2	Tug McGraw	B	yielded a major league record–tying four grand slams in one season
3	Don Lee	C	punched out the famous writer Ernest Hemingway
4	Ray Caldwell	D	was struck by lightning on the mound during a game, but rose to his feet and completed a four-hitter
5	Hugh Casey	E	picked off a record 22 baserunners in one season

ANSWER: 1—E, 2—B, 3—A, 4—D, 5—C

Garvin picked off a record of 22 baserunners for Toronto during the 1977 season. However, the statistic wasn't officially kept until 1991 (Charlie Leibrandt and Terry Mulholland picked off 16 in 1992, the high since then), meaning that Garvin's hold on the record is precarious until further research has been undertaken. . . . Ray Narleski (in 1959) and McGraw (in 1979) were joined by the Mariners' Mike Schooler, who allowed four grand slams in 1992, the Dodgers' Chan Ho Park (in 1999), and the Padres' Matt Clement (in 2000). . . . Don's father Thornton Lee also yielded a home run (actually, a few) to Ted Williams. . . . A well-mannered former amateur fighter, Hugh Casey— one of several players invited to Hemingway's place in Havana, Cuba—was taunted by Hemingway and actually forced to spar. After taking some heavy shots from the writer and baseball enthusiast, Casey used his skills to knock Hemingway out cold. The Dodgers were in Cuba for spring training in 1941. . . . Aside from Caldwell, who by the way won four of his next five starts, Indians teammate Ray Chapman was also shaken up by the lightning. But player-manager

Tris Speaker was refused by both players in his attempt to remove them for a substitute.

◆ Did you know heavyweight boxing champion Jim Corbett played in the minor leagues during and after his championship reign? Corbett gained the heavyweight title in 1892 and, for publicity, was signed to a minor league contract with Scranton (Eastern League) in 1895. Already a celebrity, "Gentleman Jim" continued to be a drawing card even after he lost his title in 1897. Corbett made an obscene amount of money. He played first base, but his baseball talents were just average. His brother Joe, however, pitched four years in the majors, with a 24-8 season for Baltimore (1897) to his credit. Joe could have spent more time in the National League but decided to play on the West Coast.

◆ Did you know Hall of Famer Ray Dandridge was a Gold Glove boxing champion before his days as a Negro League star, according to John Holway of the Society for American Baseball Research?

287. *In which year during World War II did the major leagues go without an All-Star Game?*

A 1941
B 1942
C 1943
D 1945

ANSWER: D

The 1945 All-Star Game scheduled for July 10 at Fenway Park was canceled due to travel restrictions. In the game's stead, seven interleague games were played for the purpose of raising money for war charity.

288. *Which great umpire said the following: "Umpires are supposed to keep their place. If a player was making $20,000 a year, I would have minded my own business. But I figured out that Jim Rice was making $582 for every strike I called and I was making seven cents. Seven cents! There's no way I'm going to keep my place for seven cents"?*

ANSWER: The outspoken Ron Luciano made his mark as an eccentric yet efficient major league umpire. A former pro football player with the AFL's Buffalo Bills, the six-foot-four, 300-pound Luciano became an umpire following an injury on the gridiron. Luciano was unique in that he actually cheered great plays and even shook hands with home run hitters as they stepped on the plate. Those called out by Luciano at a bag or the plate will never forget how he pumped his right arm with "a theatrical flair"—as the *New York Times* put it—in rendering the call, reiterating his decision emphatically and with great verve.

Following an 11-year career as an AL umpire, Luciano called it quits to embark on a more challenging and profitable career. He moved to the broadcast booth, serving as NBC color commentator for two years, and made public appearances. Luciano also found time to author four successful books (with David Fisher), including the hilarious *The Umpire Strikes Back*. Alas, Luciano, 57, committed suicide by carbon monoxide at his home in Endicott, New York, on January 18, 1995.

289. *Can you name the major league's first domed stadium?*

ANSWER: The Astrodome

The Astrodome, built for the 1965 season, cost $31.6 million. The transparent panels of the dome were painted to prevent glare, which in turn created another problem. Since the grass was no longer receiving its share of sun, artificial turf had to be used. With the aid of the Monsanto Chemical Co., Astro Turf arrived in baseball. Astro Turf wasn't well received by one particular slugger. Dick Allen, speaking of his dislike for the surface, said, "If a horse can't eat it, I don't want to play on it."

On April 28 of that season, New York Mets broadcaster Lindsey Nelson covered the game from a gondola attached from the top of the dome (right over second base). The apex of the dome measured 208 feet above second base.

◆ Did you know that 24 of the nation's 26 astronauts attended the historical first regular-season game in the Astrodome and, in a ceremony before that April 12, 1965, contest, received lifetime passes to major league games?

◆ Did you know the Astrodome was originally called "Harris County Domed Stadium"?

290. *What was the closest pennant race in major league history?*

ANSWER: The Federal League's 1915 season provided followers with its closest pennant race ever, which the Chicago Whalers won by finishing .001 ahead of the St. Louis Terriers and .004 ahead of the Pittsburgh Rebels. Chicago, which finished at 86-66 (.566), played two fewer games than St. Louis (87-67) and one fewer than Pittsburgh (86-67), due to rainouts. Since league rules did not require that rainouts be made up, Chicago and St. Louis finished in a virtual tie and third-place Pittsburgh ending up a mere one-half game away. Under today's rules, the three clubs would have to play the same number of games in order to decide a race that close. Chicago had finished a game and a half behind the Federal League Champion Indianapolis Hoosiers the previous season. After the Federal League collapsed, its records have been included among those of the major leagues.

The 1972 season, in which the strike cost Major League Baseball 13 days of action (not to be made up), had a similar ending. In the AL East race, division champ Detroit finished at 86-70 and Boston finished one-half game behind at 85-70, with a game in hand it could not use.

Another tight pennant race came in 1908, when the Chicago Cubs defeated the New York Giants in a one-game playoff to win by one game over the Giants and the Pittsburgh Pirates.

291. *Why did the Federal League last just two seasons?*

ANSWER: Quite simply, the Federal League owners and financial backers ran out of money defending themselves in the court room against the National and American Leagues over territorial rights. Although the NL and AL owners kept losing in court, they maintained a flood of lawsuits, knowing full well that the Federal League would eventually run out of funds. Federal District Court Judge Kenesaw Landis urged the Federal League (which filed a lawsuit of its own on January 5, 1915) and the National and American League to reach a settlement, since each side was losing money at a rapid rate. Both parties heeded Landis' advice and reached an accord, and, thus, the brief history of the Federal League came to an end on December 21, 1915.

In return for dropping its potentially devastating lawsuit, the

Federal League received various forms of compensation. Some Federal League owners were reimbursed for their losses, others were done the favor of being bought out, and Charles Weeghman and Phillip Ball were allowed to purchase the Chicago Cubs and the St. Louis Browns, respectively. Other arrangements allowed the remaining Federal League players to be sold to the highest major league bidder. It was the best solution available, as poor attendance had hindered every team in all three major leagues, with the number of clubs increasing and the fan support unable to spread as fast, especially with the prospect of a war. Also, Brooklyn Tip-Tops owner Robert Ward died in October, and the Buffalo Blues and Kansas City Packers needed help from the league just to finish the season.

Excluded from the compensation, the owners of the Baltimore Terrapins sued Major League Baseball for antitrust violations. But baseball was ruled not to be an interstate commerce, and thus not subject to antitrust regulations, so that suit proved futile.

One American League team that suffered greatly was the Philadelphia Athletics. After losing star pitchers Eddie Plank and Chief Bender to the Federal League (the St. Louis Terriers and the Terrapins, respectively) following the 1914 season, owner Connie Mack sold off some quality players to other major league clubs perhaps to prevent the new rival circuit from nabbing them from his financially unstable team. His team lost a lot of talent, but Mack became recognized as one of the major leagues' saviors for his actions, which helped to keep the two recognizable major leagues intact.

◆ Did you know that Benny Kauff, Edd Roush, Jack Tobin, Howard Ehmke, and Max Flack all made their major league debuts in the Federal League? Kauff, the league's best player, led the Indianapolis Hoosiers to the pennant in 1914 with a .370 mark, 75 stolen bases, 120 runs scored, 211 hits, and 44 doubles—all league-leading figures. In 1915 Kauff (then playing for Brooklyn after a bidding war made him one of the richest Federal Leaguers) again led in batting (.342) and stolen bases (55), but for a seventh-place team this time. After the 1915 season, Kauff was bought by the NL's New York Giants for $35,000 (Kauff had been signed by the Giants during the 1915 season as well, but the Braves then complained that the star outfielder had yet to be reinstated, as per the agreement the National and American Leagues decided on). Kauff was banned from the game by Commissioner Kenesaw Mountain

Landis in 1920 after being implicated in a stolen-car ring. Though acquitted of the charges, Kauff was not allowed back in the majors because Landis deemed him to have an "undesirable character and reputation."

◆ Did you know Claude Hendrix's 45 wins were the most in the brief history of the Federal League? Hendrix of the Chicago Whales led the Federal League with 29 wins (and a 1.69 ERA) in 1914, and he earned 16 more victories the following season, a campaign that included a no-hitter. The righthander was a combined 45-25 in that circuit's two-year history. He hadn't come out of nowhere, though, as he had already won 24 games for the Pirates in 1912. In 1918 he proved he still had it, earning 20 victories for the Cubs. He was released by the Cubs prior to the 1921 season for having agreed to throw a game the previous year. Hendrix was 144-116 over his 10-year career, bridging the National and Federal Leagues.

292. *By now you have learned that, at least in my opinion, the 1885 White Sox, 1896 Baltimore Orioles, 1915 Red Sox, 1927 Yankees, 1939 Yankees, 1942 Cardinals, 1955 Dodgers, 1961 Yankees, 1975 Reds, 1986 Mets, and 1998 Yankees are not only 11 of the best teams of all time but the best clubs of their respective decades as well. The 1905 Giants lock the door to the penthouse of my great dozen squads, staking their claim to the prestigious honor of the best team of the 20th century's first decade. Manager John McGraw was one of this team's many*

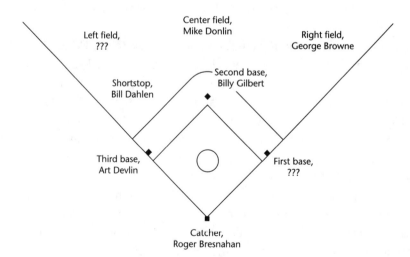

*strengths, and among the others were pitching, speed, defense, and
the majors' most feared offense. This confident squad finished at
105-48 (.686), outscoring its opponents (780-504) by 276 runs. The
1905 Giants led the league with a .273 batting average, a .368 slugging average, 39 home runs, 191 doubles, and 291 stolen bases. The
team also had the deepest pitching staff, finishing second in ERA at
2.39 and pacing the league with 760 strikeouts and 14 saves, and a
formidable defense that finished third. Complete the team's alignment, and name the squad's rarely used Hall of Fame pinch-runner, a
former speedster who saw action in three games:*

ANSWER: Left field, Sam Mertes; First base, Dan McGann. John Mc-
Graw himself was the pinch-runner who stole one base in three games.

Mertes led the team with 108 RBI (second in the National League),
and Donlin led with a .356 batting average and a league-leading 124
runs scored to accompany his 80 RBI. Dahlen drove in 81 runners, Mc-
Gann batted .299 with 75 RBI, and Browne hit .293 with 95 runs scored.
Formerly the manager of the Baltimore Orioles, McGraw brought with
him the Joe McGinnity–Roger Bresnahan battery and played a major
role in the Christy Mathewson–Amos Rusie trade. Mathewson led the
National League with 31 wins and formed one-third of the club's 20-
win trio, joining Red Ames (22) and McGinnity (21). Mathewson also
led the National League in strikeouts and shutouts.

Donlin was one of the most curious characters of his time.
Greatly talented and popular, "Turkey" Donlin battled injuries, the
law, and indecision about his own ambitions to bat .333 and slug .468
over a 12-year career. The left-handed hitter finished in the top three
in batting average and in the top ten in homers five times despite
reaching 400 at-bats in just four seasons, mostly because of frequent
injuries. In between his major league exploits, Donlin spent six
months in jail for assaulting a woman—which cost him most of the
1902 season—and married vaudeville actress Mabel Hite. His marriage
prompted him to retire from baseball after the 1908 season to lend
his energy to the vaudeville circuit. Following the death of his famous
wife, he returned, having missed two years, to bat .316 in 1911 as well
as in 1912. He retired again, missing the 1913 schedule, before giving
it one final hurrah for the Giants in 1914, after which he married another actress and continued his acting career. Including the 1907

campaign, which he sat out because of a contract dispute, Donlin's major league career spanned 16 years but included just 3,854 at-bats.

◆ Did you know "Moonlight" Graham, portrayed in the hit movie *Field of Dreams,* made his only major league appearance on June 29 for the 1905 Giants? With a win all but assured against the Dodgers, manager John McGraw sent in the 28-year-old Archibald Wright Graham to play the ninth inning in right field, substituting for George Browne. Graham didn't field a chance, as three infield outs ended the contest, and never got another opportunity to play in the majors. Although he played a few more years in the minors, Graham retired without a major league plate appearance or a chance in the field, going on to become a successful medical doctor in Chisholm, Minnesota.

◆ Did you know New York Giants rookie Bill O'Hara stole second and third base as a pinch-runner on September 1, 1909, and did the same the next day? O'Hara, who swiped 31 bases in his 124-game career, remains the only pinch-runner to steal two bases in an inning twice.

293. *Who is the only starting pitcher in World Series history to not bat ninth?*

ANSWER: Babe Ruth

Babe Ruth batted sixth in the fourth game of the 1918 World Series for the victorious Boston Red Sox. In that slot of the batting order, Ruth hit a two-run triple to deep right-center in the fourth inning to open the scoring. After the Cubs tied the game at 2-2 in the top of the eighth, the Red Sox regained the lead in the bottom half, as catcher Wally Schang singled, advanced to second on a passed ball, went to third on a sacrifice bunt by Harry Hooper, and scored on an error. When the Cubs were rallying in the ninth, a tiring Ruth was relieved and placed in left field. Righthander "Bullet" Joe Bush thwarted the rally to save the 3-2 win for Ruth and the Red Sox, who won the series in six games. For Ruth, the win marked his second of the series, for a 2-0 mark and a minuscule 1.06 ERA. Equally stellar on the mound, side-arming righthander Carl Mays also went 2-0, with a similar 1.00 ERA. Incredibly, Ruth's two RBI led the team in the fifth lowest scoring fall classic in history (a combined 19 runs were scored—four more than in the 1966 World Series, three more than in the 1950 and 1963 World Series, and one more than in the shutout-dominated 1905 classic).

Although Ruth excelled at pitching almost from the get-go and hurled a 14-inning complete game during the 1916 World Series, it wasn't until 1918 that he began exhibiting on a regular basis and to a wider audience his dual talent of pitching and hitting for power.

◆ Did you know Babe Ruth still has more shutouts than Pedro Martinez? Ruth, the very legend that Martinez said he'd "drill in the #$@!" when questioned about the "Curse of the Bambino," threw 17 shutouts, including a league-best nine in 1916. Martinez, a three-time Cy Young Award winner, enters the 2003 season with 15. Riding high, Martinez was 7-1 with a 1.44 ERA at the time of his boastful statement on May 30, 2001, but, in keeping with the Curse, the righthander didn't win again that year, because of a right shoulder injury.

◆ Did you know Babe Ruth still owns the record for most career multi-homer games, with 72 such performances? Mark McGwire retired with 67, and, according to home run researcher David Vincent of the Society for American Baseball Research, Willie Mays and Hank Aaron had 63 and 62 such games, respectively. Fifth on the list is Barry Bonds, who enters the 2003 season with 61 multi-homer games. And sixth is Sammy Sosa, who has homered at least twice in 58 games.

294. *You already know that the New York Mets have never had a pitcher throw a no-hitter for them. Yet seven hurlers they traded or allowed to leave via free agency went on to pitch one for another team. Name five of the seven pitchers.*

ANSWER: Nolan Ryan, Tom Seaver, Mike Scott, Dwight Gooden, David Cone, Hideo Nomo, and A. J. Burnett have all pitched no-hitters after their tenure with the Mets came to an end. Ryan, who pitched for the Mets from 1966 to 1971, went on to throw a record seven of them, starting in 1973 as he matured and gained better control of his blazing fastball. Seaver, who embodied the Mets organization in his 11 seasons, pitched a no-hitter for the Cincinnati Reds on June 16, 1978, a year and a day after he was traded from the organization he led to the world championship. Scott pitched for the Mets from 1979 to 1982 before being traded to the Astros, for whom he threw a division-clinching no-hitter in 1986. Gooden, who helped revitalize the Mets organization in his rookie year of 1984 and pitched for them through 1994, pitched a no-hitter for the Yankees in 1996. Cone pitched for the Mets from 1987 to 1992 but enjoyed his grandest day in a Yankee uniform, hurling a perfect game on July 18, 1999. On April 4, 2001, Nomo pitched a no-hitter in his first start for the Red Sox, three years after struggling in a Mets uniform. Then on May 12, Burnett (brought up in the Mets organization) no-hit the Padres in a Marlins uniform.

That's 13 no-hitters former Mets pitchers have thrown for other teams. Heck, even reliever Alejandro Pena, whom New York had in 1990, went on to pitch in a combined no-hitter for Atlanta in 1991. Make that 14, all by righthanders by the way. Come to think of it, Nomo also threw a no-hitter before his tenure with the Mets, but that's another list.

The franchise has had somewhat tough luck with the Cy Young Award, though the Mets are far from being blanked in this category. A total of 11 Cy Young Award winners have at one time or another pitched for the Mets during their career, but only 2—Seaver (1969, 1973, and 1975) and Gooden (1985)—have won their awards with the Mets. The other 9 are: Scott, Cone, Frank Viola, Bret Saberhagen, Orel Hershiser, Warren Spahn, Dean Chance, Mike Marshall, and Randy Jones. Of course, some of these hurlers pitched for the Mets after they had already won the award, but it's an intriguing list nonetheless.

Spahn, the 1957 Cy Young Award winner, pitched for the Mets (4-12) and the Giants (3-4) during his final season of 1965. The 1964 winner, Chance pitched a mere three games for the Mets in 1970. Marshall, the 1974 NL winner, pitched for the 1981 Mets in his last season, going 3-2 with no saves in 20 appearances. The 1976 NL winner, Jones concluded his 10-year career with mediocre seasons for the Mets in 1981 (1-8, 4.88 ERA) and 1982 (7-10, 4.60). Scott won his with Houston in 1986, Viola won his with Minnesota in 1988, Saberhagen won both of his with Kansas City (1985, 1989), Cone earned his in 1994, also with the Royals, and Hershiser won his with the Dodgers (1988).

◆ Did you know two-time Cy Young Award winner Bob Gibson was a Mets coach for the 1981 season? Gibson won his awards in 1968 and 1970 with St. Louis.

◆ Did you know six-time Cy Young Award winner Roger Clemens was drafted out of San Jacinto Junior College in 1981 by the Mets but refused to sign with them over a mere $5,000? Instead, Clemens attended the University of Texas. Clemens wanted $25,000 in lieu of the offered $20,000 to help his needy mother. The 12th-round pick of the 1981 draft was lost, as was the Mets' chance to boast Clemens and Gooden on the same team. Can you imagine? One year out of Spring Woods High School in Houston, Clemens pitched for the Texas Longhorns. In his second and last year with the University of Texas, Clemens concluded a 25-7 record for the Longhorns, including a clinching victory in the 1983 College World Series. Texas teammate and eventual Red Sox teammate Calvin Schiraldi was named MVP of the series. The Red Sox chose Clemens in the first round of the 1983 June draft after 18 other teams (including the Mets again) ignored him. By the way, Clemens also refused offers from the National Basketball Association's Boston Celtics and Seattle Supersonics.

295. *Only five batteries (a pitcher and a catcher) have ever won a Gold Glove in the same season. Choose the pair that did not:*

    A Rick Reuschel and Mike LaValliere
    B Jim Kaat and Earl Battey
    C Bret Saberhagen and Bob Boone
    D Bob Gibson and Tim McCarver
    E Rick Reuschel and Tony Pena
    F Kenny Rogers and Ivan Rodriguez

ANSWER: D

Bob Gibson won nine Gold Gloves from 1965 to 1973, but McCarver, who caught Gibson regularly in St. Louis, never won a Gold Glove. Reuschel formed a Gold Glove battery in Pittsburgh with Pena in 1985 and LaValliere two years later. Kaat and Battey did so in 1962 for Minnesota. Saberhagen and Boone each earned the hardware for Kansas City in 1989, and Rogers and Rodriguez teamed up in 2000 for Texas.

◆ Did you know Bob Boone holds the major league record of catching at least 100 games 15 times? Although he does not hold either league record in this category, Boone caught at least 100 games seven times with the Phillies (1973–80), seven times with the Angels (1982–88), and once with the Royals (1989).

296. *Which MVP catcher hit the famous "Homer in the Gloamin'"?*

ANSWER: Gabby Hartnett

Cubs player-manager Gabby Hartnett on September 28, 1938, hit the famous home run that gave Chicago a key 6-5 victory over Pittsburgh en route to the NL pennant. The win, Chicago's ninth straight in a stretch drive that featured 21 wins in 24 games, put the Cubs ahead of the Pirates for good in the standings. Tied at 5-5 with darkness descending and two out in the bottom of the ninth inning, Hartnett tagged an 0-2 offering from Mace Brown for a dramatic, walk-off home run into Wrigley Field's left-field bleachers. It took most fans a few extra moments to realize the ball's destiny. Interestingly, the umpires had gathered beforehand and decided that Hartnett would be the last batter, because of the dark.

It was a fitting story for a leader who had taken over the team's managerial duties two months earlier, bringing the team back from a five and a half game deficit while earning the MVP Award for his efforts. For Hartnett, his "Homer in the Gloamin'" was 1 of just 10 that season, a far cry from the 37 he crushed eight years earlier.

297. *Three teams played a six-inning exhibition on June 26, 1944, with the purpose of raising funds for the war. (Yes, you read right; three teams.) In front of an audience of about 50,000 at the Polo Grounds, each club played concurrent innings against the other two and then sat out a frame. Name these three clubs, and select the winning team.*

ANSWER: The Dodgers, Yankees, and Giants were the three teams. The final score was: Dodgers 5, Yankees 1, Giants 0.

◆ Did you know that two major leaguers were killed in World War II? Elmer Gedeon of Washington died in 1944, and Harry O'Neill of the Philadelphia Athletics died in 1945. Gedeon was an outfielder for the Senators and played in just five games in his only season (1939). O'Neill was a catcher who made but one defensive appearance, also in 1939.

◆ Did you know 15-year major league catcher Moe Berg served the U.S. government as a spy in Europe during World War II and in Japan a decade earlier? The Central Intelligence Agent spoke 12 languages and held degrees from Princeton University (magna cum laude) and Columbia Law School. In between, he studied philosophy at the Sorbonne. Berg's 1934 espionage mission of taking photos of Japan's harbor and industrial sections from atop that country's tallest building explains why he was a part of that year's traveling major league All-Star team, which also included Babe Ruth and Lou Gehrig. After all, Berg was a .243 career singles hitter whose only on-field forte was his defensive skill as a catcher. (It was Berg that scout Mike Gonzalez was describing when he came up with the phrase "good field, no hit.") Berg later coached baseball and became a lawyer as well as a Good Will ambassador. He also earned the Medal of Freedom by spying on the Germans, helping determine that the Nazi atom bomb plans were neither developed nor a threat, which led the agency to scratch a plot to assassinate Werner Heisenberg, the head of said A-bomb project. Berg, who came to bat as many as 200 times in a season merely twice, remains the only major league ballplayer whose baseball card is displayed at the CIA headquarters. Following World War II, the enigmatic Berg spent the vast majority of his time unemployed and stricken with poverty, despite a wealth of credentials.

298. *How did the Yankees fare on what would have been Lou Gehrig's 2,131st consecutive game played?*

ANSWER: On May 2, 1939, the Yankees crushed the Tigers at Briggs Stadium by a whopping score of 22-2, after Gehrig took himself out of the lineup due to his weakened condition. Gehrig, forced to make the decision after bewilderingly losing his power and ability to hit the ball, watched from the dugout with tears in his eyes as first baseman Babe Dahlgren homered and doubled. Gehrig hadn't yet been diagnosed with the disease that ultimately took his life two years later. Amyotrophic Lateral Sclerosis (ALS, also know as Lou Gehrig's Disease) is a progressive disease of the nervous system. To Gehrig, it felt like a paralyzing coma that never affected his ability to feel, see, hear, smell, and taste. Art Hill, author of *I Don't Care if I Never Come Back,* eloquently described the moment Dahlgren's name was announced as the starting Yankee first baseman: "the words 'Dahlgren, first base' stunned the crowd into a moment of unplanned silence, which was followed by the unprecedented sound of several thousand people sighing in unison. Then Gehrig trudged painfully up to the plate, carrying the lineup card without his name on it. It was one of the most moving moments in sports history, high drama of the sort you can not make up."

Sadly, ALS also took the life of Hall of Fame pitcher Jim "Catfish" Hunter on September 9, 1999. Two months before dying, he told me during a private dinner in his honor that he "never asked, 'why me?'" That's courage!

299. *Some years just stick out—the happy-go-lucky slugging years of 1930 and 1987, for example, or the famine days of 1968 (when the American League averaged .230 and the National League didn't fare much better). But this recent record-breaking major league season featured new standards, including a whopping total of 5,693 home runs. In which season did this free-swinging occur?*

ANSWER: 2000

As with the previous four years, the 2000 campaign will be remembered for its offensive accomplishments. A staggering average of 2.34 homers were hit per game in 2000, or 1 every 29.3 at-bats. A record-tying 103 players hit 20 or more home runs, a record 47 players hit at least 30, and 9 hit at least 43. Eleven teams accumulated at least 200 home runs, and the 100-RBI plateau was reached by 53 players. The 1999 season featured a record 59 players reaching 100 RBI and five teams with four 100-RBI players.

Some have speculated that owners and executives of Major League Baseball have "juiced" or livened up the baseball, on the theory that more offense would bring in more fans, as had happened in previous eras. Following the demoralizing 1919 "Black Sox" scandal, Babe Ruth's prowess revitalized the game. And following the onset of the Great Depression, the leagues used more tightly wound balls to create more offense and attract more fans, although the ball's liveliness varied throughout the 1930s.

    Of course, the 1994 strike was self-inflicted, but once again baseball has survived a tragedy and drew 70,589,505 fans in 1998, almost matched that total in 1999, and reached a record level in 2000. Many think both leagues have livened up the baseballs to stir the current power surge and re-create interest among those who were disgusted with the game following the strike. Another target may have been teenagers, an age group that has recently shown more interest in other sports that are faster-paced and higher-scoring. Major League Baseball has denied livening up the baseballs. But regardless of the reason—juiced or tighter-wound balls, a smaller strike zone, small, hitter-friendly ballparks, diluted pitching caused by expansion, muscled-up hitters, or any combination thereof—home runs are ruling today's game.

◆ Did you know more home runs were hit from opening day through April 7, 2000, than were hit during the entire 1918 campaign?

◆ Did you know the Baltimore Orioles and California Angels combined to hit 11 home runs in one game on July 1, 1994, tying a mark previously reached on seven occasions? Much like the 1930, 1987, and 1996 campaigns, 1994 appeared to be an explosive offensive year before it was cut short by the strike, leaving many to wonder what might have been. The mark set by the Orioles and Angels would only stand for a year, as on May 28, 1995, the Detroit Tigers (7) and the Chicago White Sox (5) combined for an unprecedented 12 home runs in one game. Lou Whitaker hit the game's final blast in Tiger Stadium, but the White Sox won the slugfest by a 14-12 score. A record 10 of the homers were solo shots. Seven years later, the same two teams tied their own mark during a 17-9 White Sox victory on July 2, 2002. (Each team hit six homers.)

◆ Did you know the Cincinnati Reds set an NL record with nine home runs in a 22-3 rout at Philadelphia on September 4, 1999, to ignite a record-breaking home run week for the club? Although the Reds fell one homer shy of the major league single-game record, set by Toronto on September 14, 1987, they cashed in on more opportunities. Cincinnati went on to hit five more roundtrippers the next day to break the major league mark of 13 homers over two games, previously held by the 1939 Yankees and 1961 Giants. The Reds ultimately tied the major league record—set by the 1977 Red Sox—of 21 homers over five games, and they tied the NL mark of 22 homers over six games.

◆ Did you know the 1967 Chicago White Sox (2.45) and the 1968 St. Louis Cardinals (2.49) are the last teams to have an ERA under 2.50 for an entire season?

300. *Match these well-known managers with their dubious achievements as players:*

1	Sparky Anderson	A	was traded four times (once for cash) in his eight-year career
2	Dick Howser	B	once drove in a mere six runs in a 307-at-bat season (a record low)
3	Ty Cobb and Tris Speaker	C	lost 46 games over two successive seasons
4	Whitey Herzog	D	could only collect a record-low 119 total bases in a 477-at-bat season
5	Roger Craig	E	escaped banishment when a witness failed to show up in court

ANSWER: 1—D, 2—B, 3—E, 4—A, 5—C

Two of the sport's greatest names almost joined Joe Jackson and Hal Chase (and later Pete Rose) among those banned from the game, but Cobb and Speaker (also managers at the time) escaped trouble once again in 1926. Pitcher Dutch Leonard (upset at Cobb, the player-manager for the Tigers, for releasing him during the 1926 season and at Speaker, Cleveland's player-manager, for not signing him) divulged a seven-year secret about himself, Smokey Joe Wood (from whom he received the incriminating evidence), Cobb, and Speaker. He claimed the aforementioned parties engaged in the "throwing" of a 1919 contest between the Tigers and Indians. According to Leonard, Cobb approached Speaker (Wood's manager and teammate on the Indians) and persuaded him to lose the game, so that the Tigers could beat the Yankees out of third-place shares. Speaker and Cobb were given the option of "retiring" so as to not tarnish their legendary names, but they decided to fight Leonard in court. However, Leonard never showed up in court, and Judge Landis dismissed the case. Although Cobb and Speaker escaped permanent banishment, neither played or managed again for the Tigers and Indians, respectively.

Cobb, oddly, finished his career with the Athletics in 1927 and 1928, reaching the 4,000-hit plateau in a Philadelphia uniform—

against his former squad. Speaker played for the Senators in 1927 and alongside Cobb with the Athletics the following year.

♦ Did you know that despite the alleged fixed game between the Indians and the Tigers, Detroit still finished one-half game behind the third-place Yankees? Cleveland, by the way, finished in second place, $3\frac{1}{2}$ games behind the "Black Sox."

301. *Aside from Joe Torre, can you name the Yankee manager who has sustained the longest uninterrupted tenure under George Steinbrenner's intimidating supervision?*

ANSWER: Buck Showalter

Buck Showalter, who was officially hired by Yankees general partner Robert Nederlander (during Steinbrenner's suspension) to open the 1992 season, managed the Yankees through the 1995 season for an uninterrupted tenure of 581 regular season games. Showalter had a winning percentage of .539 in four years, which included the team's first postseason berth in 14 years. Billy Martin, who managed the Yankees the last 56 games (30-26) of the 1975 season, the entire 1976 season (97-62 and a pennant), the entire 1977 season (100-62 and a World Series title), and the first 94 games (52-42) of New York's second straight world championship season, had the second longest uninterrupted tenure at 477 regular season games.

Torre will enter the 2003 season with credit for having managed the Yankees for 1,131 regular-season games. He missed the first 36 games of the 1999 season while recovering from prostate cancer.

♦ Did you know that since George Steinbrenner took over the Yankees, the organization has changed managers 21 times, general managers 15 times, pitching coaches 34 times, and public relation directors a dozen times?

302. *Match these pitchers with their non-pitching feats:*

1	Tom Glavine	A	was the last AL pitcher to get a hit before the designated hitter rule was adopted
2	Babe Birrer	B	hit a pair of three-run homers after entering a game in relief
3	Ed Walsh	C	has laid down 168 career sacrifice bunts, a record for pitchers

4 Larry Gowell   D comfortably holds the pitcher's record
                            with 266 chances accepted in a season

ANSWER: 1—C, 2—B, 3—D, 4—A

Glavine's total of 168 sacrifice bunts through 2002 is 21 more than that of the previous record holder, Joe Niekro. According to John Schwartz of the Society for American Baseball Research, Don Sutton (136) is third, the active Greg Maddux (135) is fourth, Rick Reuschel (135) is fifth, and Phil Niekro (129) rounds out the top six. . . . The groundball-inducing Walsh showed his tremendous defensive ability by acting as a fifth infielder in 1907. Walsh registered a whopping 227 assists (also a comfortable major league record), totaled 35 putouts, and made four errors in 1907, as he posted 24 wins and a 1.60 ERA. In addition, Walsh holds or shares the major league record by pitchers for most chances in a nine-inning game (13), extra-inning game (15), and two consecutive games (20), and most assists in a nine-inning game (11) as well as extra-inning game (12). No other pitcher in the history of the game has relied as heavily on his fielding ability or made his fielding such a key ingredient of his success on the mound. From 1906 to 1915, Walsh's range factor (chances per nine innings) dwarfed the league average. In the 1907 season, Walsh almost doubled the league average (4.68 to 2.43). . . . For Birrer, who accomplished his aforementioned feat on July 19, 1955, those two home runs represented the only two of his career. . . . Gowell's hit on October 4, 1972, came in his only at-bat.

◆ Did you know all-time saves leader Lee Smith holds the major league record for pitchers of 546 consecutive errorless games, a stretch of over 10 years? It began with a flawless defensive performance on July 5, 1982, and lasted through September 22, 1992.

303. *Match these diverse characters with their histories:*

1 Darrell Evans   A claims that his career took a turn for the
                            better after he spotted a UFO
2 Mike Hargrove   B was so disgusted with manager Leo
                            Durocher's handling of a team argument
                            that he retired and didn't return until
                            three and a half seasons later

3 Leo Durocher   C this Rookie of the Year took so long in
                            between pitches he was nicknamed "The
                            Human Rain Delay"
4 Arky Vaughan   D received a Purple Heart in World War II
5 Branch Rickey   E said "nice guys finish last"
6 Hoyt Wilhelm   F claimed that luck was the "residue of
                            design"

ANSWER: 1—A, 2—C, 3—E, 4—B, 5—F, 6—D

Vaughan, the great, left-handed-hitting shortstop, thought Durocher's suspension of pitcher Bobo Newsom in 1943 was unjust and unwarranted—another incident about which the pair didn't see eye to eye. After the season Vaughan retired, choosing not to spend more time in the ballpark with Durocher. When Durocher was suspended for an incident in 1947, Vaughan returned to the Dodgers and helped them win the NL pennant with a .444 on-base percentage in 64 games. He retired on his own in 1948. A career .318 hitter, Vaughan hit at least .300 in each of his first 10 seasons—all for the Pirates. A trade to Brooklyn, though, after the 1941 season brought him into close contact with Durocher. The 1935 batting champ led the National League in triples, walks, and on-base percentage three times for each category. Vaughan overcame sloppy defense (he led the league in errors three times early in his career) with the help of his roommate, coach Honus Wagner, as had Yogi Berra, with the help of Bill Dickey. Thanks to his work with the legendary Wagner, Vaughan went on to lead all NL shortstops in assists and putouts three times apiece—an impressive feat considering his counterparts on other teams included the defensively talented Eddie Miller and Dick Bartell. Nicknamed "Arky" because of his place of birth (Arkansas), Joseph Floyd Vaughan was elected to the Hall of Fame in 1985. . . . Durocher was referring to his sincere and friendly superstar Mel Ott when he came up with that famous line.

◆ Did you know that Tony Oliva was born Pedro Oliva but became known as Tony after he used his brother's passport to get out of Cuba? By whatever first name, the graceful Oliva proved he could hit as well as anyone when he was healthy. The Twins outfielder won three batting crowns with a fluid left-handed swing that became his trademark and finished among the top three four other times over a 15-year career that featured a .304 batting average, 220 homers, and 947 RBI. The eight-time All-Star led the league in hits five times and in doubles four times, also totaling five top-10 MVP finishes. Injuries prevented Oliva from reaching legendary plateaus, as a bad knee sidelined him in 1972 and affected his approach thereafter.

304. *Match these courageous players with their battles:*

1	Roger Metzger	A	was the first major leaguer to be killed in World War I
2	Ross Youngs	B	had four fingers amputated and retired in 1980 with a .231 career average
3	Jim Eisenreich	C	contracted tuberculosis when helping a city in Kentucky repair a damaged dike in freezing water by passing along sand bags
4	Tommy John	D	played his last season with Bright's Disease
5	Eddie Grant	E	tore a ligament in his left elbow, then underwent history's first ligament transplant, performed by Dr. Frank Jobe, which rejuvenated his career
6	Rube Waddell	F	had Tourette's Syndrome

ANSWER: 1—B, 2—D, 3—F, 4—E, 5—A, 6—C

Eisenreich had to take a leave as a Twins rookie in 1982 and retire in 1984 because he suffered from the nervous disorder Tourette's Syndrome. This driven young man, who suffered from an uncontrollable twitching when excited, removed himself from a May 4, 1982, game in Boston and didn't fully recover until 1987, when he returned to the majors for another 12 years. . . . Waddell, a man with a big heart, is said to have reportedly (at one time or another) saved the lives of 10 people, including teammate Danny Hoffman. . . . John missed the 1975 season before returning to win the NL Comeback Player of the Year Award in 1976 and register his first of three 20-win campaigns in 1977. Dr. Jobe has since performed the operation on many other pitchers, such as Orel Hershiser, Charles Nagy, Matt Morris, Mariano Rivera, Darren Dreifort, and Billy Koch. Morris became a 22-game winner two years after his surgery in 1999, Rivera became a dominating closer after his surgery in 1992, and Koch is the hardest thrower in the majors today. The procedure is now known as "Tommy John surgery."

◆ Did you know Christy Mathewson was a victim of poison gas in France during World War I? The inhalation of mustard gas weakened the pitcher and left him vulnerable to tuberculosis, which killed him at the age of 45 on October 7, 1925. According to Al Stump's *Cobb,* this happened during a drill that ended with many men trying to trample each other just to get out of a room that contained the deadly gas. "The signal was poorly given and a lot of us missed it, including Christy and me," Cobb said. "Christy was an instructor in Chemical, too. So were Branch Rickey and George Sisler. . . . When it was over, 16 bodies stretched out on the ground. Eight men died within hours of lung damage. In a few days, others were crippled."

Mathewson returned to baseball as a Giants coach from 1919 to 1921. In 1923 Mathewson served as the president of the Boston Braves. He developed tuberculosis in both lungs and spent the last years of his life as a cripple in a sanatorium at Saranac Lake, New York.

305. *Match these one-time wonders with their achievements:*

1	Luis Arroyo	A	won Rookie of the Year honors but never again hit above .214
2	Joe Charboneau	B	this 17-year-old Dodger became the youngest major leaguer to homer
3	John Paciorek	C	won 15 of 20 decisions and saved a then-record 29 games in 65 appearances (all in relief) for the 1961 Yankees
4	Tommy Brown	D	was 3-for-3 with two walks, three RBI, and four runs scored in his only major league game

ANSWER: 1—C, 2—A, 3—D, 4—B

Arroyo and Jim Coates (a middle reliever, occasional closer, and spot starter) were unsung heroes of the great 1961 Yankees team, combining for a 26-10 ledger with 34 saves. . . . Charboneau batted .289 with 23 homers and 87 RBI for the Indians in 1980, capturing the fancy of Cleveland fans, who dubbed him "Super Joe" and serenaded him with songs. But the right-handed slugger slumped miserably the following year with a .210 mark and just four homers in 48 games, a season that included a demotion to the minor leagues as well as injuries. Charboneau had just two homers and nine RBI in 1982, his final major league season. . . . Soon after his September 29,

1963, debut for Houston against the Mets, Paciorek injured his back and never returned. Paciorek remains the player to have the most career hits without making an out. . . . Brown, three and a half months shy of his 18th birthday, homered against Pittsburgh on August 20, 1945. The shortstop made his debut a year earlier, at the age of 16. Although Brown hit just 31 homers over a nine-year career, the right-handed hitter did enjoy a three-homer game during the 1950 season.

◆ Did you know Henry Schmidt in 1903 became a 20-game winner in his only major league season? The Brooklyn Dodgers' righthander went 21-13 with a 3.83 ERA, hurling 301 innings and 29 complete games that season. Incredibly, the 30-year-old Texas native refused to report for the 1904 season, saying simply that he did not like living in the East.

306. *This Hall of Fame shortstop played from 1920 to 1933, using great discipline and control to compile a .312 career batting average and .391 on-base percentage. He demonstrated unbelievable bat handling in striking out just 114 times in 7,132 at-bats. Identify him.*

ANSWER: Joe Sewell

Sewell's strikeout to at-bat ratio of .016 (only 16 Ks for every 1,000 at-bats) remains the best in major league history. Sewell owns the single-season record of fewest strikeouts among those with at least 150 games played, whiffing just four times in 1925 as well as in 1929. Sewell, who walked 844 times, retired with a ratio of 7.4 walks per strikeout, also the best in major league history—well ahead of runner-up Mickey Cochrane, who averaged 3.95 walks per strikeout. The 155-pound, left-handed Sewell also holds the mark for most consecutive games (115) without striking out—a span of 437 at-bats, according to *The Sporting News Complete Baseball Record Book.* The durable Sewell was also a great fielder with tremendous range.

◆ Did you know Rob Picciolo walked a record-low 25 times in a 1,628-at-bat career (a ratio of one walk every 65.1 at-bats)? Conversely, Roy Cullenbine (a career .276 hitter) walked in a record 22 straight games (July 2–July 24) during the 1947 season—his last.

◆ Did you know Joe Sewell's younger brother, Luke, a catcher from 1921 to 1942 for Cleveland and the Chicago White Sox (primarily), struck out only 307 times?

307. *Match these past owners with their clubs:*

1	Robert E. Smith and Judge Roy Hofheinz	A	Phillies
2	Horace Stoneham	B	Braves
3	Bob Carpenter	C	Giants
4	Lou Perini	D	Astros

ANSWER: 1—D, 2—C, 3—A, 4—B

Stoneham, who took over as the Giants president in 1936 and presided over four pennant-winning clubs and a World Series champion in 1954, decided in 1957 that the Polo Grounds could no longer attract the attendance the team deserved. Unable to receive approval for funds for a new stadium in Manhattan, Stoneham spearheaded a near-unanimous vote by the Giants' board of directors to move the team to San Francisco for the 1958 season. In a dual move, Stoneham's Giants and Walter O'Malley's Dodgers moved out West following the 1957 campaign. O'Malley is still looked down upon in some parts of Brooklyn, where columnists at the time listed "Hitler, Stalin, and Walter O'Malley" as the three most evil men of the 20th century. . . . Carpenter Sr. bought the Phillies from the banned William Cox and kept the franchise in the family for the next 38 years. Carpenter Jr. operated the club upon his father's purchase.

◆ Did you know Clark Griffith was the first player to become an owner? The Senators owner and Hall of Famer won 240 games as a pitcher and managed for 20 years (posting a 1,491-1,367 record) before buying the Washington Senators in 1920.

308. *Which pair of sluggers were involved in the closest batting race in major league history?*

A Goose Goslin and Heinie Manush
B Chick Hafey and Bill Terry
C Alex Johnson and Carl Yastrzemski
D Don Mattingly and Dave Winfield
E Snuffy Stirnweiss and Tony Cuccinello

ANSWER: E

Snuffy Stirnweiss of the Yankees edged out Tony Cuccinello of the White Sox for the 1945 batting title by .0008. Stirnweiss averaged

.30854 (195-for-632) to Cuccinello's .30846 (124-for-402). Cuccinello (a .280 career average over 15 years) was released afterward, as the White Sox (like every other team) were expecting their players back from military action in time for the 1946 season. Stirnweiss never hit as high as .261 over his last seven seasons, and he averaged .268 over his 10-year career.

In the closest batting race in the National League, Chick Hafey of St. Louis won with a .3488 mark, New York's Bill Terry hit .3486, and Jim Bottomley (also of St. Louis) hit .3481. Despite losing, Terry out-hit Hafey by 56 hits (213-157) and Bottomley by 80 hits, as Hafey and Bottomley endured sickness and injury.

California's Alex Johnson edged Carl Yastrzemski, .3289 to .3286, in the 1970 batting race. Afterward, Yastrzemski resumed his Hall of Fame career (although his averages of .297, 24 homers, and 87 RBI from 1961 to 1970 dwindled to .276, 16 homers, and 75 RBI over his next 13 years), and Johnson never again hit over .287. Johnson later played for four more teams, increasing his total number of uniforms to eight.

309. *Who is the only player other than Babe Ruth to appear in one World Series as a pitcher and in another World Series as an outfielder?*

A Joe Wood
B Bob Lemon
C John Ward
D Stan Musial
E Lefty O'Doul

ANSWER: A

"Smokey" Joe Wood appeared in the 1912 World Series as a pitcher and the 1920 fall classic as an outfielder. Wood helped the Red Sox win the 1912 World Series with a 3-1 record in the seven-game tilt with the Giants. A pitcher-turned-outfielder, Wood was used as a reserve in the 1920 World Series. He went 2-for-10 for the Indians, helping the team defeat Brooklyn five games to two. Wood retired with a .283 average and an amazing 116-57 lifetime record. He used a great fastball to post a lifetime 2.03 ERA and give opposing batters headaches (989 Ks in 1,434⅓ innings pitched).

◆ Did you know that Joe Wood was forced to stop pitching and move to the outfield because of chronic soreness in his right arm? After an unbelievable 34-5 campaign in 1912, the pain began to affect him, limiting him to 16 starts (11-5, 2.29) in 1913. He was 9-3 in 1914 before enjoying one last hurrah on the mound in 1915, when he boasted an impressive 15-5 mark with a career-best and league-leading ERA of 1.49.

◆ Did you know Cy Seymour is the only player other than Babe Ruth to win a batting title one season and 20 games in another? A .303 lifetime hitter (1,723 hits), Seymour won his batting title (.377) in 1905, and he won 20 games in 1897 and 25 in 1898. Seymour was 63-54 for his career. Ruth won his only batting title (.378) in 1924, and he won 23 games in 1916 and 24 in 1917.

310. *Which one of these players became the first player in the 20th century (or since Cap Anson in 1884) to hit five home runs over two consecutive games?*

A Ty Cobb
B Honus Wagner
C Babe Ruth
D Jimmie Foxx
E Lou Gehrig

ANSWER: A

Cobb homered three times on May 5, 1925, and twice more the next day to become the first player in 41 years to accomplish the feat, taking advantage of the end of the Dead Ball Era. (In 1911, the dead-as-duck feathers-and-rubber-core ball was replaced by the cork-and-rubber-core ball.) In total, the feat has been achieved by 24 players on 26 occasions, with Mark McGwire and Ralph Kiner being the only repeaters. Cobb, who went 6-for-6 in that May 5 game, remained the only player with three homers and six hits in the same game until the Mets' Edgardo Alfonzo accomplished the feat on August 30, 1999.

According to the biography written by Al Stump, Cobb wanted to prove that he could hit home runs if he wanted to (but preferred the excitement and strategy of scoring from first or second base.) So before his six-hit performance in that May 5 game, Cobb told writers close by, "Gentlemen pay close attention today. I'll show you something new. For the first time in my life, I will be deliberately going for home runs." And he did it! Cobb added two more home runs the next day for a since-tied record two-game total of 25 total bases. Of course, Babe Ruth had a retort of his own. "If I'd tried for them dinky singles, I could've batted around .600."

311. *Match these catchers with their achievements:*

1	Carlton Fisk	A	caught 18 20-game winners
2	Thurman Munson	B	was the third catcher inducted into the Hall of Fame
3	Pat Moran	C	was the second catcher inducted into the Hall of Fame, after Buck Ewing
4	Mickey Cochrane	D	is the only catcher with 100 career steals and 100 homers
5	Jim Hegan	E	won the 1970 Rookie of the Year and 1976 MVP awards
6	Roger Bresnahan	F	is the only catcher to average two assists a game for a season

ANSWER: 1—D, 2—E, 3—F, 4—B, 5—A, 6—C

Fisk retired with 376 home runs (a record 351 as a catcher, although Mike Piazza is only 15 short of that mark) and 128 thefts in 186 attempts. During a 24-year career, Fisk displayed a tremendous amount of respect for the Game, once even scolding Deion Sanders (a member of the opposing team!) for not running out a pop-up to short. So demanding was Fisk that he even criticized Red Sox veterans Carl Yastrzemski and Reggie Smith for insufficient leadership—as a rookie! Few cared about the image of the Game as much as Fisk. . . . The Yankees' Munson rivaled Fisk as the best AL catcher during the 1970s. Munson placed in the top ten in batting six times, reached the 100-RBI mark thrice, garnered three Gold Gloves, and earned seven All-Star Game invitations over an 11-year career. As rugged as they came, Munson served as a fierce team leader—in 1976, he became the franchise's first captain since Lou Gehrig—and marched the Yankees to three straight pennants and two world championships. In those three World Series from 1976 to 1978, Munson batted a combined .373 in 67 at-bats, playing errorless ball and totaling 17 assists. He died in a plane crash at the age of 32 in 1979. . . . Moran performed his feat for the NL's Boston Beaneaters in 1903, averaging exactly two per game in his 107 contests behind the plate. A reserve for most of his career, Moran learned enough to become a solid manager, guiding the Phillies to the 1915 NL pennant and the Reds to a world championship four years later. . . . Bresnahan (a .279 lifetime hitter) was inducted in 1945. Cochrane was inducted two years later with a .320 batting average and a .419 on-base percentage (a record for catchers) to show for a shortened 13-year career. Cochrane was enjoying yet another solid season in 1937 when a pitch by Bump Hadley almost killed the two-time MVP, ending his brilliant career. Hadley was wild, issuing bases on balls to 1,442 batters (the 11th highest figure all time) over a 16-year career marked by a 161-165 ledger. Although Cochrane had homered in his prior at-bat, he exonerated Hadley. Cochrane showed great leadership, often taking charge of pitchers, even quick-tempered ones such as Lefty Grove. Cochrane liked to lead by example. In 1936 he suffered a nervous breakdown 120 games into the season after the tasks of playing, managing, and general managing became too great.

◆ Did you know that Mickey Mantle's father, Charles, named his son after "Mickey" Gordon Cochrane, because he admired Cochrane so much? Cochrane was a highly respected figure who came to be idolized by many.

312. *This newly acquired left fielder broke his ankle in spring training one year, opening the door for Milwaukee Braves' minor league second baseman Henry Aaron. Aaron went on to hit .280 with 13 home runs and 69 RBI (in 468 at-bats) in his 1954 rookie season. Can you name this famous outfielder whose injury allowed Aaron to step right in?*

A Bobby Thomson
B Eddie Mathews
C Bill Bruton
D Johnny Logan

ANSWER: A

Thomson, traded by the New York Giants for four players and $50,000 on February 1, suffered a triple fracture in his right ankle sliding into second base, disabling him until mid-July. Thomson ended his 15-year career in 1960 with a .270 mark, 264 home runs, and 1,026 RBI. To this day he is remembered for his dramatic 1951 home run.

313. *True or False? Rather than hire a manager for the 1961 season, Cubs owner William Wrigley hired eight coaches to rotate as managers. The Cubs used this system through the 1964 campaign.*

ANSWER: True

Although there were eight coaches, one was placed in charge for each game and given the credit in the record books. Vedie Himsl was 10-21 through the first 31 games, Harry Craft was credited with a 7-9 mark, El Tappe posted a 42-53 record, while Lou Klein (5-7) was at the helm for the final 12 games of the 1961 season (in which the Cubs finished 64-90, next to last). The 1962 campaign was much of the same, as Tappe (4-16), Klein (12-18), and Charlie Metro (43-69) combined for a disastrous 59-103 mark, again finishing next to last. Miraculously, in 1963 the Cubs climbed to over .500 (82-80) for the first time since 1946 with Bob Kennedy as the only leading coach. The 1964 season saw the Cubs use only Kennedy again, but the team slipped a bit to 76-86. Back to the more ordinary managerial system, in 1965 the Cubs fired Kennedy when their record stood at 24-32 after the first 56 games and hired Klein for the remainder of the season, finishing 72-90. The managerial headaches were over when the organization hired Leo Durocher for the 1966 season.

◆ Did you know the Wrigley family sold the Chicago Cubs to the Chicago Tribune Company and Bill Veeck sold his Chicago White Sox to Jerry Reinsdorf in the same year, 1981?

314. *This hefty slugger made a habit of having "courtesy runners" continue his home run trots when he was too fatigued to continue running the bases after reaching first. Who was he?*

ANSWER: Babe Ruth

Ruth repeated this action "about eight times" over his last two seasons with the New York Yankees (1934) and Boston Braves (1935), according to the Baseball Hall of Fame. Permitted through 1949, the courtesy-runner rule was used by managers wishing to keep an injured or tired player off the bases, after he reaches by a hit or some other way. A manager had to first ask the opposing skipper for permission and, when relevant, had to allow that opposing manager to choose any runner he wanted from the bench. (Most opposing skippers granted this gesture as a courtesy but usually chose a slow runner.) It's hard to believe that the same, albeit less rotund, Ruth legged out 10 inside-the-park home runs and stole home 10 times earlier in his career.

Ruth on May 25, 1935, had one last roar, clubbing and running out three home runs in a 4-for-4, six-RBI performance at Forbes Field. Ruth's third homer that day cleared the Forbes Field roof, the first to clear the right-field grandstand there. It was the 714th and final home run in the illustrious career of "The Bambino," who played his final game five days later and retired on June 2. Pirates righthander Guy Bush yielded that final homer, the blast some insist approached 600 feet. Bush told *The Sporting News*, "It was on the outside corner. As he went around third, Ruth gave me the hand sign meaning 'to hell with you.' He was better than me. He was the best that ever lived. That big joker hit it clear out of the park for his third home run of the game. It was the longest homer I'd ever seen in baseball."

In retirement Ruth spent more time with his family, served for part of the 1938 season as a coach for the Dodgers, made public appearances, and played a lot of golf. He died on August 16, 1948, of throat cancer at the age of 53. After more than 6,000 mourners attended his funeral mass, Ruth's body was laid at Yankee Stadium, where close to a quarter of a million people attended to pay their respects. Ruth was buried in Mount Pleasant, New York.

◆ Did you know the candy bar "Baby Ruth" was not named after the slugger but rather after the daughter of U.S. president Grover Cleveland?

315. *Match these baseball pioneers with their native country (the year in parenthesis represents the season in which the player made his debut):*

1 Joseph Miller A first major leaguer from Honduras (1987)
2 Jake Gettman B first major leaguer from Germany (1872)
3 Baldomero Almada C first major leaguer from Puerto Rico (1942)

4 Gerald Young   D first major leaguer from Mexico (1933)

5 Hiram Bithorn   E first major leaguer from Russia (1897)

ANSWER: 1—B, 2—E, 3—D, 4—A, 5—C

Other pioneers of note include Osvaldo Virgil from the Dominican Republic (1956), a current gold mine of talent, Bill Phillips of Canada (1897), Alejandro Carrasquel of Venezuela (1939), Esteban Bellan of Cuba (1871, in a league now recognized as a major league), Humberto Robinson of Panama (1955), Chan Ho Park of Korea (1994), and Calvin Maduro of Aruba (1996).

◆ Did you know Armando Rodriguez became the first Hispanic umpire in 1974? Rodriguez umpired until 1975. Rich Garcia became the second Hispanic umpire in 1975, arbitrating in the American League until 1999. Rodriguez was also an American Leaguer.

316. *Match these third basemen with their accomplishments:*

1 Frank "Home Run" Baker   A set the AL record of 46 homers in a season as a third baseman

2 Pete Rose   B set what was the third baseman's home run record with 29 and 34

3 Harlond Clift   C hit a crucial World Series home run on successive days

4 Troy Glaus   D was voted the best third baseman over the first 100 years of professional baseball in a vast 1969 poll of writers

5 Pie Traynor   E made the All-Star team at five different positions

ANSWER: 1—C, 2—E, 3—B, 4—A, 5—D

Using a 52-ounce bat, Baker earned his nickname by belting two big home runs during the 1911 World Series off different Hall of Fame pitchers. Baker's two-run shot in the sixth off the Giants' Rube Marquard gave the Athletics a 3-1 victory in Game Two to even the series. With Philadelphia trailing by a 1-0 margin in the top of the ninth the following day, Baker belted a pitch by Christy Mathewson over the right-field wall to tie the game and send the contest into extra innings. The Athletics went on to take advantage of a few errors and win an 11-inning thriller, 3-2. Jack Coombs, a 29-game winner that year, outdueled Mathewson, a 26-game victor, in one of the best and most exciting World Series games ever. . . . Rose played in 16 All-Star Games, making the team as a second baseman, a left fielder, a right fielder, a third baseman, and a first baseman. . . . Glaus in 2000 hit 46 of his 47 home runs as a third baseman, breaking the old AL mark of 43 set by Cleveland's Al Rosen in 1953. Glaus, who hit 41 in 2001, has a great chance of becoming the first third baseman to reach the 50-homer plateau, especially after the confidence-boosting 2002 post-season he enjoyed. No second baseman or catcher has reached that mark either. . . . Traynor, who played from 1920 to 1937, was the pro-totypical third baseman of the era, focusing on defense and hitting for a high average. Traynor excelled at each aspect, compiling a .320 lifetime batting average (best among all third basemen) and 2,889 putouts, a figure that still represents the NL standard. Traynor, who had the range of a shortstop and an excellent arm, also led the National League in double plays four times and assists three times.

◆ Did you know Babe Ruth usually used a 54-ounce bat during spring train-ing before returning to his 34-37 ounce lumber in the regular season? The heavy bat made the normal bats seem that much lighter, allowing him to generate more bat speed.

◆ Did you know "Wee" Willie Keeler's 30-inch bat is considered the shortest in major league history? It weighed but 29 ounces.

317. *Match these pitchers with their histories:*

1	Phil Niekro	A	holds the record for 12 straight seasons aver-aging 10 Ks per nine innings
2	Jim Whitney	B	is the only pitcher to lose 19 games on a pennant-winning club
3	Randy Johnson	C	was still pitching in the minors at the age of 54
4	Larry French	D	led the league in losses four times, a record he shares with Bobo Newsom and Pedro Ramos
5	Joe McGinnity	E	was the first pitcher to lead the league in wins and losses in the same season

ANSWER: 1—D, 2—E, 3—A, 4—B, 5—C

Niekro led the league in losses four years in a row with the Braves. Niekro was 16-20 in 1977, 19-18 in 1978, 21-20 in 1979, and 15-18 in 1980. His ERA was over 3.63 only once among those four years, and he posted a low of 2.88 in 1978. . . . "Grasshopper" Jim Whitney tied for the NL lead with 31 wins and led with 33 losses as a rookie for the Boston Red Caps (later known as the Braves) in 1881. Niekro, with 20 defeats and a co-leading 21 wins in 1979, is the only other major league pitcher to do so. Whitney, who boasted a 191-204 ledger as a righthander, also played center field on occasion and was such a good hitter (.261 average, 18 homers) he batted cleanup at times. Sadly, he died of tuberculosis in 1891. . . . Johnson has averaged 10 strikeouts per nine innings each year dating back to 1991, with outstanding figures of 10.19, 10.3, 10.9, 10.7, a then-record 12.35 (shattering Ryan's previous mark of 11.48 in 1987), 12.47 (in an injury-plagued 1996 season that limited him to 61⅓ innings), 12.3, 12.12, 12.06, 12.56, 13.41, and 11.56, respectively. Ryan, who previously held the record by averaging 10 Ks per nine innings in eight seasons, averaged a strikeout per inning during a season a record 16 times, missing by a narrow margin a few other times.

Overall, Lynn Nolan Ryan Jr. retired with a record 5,714 strikeouts in 5,387 innings (fifth all time) for a career average of 9.6 Ks per nine innings. Ryan called it a career after the 1993 season with 324 wins (tied with Don Sutton for 11th on the all-time list), 773 games started (second to all-time leader Cy Young's 818), 61 shutouts (tied with Tom Seaver for eighth), and a 3.19 ERA (18th best among those with 3,000 innings). The resilient Ryan also lost 292 times (third most all time) and walked 2,795 batters (by far the most in history).

◆ Did you know Houston Astros fireballing closer Billy Wagner in 1997 set the major league record for strikeouts per nine innings with a minimum of 50 innings pitched or 100 strikeouts recorded? Wagner, a diminutive southpaw, fanned 106 in 66⅓ innings for a ratio of 14.4 Ks per nine innings. Rob Dibble was the former holder of that record—in 1992 he whiffed 110 in only 70⅓ innings for a ratio of 14.1 per nine innings, which surpassed his 13.6 ratio per nine innings from the previous season. Dibble also owns the dubious season mark of 15.72 walks per nine innings, set in 1995.

318. *Match these events with their importance:*

1	1971 World Series	A	was played at the latest date in history
2	1982 All-Star Game	B	was the first one televised
3	1950 All-Star Game	C	was the first one played indoors
4	1975 World Series	D	was the first one played outside the United States
5	1968 All-Star Game	E	was the first one played at night
6	2001 World Series	F	was the first time no 20-game winner was involved

ANSWER: 1—E, 2—D, 3—B, 4—F, 5—C, 6—A

The first World Series night game was played in Pittsburgh (Game Four, 1971, versus Baltimore). . . . The 1982 All-Star Game was played in Montreal, where the NL won by a 4-1 score. . . . The 1922 World Series was the first fall classic broadcast over the radio. WJZ of Newark, New Jersey, hired the esteemed Grantland Rice for the honor, placing him directly in the Polo Grounds to broadcast the series between the New York Giants and New York Yankees. According to William Harper, author of *How You Played the Game: The Life of Grantland Rice,* WJZ tested out their product during the 1921 World Series with a "relay broadcast," in which a sports editor named Sandy Hunt sat in a box seat and relayed play-by-play and other information by telephone to WJZ quarters, "where Tommy Cowan repeated what he heard over the air." Earlier that 1921 season (on August 5), KDKA performed the first broadcast of a major league game, choosing Harold Arlin to do the play-by-play for the contest at Forbes Field between the Pirates and Phillies, according to Gene DeLisio of the Society for American Baseball Research. . . . The 1968 All-Star Game was played in the Astrodome. The National League won, scoring the game's lone run in the first on a double-play grounder that plated MVP Willie Mays. . . . The 2001 World Series ended on November 4. The 1981 World Series between the Yankees and Dodgers ended on October 28. The earthquake-delayed 1989 World Series also came to an end on the same date.

◆ Did you know Ivory Soap, Wheaties Cereal, and Mobile Oil were the three products endorsed in commercials aired by NBC during the first televised game in 1939, between the Cincinnati Reds and the Brooklyn Dodgers? That historic game on August 26 took place in Ebbets Field and was broadcasted by Red Barber, the Dodgers' radio voice.

◆ Did you know the 1947 World Series was the first to be televised? NBC did the honors in this event as well. The classic went seven games, crowning the Yankees as world champions. The NBC camera showed much during the series, and its most memorable image came about in the sixth inning of Game Six. The camera captured Joe DiMaggio's reaction after a long drive of his was run down at the left-field fence by Brooklyn's Al Gionfriddo. DiMaggio, half-way between first and second base, kicked the dirt in stride as he watched Gionfriddo stick his glove out at the last instant to take away a sure extra-base hit with two runners on, helping the Dodgers force a seventh game. It was as much emotion as DiMaggio ever showed between the lines, or close to it.

319. *Match these pitchers with their histories:*

1	Ed Reulbach	A	ended up in an institution after suffering a nervous breakdown
2	Karl Spooner	B	flamed out early after showing great promise, becoming only the fifth pitcher to throw shutouts in his first two starts
3	Urban Shocker	C	died on July 17, 1961—same day as Ty Cobb
4	John Clarkson	D	died of heart disease and pneumonia at the age of 38

ANSWER: 1—C, 2—B, 3—D, 4—A

Al Spalding, Monte Ward, Jim Hughes, and Al Worthington all preceded Spooner in beginning their careers so spectacularly. Worthington, pitching for the Giants, was the only other pitcher to hurl consecutive shutouts at the outset of his starting career in the 1900s. Spooner, pitching for Brooklyn, turned in his consecutive shutouts in September of 1954. But the following March, in spring training, the hard-throwing southpaw hurt his arm. . . . Clarkson, an extremely sensitive man, suffered a nervous breakdown in 1906 and was institutionalized. It was said that the Hall of Famer pitched without peer when complimented. Knowing this, his managers—especially Cap Anson—made sure to boost his confidence prior to his starting assignments. However, the insecure Clarkson was not good at receiving criticism. Upon hearing such, Clarkson would sulk and on occasion refuse to take the mound.

320. *Can you name the last World Series to be played entirely in one stadium?*

ANSWER: The 1944 World Series

The 1944 World Series, which pitted the St. Louis Cardinals against the St. Louis Browns, was played entirely in Sportsman's Park, which served as home field to both teams until 1953. The Cardinals won the series, dubbed the "Streetcar Series," in six games after dropping two of the first three. Scheduled without off days, the series was the first in which all games were played west of the Mississippi River. Originally the home of the St. Louis Red Stockings (who were renamed the Cardinals) from 1876 to 1877, Sportsman's Park later became the home of the American Association's St. Louis Browns, who were invited into the American League in 1902. The Cardinals moved into Robison Field in 1893, staying there for 27 years. In 1920 the Cardinals finally left the last wooden major league park and were welcomed by the Browns (for rent, of course) to share their home games at Sportsman's Park. This was not the only time a team used another team's stadium for the World Series, however. In the 1914 World Series between the Athletics and the Boston Braves, the Braves played their home games in Fenway Park (since their park, South Ends Grounds, only seated 11,000). The Braves later returned the favor, allowing the Red Sox to borrow newly built Braves Field, which had a 40,000-seat capacity, during the 1915 and 1916 World Series.

The 1918 Chicago Cubs used the White Sox's Comiskey Park for its larger seating capacity as well, but to no avail, as World War I activities affected attendance (only 66,000 fans came to see the series' first three games at Comiskey). The Cubs, hosting the first three games in Chicago (to reduce travel), lost three of the first four games and wound up losing the series in six to the Red Sox.

321. *Match these franchises with the events in their history:*

1	Brooklyn Dodgers	A	lost a record 26 games in a row
2	Pittsburgh Pirates	B	scored 13 eighth-inning runs after two were out to win, 20-7
3	Louisville Colonels	C	pounded the Cubs, 22-0, in the most lopsided shutout dating back to 1900
4	New York Giants	D	turned a record two triple plays in the same game
5	Minnesota Twins	E	hosted the first Sunday night game ever
6	Houston Colts	F	set a 20th-century record with 31 hits in one game, a mark later tied

ANSWER: 1—B, 2—C, 3—A, 4—F, 5—D, 6—E

Brooklyn's eighth-inning eruption came at the expense of Cincinnati on August 8, 1954. . . . The 22-0 rout was dealt by Pittsburgh on September 16, 1975, in Wrigley Field (the same game in which Rennie Stennett enjoyed his 7-for-7 performance). . . . The Colonels lost 26 consecutive games during their gloomy 1889 season in the American Association. . . . The Giants' offensive attack came at the hands of the Reds (25-13 losers) on June 9, 1901. It wasn't until August 28, 1992, that Milwaukee tied the record in its 22-2 rout of Toronto. The all-time record is 36 hits by the Phillies against the Colonels on August 17, 1894. . . . The Twins turned two triple plays in Boston on July 17, 1990, during a 1-0 defeat. Each gem was started by four-time Gold Glove winner Gary Gaetti, who owns the record of assisting in seven triple plays. Gaetti's triple plays occurred on: May 29, 1982, vs. the Yankees; August 8, 1983, vs. California; July 19, 1984, vs. the Yankees; April 5, 1988, vs. the Yankees; July 17, 1990 (two), vs. Boston; and May 14, 1994, vs. Oakland. His final triple play came as a member of the Kansas City Royals.

Gaetti once told me that he actually looked for chances to turn a triple play. "I definitely play for it, and put myself in that position. I often think about it beforehand and prepare myself for the situation. A lot of times, I'll just let the second baseman know, 'hey, this is what I'm thinking.' It's a nice little highlight of my career. I definitely look back at it with pride."

◆ Did you know Rennie Stennett was pinch-run for by Willie Randolph in the eighth inning of his 7-for-7 performance on September 16, 1975?

322. *Match these pitchers with their achievements:*

1	Eddie Plank	A	this ambidextrous pitcher used to pitch without a glove to conceal the direction of his delivery until the last instant
2	Carl Hubbell	B	invented the palm ball
3	Tony Mullane	C	threw a six-hit, 18-inning shutout without issuing a walk
4	Burleigh Grimes	D	allowed a live ball era record-low one home run in 301 innings
5	Eppa Rixey	E	was the last legal spitball pitcher

ANSWER: 1—B, 2—C, 3—A, 4—E, 5—D

Plank used the palm ball to become the first lefthander to win 300 games. . . . Hubbell's 18-inning gem on July 2, 1933, included 12 strikeouts against the Cardinals. Tex Carleton started for the Cardinals and pitched 16 shutout innings. After Hubbell's performance, which equaled the major league record for longest complete game shutout, no pitcher has duplicated the feat. The other three hurlers to accomplish it were Monte Ward (August 17, 1882), Walter Johnson (May 15, 1918), and Ed Summers (July 16, 1909). Ward, Johnson, and Hubbell each won, 1-0, but Summers' battle ended in a tie. . . . Mullane used his ambidextrous abilities to post a 285-215 record, a 3.05 career ERA, and 469 complete games from 1881 to 1894. On July 18, 1882, Mullane became the first to throw right-handed and left-handed in the same game, a feat he repeated on July 14, 1893. On September 29, 1995, Montreal's Greg Harris pitched one inning right-handed and one inning left-handed against the Reds, becoming the first to do so since Mullane 102 years earlier. The others who threw from the right and left side in the same game were Elton "Ice Box" Chamberlain (May 9, 1888) and Larry Corcoran (June 10, 1884). . . . Grimes was one of 17 pitchers to take advantage of the grandfather clause put into effect when the spitball was banned in 1920, which allowed those major leaguers already using the spitball to keep using it. According to Harvey Frommer, author of *Shoeless Joe and Ragtime Baseball,* the other 16 were: Stan Coveleski, Red Faber (the next to last allowed to use the pitch), Urban Shocker, Jack Quinn, Dutch Leonard, Ray Fisher, Ray Caldwell, Dick Rudolph, Bill Doak, Phil Douglas, Allan Russell, Clarence Mitchell, Allen Sothoron, Doc Ayers, Dana Fillingim, and Marv Goodwin. Aside from banning spitballs, Major League Baseball also banned the use of any foreign substance on the ball. . . . Rixey in 1921 went 19-18 with a 2.78 ERA for the Reds (a year away from his best season of 25-13).

◆ Did you know Babe Adams' 21-inning complete game defeat during the middle of the 1914 season remains the longest pitching performance without a walk? On July 17 of that season, Adams of the Pirates went head-to-head against the Giants' Rube Marquard and pitched the entire, extra-inning affair without issuing a single base on balls. Adams did, however, permit a pair of Giants to score in the top of the 21st inning, allowing New York to win the pitching battle, 3-1. Adams yielded 12 hits and struck out six. Marquard displayed good control as well, walking two, whiffing two, and permitting 15 hits in the marathon victory.

323. *Match these great hurlers with their accomplishments:*

1	Ed Walsh	A	was the second-oldest pitcher to homer in the 20th century
2	Larry French	B	hurled 45⅓ consecutive scoreless innings
3	Phil Niekro	C	is the only pitcher to ever lead the league in ERA and losses in the same season
4	"Three Fingers" Brown	D	led the league in saves for four straight years, becoming the first pitcher to save 10 games in one season
5	Carl Hubbell	E	remains the only pitcher to throw a one-hitter in his last career start

ANSWER: 1—C, 2—E, 3—A, 4—D, 5—B

In 1910 Walsh led the American League with a 1.27 ERA and 20 losses (his White Sox's futile offense rewarded "Big Ed" with only 18 wins). In 1987 Nolan Ryan came awfully close to duplicating Walsh's "feat," finishing one loss off the mark. . . . In 1982 Niekro homered at 43 years of age—three years shy of the record held by Jack Quinn, who homered for the last time in 1930, shortly before his 47th birthday. . . . Hubbell's 45⅓ scoreless inning streak in 1933 remains the longest by a lefthander. Later that October, "King Carl" allowed nary an earned run in 20 World Series innings, helping the Giants oust the Senators in five games for the title. The 1933 campaign marked the first of Hubbell's two MVPs and the first of Hubbell's three ERA and victory crowns. Hubbell used a high leg kick, similar to that of righthander Juan Marichal.

324. *Match these managers with their ledgers:*

1	Bill McKechnie	A	finished first or second in 15 of his 23 seasons
2	Dick Williams	B	managed only one team to a first- or second-place finish
3	Walter Alston	C	is one of only three managers to win the World Series with two different teams
4	Danny Murtaugh	D	managed the 1960 champion Pittsburgh Pirates
5	Lou Boudreau	E	is one of only two managers to take three different teams to a World Series

ANSWER: 1—C, 2—E, 3—A, 4—D, 5—B

Sparky Anderson (1975–76 Reds, 1984 Tigers) and Bucky Harris (1924 Senators, 1947 Yankees) joined McKechnie (1925 Pirates, 1940 Reds) as the other managers to win a World Series with two different teams. Anderson remains the only manager to win a World Series in each major league, defeating Williams' Padres in the 1984 fall classic with that honor on the line, going to the victor. . . . McKechnie, who also took the Cardinals to the 1928 World Series, became the first manager to take three different teams to the fall classic. Williams, of course, became the second. Williams guided the Red Sox to the 1967 World Series, then managed the A's to World Series victories in 1972 and 1973, before guiding the Padres to the 1984 NL pennant. . . . Alston also led his club to six pennants and four world championships. . . . Boudreau, who managed the Indians to their last series title in 1948, managed four different teams over 16 years.

◆ Did you know the Cincinnati Reds are the first team to have three members of its organization enter the Hall of Fame in the same year? Manager Sparky Anderson, first baseman Tony Perez, and long-time broadcaster Marty Brennaman were all elected in 2000.

SECOND POSTSEASON

Best-of-Seven League Championship Series

Game One Question:

En route to the 1986 World Series, the Mets had to endure the Houston Astros and Mike Scott in the NL Championship Series. The Mets couldn't solve Scott, but their drive and motivation made them an almost impossible team to defeat. Aside from being talented and arrogant, this Mets club was one of the most resilient squads ever put together, overcoming seemingly insurmountable odds time and time again. Can you name the only pitcher aside from reliever Jesse Orosco to win a game for the Mets in the 1986 NL Championship Series?

ANSWER: Bob Ojeda

Bob Ojeda tied the series with his Game Two complete game win, 5-1. Orosco, who struck out 10 and yielded just five hits over eight innings, went on to win Game Three, Game Five, and Game Six, setting the League Championship Series record. The Mets took a two games to one series lead following a dramatic ninth-inning comeback in the mold of Cookie Lavagetto and Kirk Gibson. The Mets, who had already overcome a 4-0 deficit earlier, found themselves trailing, 5-4, in the bottom of the ninth inning with two out, with Wally Backman on first and Lenny Dykstra, "the man they call nails" (as Hall of Fame voice Bob Murphy put it), at the plate. Dykstra sent a delivery from closer Dave Smith into the right-field bullpen for a dramatic 6-5 victory. It was a preview of things to come. Their resiliency was also evident in the regular season, as the Mets relievers combined to win or save 80 of the team's 108 victories, a statistic that reveals the team's knack for late-inning success.

◆ Did you know that during the first 18 years (1969–86) of League Championship Series and World Series play only two teams (the 1973 A's and the 1976 Reds) won the fall classic when they were given home-field advantage in both rounds? Interestingly, no team later would waste that opportunity, beginning with the 1987 Twins and ending with the advent of the three-tier playoff format in 1995.

Game Two Question:

After another complete game by Mike Scott tied the 1986 NL Championship Series at two Games apiece, these two hurlers pitched a combined 19 innings in a 12-inning Game Five nail-biter. Can you name them?

ANSWER: Dwight Gooden and Nolan Ryan

Gooden went 10 innings and Ryan pitched 9, as the game remained knotted at 1-1 until the bottom of the 12th inning. That's when Gary Carter (in a 1-for-21 slump) sent Charlie Kerfeld's pitch right up the middle to drive in Wally Backman for the 2-1 victory.

Game Three Question:

Have you ever wondered how the Mets would have fared against Mike Scott had there been a Game Seven in the 1986 NL Championship Series? That possibility was on the cusp of becoming reality but for another Mets miracle. Can you name each starting pitcher from the exhilarating 16-inning Game Six thriller?

ANSWER: Bob Ojeda and Bob Knepper

The Mets' Ojeda allowed three runs in the bottom of the first and was gone by the sixth inning. The Astros' Knepper shut out the Mets over the first eight innings before yielding three runs in the ninth to the ever-so-resilient Mets, who forced extra innings. Mets reliever Roger McDowell followed with the performance of his life in pitching five scoreless innings (from the ninth inning through the 13th). Wally Backman's RBI single in the 14th off Aurelio Lopez handed the Mets a 4-3 lead before Jesse Orosco yielded the advantage right back, serving up a game-tying home run to Billy Hatcher in the bottom half of the inning.

Game Four Question:

Thanks to Ray Knight's RBI single, a wild pitch, and an RBI single by Lenny Dykstra, New York entered the bottom of the 16th inning ahead, 7-4, in Game Six of the 1986 NL Championship Series. The Astros pulled within 7-6 with runners on first and third, two outs, and a reliever (Jesse Orosco) so exhausted he couldn't throw a fastball. Can you name the Astros batter who swung and missed on the three-ball, two-strike pitch with the 1986 NL pennant on the line?

ANSWER: Kevin Bass

Outfielder Kevin Bass struck out on Orosco's sixth straight slider. The southpaw reliever reacted by throwing his glove high into the Astrodome air. Among the most famous strikeouts of all time, Orosco's punchout ended the most exciting League Championship Series game in history and gave the Mets their first pennant in 13 years. The only other League Championship Series that can compare in drama is the 1980 NL Championship Series between the Phillies and Astros. Although not a League Championship Series game, Game Five of the 1995 AL Division Series between the Yankees and the Mariners was every bit as exciting. For that matter, so were Game Two and Game Four of that memorable AL Division Series.

Game Five Question (if necessary):

Can you name the 1980 NL Championship Series MVP?

ANSWER: Manny Trillo

Philadelphia Phillies second baseman Manny Trillo stood out above the rest in the best-of-five series in which the last four games were decided in extra innings. Best known for his fielding prowess (he retired in 1989 with a .263 career average), Trillo hit .381 with two doubles, a triple, and four RBI. Trillo followed Greg Luzinski's go-ahead RBI double in the 10th inning off loser Joe Sambito with one of his own to give the Phillies a 5-3 win in Game Four and force a deciding game. Warren Brusstar won Game Four in relief, and Tug McGraw recorded his second save of the series.

◆ Did you know Manny Trillo, who was born in Venezuela as Jesus Manuel Marcano, was the first non–American-born player to earn a League Championship Series MVP? Toronto's Roberto Alomar (a native of Puerto Rico) later won the 1992 AL Championship Series MVP. A pair of Puerto Ricans swept the 1996 League Championship Series MVP honors, as Atlanta's Javier Lopez and the Yankees' Bernie Williams led their respective teams to the World Series. Two non–American-born players also swept the 1999 NL Championship Series MVP honors—Atlanta's Eddie Perez (Venezuela) and the Yankees' Orlando Hernandez (Cuba). Puerto Rican Benito Santiago won the 2002 NL Championship Series MVP award for the Giants. In 1997 the Marlins' Livan Hernandez (Orlando's brother) earned MVP honors in the NL Championship Series and the World Series. Other non-American World Series MVP heroes include Puerto Rican Roberto Clemente (1971), Dominicans Pedro Guerrero (1981) and Jose Rijo (1990), and Panamanian Mariano Rivera (1999).

Game Six Question (if necessary):

Can you name the Astros pitcher who was within six outs of delivering Houston its first pennant but blew a 5-2 lead in the eighth inning to allow the Phillies to win the 1980 NL Championship Series and pennant?

ANSWER: Nolan Ryan

The Phillies got to the Astros' million-dollar-a-year superstar for four runs in the eighth, as the fireballer was relieved without retiring a single batter during the frame. The Phillies added another run off Ken Forsch (the Game One loser) to cap off a five-run eighth that gave them a 7-5 advantage. The resilient Astros added two runs in their bottom half of the eighth to tie the game at 7-7, but Garry Maddox's RBI double off loser Frank LaCorte clinched the Phillies' first pennant in 30 years.

In 1979 Houston finished 89-73 (one and a half games behind Cincinnati). In 1980 Houston (93-70) overcame the midseason loss of fireballer J. R. Richard to win its first division title. The Astros benefited from the rookie luck of reliever Dave Smith (1.92 ERA), Vern Ruhle's career year (12-4, 2.38 ERA), and the acquisitions of veterans Joe Morgan and Ryan. Affected by the loss of Richard (10-4, 1.89), the dampened spirits of the Astros were evident as they slumped in the second half of that 1980 season. The Astros lost their last three scheduled games to the Dodgers in Los Angeles and had to play a one-game playoff victory at Dodger Stadium to clinch the division. Houston's winningest pitcher, Joe Niekro, pitched them to a 7-1 win (his 20th) in the one-game playoff, but because of the extra assignment Niekro was available for just one NL Championship Series start instead of two.

◆ Did you know the Houston Astros enter the 2003 season having lost all seven of their postseason series? The same franchise that has never won a postseason game when facing elimination has lost three times to Atlanta, once to San Diego, once to the New York Mets, once to Los Angeles, and once to Philadelphia.

Game Seven Question (if necessary):

Can you name the only player to homer during that exciting 1980 NL Championship Series?

ANSWER: Greg Luzinski

Greg "The Bull" Luzinski hit a game-winning two-run homer in the sixth inning in a 3-1 Phillies victory in Game One. Steve Carlton won that game. In Game Two, tied 3-3 going into extra innings, the Astros won on the strength of a four-run 10th, highlighted by Jose Cruz's RBI single and Dave Bergman's two-run triple, to even the series. Game Three featured Joe Niekro at his knuckleballing best, baffling the Phillies' lineup for 10 innings of six-hit, shutout ball. Winner Dave Smith pitched a scoreless 11th inning for Houston as the Astros took a two games to one series lead. Joe Morgan led off the bottom of the 11th inning with a triple and scored on Denny Walling's sacrifice fly.

If you have won four League Championship Series games, you advance to the World Series.

Best-of-Seven World Series

Game One Question:

> *The Yankees' John Wetteland and Mariano Rivera became the third and fourth relievers, in 1996 and 1999, respectively, to earn World Series MVP honors. Can you name the first two?*

ANSWER: Larry Sherry and Rollie Fingers

Dodgers rookie Larry Sherry earned the honor in 1959 by becoming the first pitcher in World Series history to either win or save a combination of four games. The righthander (who allowed just one earned run in 12⅔ innings versus the White Sox) saved Game Two and Game Three and won Game Four and Game Six.

Oakland's Rollie Fingers was the second reliever to earn the honor, in 1974. He won Game One by hurling 4⅓ innings and went on to save Game Four and Game Five. By today's rules, Fingers would also have been awarded a save in Game Three, which would have given him a victory and three saves. Fingers entered the eighth inning with one out and no runners on base and was charged with preserving a 3-1 lead. Fingers yielded a home run to Dodger outfielder Willie Crawford in the ninth but hung on to preserve the 3-2 win. The decision not to award him a save was the official scorer's judgment.

In the 1996 World Series, Wetteland was awesome in nailing down a record four saves. The righthander allowed one run and four hits over 4⅓ innings spanning five appearances, during which he struck out six and walked one. Wetteland took advantage of the relatively new three-tiered postseason format to chalk up seven saves, a new standard for a single postseason.

In 1999 Rivera (Wetteland's setup man three years earlier) became the fourth reliever to win the award, with two saves and a victory.

◆ Did you know Arizona's Randy Johnson in 2001 became the first pitcher to win five games in a single postseason? After losing his NL Division Series start against St. Louis, Johnson won both his assignments against Atlanta in the NL Championship Series. In the subsequent World Series, the "Big Unit" started and won Game Two and Game Six, then came on in relief to win the decisive Game Seven without any rest. For his incredible effort, Johnson earned a share of the fall classic's MVP Award, with Curt Schilling, marking only the second time in series history that the award has been shared. The duo combined for 9 of the Diamondbacks' 11 postseason victories.

In 2002, sensational rookie middle reliever Francisco Rodriguez matched Johnson's five wins in a single postseason to help the Anaheim Angels win their first world championship. The smooth yet hard-throwing righthander stormed into the spotlight after pitching just $5\frac{2}{3}$ innings during the regular season. In the postseason the 20-year-old went 5-1 with a 1.93 ERA over $18\frac{2}{3}$ innings, during which he struck out a whopping 28 batters.

Game Two Question:

In 1979 Willie Stargell became the first player to follow up a League Championship Series MVP Award with an MVP Award in the World Series. Orel Hershiser became the third in 1988, and Livan Hernandez became the fourth nine years later. Can you name the only other player to earn both awards?

ANSWER: Darrell Porter

Darrell Porter earned the 1982 World Series MVP by performing well behind the plate and with his bat, hitting an important .286. The catcher drove in five runs with one home run and two doubles— the latter of which drove home two runners to tie the game during the sixth inning of Game Two. The Cardinals went on to win the game by a 5-4 margin, making their 10-0 defeat to Milwaukee in Game One seem a dim memory. That was the game in which Paul Molitor set the record for five hits in a World Series game and Robin Yount had the first of his record two four-hit games. Joaquin Andujar won both his starts (including Game Seven) with a 1.35 ERA.

◆ Did you know Livan Hernandez is a Cuban defector who had still been pitching in Cuba as recently as two years before his unforgettable October performance for the Florida Marlins in 1997? Hernandez, who left his family behind in Cuba, received a $2.5 million bonus from the Marlins shortly after the 1996 New Year's celebration. He became just the second rookie—Larry Sherry was the first—to win World Series MVP honors, after earning the NL Championship Series honor with a 2-0 record. As an emergency starter in Game Five against the Braves, Hernandez struck out an NL Championship Series record 15 in a three-hit, 2-1 victory. In the fall classic against the Indians, the 22-year-old Hernandez won Game One (becoming the youngest to win an opener) and Game Five—each against postseason stalwart Orel Hershiser. Hernandez had come a long way from being a guy whose future looked bleak just 12 months earlier, after he had pitched ineffectively in the Marlins' farm system in his first season in the United States. He had gained a significant amount of weight and appeared unable to shake the effects of being all alone in a new world. But he got comfortable in his new surroundings, regained his confidence, and lost some weight to reclaim his winning form, leading the underdog Marlins to the world championship.

◆ Did you know Livan Hernandez in 1997 became the sixth pitcher to win four games in a single postseason? Hernandez, who earned two NL Championship Series and two World Series wins for the Florida Marlins, made it a third straight year that the feat was accomplished, following Cleveland's Hershiser (in 1995) and Atlanta's John Smoltz (in 1996). Smoltz and Hershiser each had one win in the Division Series, two in the NL Championship Series, and one in the World Series. During the strike-shortened 1981 season, the Dodgers' Burt Hooton became the first to do so, with one win in the Division Playoffs, two in the NL Championship Series, and one in the fall classic. Oakland's Dave Stewart and Minnesota's Jack Morris each achieved the feat, in 1989 and 1991, respectively, with two wins each in the AL Championship Series and World Series. Since Hernandez, the Yankees' David Wells (1998), Arizona's Curt Schilling (2001), Arizona's Randy Johnson (five, in 2001), and Anaheim's Francisco Rodriguez (five, in 2002) have achieved the feat.

Game Three Question:

John Wetteland's record four saves surpassed the mark of three shared by a pair of relievers, including Kent Tekulve in 1979. Who was the first?

ANSWER: Elroy Face

Pittsburgh's Elroy Face saved Game One, Game Four, and Game Five before being attacked for four runs during Game Seven of the 1960 World Series. In his attempt for a fourth save, Face (who entered the game with a 2.46 series ERA) saw his series ERA jump to 5.23, ruining his MVP chances. In 1979 Tekulve saved Game Two, Game Six, and Game Seven to redeem himself for a loss in Game Four. In that contest, the Pirates lost a 6-3 lead in the eighth inning to fall, 9-6, and find themselves down three games to one. That's when the comeback began.

Game Four Question:

Only one player has ever won the World Series MVP in a losing cause. His total of 12 RBI in that classic still stands as the series record. Who is this reliable contact hitter better known for his smooth ability with the glove?

ANSWER: Bobby Richardson

Richardson, a five-time Gold Glove second baseman who didn't drive in more than 59 runs in any of his 12 seasons, teed off on Pittsburgh Pirates pitching during the 1960 World Series. His unforeseen 12 RBI in that seven-game set represented almost half of his regular-season total (26), which had come in 150 games. The right-handed batter walloped Pirates pitching that October for 11 hits, including a homer, two triples, and a pair of doubles. He also scored eight times and slugged .667 in the losing effort. In Game Three, Richardson belted a grand slam and collected a record six RBI. His dozen total RBI also represent the mark for any postseason series (Boston's Nomar Garciaparra came close with 11 in the 1998 Division Series). In addition, Richardson recorded 21 putouts and 28 assists for the Yankees, who lost in seven games.

Richardson remains the only second baseman to earn the award, as officially given out by *Sport*. However, second basemen Jerry Coleman (1950), Billy Martin (1953), Bill Mazeroski (1960), and Dick Green (1974) each have won the Babe Ruth Award, the less-heralded World Series MVP honor given out by the New York chapter of the Baseball Writers Association of America.

◆ Did you know Edgar Martinez, Mo Vaughn, and John Valentin share the postseason record of seven RBI in one game? Martinez accomplished his feat in Game Four of the 1995 AL Division Series for Seattle against the Yankees, slugging a three-run homer and a grand slam to help the Mariners force a Game Five. Vaughn drove in seven runs in Boston's AL Division Series–opening win against Cleveland in 1998, with a three-run homer and a pair of two-run hits. Boston's Valentin had two homers, a double, and a single in Game Four of the 1999 AL Division Series against Cleveland.

Game Five Question (if necessary):

Match these pitchers with their World Series MVP year:

1	Whitey Ford	A	1957
2	Bob Turley	B	1958
3	Ralph Terry	C	1961
4	Lew Burdette	D	1962

ANSWER: 1—C, 2—B, 3—D, 4—A

Ford went 2-0 (no runs, six hits in 14 innings), including a two-hit shutout over the Reds in Game One of the 1961 World Series. Ford, who pitched 18 scoreless frames in the 1960 World Series, also pitched five scoreless innings in Game Four of the 1961 Series to surpass Babe Ruth's fall classic record of $29\frac{2}{3}$ consecutive scoreless innings. Ford left the latter start in the sixth inning because of a bruised toe, but he got a chance to extend the streak some more the following October against the Giants. After a scoreless frame in the 1962 Series opener, Ford finally permitted a run with two out in the second, bringing to an end his streak at $33\frac{2}{3}$, although it's in the current record books as 33 (according to Elias Sports Bureau, fractions of an inning are only included in a scoreless frame). Christy Mathewson threw 28 consecutive scoreless innings in World Series play (27 goose eggs in 1905 and one in 1911). . . . Turley was knocked out of the box in the second game of the 1958 classic, as he could only retire one batter before allowing four earned runs in the Braves' seven-run first inning. But, unbelievably, a reinvigorated Turley bounced back with a five-hit shutout in Game Five, a pressure-packed save in Game Six (he was brought in to retire Frank Torre in the 10th with the tying run on third and two out), and a win in relief in Game Seven (pitching the final 6⅔ innings). . . . Trying to rebound from a forgettable 1960 World Series effort, Terry lost Game Two, 2-0. However, the righthander received enough run support to win his Game Five complete game and his Game Seven four-hit shutout of the Giants, finishing with a series ERA of 1.80. . . . Burdette (0.67 ERA) yielded only two earned runs in hurling three complete games, not allowing a run over the last 24 innings. Burdette went the distance in Game Two, Game Five, and Game Seven; the last two victories were shutouts. Burdette not only brought the Braves their first world championship in 43 years but enjoyed what is perhaps the second-best pitching performance in fall classic play, behind only Mathewson's quasi-perfect pitching exhibition in the 1905 World Series.

◆ Did you know Mariano Rivera in 2000 set a postseason record by extending his streak of consecutive scoreless innings to 33⅓? Rivera broke Whitey Ford's mark of 33 (which came exclusively in World Series play). Rivera, who started the streak in 1997 and saw it end in the 2000 AL Championship Series, went 23 straight postseason appearances without allowing a run. In 19 of those outings he pitched more than an inning.

Game Six Question (if necessary):

Alan Trammell owned San Diego pitchers during the 1984 World Series while becoming the second of three shortstops to win the World Series MVP Award. Derek Jeter was the last. Can you name the first?

ANSWER: Bucky Dent

Bucky Dent earned the honor by hitting .417 with 10 hits and seven RBI in the Yankees' 1978 World Series triumph over Los Angeles. Trammell hit .450 with nine hits, two home runs, six RBI, and five runs scored. Jeter homered twice, doubled twice, and tripled among his nine hits, batting .409 in addition to playing solid defense.

◆ Did you know Toronto's Tony Fernandez broke Bucky Dent's single-series record of seven RBI by a shortstop with nine in the 1993 World Series? Fernandez hit .333.

Game Seven Question (if necessary):

Can you name the Yankees second baseman who hit .438 in the 1978 World Series?

ANSWER: Brian Doyle

Rookie Brian Doyle, playing for the injured Willie Randolph, scored four runs, drove in two, played flawless defense, and equaled Bucky Dent's three-hit performance in the finale (Game Six). Doyle, who went 7-for-16 in the series and slugged .500, also had three hits in Game Five, helping the Yankees untie the series. Doyle and Dent combined for five RBI in Game Six. The keystone duo even over-shadowed Reggie Jackson, who hit .391 with two home runs and a series-high eight RBI.

For Doyle, it was an unforeseen performance, given that he never batted higher than .192 and averaged a mere .161 over a four-year career that spanned just 199 at-bats. In his 110 regular-season games, Doyle slugged just .191.

Allow me to congratulate you on your world championship if you answered four questions correctly!!!!

Your two-year contract is over. The team must decide your future. The club will grant you a contract extension if you won: (a) one world championship over the past two years; or (b) one pennant; or (c) 170 regular-season games.

Try managing again to test your learning abilities and absorb more baseball nuggets.

Sign Here _____

Barnstorming Tour

In the early days, when players sought to supplement their incomes during the offseason, they traveled on planned barnstorming tours in groups and played exhibition baseball in warm spots throughout the country. With the conclusion of this book's second season, I invite you to attend a barnstorming tour of your own. Here are a few more "Did You Know?" tidbits to keep you entertained. Enjoy!

◆ Did you know Amos Otis admitted to using a corked bat throughout his entire career? The lean and lanky center fielder hit .277 with 193 home runs and 1,007 RBI over a 17-year career, spent mostly in Kansas City. Otis, who also pilfered 341 bases, was a tremendous performer in postseason play. In the 1980 World Series, Otis hit .478 with three homers and seven RBI. By drilling a hole into the bat's barrel and filling it with lighter material such as cork, glue, and rubber, cheating players are able to generate more bat speed without sacrificing the size of the bat's sweet spot.

◆ Did you know that 3-2 was the most common score throughout the National and American Leagues from 1901 to 2000? According to the Hall of Fame, 8,947 games in that period ended in that score. Over that same time, 8,500 games ended 4-3, the second most common score. The third most common was 2-1, followed by 5-4 and the ever popular 4-2.

◆ Did you know Hank Aaron hit 17 of his 755 home runs off hard-throwing Hall of Famer Don Drysdale? The intimidating hurler was 1 of 12 Hall of Famers and 310 different hurlers Aaron connected off of for a home run. In his autobiography, *I Had a Hammer*, Aaron wrote of Drysdale, "We had a great rivalry going and there was nothing bitter about it." Aaron's favorite month to homer in was July (152), his favorite team to homer off was Cincinnati (97), and his favorite inning to homer in was the first (124).

◆ Did you know Pete Rose reached base a record 29 times on catcher's interference? The tireless Rose truly used every resource available to him to reach his maximum potential.

◆ Did you know stellar batsman Lance Berkman was not drafted out of high school since scouts said he "didn't look like a player," because of his boyish face? I kid you not; that was the reason given for not drafting Berkman, who went on to bat an obscene .438 with 41 homers and 134 RBI for Rice University in 1997. The boyish Berkman, who is continuing his onslaught in the big leagues, carries a .304 batting average, a .406 on-base percentage, and a hefty .578 slugging figure into the 2003 season.

◆ Did you know Clyde Sukeforth, the talented scout who discovered Roberto Clemente, also had a hand in bringing Jackie Robinson and Don Newcombe to the major leagues? With help and direction from Oscar Charleston, the respected and valued Sukeforth decided that Robinson was the right man to break the color barrier. Sukeforth, a mediocre major league catcher for 10 years in Cincinnati and Brooklyn, became a scout for the Dodgers in the 1940s. He passed away on September 5, 2000.

◆ Did you know a total of 15,929 players have participated in either the National Association or the major leagues through 2002?

◆ Did you know that San Francisco Giants slugger Barry Bonds came around to score just three times after his 68 intentional walks in 2002? In fact, his Giants scored just 27 runs after his 68 intentional passes that year, perhaps a reflection of the poor protection Bonds had in the batting order. Jeff Kent, Reggie Sanders, and Benito Santiago took turns batting cleanup behind Bonds, but the team performed at its best after manager Dusty Baker flip-flopped Kent to the third slot and Bonds to the cleanup spot. The Giants then surged offensively en route to the NL pennant. Bonds earned his record-extending fifth MVP Award for a second straight spectacular campaign. Aside from winning his first batting title (with a .370 mark), smashing 46 home runs, driving in 110, and scoring 117 times, Bonds set major league records with 198 walks, a .582 on-base percentage, and a 1.381 OPS (on-base plus slugging percentage).

Acknowledgments

In researching material for this book, I was quite humbled by the informational support I received from great organizations and many passionate individuals, who supplied answer after answer to my endless questions. I don't know where I'd be as a baseball researcher without the Society for American Baseball Research (SABR), a resourceful organization for baseball history enthusiasts such as myself. From that venerable brotherhood of historians and researchers, I would like to thank four in particular for sharing their findings with me, inspiring me, and teaching me more about the game's history than I ever dreamt possible. That glorious quartet is composed of Bill James (the best baseball historian of all time), David Smith (the hardest-working researcher in the business today), David Vincent (SABR's best ambassador), and Frank Russo (a tireless researcher whose unselfishness epitomizes SABR). I'm ever mindful of the innovative efforts of Mr. Bob Davids, the late founder of SABR, who made it possible for historians, researchers, and enthusiasts to uncover a tremendous amount of information that has given us invaluable descriptions of the game and its characters. Because of Mr. Davids, we have inherited the ability to better understand the game's past, present, and future. Because of Mr. Davids, we are all part of an information-finding team.

Dominick Balsamo of the Major League Baseball's Media Relations Department was integral to my research, supplying help in many areas throughout the major league season and afterward. I'd be remiss if I didn't acknowledge the help of Matt Gould and Richard Levin as well. The ever-so-professional Jeff Idelson, Bill Francis, and Bruce Markusen of the National Baseball Hall of Fame were my "Meal Ticket," coming through when I most needed an answer. Also helpful in one way or another were the following: Glenn Argenbright, Paul Lanning, Neil Scott, Steve Powderly, Lyle Spatz, Joe Cronin, John

Holway, Dan Latham, Michael Westbay, James Albright, Jules Tygiel, Buck O'Neil, Vera Clemente, Josh Gibson Jr., Lee Sinins, Sue Lukasik, Justine Warren, Chuck Brodsky, Jerome Holtzman, Norman Macht, Dave Gush, Merrit Clifton, Steve Constantelos, John Schwartz, John Reyes, Gene DeLisio, Cliff Blau, Gary Garland, Clifton Parker, Daniel O'Brien, Dick Clark, Larry Lester, John Coates, Herm Krabbenhoft, Sean Holtz, Paul Wendt, Norman Macht, Maxwell Kates, Doug Pappas, Dick Adams, Tom Simon, Frederick Ivor-Campbell, Bill Deane, Harvey Frommer, Eddie Deezen, Mark Alvarez, John Zajc, Chris Bernucca, Daren Smith, Joe Rizzo, Anthony Mormile, John Pezzullo, John Palmeri, Joe Carnecelli, Chris Mattia, and Felix Modestin.

The following sources were also helpful: all 30 Major League Baseball teams (special thanks to media relations directors Glen Serra, Bill Stetka, and Jay Horowitz), many major league players, the Office of the Commissioner, the MLB Players Association, the *Boston Globe*, Nikkan Sports, Japanesebaseball.com, Retrosheet, Negro League Hall of Fame, Elias Sports Bureau, *The Sporting News*, *The Sporting Life*, *Sports Heritage*, SportsTicker, *Baseball Weekly*, Baseball Library, Little League Baseball, the *New York Times*, ESPN, the Nolan Ryan museum, the Associated Press, SABR's Records Committee, SABR's 19th Century Committee, SABR's Dead Ball Era Committee, SABR's Umpires and Rules Committee, and SABR's L archives.

I am ever grateful to the staff at the Johns Hopkins University Press for making the publishing experience rewarding and fulfilling. I'm not sure I can ever thank Trevor Lipscombe enough for taking a chance on an unproven author a few years back. His belief in my ability has given me the confidence to author books for the rest of my life. Thank you, Trevor. I am thankful for Tom Roche's excellent editorial skills, which improved the quality of my book. I also appreciate the promotional energy of Mahinder Kingra, as well as the editorial advice given to me by Cyd Westmoreland.

I wouldn't be invited for Thanksgiving dinner if I didn't thank my fun-loving family, everyone from my parents, uncles, and aunts down to my siblings and cousins. I owe the most to the person to whom this book is dedicated, my cousin Suzie, the most encouraging, helpful, and unselfish person I've ever known. I love you Suzie, and thank you for your guidance. Thank you for believing in me.

Bibliography

Aaron, Hank, and Lonnie Wheeler. *I Had a Hammer: The Hank Aaron Story*. New York: HarperCollins, 1991.

Allen, Lee, and Tom Meany. *King of the Diamonds*. New York: G. P. Putnam's Sons, 1965.

The Baseball Encyclopedia. New York: Macmillan, 1969, 1993.

Baseball Research Journal. Cleveland: Society for American Baseball Research, 1991, 1992, 1993, 1994, 1995, 1996, 1997, 1998, 1999, 2000, 2001.

Baseball's First Stars. Cleveland: Society for American Baseball Research, 1996.

Bouton, Jim. *Ball Four*. New York: World Publishing Co., 1970.

Brashler, William. *Josh Gibson: A Life in the Negro Leagues*. New York: Harper and Row, 1978.

Bryant, Howard. *Shut Out: A Story of Race and Baseball in Boston*. New York: Routledge, 2002.

Burns, Ken. *Baseball: A Film by Ken Burns*. PBS Home Video, 1994, videorecording.

Charlton, James. *The Baseball Chronology*. New York: Macmillan Publishing Company, 1991.

Cohen, Richard, and David Neft. *The World Series*. New York: St. Martin's, 1976, 1990.

Epstein, Eddie, and Rob Neyer. *Baseball Dynasties*. New York: Norton, 2000.

Fleming, G. H. *The Unforgettable Season*. New York: Simon and Schuster, 1981.

Frommer, Harvey. *Shoeless Joe and Ragtime Baseball*. Dallas: Taylor, 1992.

Garagiola, Joe. *It's Anybody's Ball Game*. Chicago: Contemporary Books, 1988.

Greenberg, Hank, and Ira Berkow. *Hank Greenberg: The Story of My Life*. Triumph, 2001.

Hageman, William. *Honus: The Life and Times of a Baseball Hero*. Champaign, Ill.: Sagamore Publishing, 1996.

Harper, William. *How You Played the Game: The Life of Grantland Rice*. Columbia: University of Missouri Press, 1999.

Hill, Art. *I Don't Care If I Never Come Back*. New York: Simon and Schuster, 1980.

Honig, Donald, and Lawrence Ritter. *The 100 Greatest Baseball Players of All Time*. New York: Crown Publishers, 1981.

James, Bill. *The Bill James' Historical Baseball Abstract*. New York: Villard, 1986.

Kahn, Roger, and Pete Rose. *Pete Rose: My Way*. New York: Macmillan, 1989.

Kaplan, Jim. *Lefty Grove: American Original.* Cleveland: Society for American Baseball Research, 2000.

Kavanagh, Jack. *Walter Johnson: A Life.* South Bend, Ind.: Diamond Communications, 1996.

Kavanagh, Jack, and Norman Macht. *Uncle Robbie.* Cleveland: Society for American Baseball Research, 1999.

Kurkjian, Tim. "The Name Game." *Sports Illustrated,* 23 April 1990, p. 72.

Lansche, Jerry. *Stan the Man Musial.* Dallas: Taylor, 1994.

Longert, Scott. *Addie Joss: King of the Pitchers.* Cleveland: Society for American Baseball Research, 1998.

Markusen, Bruce. *Roberto Clemente: The Great One.* Champaign, Ill.: Sports Publishing, 1998.

The National Pastime. Cleveland: Society for American Baseball Research, 1984, 1988, 1990, 1992, 1995, 1996, 1997, 1998, 1999.

Palacios, Oscar. *Diamond Diagrams.* Illinois, STATS Inc., 1997.

Phillips, Bill. *Who Was Who in Cleveland Baseball in 1901–1910.* Cabin John, Md.: Capital Pub. Co., 1989.

Riley, James. *The Biographical Encyclopedia of the Negro Leagues.* New York: Carroll and Graf Publishers, Inc, 1994.

Robinson, Ray. *Iron Horse.* New York: Harper Perennial, 1990.

The Sporting News Complete Baseball Record Book. St. Louis: Times Mirror Magazine, 2000.

Stevens, David. *Baseball's Radical for All Seasons: A Biography of John Montgomery Ward.* Lanham, Md.: Scarecrow Press, 1998.

Stewart, Wayne. "The Man Who Owned Babe Ruth." *Sports Heritage,* May/June 1987.

Stump, Al. *Cobb.* Chapel Hill, N.C.: Algonquin, 1994.

Thompson, Joe. *Growing Up with "Shoeless" Joe: The Greatest Natural Player in Baseball History.* Laurel Fork, Va.: JTI Publishing, 1998.

Total Baseball. Ed. by John Thorn, Peter Palmer, Michael Gershman, and David Pietrusza. New York: Total Sports, 1988, 1999.

Veeck, Bill, with Ed Linn. *Veeck as in Wreck: The Autobiography of Bill Veeck.* Chicago: University of Chicago Press, 2001.

Wendel, Tim. "Close Shot." *USA Today Baseball Weekly,* April 15, 1992, p. 4.

When It Was a Game, produced by George Roy, Steven Stern, and David Harmon, written by Steven Stern. New York: HBO Video, 1991, videorecording.

About the Author

Mike Attiyeh, author of *Who Was Traded for Lefty Grove? Baseball's Fun Facts and Serious Trivia*, is a published sports historian and poet whose works have appeared in such publications as *Baseball Digest*, *Pirate Report*, and *Birch Brook Press*, as well as on numerous Web sites. Attiyeh, an active member of the Society for American Baseball Research who has appeared as an expert guest analyst on sports radio talk shows throughout the United States, is best known nationally for breaking the story of Tony Gwynn's blood clot in 1997.

In 1999 Attiyeh provided the majority of the content for "This Day in Baseball History," a segment in the Oakland Athletics' official pre-game radio show. He has interviewed and written about a score of athletes and was a semi-finalist in a National Trivia Contest, held by the Society for American Baseball Research. He attended Rutgers University and Piscataway High School.

Attiyeh, a former Sports News Director for Todays Sports and Sports Extra, and an earlier editor for ESPN SportsTicker, is devoting his immediate future to authoring more books. He currently lives in Elk Grove, California.